C0-BXA-463

AISLINGE MEIC CON GLINNE

AISLINGE
MEIC CON GLINNE

EDITED BY KENNETH HURLSTONE JACKSON
CBE, Litt.D., D.Litt.Celt., Hon. MRIA, FBA

School of Celtic Studies
Dublin Institute for Advanced Studies
1990

© Dublin Institute for Advanced Studies 1990
ISBN 0 901282 94 4

Printed by
Dublin University Press

For Brian Ó Cuív
great scholar and generous friend

CONTENTS

PREFACE

This book was originally intended as one of the volumes of the Mediaeval and Modern Irish Series published by the Dublin Institute for Advanced Studies. I began it in 1955 but was unable to find time for it until I retired in 1979. It soon developed into a much larger work, with special stress on the Middle Irish of the *Aislinge*, as evidenced, not only in the Notes, but above all in the Appendix on the language and in the Glossary. Apart from Dottin's *Manuel d'irlandais moyen*, which is long out of print and out of date, there is so far no exhaustive morphology of Middle Irish in existence; the present book is intended as a broad sketch of the language of the *Aislinge*, with special reference to the dating. It has always been my ambition to edit this text for students: purely Middle Irish texts are sometimes lacking in real literary interest, whereas this one is unique in its combination of humour, burlesque, satire, fantasy and variety, which makes a delightful contrast with works such as the *Passions and Homilies*, in spite of their great linguistic importance.

Part of this work consists of a complete glossary of words. It is far from being a mere vocabulary, rather it is a concordance of the language of this important text, and is the key to the whole. It also serves the purpose of containing the collections of forms on which the statistics and conclusions in the Appendix are based.

A stroke which I suffered in 1984 and a subsequent serious illness made it impossible for me to see this work through its final stages. I wish to express my profound thanks to a number of scholars who came to my aid. I am above all grateful to Brian Ó Cuív and to the late Gordon Quin. I cannot even begin to thank Brian Ó Cuív adequately for the kindness with which he wrestled with the problems of editing and tidying my hand-written version of the book in addition to answering many queries regarding details of language and manuscript readings. (I had worked from the excellent photostats of the two manuscripts given me by the late Myles Dillon, but the Leabhar Breac was not invariably clear enough to be trusted.) I am also most grateful to the late Daniel Binchy for his liberal and expert advice on some of the questions of early Irish law which characterize the *Aislinge*. Early in 1987 the task of getting the work into typescript and seeing it through the press was handed over to Dr. Pádraig Ó Macháin. He was also asked to revise and condense the Glossary. This has been a laborious and time-consuming task for him, and I am very grateful to him for taking it in hand and doing it so successfully.

Other scholars to whom I want to express my gratitude are Dr. Breandán Ó Cíobháin, formerly of An Oifig Logainmneacha, for his kind help in the identification of several places mentioned in the text (§§ 13 etc.); Fr. Pádraig Ó Fiannachta, St. Patrick's College, Maynooth, for comments on the Seven Things and the Tenth Order (§ 41); Mr. Jürgen Uhlich, Sprachwissenschaftliches Institut der Universität Bonn, for elucidating line 888 and for much other assistance; and Dr. Michael Guiry, University College, Galway, for his research for me on the obscure word *bundraisse* (line 1088). Finally, thanks are due to Institute staff who helped in bringing the work to completion: R. Baumgarten, P. Dunne, K. Elson, S. Farrell, K. Hollo, A. Nic Dhonnchadha, E. Nic Dhonncha, M. Uí Chinnseala.

Kenneth Jackson

INTRODUCTION

THE MANUSCRIPTS AND TEXT

This Middle Irish tale (abbreviated AMC[1]) has been edited only once before, by Kuno Meyer, 'Aislinge Meic Conglinne, The Vision of MacConglinne' (London, 1892), with a translation, notes, glossary, etc. It had been translated previously by W. M. Hennessy in Fraser's Magazine, LXXXVIII, September 1873, pp. 298–323, with serious shortcomings which Meyer discusses on his p. viii f.

Two MS versions are extant, one in the well-known vellum Leabhar Breac ('B') in the Royal Irish Academy, formerly no. 23 P 16, now no. 1230, AMC being on pp. 213–219; the other on pp. 732–743[2] of the MS H.3.18 ('H'), now numbered 1337, in Trinity College, Dublin. B was written by a single hand between 1408 and 1411; see T. Ó Concheanainn in Ériu XXIV, 64ff., and the Royal Irish Academy's catalogue of Irish MSS in its possession, XXVII (Dublin, 1943), no. 1230, pp. 3379ff. Ó Concheanainn discusses the hand on his pp. 68ff. A lithographic facsimile of a transcript of the whole MS made by Joseph O'Longan was published by the Academy in Dublin in 1876, 'Leabhar Breac, the Speckled Book'. Though its text of AMC is on the whole very accurate, it does contain a number of errors, presumably due to O'Longan. The manuscript H was described by T. K. Abbott and E. J. Gwynn in their 'Catalogue of the Irish Manuscripts in the Library of Trinity College, Dublin' (Dublin and London, 1921), pp. 140–158. The text of AMC is on paper, in a clear hand of the 16th–17th centuries.

Meyer took B, much the older MS, for his text, but printed the very much shorter H version, not without errors, in an appendix on pp. 114–129, and translated it on pp. 148–155. The prose parts of H are of very little use in supplying variant readings; see p. xxxi below. It is unfortunate that Meyer did not use the

---

[1] This abbreviation means both the text in the MSS and Meyer's edition of it.

[2] The page in H after 736 is also numbered 736, and 737 follows. The extra 736 is here called 736a.

original MS of B in making his edition, because in his text he reproduced faithfully the errors of the Facsimile. He noted and corrected some (but not all) of these on his pp. 205–207 after having seen the MS itself (see his p. viii), with a few corrigenda on his text of H. These corrigenda on both texts seem to have been missed by the editors of DIL. In addition to the mistakes copied from the Facsimile of B, Meyer made some more mistranscriptions of his own. These and those mentioned already are noted in the variant readings.

The text offered here is made from an excellently clear set of photostats from B sent me by Myles Dillon, along with a similar set from H. I have used H for significant variants, particularly for the poems, eight of which it contains in whole or part (cf. THE METRES OF THE POEMS below), but as just noted it is almost impossible to use it otherwise. It is shorter than the B version, but to repeat the whole would not only lengthen this book considerably but would also be superfluous, in view of Meyer's more or less satisfactory text and translation of it. However, a summary of its contents, with references to corresponding passages in B, is given below, pp. xxvi ff.

As matters of editorial policy, I have adopted the following practices:

(1) *The use of square brackets.* Wherever letters not in the MS are inserted because they are required grammatically or historically they are printed in square brackets. So, *do C[h]athal, Mo[i]li Dúin*, etc. Similarly with verbal forms; see the Appendix § i.

(2) *Lenition and nasalisation.* B indicates lenition of *c, p, t, f* and *s* either by writing h after the lenited consonant or by using a suprascript rudimentary *h* or a suprascript dot. He occasionally uses the suprascript marks with *b, d, g* and *m*. I use roman *h* to represent both scribal *h* and the suprascript mark in all such instances. Where lenition of *c, p, t, f* or *s* would be appropriate but is not marked in the manuscript, I supply *h* in square brackets as stated above under (1). I also supply [*h*] where use of a suprascript contraction, such as ⁰ or ⁱ, inhibits marking of lenition, thus *t[h]rostán*. Sometimes scribal *fh*, or *f* with suprascript lenition mark, is found where nasalisation would be regular. In such instances I use italic *h* in the text, thus *dia*

fhesmais.[3] I also use italic *h*, (i) in a few instances where the suprascript mark is used to indicate prefixing of *h* to a following vowel, thus *bahé* and (ii) in expanding scribal ꝝ as *edh*. Note that nasalisation of *t-* is once spelt *d-* (*a dochrat*, l. 1182 f.).

(3) *Length-marks.* Like many other scribes, B frequently omits the accent on long vowels, but also he is notorious for wrongly marking short vowels long, particularly but not exclusively where they had become lengthened in EMod.I later than the period of AMC. These faults are silently corrected (silently because explicit correction would grossly clutter the apparatus criticus, and KM's edition represents them anyway), and the acute accent is used rather than the macron for typographical reasons. The only exception in my editorial treatment of the inherited short/long vowels is in those parts of the verb where the endings were short in OI but became lengthened later, such as first plural imperfect *-m(a)is* giving *-maís* etc.; cf. Ériu XXIV, 124 f. This feature was developing during the MI period. In B there are twice as many examples of failure to indicate length in such cases as there are of marking it; see § lxxxi. How far this is a scribal matter rather than linguistic fluctuation in the original it is impossible to tell, and therefore impossible to normalise either by marking all long or all short. I therefore follow the MS in each case.

(4) *Contractions.* Italics are perhaps rather more frequent here than is strictly necessary, including cases where the 'doubt' is merely a matter of spelling, but this is probably better than the converse. B is unfortunately very fond of using the suspension-mark identical with the contraction for *n* instead of the standard contractions, but there is usually no real doubt about the expansion. There is, however, one more important matter of ambiguity, in the *r*-endings of the deponent and passive. For a discussion of this and of the policy adopted see §§ lvii f.

(5) *Emendations.* AMC contains an unusually large number of hapax legomena, particularly among the words for foods; also some passages where the text appears to be corrupt, and two or three small lacunae. I have therefore had to resort to emendation to what may seem an excessive degree; but where an emendation

[3] Cf. MIM p. 7.

is not in itself palaeographically improbable and the sense it gives is suitable, particularly where it is supported by metre, these circumstances would seem to warrant it.

For a discussion of several points which affect the use of the Glossary see the introductory note to that section.

THE METRES OF THE POEMS

The syllabic metres of the poems in MI (and OI) narrative[4] are generally looser, often much looser, than those of the strict *dán direch* of the classical EMod.I bards, though it is mostly possible to see in them the germs of the later strict metres, qualified here by 'loose'. The strict varieties are familiar to students in Eleanor Knott's 'Irish Syllabic Poetry, 1200-1600' (ISP), and more fully in Gerard Murphy's 'Early Irish Metrics' (EIM).

There may be considerable irregular variation in the number of lines to a verse, in that of syllables to a line, and in that of the rhyming or consonating words; the rhymes and consonances are often imperfect, sometimes very much so; internal rhyme is often lacking; alliteration, whether within the line or from line to line, may be scanty or quite absent where *dán direch* requires or encourages it; and elisions of a kind not tolerated in the latter may occur.

In the following descriptions the syllabic construction of the verses will be analysed according to formulae of which this is an example: $8^2 + 7^1 + 8^2 + 7^1$, meaning that the first and third lines ('*a*' and '*c*') have eight syllables, and end-words of two, and '*b*' and '*d*' have seven and end-words of one respectively. In such a verse, *b* and *d* will rhyme together; there may be *aicill* between lines *c* and *d* (i.e. the final word of *c* rhymes with one in the interior of *d*); and *a* may be tied to *b* by *aicill* or by having its last word alliterate with the first stressed word of *b*. An example is verse 6 in § 51 a. The *dán direch* version of this is called *Sétna* (ISP p. 16) or *Sétnad Mór* (EIM p. 49); and these names for the various metres will be used below purely in the sense 'The name of the descendant of this in *dán direch* is . . .'.

[4] For a discussion see A. Mac an Bhaird, 'Dán Díreach agus Ranna as na hAnnála', Éigse XVII, 157 ff.

The metres of the poems in AMC may be analysed as follows:

§4 (not in H). Verse 1, $4^1+8^3+4^1+8^3$; v. 2, $4^2+8^3+4^2+8^3$. Types of Ollbairdne (EIM p. 61). Lines *b* and *d* rhyme (imperfectly in v. 1); there is *aicill* in *c* and *d* and a rough one in *atuaid : Dúin*; internal rhyme in *láim : táir*; and alliteration in vv. 1 *c* and 2 *a*. The scribe lengthens lines *a* and *c* in v. 1 by repeating them, as often happens in MSS when short lines precede longer ones in a couplet. On B's *dia-nus táir* see Note to l. 34.

§8 (not in H). V. 1, $7^1+7^2+7^1+7^3$; v. 2, $7^2+7^2+7^1+7^2$; v. 3, $7^1+7^3+7^1+7^2$; v. 4, $7^2+7^3+7^1+7^2$; v. 5, $7^1+7^1+7^1+7^2$. A very loose Deibide Scáilte (ISP pp. 18 ff., EIM pp. 28 n. 1, 29, 65 ff.). There are violations, typical in MI verse in narrative, of the normal *dán dírech* rule about numbers of syllables in Deibide rhymes in *a : b* and *c : d*. There is only one perfect internal rhyme, in v. 5, *c : d*; and two imperfect, v. 1 *c : d* and v. 3 *c : d*. Considerable alliteration throughout, not limited to *c : d* couplets; note specially v. 4, *b : c*.

§19 (H has vv. 1 and 3 only). The metre varies from verse to verse, as in §8. V. 1, $3^2+7^2+7^2+7^2$; Rannaigecht Chetharchubaid Gairit Récomarcach (ISP p. 14 f., EIM p. 55). The *b : d* rhyme is perfect, and *a* and *c* consonate (imperfectly) with each other but not with *b* and *d*. There is no *aicill* in either couplet; only one internal rhyme, in *c : d*; no alliterations.

V. 2, $8^2+4^2+4^2+6^2$. Apparently a variant of Dechnad Cummaisc (ISP p. 18, ll. 2–3; cf. an ex. in op. cit. p. 58 vv. 21 and 24; and EIM p. 50). Here, 6^2 in *d* seems irregular; perhaps some disyllable has dropped out. There is rhyme in place of consonance between *a* and *d* instead of between *b* and *d*, and no consonances; *aicill c : d*; and alliteration in *b* and *c* and between them.

V. 3, $7^3+7^2+7^3+7^2$; the basic essential of Ae Freislige (ISP p. 13, EIM p. 62). But although *b* and *d* rhyme together, *a* and *c* do not, here. The *aicill* and internal rhyme between *c* and *d* are due to a clumsy repetition. There is complete alliteration in and between both these lines.

V. 4, $7^2+7^2+7^2+7^2$, imperfect Rannaigecht Becc (ISP p. 15, EIM p. 53). There is rhyme between *b* and *d*, as emended (see Note to l. 190); imperfect consonance of *a* with *b* and *d*; *aicill* between c and d; no internal rhymes; and two alliterations, one each in c and d.

§ 31 (also in H). All verses are varieties of the ancestor of *dán direch* Rinnaird (ISP p. 16, EIM p. 64), formula $6^2 + 6^2 + 6^2 + 6^2$, properly with rhyme between b and d; alliteration between the end-word of a and the first stressed word of b; *aicill* between c and d; and alliteration between the last word of each verse and the first stressed word of the next ('*fidrad freccomail*'; EIM p. 38). This basic description applies to vv. 1, 2, 4, 7, 10, 11, and (but lacking the $a:b$ alliteration) 12. The 'varieties' just mentioned are the following:

V. 3, in addition, a and c rhyme with each other and consonate with b and d.

Vv. 5 and 9 lack the alliteration between a and b, but this is compensated for by a consonating with b and d in both.

V. 6 is the same as 1, 2 etc. as listed just above, but also c consonates with b and d.

V. 8 is also the same as 1, 2 etc., but lacks the $a:b$ alliteration, unless *meic Fhína* is treated, metri gratia, as *mei Cína*.

There are no true internal rhymes in the poem, but there are many alliterations, continuing in some cases from one line to the next, in addition to the $a:b$ link; in v. 2 there is alliteration in b- throughout the verse. The *fidrad freccomail* characteristic of Rinnaird is missing in vv. 10-11 and 11-12. *Meic* is treated as not counting for alliteration throughout the poem; cf. EIM p. 41.

§ 33 (also in H). Formula $7^3 + 7^3 + 5^1 + 7^3 + 7^3 + 5^1$. A variety of Eochraid (EIM p. 79); cf. also § 58. In vv. 2 and 11 there is an extra long-line in the second half-verse. The long-lines do not rhyme at all, and only the short-lines do so, $c:f$; nor is there consonance, *aicill*, or internal rhyme. Instead, there is frequent alliteration, sometimes spreading from one line to the next or the next two, or in v. 5 to the next three.

§ 51 a (also in H except for vv. 2 and 3). There is the same variation in the metres as in § 19. V. 1, $7^1 + 7^1 + 7^2 + 7^1$, with b and d rhyming and *aicill* in c and d. Loose Rannaigecht Mór (ISP p. 13 f., EIM p. 52), except for the disyllabic end-word, and consequently *aicill*, in c, as if Rannaigecht Becc (cf. § 19 v. 4); cf. Murphy, EIL, no. 2, v. 2.

Vv. 2 and 3, $7^3+5^1+7^3+5^1$, loose Cró Cummaisc etir Chasbairdne agus Lethrannaigecht (EIM p. 61). Here, *b* and *d* rhyme but *a* and *c* neither rhyme nor consonate, nor are they connected with *b* and *d* in any way except for the *a* : *b* alliteration link in v. 2. No internal rhymes and no other alliterations except in v. 3 *a* and *b*.

Vv. 4, 5, 6, 7; $8^2+7^1+8^2+7^1$. Loose Sétnad (cf. the introductory note to the metres, p. xiv). Vv. 4, 5, and 7 lack alliteration between *a* and *b*, which is compensated for in v. 7 by the *aicill* between them. Other alliterations are frequent, but there are no internal rhymes except the imperfect one in v. 5, *c* : *d*.

§51 b (also in H). Metre very loose indeed in the MSS and KM, though improvements are possible by emendation.

Vv. 1, 2, 3, and 4 seem meant for Snédbairdne, $8^2+4^2+8^2+4^2$ (ISP p. 17 f., EIM p. 51), with *b* and *d* rhyming, but in v. 2, *a* consonates with *b* and *d*, and in v. 3, *a* and *c* consonate with each other. There are no internal rhymes except the imperfect one in v. 2, *c* : *d* and the perfect one in v. 3, *c* : *d*. I have emended, or suggest emending, the MS text of these verses (for which see the variants) as follows:

In v. 1 the monosyllabic end-words *a-raír* and *dam* are irregular. The first is demanded by the phrase, but *c* could be improved by reading *dam co tárfas* or *dam do-árfas* (cf. v. 4 *a*). In *a* the required eight syllables can be found by ignoring the expected elision *'t-chondarc*; for this licence in MI see EIM p. 39, and cf. vv. 3 *c* and 4 *a* here and § 57 a v. 3 *c*. In v. 2 both MSS make *c* too long by two syllables and give it an irregular trisyllabic ending; hence I have omitted *imme* and transposed *carrach* and *do minscellcib*. This move also provides rhyme with *barrach* and *aicill* with *tanach* (*carrach* still qualifies *caisel*). The fact that there is now rhyme between *a* and *c* would be irregular, but the consonance of both with *b* and *d* would give the variety of Snédbairdne called Lethdechnad (cf. EIM p. 51). V. 3 *b* would be hypermetric if elision of *a* after *do-rónta* is rejected, with EIM p. 39 n. 2. If so, read simply *colbai cadlai*. For the lack of elision in *c* cf. on vv. 1 *a* and 4 *a*. V. 4, both MSS have only six syllables in *a*, or seven if we allow hiatus (between *amra* and *in*) as in vv. 1 *a* and 3 *c*; but eight, with the necessary disyllabic ending, can be got by reading *dam do-árfas* (cf. v. 1 *c*). There are five

B

syllables in b, but the $(h)i$ of the MSS can easily be omitted to give four; cf. DIL C 1.122. 3–8.

If v. 5 is also intended as Snédbairdne its formula, $7^2 + 4^2 + 7^2 + 8^2$ (or 7^2, see below), is very irregular. The hypometric a could be made into eight syllables by reading *mo Dia*, and c by reading *dam-sa hi* without elision. The metre allows eight syllables in d, but only if one of the two normally 8^2 lines is reduced to 4^2 to compensate (cf. ISP p. 181. 2). If the poet really intended $7^2 + 4^2 + 7^2 + 7^2$ this could be got by substituting H's *laad* for B's *láitea* and taking it for monosyllabic *lád*; but that would not be Snédbairdne. I do not attempt to emend this verse.

§ 57. This too consists of two poems with a change of metre, though they are not so completely separate as in § 51. The *dúnad* in ll. 954, 967 and 972 does not of itself imply separateness.

§ 57 a (also in H, except for vv. 5 and 6). There is an unusual variation of detail in the metrical construction here, and the omission of two verses by H is unfortunate. Vv. 1, 2, 3, 5, and 6 appear to be loose varieties of Ochtfhoclach (EIM p. 70 f.). Each verse consists of two (or more) half-verses of relatively long lines with polysyllabic end-words which may or may not rhyme or consonate with each other, plus a normally shorter one following each group of long ones, the two short ones with monosyllabic end-words rhyming together. There may be *aicill* in one or both halves. The chief loosenesses in § 57 a are the variations in the number of syllables in the lines and in the end-words, and the absence of end-rhyme or consonance in the long-lines. There are no internal rhymes, but a fair amount of alliteration.

The 'tightest' verse of the group 1, 2, 3, 5, and 6 is 5, with the formula $4^2 + 4^2 + 3^1$, $4^2 + 4^2 + 3^1$, and v. 6 (q.v. below) is almost the same. The long-lines a and b in v. 1 rhyme, and so do d and e, and the short-lines c and f. For the others, v. 1, with the pattern $7^3 + 6^3 + 4^2$ (H 6^2), $4^1 + 4^1 + 3^1$ in both MSS, is highly irregular, particularly since c's 3^1 in l. 921 is an emendation for B's 4^2 and H's 6^2, and the end-words in c and f do not rhyme in B and H, though a simple emendation in c solves this last. I can make no suggestion for dealing with the very irregular a and b, with their seven and six syllables respectively and their trisyllabic end-words, not to mention their lack of rhyme, which however is paralleled elsewhere in the poem. In the second half-verse the end-words of d and e are monosyllables, but the confusion in a and b prevents us knowing whether this is regular or not.

V. 2 has the formula $4^2 + 4^1 + 3^1$, $4^1 + 4^1 + 4^1$, again irregular in having four syllables in f (cf. v. 3 f). One suspects the pattern should be $4^1 + 4^1 + 3^1$, $4^1 + 4^1 + 3^1$, as probably also in the case of v. 1. There is consonance between b, d, and e, and alliteration a-b, b-c, and c-d. The pattern of v. 3 appears to be $4^2 + 4^2 + 3^1$, $4^1 + 4^1 + 4^1$, again irregular in the syllable-counts, but close to that of v. 2; c could be 4^1 if we allow hiatus between $gile$ and a $glond$ (cf. the note above on § 51 b, v. 1 a), but I see no way of reducing f to three syllables.

V. 6, with the formula $4^2 + 4^2 + 4^2 + 3^1$, $4^2 + 4^2 + 3^1$, is identical with 5 except that it has an extra long-line in the first half-verse, and these three long-lines lack rhyme. On disyllabic $diaid$ see the Note.

V. 4 is the really odd man out. It is a quite different metre, with the formula $3^2 + 7^1 + 3^1 + 7^1$, apparently a loose inversion of Cró Cummaisc etir Rannaigecht agus Sruth di Aill (EIM p. 56); 3^1 would be expected in a. Lines b and d rhyme: there is $aicill$ in $c : d$; alliteration in a, c, and d; but no internal rhymes.

§ 57 b (also in H, where it lacks vv. 1 and 2). These four verses are evidently intended to have the formula $8^2 + 3^1 + 8^2 + 3^1$, which is that of Sétnad nGairit (EIM p. 50); b and d rhyme together, and so should a and c in *dán dírech*, but in this loose predecessor this is the case in v. 1 only. There are no internal rhymes here, and apart from v. 1 there is not much alliteration. A fair amount of emendation is necessary in this poem, for some of which see the Notes.

Vv. 1 and 2 keep to the above formula. In v. 1, KM's emendation [a] *adastar* is quite unnecessary; 'a bridle and its harness' is quite adequate, and cf. *mór-mhuince* without possessive in a.

In v. 3 c the treatment of B's *nibras* as *ní bras* gives sense but makes the line-end monosyllabic instead of disyllabic. B's d is hypermetric but can be corrected to 3^1 by omitting *don*. On these points, and the confusions in vv. 2 and 4 c and d, which are matters of semantics rather than metre, see the Notes on ll. 963–970.

V. 4 a, B's *immum-sa féin*, supported by H's *immun fadéin*, makes this line hypermetric too, but it is cured here by leaving out *féin*, though this renders the line 8^3 instead of 8^2.

§ 58 (H omits this poem). The metre is the same as that of § 33, except that there are three long-lines in the first half-verse, not two; though § 33 has three instead of two in its second half-verse. The alliteration is particularly full here; no line is without it.

§ 76 (also in H); $7^1 + 7^2 + 7^1 + 7^2$. Debide Scaílte, the same as § 8, but much more regular. The only irregularity is that vv. 2 and 3 have three *debide* couplets each instead of the classical two, which is not unusual in MI verse. There is the common MI lack of internal rhyme except in v. 2 $c:d$ and v. 3 $c:d$, and the imperfect *dathaib*: *Cathal* in v. 2 $e:f$.

DATE

The chief sources for the historical development of MI are as follows:

(1) Saltair na Rann. It is usually agreed that this was composed in 988; cf. Professor G. Mac Eoin in ZCP XXVIII, 51 ff., Ériu XX, 112 ff., and ZCP XXXIX, 1 ff. A more recent attempt to show that it is more than a century older—in effect, Old Irish—is scarcely likely to be generally accepted (Éigse XIX, 177 ff.).

(2) The MI texts in LU, 10th or probably mostly 11th century. The date of the scribes is crucial, but it has become controversial in late years. However, I think the 'canonical' date of c. 1100 for the scribes A and M must stand; and certainly the linguistic evidence shows the interpolator H was writing at least as late as the second half of the 12th century, though hardly in the 13th (cf. PSIC p. 3 f.). I have seen no good reason to revise this opinion; such linguistic arguments as have been advanced are slight and controvertible.

(3) Togail Troí in the H.2.17 version, as analysed by Professor Mac Eoin in ZCP XXVIII, 73 ff. (= TTr. 1). He dates this 11th century (op. cit. p. 202); one might suggest some time in the second half of that century.

(4) The Passions and Homilies. On this see PSIC p. 6 f., where I pointed out that by no means all the texts are of the same

date. I would suggest that not counting the few obviously very late ones and one or two very early ones, about half of them may belong to the later 11th century and the rest to somewhere about the middle of the 12th or a little earlier. This may account for the hesitation between c. 1100 and c. 1150 among previous scholars, who took it for granted that PH is a single contemporaneous whole. Dillon, one of these, who dated it as c. 1150 in ZCP XVI, 321, explained (p. 319) that this was because he took its language to be about half-way between that of TBC II L (q.v. below) and of AS, which he dated c. 1200; thinking that the condition of the infixed pronoun and the attributive adjective in PH is later than that of TBC II L. But he admitted that if TBC II L 'preserves an archaic language' [as it certainly does in part], PH may be as early as TBC II L [i.e. c. 1100]. This date is accepted by McE in IMN 1961 p. 43. Unless otherwise stated, references to the language of 'PH' in the Appendix below belong to those sections of the text to which I would provisionally assign the earlier of the two dates suggested above.

(5) The Book of Leinster version of TBC (TBC II L; see Máirín O Daly's VST). Thurneysen's date of 1100–1125 is severely and rightly criticised by McE in IMN, 1961, p. 43 and in PBA LXVIII, 117 for the inadequacy of the grounds for it. See these for the difficulties about the date and about using it as evidence on that of other texts, including the very early character of much of its main source (TBC I), and its tendency to archaise (e.g. it has at least ten verbs still deponent, some of them in -(a)ig-, and has created new ones). In using it for dating purposes caution is necessary, for the reasons pointed out in PSIC p. 9 f., but at least it does give a *terminus ad quem* for MI forms not known to occur in older texts. For purposes of MI history the 'date' assigned to TBC II L must mean primarily the date of its compiler, whose MI language constantly appears in a text derived from older sources. It may well be that Thurneysen's date for him is after all fairly near the truth, but this is a coincidence. Dillon's date for it was c. 1100 (ZCP XVI, 320), and so is McE's (PBA LXVIII, 117 f.); one might suggest 'very early 12th century'.

(6) In Cath Catharda. The verbal system is painstakingly described by Sommerfelt in RC XXVI, XXVII and XXVIII.

His final date for it, in RC XXVIII, 36, n. 3 would appear to be c. 1150 (contrast 38 f., where he seems to have been influenced by a wrong date for AS as well as an ill-defined one for PH). This may not be far out, or perhaps a little later. M. O Daly would put it earlier, in the second quarter of the 12th century. One must remember, however, that this tale is to some extent in the tradition of late MI and EMod.I heroic-romantic story, which tends to sporadic archaisation.

The difficulties in trying to date MI texts are very great, as was noted recently by myself in PSIC p. 1 ff. and by McE in PBA LXVIII 109 ff., particularly the hazardous nature of the so-called 'proportional method', as pointed out by G. Mac Niocaill in Studia Celtica III 47 ff. and by the two authors just mentioned in opp. citt. pp. 5 f. and 135 f. respectively. But I think one should not condemn it totally. When comparing two texts of very different lengths there is clearly not very much point in adding up and comparing the totals of the occurrences of some particular early feature X and deciding that text A is older than text B because it has more cases of X if A is significantly longer than B. The proportional method was designed to meet this. One takes not only X but also Y, the later development of or substitute for X; works out the *proportion* of occurrences of X to Y that each text contains; and always provided that the 'statistical sample' is adequate, it is reasonable to think that the text with an obviously markedly larger proportion of the old form is probably older. Extending this to more than two texts should, in theory, make it possible to rank a number of different ones in chronological order, since discrepancies in the lengths of texts would be irrelevant provided that the statistical samples provided by all of them are adequate. The chief objection to all this is that it has been used for dating texts in which the samples are far too small to justify any conclusion at all, and also to set up a kind of series of absolute proportional criteria applicable to any and all texts. None the less I should like to emphasise that when used with caution, taking these objections into account, the method may still give significant results.

AMC is a MI text. It has become customary to speak of Early MI (EMI) and Late MI (LMI). I do not think these terms have been clearly defined chronologically, though my impression is that the period c. 900–c. 1200 is thought to be divisible at c. 1050. I am not sure of the validity of this, and should prefer to refine it a little by suggesting three divisions. Early MI would cover the 10th century, with SR as a characteristic text; Intermediate MI (IMI) roughly the 11th century, the MI texts in LU, TTr. 1, and the earlier parts of PH belonging here; and Late MI (LMI) would describe the 12th century and include TBC II L, most of the later texts in PH, and the MI element in CCath. But the traditional division into EMI and LMI is used in this book (cf. Abbreviations svv. EMI, IMI, and LMI), though LMI beginning c. 1100 rather than c. 1050 would in any case seem more appropriate.

The Appendix on the language of AMC below is intended in part as an attempt to arrive at a possible date for the composition of the B text. What it shows, very broadly speaking, seems to be that it belongs in the range of the 'IMI' and very early 'LMI' texts[5] TTr. 1, most of the early parts of PH, and the MI element in TBC II L; it is of course much later than SR, and clearly earlier than CCath. To narrow this down more closely, I should suggest that it seems on the whole rather later than TTr. 1 and perhaps contemporary with most of the earlier parts of PH; that is to say, if an approximate AD date is to be hazarded, somewhere in the last quarter of the 11th century.

The chief aspects of the language which may support, more or less strongly according to their weight, a date of this kind rather than the usual 'mid- or late 12th century' one are the following: Perhaps survival of the ending -ib in the pl. dat. of the adjective (Appendix §xxvi). Absence of pronoun subjects of active non-copula verbs (§xxx). The lack of -th- forms in the prepositions for, ó, and oc, and the rarity of fri for la (§xl). The rarity of compound nominal conjunctions (§xliii). Sech ni . . . ní (ibid.), and the absence of mar as conjunction (§xliv). Ro and do not yet displacing preverbal no (§xlv). The rarity of ro- for do- and do- for ro-, and the lack of confusion of other preverbs (§l; contrast TBC II L). The evidence of nícon and noc(h)o(n) (§li). The rarity of the deponent verb (§lvi). The state of the past indicative passive pl. (§lxii). The proportion of surviving original deuterotonics to new 'simple prototonics' (§lxxiv). The

---

[5] To use here the definitions just employed; but the traditional 'early/late MI' are otherwise used in the book, and 'IMI' is ignored.

infrequency of *t*-preterites and suffixless preterites having joined the *s*-preterites (§ lxxxix). The evidence of the infixed versus the independent object pronoun (§§ xxxvii f.) and that of infixed versus prefixed *ro* (§§ xlvi–xlix). All this would suggest, and rather strongly, that AMC is older than TTr. 1; but this is hardly supported by the rest. Another feature is that the interrogative pronoun is almost invariably *cia* in AMC, only once *cé*, and never *gia*, *gé*, *cá*, or *gá*, the last four apparently belonging to the 12th century; but the fem. *cissí* is found once. On *cémad* and *gémad* see the next paragraph. *Cissí* looks like an archaism, but in general AMC eschews archaisms except for a couple in verse (*sceó* and disyllabic *diaid* once each) and a few neuters in chevilles (§ vii). On the other hand there are no features of any substance which clearly suggest the 12th century, unless possibly the few cases of *feib* in the sense 'when'.

It is true that there are certain forms in AMC which in some cases are even *later* than the 12th century, or at least uncharacteristic of the text, but their isolation and the fact that they are all words or forms carrying no stress would suggest that they are simple inadvertencies by the copyist, who, after all, was writing some three centuries later than the date of the composition proposed above, unconsciously or carelessly substituting linguistic features of his own day for those of his exemplar (cf. PBA LXVIII, 113). Such things may well be suspected when they are very few as against considerably more examples of the older form, particularly when they are trifling matters likely not to be noticed by the scribe; e.g. the three cases of definite article *an* beside innumerable ones of *in* (§ vi). This is of course a well-known feature in the copying of MSS, and may be conveniently described as 'scribal'. Other examples are *cé* once for *cia*, and *cémad* and *gémad* once each, as above; some of the prepositional forms (§ xl), as *esti* once for *essi*; *dá* 'to their' for *dia*; *ba* once for *fo* and *fóthib* once for *foib*; *air* 'in addition to' once for *fair*; *ar* once for *iar*; *re* once for *la*; *um* and *ba* once each for *im(m)* and two exx. of *ma na*; *'ga* 'with whom' (*oc*), the only example of -*g*- in this preposition in AMC; *rom-* once for *rem-* (*ré*); *seoch-* once beside *sech-*. In the verb, *ro-chóid* for *do-chóid*, *do thomail* for *ro thomail*, and *do-géba* for *fo-géba*, all once each (§ l); *da-ní* for *do-gní* (§ lxxvi), the only example in AMC of /jni:/ becoming /ni:/ in this verb; *no ragaind*, the only example of *rag-* for *reg-* in the future stem of *téit* (§ lxxxviii (4)); and *dámad* (§ cii) and *conad*, *dianad* (§ civ) for *diamad*, *conid*, and *dianid* in the copula. Note that there are over 90 instances of *ol* 'said', about 40 each of *or* and *ar*, but only one of *for*.

The opinions of scholars on the date of AMC have been various. Meyer suggested the end of the 12th century (KM p. x), on two grounds. One, he thought the language could be compared with that of a fair number of dateable poems in LL (c. 1160–1200; cf. Best, Bergin and O'Brien, 'The Book of Leinster', I, xv ff., Dublin, 1954); as he did not specify which poems, this is valueless. Two, the mention of tithes in B § 23. While he admitted that tithes are mentioned earlier, they were not generally paid in Ireland, he said, till the second half of the 12th century, and then only with much opposition; e.g. at the Synod of Kells in 1152 the papal legate ordered that they should be paid. This seems to have hypnotised subsequent writers in such a way that the date 'c. 1150' appears to have become accepted without question by some. As we have seen, Dillon, dating it c. 1150 in ZCP XVI, 321, thought AMC older than PH, adding 'my date is tentative'. But his 'c. 1150' for PH must be withdrawn, as explained above. Later, in 'Early Irish Literature' (Chicago, 1948), p. 143, he says briefly 'in the 12th century'. Flower, 'The Irish Tradition' (Oxford, 1947), p. 77, thought 'it can hardly be earlier than the 12th century, but the traditions it reflects certainly go back to an earlier period'. So too Murphy, in 'Saga and Myth in Ancient Ireland' (Dublin, 1955), p. 56 speaks of AMC as 'extant in two twelfth century versions'. But no one has ever rigorously examined the language, apart from Hull, whose (somewhat unsatisfactory) treatment of the verb in ZCP XXIX led him to conclude the tale was composed about 1100.

Meyer was scarcely yet an expert in MI when his AMC was published, and his opinion on the date of its language is not supported by evidence. As to the matter of tithes, which has probably been largely responsible for the confident treatment of AMC as mid or late 12th century, Hull was quite right to point out (op. cit. p. 325 n. 1) that Meyer's admission that tithes are 'mentioned earlier' than the middle of the 12th century does not 'confirm' his date. The fact is that the claim to the payment of tithes was well established in Ireland from at least the 7th century, as the late Kathleen Hughes remarked to me with

reference to the ecclesiastical discussion of them printed in L.
Bieler's 'The Irish Penitentials' (Scriptores Latini Hibernici, 5;
Dublin, 1963), pp. 166 ff. R. D. Nuner, in ZCP XXVII, 233,
lists a number of out of date writers whom he takes to show that
the payment of tithes scarcely existed before the late 12th
century, implying that AMC can be no earlier, though he admits
the mention of them (as an existing institution) in Fís Adomnán
in LU M 2177. In any case it is most unlikely that strong
opposition to and non-payment of tithes must have preceded the
Synod of Kells by only a short time. The movement may have
been gathering strength for a very long time, and we should note
that it was not the actual payment of them that Mac Con Glinne
was satirising but the *claim* to them. If the generally accepted
view that Acallam na Senórach and the standardisation of the
Classical Bardic language both date from about 1200 is correct,
everyone must agree, on linguistic grounds, that AMC cannot be
anything approaching as late as only half a century before them;
and Nuner's statement (loc. cit.) that 'tithes were very little
exacted in Ireland till the establishment of English power' (in
1170) is valueless as a basis for dating AMC later than that or
anywhere near it.

Taking the foregoing discussion together with the detailed
examination of the language of AMC in the Appendix below, I
conclude, then, that the last quarter of the 11th century is a
reasonable date for the composition of Version B.

ANALYSIS OF THE TALE

THE RELATION OF B TO H

Some matters relevant to the following are discussed by
Wollner in his Introduction to Meyer's edition, but there is no
space to treat some of them here. The reader is referred to KM
pp. xiv–xxxix, though I do not always agree with his views,
which for one thing do not always allow for the considerable
differences between mediaeval Irish and Continental society and
literature.

The Version of H

The essence of the tale in both versions is a fusion of two
widespread popular elements. One is the belief about curing a

sick man of a tape-worm by starving him—and the worm—and
then setting food which it likes in front of the victim's nose and
open mouth, so that the hungry worm, attracted by the smell,
pops its head out and is caught and destroyed; see Note to l. 9.
The other is the familiar early Irish theme of 'The Land of
the Living', the Earthly Paradise across the ocean, where the
wonderful apples grow, the rivers flow with mead and wine,
and the Immortals feast eternally; which land may occasionally
be reached by mortal heroes and their men after a long sea
voyage, in some versions passing islands full of marvels on the
way. This is used—and parodied—in AMC as part of the
recitation of foods which lures out the tape-worm Demon. How
far it is influenced by the international popular motif of the
wonderful Land of Cockayne (AT 2. 1930), if at all, is not quite
clear, because although abundance of food for the taking is one of
its features (roasted pigs running about crying 'Eat me!' etc.),
marvels of quite different sorts are more prominent there.

In H, Cathal has a monstrous appetite, due to a demon of
gluttony inside him (= B §2). Mac Con Glinne, of the
monastery of Fathan Mura north of Derry (not in B), travels to
Cork with a lay-brother; their route through Armagh etc. is
described (cf. B §§ 10–13). They stop at Kells, where they get no
food (not in B), and MC composes a satirical verse in the hearing
of the monks, 'Lay Brother, let us compose two antithetical
verses' etc. (= B § 19, v. 1). They reach the monastery guest-
house at Cork when the Munstermen are arriving for its saint's
day festival (the last not in B). Manchín sends a clerical student
to see whether there are any guests; he reports there is a
master-poet who will satirise the monastery for giving him no
attendance. Manchín orders a wretched fire and a bowl of oats
for them (cf. B §§ 17–18). Angered by this meanness, MC
composes a satirical verse (= B § 19, v. 3). The student reports,
and Manchín, alarmed by the satire, orders MC to be hanged
next day (cf. B § 20). MC begs a favour in the name of the patron
saint—plenty of food and drink, and to sleep in M's comfortable
bed (cf. B § 28). M grants it, and MC dreams there, and that his
patron St. Mura tells him to relate the dream to Cathal and so
rescue him from the Demon (cf. B § 29); MC then sings the
Vision poem (= B § 33, quoted in H later, KM p. 120. 4 ff.). MC
is brought before Cathal and the assembly, but C refuses to hang

a poet himself and hands him over to the monks (not in B). C grants him a favour, to drink his fill of water; at the well, MC dips his brooch-pin and keeps dripping water into his mouth, thus delaying the execution. C allows a respite till morning (cf. B §§ 21–25).

Cathal goes to the house of Pichán, sub-king of Iveagh, and MC joins him there (cf. B §§ 34 and 36). C munches apples, and MC, who makes chewing motions though without food, explains he is ashamed to let him eat alone; he begs thirteen apples, justifying each by religious analogies, till C loses his temper (cf. B §§ 40–42). MC, dressed as a cook, roasts meat (= B § 48). C is pleased, and permits him to describe his Vision, though he threatens to hang him next day (not in B). MC recites the poem about it (= B §§ 51 a and 51 b). That night, in his comfortable bed, an Apparition calls him to get up to avoid being drowned in gravy, and asks him who he is (cf. B § 52). 'A poor scholar, seeking to cure C of his gluttony.' 'I will guide you to the O'Early-Eatings and the "retreat" of the Prognostic Physician,' says the Apparition, naming himself as Dirty Belch son of Fluxy (cf. B §§ 54 and 55).

MC now gets up as swiftly as a fox to his food etc. (cf. B § 59), takes a boat of corned beef etc., and with unspecified companions rows across Milk Lake, through stormy seas of curds and whey etc. etc., and reaches port at the Prognostic Physician's 'retreat' in the land of the O'Early-Eatings (cf. B § 60). There he recites the Vision poem mentioned above describing his voyage, the PP's fort and its surroundings, all made of foods, and the inhabitants dressed and armed with foods (= B § 33). He tells how they landed and saw the PP's servant fishing in Milk Lake with a hook of marrow and line of lard etc., catching salmon made of bacon etc., and told him he was seeking the PP (cf. B § 64). The servant advises him to ask protection of the chiefs of the Tribes of Food against the waves of gravy (cf. B ll. 1000–5). Next morning MC meets Fatty Becnat, ancestress of the Tribes of Food, on her horse of suet etc., in her cloak of corned beef etc., and she tells him the PP lives nearby (not in B).

MC comes to the precinct between Butter Mountain and Milk Lake in the land of the O'Early-Eatings, built of various foods (cf. B §§ 60–61). The two porters cannot open the door in the precinct wall, but MC squeezes in past the door-post (cf. B § 62), and sees a church made of foods, and the chief priest, i.e. the PP (not in B). MC greets him with the poem 'Bless us, priest' etc. (= B §31). The priest is on a horse of bacon, etc. etc., and dressed in and accoutred with various other foods (cf. B §63, where the priest has become the PP's porter). He puts MC under the protection of good food and drink (not in B, but cf. below). MC says he has come to be cured of fearful voracity, which he describes (= B §66). The priest says that is nothing in this island, where a month-old child could consume all that (not in B); and to MC's intention of demolishing food there (not in B) he compares a list of nineteen futile actions (= B §53; see Note). He offers to cure MC, who is to fast, light a great fire, and get a woman to feed him (briefly described; vastly expanded in B §67). This will cure any illness except diarrhoea (cf. B ll. 1215-18). MC asks his name, and the PP, which he is now explicitly called, says he is Little Wheat son of Little Fresh Milk, etc. (= the poems §57 a and 57 b in B). He hangs a Gospel-book of bacon round MC's neck as an amulet, and puts him under the protection of various foods etc. (= B §58). MC now sets off to the chiefs of the Tribes of Food, a long list of metaphorical names of foods (= B §69), ending with gulps of thick and thin milk which talk together as they are swallowed (= B §70).

While describing all these adventures to Cathal, MC has been roasting steaks on spits and passing them close under C's nose. Now the Demon pounces out of his mouth after one, grabs it, and jumps into the mouth of a priest's servant-boy who is beside a cauldron by the fire, and thence on to the spit in MC's hand. MC thrusts the Demon, spit, steak and all, into the fire and inverts the cauldron over them; and C is rushed out of the great hall, which is deserted by everyone and set on fire (cf. B §72); and the Demon screams as it is burned (not in B).

C gets up next day, 'Aren't you pleased I cured you?' says MC, and 'Aren't you pleased I'm not going to hang you?' says C (not in B). He offers MC permanent employment as his carver, and clothing and an arm-ring, and a hundred cattle, as his reward (cf. B §75). Manchín indignantly asks 'Is it thus you remove from me the man who satirised the Church?' MC however demands a trial and legal acquittal; judges must be summoned, Manchín must put a pledge in Cathal's hands and MC himself will do likewise, and the judges shall declare which of them shall have the right to compensation for damage. The judges declare for MC because he made no satire but only said he would not eat the oats of Cork. 'I want no honour-price or compensation,' says MC, 'except the cowl which is in the church' (cf. B § 35). 'You shall have it with my blessing,' says M (almost nothing of this whole paragraph is in B). Then a buffoon and his son and daughter recite the poem 'Manchín came—a glorious task—to prosecute Mac Con Glinne' (= B § 76); and the version of H ends there with 'And so Cathal son of Finguine was cured of gluttony and Mac Con Glinne was exalted'.

Before discussing B's version, a word must be said on the relation of the two. This has been treated by Wollner in Meyer's edition. H's version is economical, straightforward, logical, and well-constructed in its sequence of events, though there are a few contradictions and doublets, whereas B is diffuse, illogical, and very badly constructed. It is evident that H represents a relatively primary compilation and B a secondary one. Not chronologically, however, for there appears to be nothing in their language to suggest at all clearly that either is older than the other. According to KM, p. x, H is much more modern in its language, but he made no attempt to show this, and at this early date in his career was perhaps hardly qualified to do so. He may have been led astray by H's orthography. Myles Dillon, in his 'Early Irish Literature', loc. cit., curtly says of H 'the language is later', but his view of the relationship seems coloured by Meyer. Gerard Murphy, loc. cit., treats the two as both 12th century without discussing which is prior. The only scholar who has compared the language of both in detail (for the verb and infixed pronoun only) is Vernam Hull, who concluded that H is 'somewhat older' than B (ZCP XXIX, 373 ff., specially 377), though his use of part of TBC II L as his standard is not satisfactory, and his evidence for this conclusion is hardly decisive; nevertheless it is closer to probability than the reverse dating is.

It is very clear, however, that the *content*, the version, of H is prior, and that B is a secondary elaboration of a previous common ancestor tale (call it X) which H pretty faithfully preserved. Now, anyone who compares the two texts in detail must be struck by two conclusions. One, that the texts of the poems which occur in both MSS are almost always very close to each other, so that in most cases H can freely be used for variant readings (and this applies also, but *very* much less closely, to one or two 'rhetorical' prose passages or 'runs', somewhat analogous to verse, notably §§ 41, 53, and 69 in B compared respectively with H p. 116 ll. 29 ff., p. 125 ll. 18-27 and p. 127 ll. 12-27). Two, that otherwise the whole of the rest of the prose in H, however much it may tell the same *story* in the various episodes, is of little use for more than occasional variant readings, since the actual wording is so consistently different. The conclusion is obvious. The composer of B was not using a written text of X (or of H), but the prose parts of AMC were known to him as an oral tale, which, in the manner familiar to students of Irish literature and folklore, was preserved and handed on by memory but not necessarily so closely preserved that the one version must be a word for word rendering of the other. This would also account for the confusion into which the plot of the tale has fallen in the B version. With the poems however it is different. Between X and B/H the reciters either had written texts of these, or had memorised them pretty carefully, though not without a few lapses. Like verse, the 'rhetorical' prose passages were also more easily remembered than ordinary prose. This, of course, is comparable to Ifor Williams' convincing theory of the preservation of the early Welsh Llywarch Hen poems contrasted with the in this case total loss of the linking prose narrative;[6] a theory which has recently come under ill-informed and ill-considered attack in some quarters. It does not at all follow that X must have been *much* older than H or B—it may well have been almost contemporary, though the discussion of the character of Mac Con Glinne below may suggest that tales about him were older than X.

B'S USE OF THE STORY

It seems likely that H did little with X except to repeat it in the usual way. B however used it for his own very different purpose—a satire on or perhaps better a mockery of the Establishment of his own day, with all the humour of extraordinary situations and fantastic exaggerations so typical of some

[6] A good instance of an exact Irish parallel to this is seen in the MI poems about St. Mo Ling and Suibne Geilt in Anecd. II, 20 ff., evidently from a Life of the saint or version of *Buile Shuibhne* of which the prose parts were not recorded. Cf. Féil. Mhic Néill pp. 536 ff.

aspects of Irish storytelling. This is presented as a rollicking and mostly good-natured caricature or burlesque, mock-heroic or mock-pious in part, the humour characterised by an incongruous application of high-flown treatment to essentially mundane subjects, and by the frequent use of parody. Adventure is mixed in in a way recalling Gulliver's Travels; the gusto suggests Rabelais or Hudibras; the parody and general *weltanschauung* remind one of James Joyce. There is a certain element of this in H already, presumably derived from X, such as the passage about MC's demands for apples in B § 41 = H pp. 116 l. 29–117 l. 12, and of course the poems and some other passages playing on the repeated names of foods. Such things probably gave B the idea of using AMC as a vehicle for his mockery, which however he expanded vastly by comparison with H. This may have played a part in bringing about the disintegration of the coherent tale seen in H into the disorganisation of the B text, and would explain why it is so much longer than H. B muddles the order of some episodes and inserts his own inventions in unsuitable places. There are unnecessary repetitions, widely scattered, and some contradictions, and the loose structure has allowed small essentials to drop out, so that it is not always clear what is happening and why. The point has been discussed by Wollner in KM, pp. xv–xxii, and need not be dealt with here, though some of his conclusions on pp. xxii–xxxi suffer from unfamiliarity with early Irish literature and society, among other drawbacks.

Most of the passages of any length in B which are not in H—and they are numerous—are examples of what the composer of the B version was doing, i.e. making fun of the Establishment. Since so much of the tale is devoted to it is important to understand this. There are three social groups or professions at which B's mockery is chiefly aimed. First and most obvious, the monks, particularly those of Cork. He makes MC abuse them in surprising language as 'curs, robbers, and shit-hounds' (§ 24, cf. §§ 26 and 28), and calls them 'You illiterate beasts, you shifty, bungling, hangdog monks of Cork'. Yet he butters them up outrageously elsewhere as 'noble, wise, chaste, and men of integrity' (§ 73), though as this is put in the mouth of the Demon it is perhaps meant to be ironical. The monks are attacked for their meanness to guests and the filth of their guest-house (§§ 14, 15, 17, and 18); there is a small germ of this in H, and it was no

doubt in X as it is essential to the story, but the mocking
expansion of it in B is typical of him. MC composes a verse
satire, and bitterly refuses to touch the miserable ration brought
him (§ 19), so that the servant has to take it back again; which also
has its meagre roots in H. This episode is derived from an older
tale with no connection with AMC or with monks (see the Note
to ll. 118 ff.), which shows that though X and H had the original
idea about the meanness of Cork, B expanded it under this
influence. MC is so angry with the reaction of Manchín and his
monks that when, later, he asks permission to eat the scanty
picnic he brought with him to Cork he cuts off a tenth part of the
food and sarcastically offers this to the monks as tithes (§ 23).
Then, he has the impudence to tell Manchín that the saints in
Heaven are all chanting in eager expectation of his soul, and the
Nine Orders of Angels and the Cherubim and Seraphim are
awaiting him; and that he does not care though Cathal and the
nobles of Munster and of all southern Ireland, with the monks of
Cork and Manchín above all, should die and go to Hell on a
single night, because he knows that he himself will be in Heaven
along with the Trinity (§ 34; cf. § 26). The elaborate scene in
Pichán's hall in § 41, concerning the number of apples MC begs
of Cathal, is meant as a send-up of mediaeval Irish erudition,
including the symbolical lore of numbers dear to the early Irish
clerical mind, but incongruously applied here to a trivial object.
This is one of the very few of B's skits that were already in X.
See the Notes to § 41. The rest is chiefly a matter of parodies of
situations or motifs. In § 16 MC can be heard a mile away from
the monastery as he sings his psalms, which is a take-off of a
motif found in some saints' Lives, e.g. Adamnán's Life of St.
Columba, which tells how when Columba sang psalms he could
be heard, miraculously, half a mile or a mile away (Anderson,
1961, p. 286). A more extreme case is spread through §§ 20–29
where some of the elements of Christ's Passion are apparently
applied to MC, though not all in the correct order (it is
significant that on hearing his sentence of hanging he says he will
go obediently, 'as our Lord Jesus Christ went to his Passion';
§ 27). That is, he is arraigned before Manchín, condemned to be
hanged, stripped and flogged, made to cut his own gallows-tree
and carry it to the place of execution and set it up, and stripped
again and tied to a pillar-stone (in that order). The blasphemous

parody is no doubt intentional, but too much has been made of it owing to KM's repeated rendering of the verb *crochaid* as 'crucifies' which is its etymological but not, in Irish custom, its practical meaning;[7] though presumably it would remind the listeners of the Crucifixion. Other passages involving parodies of religious concepts are (1) the use of protective written prayers or small copies of the Gospels worn hung round the neck as amulets against harm, familiar in Ireland (cf. § 12), which is guyed in § 58 by having the gospel-book made of dry cheese; and the custom of putting the wearer under the protection of various holy powers is parodied by making MC's protectors bacon, clotted cream, and porridge. And (2), where in the 'Lives' of the Irish saints demons and other wicked beings may do homage to saints and acknowledge them as superior powers, we see in § 73 the Demon rather absurdly applying this to MC; the same being implied also of St. Bridget, though without explanation or any other mention of her in the tale.

The second Establishment body that gets ribbed by MC is the lawyers, whose legal learning and practice was of great importance in early Irish society. In this case there is no explicit, direct attack on them, but only a mild poking of fun. We see this in the way that MC demands that binding pledges should be given and sureties appointed to guarantee the due fulfilment of any agreement by which he profits, however informal. In § 23 he asks a boon of Manchín, but will not say what it is until he has binding legal guarantees for its fulfilment—and then reveals that what he asks is to be allowed to eat his picnic as a gallows-meal before he is hanged; an episode which mocks at legal formality by its very triviality. Again Pichán offers MC a reasonable reward for keeping Cathal away from his house, which MC rejects (§ 38). Pichán has to raise his offer to an unreasonable one, levied on his kingdom of Iveagh, which MC graciously accepts, provided certain outrageous conditions are met concerning guarantees of due performance, which MC binds legally on the guarantors— kings to enforce it, great landowners to maintain MC during the levying, and poets to lampoon Pichán and his family and satirists to spread the lampoons abroad if MC is cheated of his dues. In this farcical scene we have a glimpse of the way the early Irish

---

[7] Cf. V. Mercier, 'The Irish Comic Tradition' (Oxford, 1962), 214 ff.

aristocracy feared satire, because their reputations and social standing could be seriously damaged by ill-fame. MC's demands are preposterous; no king would have stooped to enforce private claims, particularly of such a nature (see Note to l. 569). This is a good example of the mocking humour of fantasy and exaggeration typical of AMC. Similarly, in § 45 Cathal tries to bribe MC not to insist on his fasting with him against God to save him from the curse of the monks, some of his offers being similar to those MC demanded of Pichán; but in Cathal's case the payments are of course to be levied on the whole of Munster. Part of this reappears in §§ 75 and 76 (but in 76 with the illogical condition that the payments are levied on Iveagh) as Cathal's reward to MC for saving him from the Demon, but without the legal feature of guarantors etc.

The passage in § 35 where MC demands Manchín's cowl as his reward for his projected cure of Cathal makes Manchín reluctantly agree to give it, but it is delivered into the keeping of the Bishop of Cork to hold until MC fulfils his pledge. This legal obligation on the bishop is duly fulfilled at Cathal's instigation in a brief sentence in § 75, but in H p. 128 ll. 23–24 there is a lawsuit brought by M against MC for compensation for the insult of MC's satire on Cork. MC demands a tribunal of judges to decide which of the two should be adjudged compensation to be paid by the other, and that both should deposit pledges with Cathal for the payment. The judges find for MC, on the ground that he did not compose a satire, but MC waives compensation, saying that all he wants is Manchín's cowl (which had been deposited with the Bishop of Cork, to be given to MC if he cured Cathal, in B § 35, but not yet handed over); and Manchín agrees. This is another little sketch of legal procedure intended as gentle burlesque. Incidentally, neither text gives the slightest indication of why this cowl was regarded as such a valuable object.

The custom of 'fasting against' someone to obtain a concession or enforce a claim, that is to say hunger-striking, was an ancient and accepted part of Irish legal practice, and appears here in § 35. Composers of 'Lives' of the Irish saints sometimes extended it to making their saints 'fast against God' to obtain requests. On this see D. Binchy in Whitelock, McKitterick, and Dumville (edd.), 'Ireland and Early Mediaeval Europe' (Cambridge, 1982), pp. 168 ff. But B typically uses this for a preposterous burlesque in having MC persuade Cathal and all the company in Pichán's hall to fast with him against God to save him from the curse of the monks of Cork (§ 44 f.).

There is a humorous episode in § 43 where Cathal grants the clergy (of all Ireland) exemption from military service, something which they had never had before. However, in Irish tradition this 'Law' was ascribed to various saints, but with most probability to Fothad na Canóine, who is said to have obtained it from Aed Oirdnide, king of northern Ireland, in 804, more than sixty years later than Cathal's reign. Compare K. Hughes, 'The Church in Early Irish Society' (London, 1966), pp. 191 f., and Fél. 2 pp. 4 and 10. This passage is hardly a mockery of the lawyers, but like some others mentioned above its incongruity does give a humorous context to the Law.

The third Establishment body mocked in B is the literary men, in the form of examples of their style which are made to look foolish. The composer scarcely criticises the highest levels of the poetic Establishment, but confines himself chiefly to burlesquing traditional features of prose narrative and native lore. The story opens with an example, of ecclesiastical origin but sometimes applied to secular literature, 'the four things which are to be asked about any literary composition' (see Note to l. 3). Here the joke lies in the incongruity of using this high-flown learned passage to introduce a farcical work like B's version of AMC. Parody is much in evidence; quite often in the mock-heroic style, as in § 15 where the vermin in the guest-house bed are ludicrously said to be 'as many as the sands of the sea or sparks of fire or dew-drops on a May Day morning or the stars of Heaven'—a passage well-known in various forms in the hero-tales applied to the enemies killed by the hero in his battle frenzy. The long genealogical poem in § 31 is a blatant send-up of the innumerable genealogies of kings and nobles, sometimes—as here—tracing them back to Adam,[8] which were part of the stock of learned literary men at their courts. There is a clear take-off of the hero-tales in § 42, about the hideous distortions undergone by warriors when enraged. After which, Cathal forces his back against the wall of the palace so hard that the house-posts etc. were all twisted; which looks like a reminiscence of the episode in

[8] V. Mercier, op. cit. p. 216 takes this as a parody of Christ's genealogy in Luke III, 23-38. But this ignores all early Irish history and literature.

the 'Feast of Bricriu' where Cú Chulainn grips the sill of the palace wall and heaves it right up so that his wife and her ladies can get in from outside (ed. G. Henderson, Irish Texts Society II, 30). In both passages the humour consists of the incongruity between the feats of traditional heroes and the (supposed) doings of historical kings. Still another example is the way in which the Apparition warns MC in a dream to beware of getting drowned in gravy (§ 52) and advises him to go to the Prognostic Physician to get a cure for his ravenous appetite (§ 55). This parodies the motif of the wise man or woman who warns a hero about his difficult journey and advises where to go for help, in Irish tales of adventure.

One of the most characteristic features of such stories is the elaborate decorative rhetorical passages, often with strings of alliterating nouns and adjectives, sometimes quite long, called 'runs'. These lend themselves to parody and burlesque, and in AMC they get it. We have seen how the Voyage to the Earthly Paradise, perhaps mixed with the international theme of the Land of Cockayne, is employed, and parodied, to stir up the greed of the Demon in Cathal's throat. The point is made again and again, including in the form of verse and of runs. The first two verses of § 33, and the whole of the prose § 60, parody the 'sea runs' which were a favourite in Irish tales of adventure, describing how the warriors prepare their boat, set off across stormy seas, passing various perils, until they come safely to their goal. The most remarkable of these in Irish literature is probably §§ 32 to the beginning of 35 in CML 2. Other burlesque runs in AMC are in §§ 48, on MC's behaviour and dress as a cook; 53, on the Futile Actions (see the Note); 59, MC's wild rush to the Land of Food; 63, the Prognostic Physician's porter and his horse; 65–66 and the first part of 67, the Physician's diagnosis of MC's symptoms and MC's own description of them; and 67–70 the regimen recommended. Incidentally, §§ 65–70 are evidently a send-up of another profession, the medical practitioners. The long passage in the second part of § 67 describing the kind of nurse MC needs is particularly striking, since it is a parody of similar runs in early Irish story about the beauty of a heroine, the best and best known being that describing Étaín in the 9th-century tale 'The Destruction of Da Derga's Hostel'. Of course, parodies of the Earthly Paradise theme or

xxxviii   INTRODUCTION

representations of the Land of Cockayne motif in terms of
foods are common in AMC in prose passages hardly constituting
runs, or in verse. The poem which is §33 is a parody of
descriptive poems sung by heroes on their return from the
Earthly Paradise.

Other episodes or themes which are more or less parodies, or
at least incongruous uses of themes familiar in Irish story, may
be mentioned briefly. First the *serc écmaise* motif in §3 (see Note
to l. 21); the use of the 'eight universal things' motif in §6 (see
Note to ll. 50 f.); §13 MC's incredibly rapid journey to Cork,
possibly a take-off of the Connaught army's march to Ulster in
the Cattle Raid of Cooley; and §77, the list of the reputedly 30
(actually only 6) benefits which will accrue to those who listen to
the tale—ending with the rewards expected by the reciter. The
basic idea of MC's mean reception at Cork, already present in H
and therefore derived from X, is influenced in B by a similar
passage in a 'Mythological' tale (see Note to ll. 118 ff.), and is
therefore an imitation rather than a parody. Other minor items
borrowed humorously from old tales are the several appeals to
the authority of 'the Books of Cork' (ll. 139, 593, 708, 1236,
1292, 1334); the mention of 'other versions', 'story-tellers,
sages', or 'learned men' as sources (ll. 592, 708, 1232-7, 1290-3
and 1333 f.; cf. DIL S 271. 85 ff.) and the variant versions of the
fate of the Demon (ll. 1232-7), one of which is the version of H.
Other such are the (erroneous) etymological speculation in ll.
1230 f., which is also in H; the use of what appear to be or are said
to be traditional sayings (ll. 752 ff., 765 ff., 775 ff.); and a typical
supposed explanation of a place-name (l. 351).

The only important element in the early Irish Establishment
not guyed or burlesqued is the nobility. Cathal appears in a
rather ludicrous light, of course, but that is essential to the tale;
the sub-king of Iveagh, Pichán, is treated with respect. There is a
nice point of aristocratic tact in §§39 f.: Cathal throws himself
greedily and impolitely on the food as soon as he enters Pichán's
hall, but MC makes his own hunger so evident that Cathal
pauses to enquire what is wrong. MC replies with a polite
reproof, that he could not bear to see the great king of Southern
Ireland eating alone when everyone else was fasting (sc., making
a spectacle of himself), when anyone who did not know the

special excuse for his greed might despise and abuse him (for his
bad manners). This is a tactful way of pointing out to Cathal that
he was behaving with a lack of generosity unworthy of a king. If
we can safely infer anything about the original Author from this
non-satirical attitude to the nobles, we might conclude that like
MC he was a disgruntled cleric who took up the profession of
poetry, as other early Irish clergy known to us did, and hence
became a client, and therefore partisan, of the nobility.

THE FIGURE OF MAC CON GLINNE

One problem remains. Who was MC supposed to be? How
was he envisaged by the Author? Is this a picture of a genuine
type in society? What were thought to be his origins?

Our information on the last is contradictory. In H he is an
Ulsterman, a clerical student, a member of the monastic
community at Fathan Mura (Fahan) in the Inishowen peninsula
north-west of Derry; and it is his Ulster patron saint Mura who
sings the Vision poem to him in H p. 120 ll. 4 ff. (quoted, later in
the tale, in B's § 33), the part played by 'the Angel' in B § 29. In B,
however, MC is a Munsterman (l. 1038), and even one of
Cathal's royal kindred of the Eóganacht of Glennamain (l. 6; see
the Index of Places etc.). But this is probably secondary, for his
northern connections seem encapsulated in B, where in § 8 he is
'Aniér from the bank of the Bann' and one of the eight strange
characters said to be 'in Armagh' (see the Note on § 8); and it is
from Armagh that he sets out for Cork. The poem is not likely to
have been composed by B, because it clashes in this matter with
B's version of the tale, nor indeed by the original Author, for its
connection with MC is so tenuous. It appears more probable
that it comes from independent traditions about 'Mac Con
Glinne' now almost completely lost, belonging to the Ulster
connection, which were already part of the 'saga' of MC at an
early stage, and that it was included in his version by B because it
was already an established part of it. The verse quoted in the note
to the Féilire of Oengus, Fél. 2 p. 208 (see the Note to l. 6 below)
is more likely to have come from an early variant version of the
poem used by B in his § 8 than the other way round. There has
evidently been some displacing of lines, presumably oral. It
seems probable, then, that the figure of a peculiar character

called Mac Con Glinne, who was thought at some early stage sufficiently similar to the other oddities to be included with them in the poem used in §8, was already known in story before the composition of the original AMC by the Author; that this oldest tradition made him an Ulsterman; and that it was due to some secondary influence that the strong association with Munster took over. Perhaps B was a Munsterman himself, which would explain the close familiarity with Munster place-names and other features seen in his version. In any case Cathal was king of Munster and Cork was its chief monastery, though this does not explain why Munster was the scene of events in X instead of Ulster, unless indeed the tape-worm story was so firmly linked with Cathal that it had to be there.

In H, MC begins as 'a splendid scholar' or 'student' (*scolaige*; KM p. 114, l. 5), but when they reach Cork his travelling companion, the lay-brother 'Scabby', plans to pass him off as a *fer dána*, 'poet' (p. 114, l. 28) or even, preposterously, as an *ollam*, the highest grade of qualified professional poet (H p. 115. 10), thinking this would procure them better treatment. Manchín and Cathal both call him *fer dána* (KM, pp. 115. 22 and 116. 27), and Cathal refuses to hang him because he is a *bard* (116. 10). As to B, MC is there often called *scolaige*, and in l. 84 is 'a wonderful *scolaige* with abundant erudition', but in ll. 89-91 he is a *scolaige* who has grown sick of his studies and wants to abandon them to become a *file*, a high-ranking poet and sage; and in l. 344 he is actually described as an *ecnaid* ('sage'). Cathal, however, constantly addresses him as *mac cléirech*, 'clerical student'. The Prognostic Physician speaks of him as 'a noble satirist and brilliant entertainer' (§81). Of course most of this is an aspect of B's fondness for exaggeration. The verse quoted in the MI notes to the Féilire of Oengus says 'he made many lays'.

It appears then that tradition said he began as a clerical student in Ulster, probably at Fathan Mura, but abandoned the Church for the profession of poet. The fact that in H he travelled with such a wretched 'retinue' as 'Scabby' and with none at all in B means that he cannot have been envisaged as having yet attained any recognised grade of professional poet, and that all the talk about 'sage' and *file* is mere hyperbole. Evidently all he 'really' was was a lapsed clerical student, a *mac cléirech* or *scolaige*, with an ambition to be a poet and enough knowledge of

versification to compose simple poems and low minstrelsy. In
§ 36 MC dresses himself as a kind of jester or buffoon or vulgar
satirist of very low rank, a *drúth* or *crosán*. The queer costume
he puts on, reminiscent of the layered shoulder-capes of a
Dickensian coachman, is presumably the uniform of such a
person, and his conduct in Pichán's hall is justly described as
'unseemly', though his satirical songs are admired by the
company. In KM pp. xli f. Wollner sees in this aspect of MC a
Continental *clericus vagans*, 'a wandering scholar', a Goliard,
and the parallel is striking, even, according to Wollner, to the
costume;[9] but there seems no reason to suppose that this very
European institution had found its way to Ireland, or cause to
think that the *drúth* or *crosán* is not a wholly native Irish figure.
Once again, it can be risky to see Continental characteristics in
early Irish institutions without an adequate knowledge of Irish
conditions.

[9] Actually the only real similarity to MC's costume in W's account of the dress
of a Continental minstrel is that MC's is described as 'short clothing' (l. 545).
Moreover the fashions in English male dress in the reign of Edward III can have
no relevance to those of Irishmen in the 11th to 12th centuries.

INCIPIT DO AISLINGE
MEIC CON GLINNE

[213a26]   **1** Cethardai as c[h]uintesta da cach elathain, iss
ed as c[h]uintesta don eladain-se, .i. locc [7 persu]¹ 7 aimser
7 *fáth* airicc. Locc don eladain-se Corcach mór Muman, 7   5
persu dí Anér Mac Con Glinde di Eóganacht Glenn-
amnach². I n-aimsir C[h]athail meic Fhinguine meic Con
cen Gairm nó meic Con cen Máthair do-rónad. Is hé di*diu*
fáth airicc a dénma .i. do díchor in luin c[h]raeis bhoí i
mbrágait C[h]athail meic Fhinguine.   10
   2 Cathal mac Finguine, rí maith ro gab Mumai; araile
laech-mál mór e-sside. Amlaid boí in laech-sin, co ngéri
chon, co longad chapaill. Sáttan, ¹.i. lon craís boí i n-a
brágait,¹ no meled a chuit laiss. Mucc 7 mart 7 ag *teóra*
ferglacc, la trí fichte bairgen do fhír-c[h]ruithnecht, 7   15
dabach do nua chorma 7 trícha og rerchirce, ba h-í in sin.
a p[h]rím-airaigid, cenmothá a [fh]rith-airaigid, comba
h-erlam a mór-fheiss dó. Dáig in mór-fheiss, ní thalla rím
nó áirem *fu*rri-sene.
   3 Is hé trá *fáth* airicc in luin c[h]raís i mbrágait   20
C[h]athail meic Fhinghuine, dáig boí cét-sher*cus* écmaise
dó fria Lígaig ingin Moíle Dúin, ríg Oilig, 7 derbshiúr-side
do Fhergal mac Moíle Dúin, rí Oilig beós; 7 ba cosnamaid¹
Érenn e-sside an inbaid-sin i n-agaid Cathail meic Fhinguine, am*al* is f[h]ollus a h-imarbáig in dá chaillech dia   25
nd*ern*sat in dí chammrand i nAchad Úr saindrud:

   4   I. ¹'Do-s fil atuaid¹
        mac Moíle Dúin dar ailechu,

---

1 ¹ B *om., but cf. l. 6.*   ² B Glennabrach; *see Index of Place-*
Names, Glennamain.
   2 ¹⁻¹ *Interlinear gloss.*
   3 ¹ B cosnamaig
   4 ¹⁻¹ B *repeats, hypermetrically.*

¹dar Berba brú;¹
30   co ruca bú ní aineba.'

2. 'Anfaid, anfaid,   (ar in chaillech aness)
bid buide lais dia n-érnaba;
dar láim m' athar
²dia táir² Cathal, ní-s béraba.'

35   **5** Do-bertis iarum ettne 7 ubla 7 il-blassa ó Lígaig ingin
Mo[í]li Dúin do C[h]athal mac Fhinguine for a sheirc 7
inmaine. At-c[h]uala Fergal mac Moíle Dúin in ní-sin, 7
do-garad a shiúr a dochumm, 7 do-mbert bennachtain dí
for fír d' indissi dó 7 mallacht dia s[h]énad fair. Ro indis in
40   [t]shiúr dó, ar cia boí dia sheircc 7 grád C[h]athail meic
Fhinguine aicce, rop omun lee mallacht a bráthar dia
rochtain. Ro indis iar sin in scél fíre.

6 At-bert in bráthair fria na h-ubla do t[h]achor chuice,
7 ro gairmed scolaige i n-a dochumm, 7 do-ruachell lógu
45   móra don scolaigi ar thuathi do chur isna h-il-blassaib út
do admilled C[h]athail meic Fhinguine. Ocus ro lá in
scolaigi tuathi 7 gentlecht isna h-il-blassaib-sin, 7 ¹ro
tidnacit¹ chuca ina h-il-blassa, 7 cartaid timthirid dia
tidnocul do C[h]athal. Ocus ro gáidetar for nach ochta²
50   coitc[h]end, .i. grian 7 ésca, drúcht 7 muir, nem 7 talam, lá
³[7 adaig, im ithe]³ na n-uball út, uair is ar a grád 7 inmaine
tuccad ó Lígaig ingin Mo[í]li Dúin.

7 Do-romel Cathal na h-ubla iarum, 7 do-rigne míla
eptha díb i n-a medón, 7 timoir[c]sit na míla eptha-sin i
55   mbroind oen ¹[míl díb, cor fhásatar]¹ isin anmunna-sin, co
nderna lon craís de; conid hé sin fáth oricc in luin chraís do
attreib i mbrágait C[h]athail meic Fhinguine, do aidmilled
f[h]er Muman co cend teóra leth-bliadan, 7 is dóig no
mille[d] Éirinn co cend leth-bliadna ele.

---

²⁻² B dianustáir
6 ¹⁻¹ B ro thidnacit   ² B .uiia.   ³⁻³ *Lacuna with space for*
about nine or ten letters.
7 ¹⁻¹ *Lacuna with space for about sixteen or seventeen letters.*

8 Boí ochtar i nArd Macha an inboid-sin, 7 is dóib-side 60
ro canad[1] in laíd-se:

1. 'At-c[h]uala ochtar anocht
   i nArd Macha iar midnocht,
   for-t-gillim co mbuidnib band
   nidat c[h]uibde a comanmand.   65

2. Comgán [213b] ar Mac Dá Cherda,
   ba *h*-erdraic i ndiaid shelga;
   Crítán for Mac Rustaing rán,
   ba *h*-ainm comadais comlán.

3. Dub Dá Thuath, ba togairm nglé,   70
   ba *h*-é ainm meic Stéléne;
   Don[n]-Fhiach; Caillech Bérre bán;
   Garb Daire for Mac Samán.

4. Aniér for Mac Con Glinde
   do brú Banda barr-binde;   75
   Becán, Becnait, bolg don[2] ár,
   athair sceó máthair Marbán.

5. Mo rí-se[3], rí nime náir[4],
   do-b*eir* for buidne [5]buad n-áir[5],
   mac muad Maire[6], mod nát[7] bá,   80
   comur ngaire ro-chuala.'
                                   At-c[h]uala ochtar.

9 Ba h-aen trá don ochtar-sin, .i. Aniér Mac Con
Glinne, scolaigi amru e-ss*ide* co n-immad eólais. Is aire
at-bertha Aniér friss, .i. no aerad 7 no molad cách. Deithbir 85
ón, uair ní thánic remi 7 ní t[h]icc dia éissi bu duilge aer nó
molad; conid aire at-bertha Anéra friss, iarsinní ní fétta éra
fair.

10 Tánic móit mór for me*n*main don scol*aige*, .i. dol ra

---

8 [1] B canait; *see Note.*   [2] KM's doní *is imaginary.*   [3] B
rigse   [4] B nais; *see Note.*   [5-5] B buadnais; *see Note.*   [6] B
Muire   [7] B not

90 filidecht 7 a légend do [fh]ácbáil, ar ba doinmech dó a betha
for scáth a fhogluma; 7 ro scrútustar[1] i n-a menmain cia leth
no berad a c[h]ét-chuairt fhilidechta. Iss ed trá tucc dia
scrútain a dula co Cathal mac Finguine, boí for cuairt ríg i
nUíb Echach Muman. At-chuala in scolaige immad 7 oirer
95 cacha bánbíd do fhagbáil dó, uair ba sanntach so-accobrach
mbánbíd in scolaige.

11 Is and tánic in ní-sin i mmenmain in scolaige, aidche
Sathairn saindrud ic Russ C[h]ommán, ór is ann boí oc
dénmus[1] a légind. Iar sin recaid in mbec sprédi boí acca, .i.
100 for dá bairgin do chruithnecht 7 for thócht sen-s[h]aille co
síthfi[2] dar a lár. Do-s-rat sin i n-a théig libair; 7 cummais dí
chuarán corra coidlide[3] do dond-lethar secht-fhillte dó in
adaig-sin[4].

12 At-racht moch iar n-a bárach 7 gabaid a lénid i
105 n-ard-gabáil ós mellaib a láruc, 7 gabaid a lummain find
fortócbálta i forcipul imme. Mílec[h] iarnaide[1] uasu i n-a
brutt. Tuarcaib a théig libair for stuag-leirg a dromma.
Ro-t gab a t[h]rostán comthromm coíc-duirn cutruma[2] ([3].i.
ón beind co a chéli[3]) for bolcsén i n-a des-láim. Do-lluid
110 desel relci. Bendachais dia f[h]ithir, .i. aite[4]. Atn-agar
soscéla imme.

13 Do-c[h]ummlai i cend sétta[1] 7 imdechta dar crích
Connacht, i nEchtgi, do Luimnech, do Charnd F[h]er-
adaig, do Berna Trí Carpat, i Sléib Caín, i tír Fer Fhéni
115 frisi ráiter Fir Muige indiú, dar Mónaid Móir, co ndessid
sel becc ria n-espartain i taig aíged Chorcaige. Ó Ross
C[h]omán co Corccaig dia Sathairn saindrud.

14 Is amlaid do-rala in tech aíged, oslaicthe for a chind.
Hi llathi na teórai in lá-sin, .i. gaeth 7 snechta 7 fleochad
120 i n-a dorus, co ná fárcaib in gaeth sifind tuga nó minde

---

10 [1] KM scrútustair; *sed pr.*
11 [1] B denmuus   [2] B tithfi   [3] B coidlige   [4] B agaidsin
12 [1] B iarnaige   [2] B cuthruma   [3-3] *Interlinear gloss.*
[4] *Interlinear gloss.*
13 [1] B shetta

luatha cen scuabad lee dar in dor*us* aile fo cholbaib 7 fo
immdadaib 7 fo c[h]liathaib in rígthige. Sétigi in tige aíged
¹*is*s é¹ timmthasta timmaircthi i n-a lebaid, 7 ba mílac[h]
dergnatach e-side. Deithbir ón, ar ní-s fagbad² a grianad i
lló nó a thócbáil i n-aidche, ar níba gnáth dó beith folam   125
fri a thócbáil. Lothomur in taige aíged co n-us*ce* na
h-aidche remi ind, co n-a c[h]lochaib hi taíb na h-ursand.
15 Ní*con* f[h]uair in scolaige aen do-gneth a fhosaic.
Benais fén iarum a chuaránu de, 7 indlais asin aithindlat út.
Mescais a chuaránu and iarum. Tócbais a théig lib*air* for a   130
luirg isin fraigid, 7 tecbaid a chuaránu 7 teclumaid¹ a lámu
laiss isin sétigi 7 imnaiscis imma chossa. Acht c[h]ena ba
liridir fri gainem mara nó fri drithlenna² tened nó fri
drúcht i mmatain c[h]étamain nó fri renna nime míla 7
dergnatta ic guilbniug*ud* a choss, co-nda gaib emeltí*us*; 7   135
ní-s tánic nech dia fhiss nó dia umalóit i n-a dochum.
16 Tucc fadessin a théig lib*air* chuca 7 benais a shaltair
essi 7 fo-*r*[ó]bairt cantain a shalm. Iss ed at-fiadat eól*aig* 7
libair Chorccaige co closs míle cémend sechtair c[h]ath*raig*
immach son a gotha in scolaige oc cétul a shalm tria rúnib   140
spirtálta¹, for aillib 7 annálaib 7 ernalib, for diapsalmaib 7
sinsalmaib 7 decáidib, co paitrib 7 cantaccib 7 immnaib hi
forba cacha *coec*ait. Ba dóig im*orro* fria cach fer i Corccaig
ba isin tig ba nessa dó no bíth son in f[h]oguir. Iss ed ro
imf[h]ulaing, in c[h]omra*r*gu bunatta 7 a p[h]eccad bunad-   145
gendi 7 a mí-rath foll*us*-gnéthech fodéin, cor erfhuirged
cen dig cen biad cen indlat, co ndech*aid* cach duine i
Corccaig i n-a immdaid.
17 Con[id] ann as-bert Manchín abb Corccaige iar ndul
dó i n-a lep*aid*, 'A scolócc,' ol sé, 'in filet aígid occaind   150
innocht?' 'Ní f[h]ilet,' ol in timthirid. Ar sé in timthirid
aile, 'It-c[h]onnarc-sa aen co díscir dénmnetach dar fiarut
na faithgi¹ gar becc ria n-espartain ó chianaib.' 'Is ferr a
fhiss,' ol Manchín, '7 a chutig do br*eith* dó.' Ór boí dia lesca

14 ¹⁻¹ B 7se   ² B fadbad
15 ¹ B theclumaid   ² B drithrenna
16 ¹ KM *corrects as* spírtalda (*p. 205*), *sed pr.*
17 ¹ B faigthi

155 les-side tidecht 'n-a [fh]rithing aridisi for cend a chota, 7
boí trá d' olcc na h-aidche.

18 Berar a chutig[1]-sium [214a] amach, 7 is í proind
ruccad ann, cuachán, .i. corcca,[2] do medg-us*ce* na h-ecl*a*sa,
7 dá oíbell tened i mmedón suipp sí̇l c[h]átha corcca, 7 dá
160 fhót do úr-mónaid. Ticc in timt[h]irid co dorus in taigi
oíged, 7 ro-s gab gráin 7 ecla frisin tech n-óbéla n-oslacthi
n-imdorcha. Ní*con* f[h]etar in rabi aen and fó ná rabi.
Conid ann at-bert in dala n-aeí oc tabairt a choisse dar in
tairsech, 'In fil nech sund?' ol sé. 'Fil aen,' ar Mac Con
165 Glinde. 'Is coll gessi don tig-sea a thac*ar*[3] for aenf[h]er.'
'Má ro collit riam a gessi,' ar Mac Con Glinne, 'ro collit
innocht, .i. boí a ndán a coll, 7 is mé choilles.' 'Ér[i]g,'[4] ol in
timthirid[5], '7 tomil do p[h]roind.' 'At-biur mo debroth,' ol
sé, 'ó ra-m f[h]uirged c*u*sin tráth-sa, nó co fessur[6] cid fil
170 and, nocon ér*us*.' Atn-aig in gilla in dí oíbill a medón in
tshuip shíl-c[h]átha corcca isin tell*ach*, 7 ticc sopp asin lepa
chuca. Cóirgis in dí f[h]ót úr-mónad im na suppu, sétis ind
oíbill, lassais in sopp, 7 follsigis dó a p[h]roind.

19 Ut dixit Mac Con Glinne:

175   1. 'A scolóc   (ar Mac Con Glinne)
                    cid ná dénum dá chammrand?
                    Déna-su rand ar arán
                    [1]co ndén-sa[1] rand ar annland.

                 2. Corcach i fil cluca binde,
180   goirt a gainem,
                    gainem a grian;
                    nocon f[h]il biad inde[2].

                 3. Co bráth nocon ísaind-sea
                    [3]acht minu-s tecma gorta[3]

18 [1] KM *and facsimile* chuitig, *sed pr.*   [2] *Supralinear gloss.*
[3] B thach*or*   [4] B erg; *see Note.*   [5] B timthirig   [6] B fesser;
see Note.
19 [1-1] B ɔdhensa, H digensa   [2] B sinde   [3-3] H acht maine
bein ri gortae

cuachán corca Corccaige,   185
cuachán Corccaige corca.

4. Geb-si chucat in n-arán
   ima ndernais-[s]iu t' oróit;
   in chuit-si is mairg do-s-méla;
   is iat mo scéla, a scoló[i]c.'   190
                          A scolóc.

Mebraigis in scolaigi na runda, uair ba h-áith a inntlecht.
20 Atn-agut leó in mbiad co h-airm a mboí Mainchín ⁊
taisselb*ait* na runna don abbaid. 'Maith,' ol Manchín,
'admait[1] meicc mí-fhoccuil. Gébdait me[i]cc beca na runda- 195
sin mina dígailt*er* forsint-í do-rigne.' 'Cid fil lat-su de-sin?'
or in gilla. 'Fil liumm,' or Manchín, 'dul cusint-í do-rigne
⁊ ulidetaid [2]a étaig[2] do bein de; slipre ⁊ echla*sc*a do gabáil
dó, co ro muide ⁊ co ro et*ar*scara a fheóil ⁊ a chraiccend ó [a]
chnámu, acht nammá ná ro brist*er* a chnámu; a chor isin 200
Sabraind, ⁊ a bodar-sháith d' us*ce* na Sabrainde dó; a chor
isin tech n-oíged iarum cen meth*er* n-étaig do lécud leis
inund.' (Ocus ní boí t[h]all d' étach acht in sétige, ⁊ ba
lilith*ir* drúcht cétemain a míla-side ⁊ a dergnuta. Fessid ind
in aidche-sin feib as doc*cra* ⁊ as dorcha boí riam remi.) 205
'Foriatar in tech fair co matain dianechtair ar dáig ná ro
élád, co raib mo chomairle-si fair la comarli munt*ir*i
Corccaige i mmbárach i fiadnaise in Dúilemun c[h]ena ⁊
Barre 'ga tó-sa. Níba comairle aile acht a c[h]rochad i
mbárach i mm' enech-sa ⁊ en*ech* Barra ⁊ ina h-ecla*i*si.' 210
Do-rigned am*al* sin[3], ⁊ is ann sin tánic a chomrarcu bunata
⁊ a p[h]eccad foll*us*-gnéthech fén fris-[s]ium. Ro benad
ulidetaid a étaig de ⁊ ro gabad slipre ⁊ echla*sc*a dó. Ro
fuirmed hé isin Sabraind, co tartad ní *for* a[4] sháith do
bodar-us*ce* na Sabrainde dó. Fessid iar sin isin tig oíged co 215
matain.

   21 At-r*acht* Manchín matain moch iar n-a bárach, ⁊ ro

---

20 [1] B atmait   [2-2] *Interlinear.*   [3] *Interlinear.*   [4] B
repeats a.

D

tinólit muin*nter* Chorccaige ó Manchín co mbátar i n-aen
baile, .i. isin tech n-oíged. Auroslaicther rempu, 7 fessait
220 for colbadaib 7 immdadu in tigi. 'Maith, a t[h]róig,' ol
Manchín, 'ní dernais cóir in ecl*ai*s do écnach aréir.' 'Nírbo
fherr do lucht na h-ecl*ai*si,' ar Mac Con Glinne, 'mo
bet[h]-si cen biad occu, 7 rob uathad mo dám.' 'Nír beith
cen biad deitt, cein co fagtha acht ablaind mbic nó dig do
225 medg-us*ce* isind ecl*ai*s. Fil tréda dar ná dlegar oirbire i
nd-ecl*ai*s, .i. nua-thorud 7 nua cormma 7 cuit aidche
Domnaig; ar cid bec isna h-aidchib Domnaig, iss ed is
nessam ar a bárach, sailm do ghabáil, cloc iar sin, celebrad
la *pre*cept 7 oiffrend, sásad bocht. Esbuid na h-aidche
230 Domnaig, is dia Domnaig nó aidche Luain fo-gabar; 7
moch do-rindis oirb*ire*.'

22 'Fuísidim-si trá,' ar Mac Con Glinne, 'co nd*ern*samm
i n-umalóit 7 fuilled ro-imarcr*a*id ind aithi.' 'Acht gillim
fiad nDúilemain 7 Barri,' ol Manchín, 'níba h' aír bess duit.
235 Tucc[th]*ar* lib siút co croch[th]*ar* i n-enech Barri 7 na
h-ecl*ai*si 7 i m' en*ech*-sa forsin fhaithche[1].' 'A c[h]lérig,' ar
Mac Con Glinne, 'ní-dam c[h]rocht[h]*ar*, acht berar br*eth*
f[h]írián indraicc form is f[h]err oltá mo[2] chrochad.'
Atn-agar ann sin hi cend br*eth*i do br*eith* for Mac Con
240 Glinne. Atn-aig Manchín oc taccra fris. Atn-agar cach fer
iar n-urd do m*uin*tir Chorcc[aig]e co Mac Con Glinne. Cia
boí d' immbud ecnai 7 eólais 7 airc*et*ail leó, ní [fh]ríth loc
[214b] laburtha i ndligud dó triasa crochthá.

23 Berair iar sin cen dlig*ed* co Ráthín Mac nAeda i
245 ndescert-leth Cho[r]ccaige, .i. fai[th]chi. Co n-epert
budessin, 'Asccaid dam, a Manchín 7 a m*uin*ter Chorccaige!' 'Ó t' anocul sin?' ol Manchín. 'Ní h-ead chondaigimm,' ar Mac Con Glinne; 'fó liumm cé no t[h]ísad de.'
'Apair,' ol Manchín. 'Ní epér,' ar Mac Con Glinne, '[1]co
250 *m*bet[1] cuir dam fria.' Atn-agar rátha 7 nadmand tenna 7
tr*ebai*re for m*uin*tir Chorccaige fri a comall, 7 naidmis for a

22 [1] B fhaichthe   [2] B mo mo
23 [1-1] B ɔbet

churu. 'Apair,' ol Manchín, 'cid chondige.' 'At-bér,' ar
Aniér, '.i. pars fil a m' théig lib*air* do chaithem ré ndul for
cel, ar ní dlegar escomlád cen dol do láim. Tucth*ar* mo
thiag lib*air* dam.' Do-berar a théig dó, 7 oslaicis hí, co　255
mben dí bairgin, .i. cruith*nechta*,[2] essi la tócht sen-shaille; 7
gab*aid*[3] dechmaid cechtar n-aí, 7 b*e*nais dechmaid in tóchta
co h-imargide 7 co *h*-indraicc. 'Fil dechmaid sund, a
m*uinter* Chorccaige,' ar Mac Con Glinne; 'dia f*h*esmais
int-í bud chóru nó is bochta a c[h]éli, dó do-bérmais ar　260
ndechmaid.'

24 An ro boí ann do bochtaib at-*racht*atar s*ua*s ic
décsi[n] na dechmaide 7 sínid a lámu uadib; 7 gab*aid*[1] silled
forru iarum, 7 at-bert, 'Fia Dia ám,' ol sé, 'ní f*e*sta cid mó
no ríssed aen uaib a less in dech*mad*-si oldú-sa[2] fessin. Níba　265
mó uide neich uaib indé oldá m' uidi-sea, .i. ó R*us*
Chommán co Corccaig. Nír thoimless mír nó banna iar
tidecht, ní ro chaithes for s*ét*, ní f[h]uarus fiad f*h*ír-oíged iar
tidecht, acht fuarus [　　　　　　]³, a matadu 7 a latrannu 7
a c[h]onu cacca, .i. a m*uinter* C[h]orccaige! Ro benad　270
uilideta[i]d i*n* étaig[4] dímm, ro gabad slipre 7 echl*as*ca dam,
do-m-ratad isin Sabraind, ro h-imred fír n-indlig*id* form,
ní ro damad fír dlig*id* dam. I f*h*iadnaise in Dúileman,' ar
Mac Con Glinne, 'níba h-é cét-ní aicéras Demun form-sa
iar ndul anund, in dech*mad*-sa do thabairt dúib-si, ar ní-s　275
dligthi.' Conid é cét-mír ad-uaid ind sin, a dech*mad*, 7
caithis a p[h]roind iarum, .i. a dí bairgin co n-a thócht
sen-shaille. Tócbaid a lámu 7 atlaigis buide dia Dúil*e*main.

25 'Mo br*eth* i nndochum na Sabrainne festa,' ar Mac
Con Glinne. Iar sin berair hé, lín a chuimr*ig* 7 a chométaig,　280
a dochum na Sabrainne. In tan ro-siacht in tiprait dianad
ainm Bithlán, ro mben a lumain f*h*ind de 7 do-s-rat fo a
thoeb, 7 a théig lib*air* fo leirg a droma. Ro-s léic faen for a
lummain, atn-aig a mér tria drol a delci, 7 tummais rind in

---

² *Interlinear gloss.*　　³ KM gab*ais, sed pr.*
24 ¹ KM gab*ais, sed pr.*　　² B oldásu　　³ *One or more words*
must have been omitted here.　　⁴ B étaid

285 delgai dar a ais isin tiprait. In céin no bíd banna oc snige a
cind in delca sís, no bíd in delc uas a anáil. Ro-s torsig in
lucht coiméta 7 cuimrig.

26 'Tánic in bréc for timchell, a matuda 7 a latranda, a
muinter Chorccaige! Inbuid ro bá-sa 'com' boith, iss ed
290 do-gnínd, ina-m t[h]oirched co cend cóic tráth nó sé do
blogaib, a taiscid co caithind i n-oen adaig[1]; mo sháith do
usce i n-a ndiaid-sin. No-[m] bered co cend nómaide cen ní
iar sin, 7 ní láud form. Bet nómaide for ar chaithius ó
chianaib, bet nómaide aile oc athrige, 7 nómaide aile ic ól
295 usce, ór atáut cuir fri m' lámaib. For-t-gellaimm Dia 7
Barre 'ca tú,' ar Mac Con Glinne, 'cen co tig uasal nó ísel do
muintir C[h]orccaige asin baile i tát, co ndigset écc uli i
n-aen aidchi, 7 Manchín ria cách 7 iar cách do bás 7
dochumm n-iffirn; ór am derb-sa do nim, 7 biat i frecnarcus
300 forsná fil crích nó erchra.'

27 Ro h-indissed do muintir Chorccaige in scél-sin, 7
do-rigset luath-chomarc, 7 iss ed tuccad asin chomarc,
bendacht do Mac Con Glinne for a dul fén ar umalóit dia
chrochad, nó nónbur timchillid dia chomét co ndiged éc áitt
305 a mboí, 7 co ro crochtha iar tain. Ro ráided fri Mac Con
Glinne in ní-sin. As-bert Mac Con Glinne, 'Is matroga' (.i.
is roga mataid nó is matad int-í hó tuccad in roga), 'acht oen
ní chena, cid ed bess de, regmait fri h-umalóit feib ro-chóid
ar magister Íhsu Críst fri a c[h]ésad.' At-raig co h-áit i
310 mbátar muinter Chorccaige; 7 táncatar crícha espartan ann
sin. 'Ascaid dún, a Manchín,' ol muinter C[h]orccaige
fodéin. 'A mo Dé, cissí ascaid?' ol Manchín. 'Dál co
mmatain cen crochad don tróg út. Ní ro-s bensum clucu,
nó ní dernsamm celebrad nó precept nó oiffrend. Ní ro
315 sásta boicht lind. Ná caithium co cend in Domnach cen
sássad dún fessin. Cairde dún co matin dó.' 'At-biur
bréthir,' ol Manchín, 'ná rega in dál-sin, acht lathi a
imorbois, bid hé lá a phennati.'

26 [1] B adaid

28 Monuar! Isin uair-sin berair Mac Con Glinne fo
Chaill na Sindach 7 do-berair biail 'n-a láim, 7 lucht 320
coiméta immaille friss. Benais fén a chésad-c[h]rand 7 no-s
imarch*air* fri [a] ais co faithc[h]i Chorccaige. Sáidis fén in
crand; 7 lingis ind amser dar crích n-espartan, 7 ní boí
comairle aile leó acht a chrochad in tan-sin. [215a] 'Ascaid
dam, a Manch*í*n 7 a m*uin*ter Chorccaige!' ar Mac Con 325
Glinne. 'At-b*e*rim mo br*éth*ir trá,' ol Manch*í*n, 'co ná
taet ascaid uaind.' 'Ní maithem n-anocuil c[h]onnaigimm
foraib, ór cia chuinger ní-s tá dam dia b*ar* ndeóin, a matuda
7 a latranda 7 a chonu cacca 7 a brúti nem-literdhai, .i. a
m*uin*ter chorrach comrairc*nech* cend-ísel C[h]orccaige, 330
acht mo sháith do biúd olardai inmardai 7 do lind sho-óil
sho-mesc s[h]o-milis, 7 clith n-álaind n-étrom do étach
thana t[h]irmaide torum, ná ro-m f[h]orrgi fuacht nó tess,
corup lón-fheiss coíct[h]igisi dam ria ndul i ndáil báis.'
'For-t-gill*im*,' ol Manch*í*n, 'ní fhuigbe-siu[1] in ní-sin. Acht 335
is deriud laí, is Domnach and[2]; fil di*diu* in pop*ul* oc irguide
dála duit. Acht benfaider dít do bec n-étaig 7 [3]no-t
c[h]engélt*ar*[3] don chorthi út corob[4] frithpian fo-gab*ar*
résin mór-phéin i mbárach.' Do-rónad fon samail-sin;
bent*air* de a bec n-étaig 7 ro cenglad téta 7 refeda taris don 340
chorthi.

29 Tiagat uad dia tig. Luid Manch*í*n don tig abbad co ro
sásta boicht 7 oígid leó. Ro thomailset fén ní. Ro lécsit
troscud in ecnadu út tánic iar n-a f[h]oíded do Dia 7 don
Choimdid do thesarcain C[h]athail meic Fhinguine 7 fer 345
Muman 7 Lethi Moga N*uadat* ol chena. Nocho damad fír
ndlig*id* dó. Fessid co medón oidche ann. Iar sin ticc aingel
Dé chuci for in corthi 7 fo-rórbairt in aislingthi do
f[h]oillsiug*ud* dó. Céin boí in t-aingel forsin c[h]loich ba
ro-the dó; in tan téged for imaire uad ba so-f[h]ulaing dó. 350
Conid de-sin fil Imaire in Aingil hi f*haithchi*[1] Chorccaige;

28 [1] B fhúidbesiu   [2] *Interlinear*.   [3-3] B cengelt*ar*
[4] B coro*m*
29 [1] B f*haichthi*

ní boí-sium matain cen drúcht. Do-ll*uid* uad in t-aingel
deód n-aidche. Cumaid-sium[2] iarum cennp[h]urt mbec
uad fodén bid imchubaid ré ais*néis* am*al* ro f*h*aillsiged[3] dó,
355 7 at-aig ann sin co matain co cendp[h]ort a aislingt[h]i do
léri lais.
   30 Bent*air* cloc tinóil oc m*uin*tir C[h]orccaige matan
moch iar n-a bárach. Tecat uli c*us*in corthi. 'Maith, a
t[h]róig,' ol Manchín, 'cind*us* filt*er* lat indiú?' 'Is maith,' or
360 sé, 'dia lécther dam in c*u*mair mbriathar fil occ*u*m do rélad
duit-siu .i. aislingt[h]i do-*m*-árfaid arér,' ar Mac Con
Glinne; '7 dia lécth*er* dál dam, indisfet in aislingthi.'
'At-biur do m' brét*h*ir,' ol Manchín, 'dia mbetís síl nÁdaim
do m' réir, co ná tibratis dál laí nó aidche duit. Mé fén,
365 n*icon* tibér.' 'At-beram ar mbrét*h*ir,' ol in pop*ul*, 'cid lonn
lat-su, lécfith*ir* dál dó co ro indise a aislinge. An *us* tol lat-su
iarum, tabair fair.'
   31 Conid ind sin ruc-som Manchín iar ngen[e]l*ach* bíd
co hÁdam:

370   1. 'Bennach dún, a c[h]lérig,
                      a c[h]lí c[h]loth co comgne[1];
                      mac Midbuilce[2] mela[3],
                      meic Bela[4], meic Bloince,

                   2. meic Buaidrén, meic Brothcháin,
375   meic Borr-Thoraid brec-báin,
                      meic Borr-Chrothi bláth*i*,
                      m[ei]c Bláithche, meic Brechtáin,

                   3. meic Beóiri, buaid mbainde,
                      meic Brocóti binde,
380   meic Cainninde caimme,
                      meic Shaille, meic Imme,

                   4. meic Indrechtáin lán-méith,
                      meic Lemnachtai immglain,

   [2] sium *interlinear*.   [3] *See Note.*
   31 [1] H comge   [2] H milbuilci   [3] B mhela   [4] H smeru

meic Messai, meic Thoraid,
meic Holair, meic Inmair,   385

5. meic Hítha, meic Árand,
   meic Cléthi, meic Gualand,
   meic Lón-Loingén láin-te,
   meic Láirce, meic Luabann,

6. meic Lessi, meic Leth[ch]ind[5],   390
   meic Loinge Brond ballai,
   meic Míre, me[i]c Lommai,
   meic Drommai, meic Tharrai,

7. meic Thremantai thanai,
   meic Thainghe cen traethad,   395
   meic Éisc Inbeir Indsén,
   [6]meic Millsén,[6] meic Moethal,

8. meic Meda, meic Fhína,
   meic Carna, meic Corma,
   meic Cruithnechta rigne,   400
   meic Inbe, meic Onba,

9. meic Fhind-Litten gile
   d' ass choerach co nglaine,
   meic Scaiblín buic bladmair
   co n-a gablaib[7] gaile,   405

10. meic Gruthraige gairge,
    meic [8]Garbáin cháin[8] chorcca,
    meic Craíbechán c[h]raebaig
    co n-a choeraib corccra,

11. meic bairr Braisce bíthe,   410
    meic Bolgáin[9] buic bán-ghlain,
    meic Cnó-Messa cnáim-fhéil,
    meic Ábéil, meic Ádaim.

[5] H lethcind   [6] [6] B *repeats*.   [7] H agabraib   [8] [8] H
garbarain   [9] H blogan

12. Maith do dú[th]ch*us*[10] deg-bíd
415   is milis re[11] tengaid;
          a chéim f[h]osad f[h]ostán
          a llos[12] trostán b*enn*aig.'

                                   b. b. d.

32 'Nocon olc dam-sa ón, a M*eic* Con Glinne,' ol
420 Manchín; 'bec lat-su ail form-sa 7 forsi[n]d ecl*ais*, co
ndernais gen[e]l*ach* bíd i cumni dam ná dernad do duine
romum is ná dignest*ar* [1]co brunni brátha[1].' 'Ní h-ail et*ir*
sin, a c[h]lérig,' ar Mac Con Glinne, 'acht aislingt[h]i
do-m-árfas aréir. Is *ed* siút a cennp[h]ort. [2]Ní [h-i]n-
425 c[h]ubaid[2] in aiss*linge*, 7 dia tucth*ar* dál nó cairde dam
innisfet in aislingt[h]i iar sin.' *Ocus* at-bert Manchín
in cétnai, ná tibred dál. Téit-sium iar sin hi cend a
aislingt[h]i; 7 at-berut is óthá sin sís ro f[h]aillsig in t-aingel
dó, ut dixit:

430   **33**   1. 'Aislingi do-m-árfas-[s]a,
                    taidbsi ingnad indisimm
                    i f*h*iadnaise cháich;
                    curchán gered gerthide[1]
                    i purt Locha Lemnachta
435   ós lind betha[2] bláith.

                2. Lodmar isin loech-lestar,
                    laechda in chongaib chonaire
                    dar bolc-lenna lir,
                    [3]cor b*en*summ[3] na sesbémend
440   dar muncind in mur-t[h]ráchta
                    co tochrad a mur-thorud,
                    mur-grian am*al* mil.

                3. Coem in dúnad ránc*u*mar
                    co n-a ráthaib ro-brechtán

---

[10] H duthaig   [11] H ro   [12] H llus
32 [1-1] B co bratha co brunni, *with transposition marks.*   [2-2] B
nim*c*ubaid
33 [1] B gerthige   [2] B, H bethad   [3-3] *sic* H; B *om.*

resin loch anall; 445
ba h-imm úr a erdrochat,
a chaisel ba gel-chruithnecht,
a shondach ba sall.

4. Ba suairc ségdae⁴ a shuidiug*ud*
   in tige treóin trebarda 450
   i ndechad iar tain;
   a chomla do thirm-charnu,
   a thairsech do thur-arán,
   do maethluib a⁵ f[h]raig.

5. Uaitne slemnai [215b] sen-cháise, 455
   sailghe saille súgmaire
   serndais ima-sech;
   sessa sena⁶ sen-chrothi,
   fairre finda fír-grotha,
   fo-loingtis in tech. 460

6. Tipra d' fhín 'n-a fhír-iarthar,
   aibne beóri is brocóti,
   blasta cech lind lán;
   lear do braichlis bláith-lendai⁷
   ós brú thopair threm*a*ntai 465
   do-roi[ch]⁸ dar a lár.

7. Loch do braisig bélaithe⁹
   fo barr úscai olordai
   et*a*rru *ocus* muir;
   erbi imme¹⁰ oc imaire 470
   fo chír blonci brat-gile
   imon múr amuig.

8. Ecor d' ablaib fír-ch*u*mra,
   fid co n-a bláth barr-chorccra

---

⁴ *sic* H; B si*n* ⁵ *sic* H; B do ⁶ H segda ⁷ H braitlenda
⁸ B doroí, H dorroi; *see Note.* ⁹ B belaiche, H belaithi
¹⁰ H uibe

475   et*arr*a *ocus* sliab;
                     daire forard fírlossa
                     do chainnind, do cherrbaccán,
                     for[11] cúl tige t[h]iar.

                  9. Muin*n*ter enig inchinni[12]
480   d' ócaib dercaib tenn-s[h]ádchib
                     im thenid astig;
                     secht n-allsmaind, secht n-episle
                     do cháisib, do choelánaib,
                     fo brágait cech fhir.

485   10. At-c[h]onnarc ní[13], ind[14] airchindech
                     co n-a brot[h]raig bóshaille
                     má mnaí miadaig maiss;
                     at-c[h]onnarc in luchtaire
                     fo[15] inb*iur* in ard-chori
490   's a ahél[16] ri a ais.

                                                          .A.

                  11. Cathal maith mac Finguine,
                     fó fer dianad oirfited
                     airscéla bíd[17] braiss,
495   maith in monar [18]oen-uaire
                     is aíbind ri a indisi
                     immram lúipe laech-lestair
                     dar ler Locha Ais[19].'

                                                    A. d. a.[18]

500   **34** Ro indis-[s]ium a aisl*i*ngi uli ann sin i fiadnaise
       m*uin*ti*re* Corccaige co ro*ach*t a deriud, cen cop é so a
       deriud, 7 ro fallsiged do Manchín rath in aisl*i*ngi. 'Maith, a
       t[h]róig,' ol Manchín, 'eirg do s[h]aigid C[h]athail meic
       F[h]inguine 7 indis dó in aisl*i*ngi, uair ro fallsiged dam-sa
505   aréir in t-olc-sa fil i Cathal do híc triasin aisl*i*ngi-sin.' 'Cia

---

       [11] H ar   [12] B inichin, H inicin; *see Note.*   [13] H *om.*
       [14] *sic* H; B in   [15] H os   [16] B aéhel, H ael   [17] B b*i*nd, H
       bid; *see Note.*   [18-18] *In upper margin in* B   [19] *sic* H; B lais

lóg do-bérad dam-sa aire?' ar Mac Con Glinne. 'Nach mór
in lóg,' ol Manchín, 'do chorp 7 t' anim do lécud duit?'
'Cumma lem in ní-sin cia do-gnether. Senistre nime at
urslacthi frim, 7 in uile f[h]íreón ató Ádam 7 Ábél a mac 7
cosin fírián frecnairc do-lluid doc[h]umm ríchid isin   510
p[h]unc amsire hi támm, atát uli oc clas-c[h]étul for cind
m' anma co tias i nnem. Atát noí ngráid nime, im hirophin
7 sarophin, i frestul m' anma. Is cumma leam cia dig Cathal
mac Finguine 7 fir Muman co Leth Mog[a] Nuadat 7
muintir C[h]orccaige, 7 Manchín ria cách 7 iar cách, i nd-éc 515
7 i nd-iffern a n-aen oidche, uair bet[1] fessin i n-aentaid in
Athar 7 in Meic 7 in Spiruta Naíb.'

35 'Cia lóg chondigi?' ar muinter C[h]orccaige. 'Ní[1] mór
ém an condigim,' ol Mac Con Glinne, '.i. in cochall bec ima
ro éraid clérig Lethi Moga 7 bár t[h]roiscset[2] in aen aidchi, 520
.i. cochall Manchín.' 'Bec fiad[ut]-su in ní-sin 7 mór
fiadum-sa,' ol Manchín; 'acht aen ní,' ol Manchín, 'do-
biur-sa bréthir i fiadnaise Dé 7 Barri, dámad[3] lemm-sa[4] a fil
eter Corccaig 7 a termund, robad usa a sechna uli oltás in
cochall a aenar.' 'Mairg nach tibre,' ol cách, 'in cochall, ol is 525
ferr in Cathal 7 Leth Moga do t[h]esarcain oldás in
cochall.' 'Do-bér-sa amal seo,' ol Manchín, '7 ní t[h]ardus 7
ní thibar ascaid is andsa lemm; .i. do-bér hé i n-erláim
espuic Corccaige fri a aisec don scolaige dia cobra Cathal
mac Finguine.' Ro h-aithned iar sin i n-erláim espuic   530
Corccaige, 7 muinter C[h]orccaige dia idnocul[5] leis in
c[h]ochaill, acht is a lláim in espuic ro fácbad.

36 'Imthig fodecht-sa do s[h]aigid C[h]athail!' 'Cia
h-airmm i fil Cathal?' ar Mac Con Glinne. 'Ní h-annsa,' ol
Manchín, 'i taig P[h]icháin meic Moíle Finde, ríg hUa   535
nEchach ic Dún Choba i cocrích hUa nEchach[1] 7 Corco
Laígde; 7 so[i]ch-si innocht connice ind sin.' Luid Mac

34 [1] *Interlinear.*
35 [1] B nit; *see Note.*   [2] *See Note.*   [3] mad *interlinear.*
[4] sa *interlinear.*   [5] B hidnocul
36 [1] *Interlinear.*

Con Glinne iarum co dedbirech[2] díscir déinmnetach, 7
tócbais a lummain coíc-diabulta cengalta i fán a dá gualand,
540 7 cenglaid a lénid ós mell*aib* a lárac, 7 cingis dar fiarlaít na
faithchi[3] fon samail-sin co tech Pichán meic Moíl[e] Finde,
co Dún Coba i cocrích h*Ua* nEch*ach* 7 Corcu Laígde. *Ocus*
cingis co dian a dochumm in dúnaid fon tochim-sin, 7 feib
ro-siacht in sluag-t[h]ech saindrud i mbád*us* oc tinól na
545 slóg, gab*aid*[4] gerr-chochall 7 gerr-étach imme, girru cach
n-uachtarach lais 7 libru cach n-íchtarach. F*o*-rórbairt
f*ui*rseóracht fon samail-sin don ts[h]lóg do lár in rígthige,
.i. ní nárba comadais dia p[h]ersaind—cáintecht 7 bragitóracht 7 duana la filidecht do gabáil, co ro h-asblad[5] hé
550 ná tánic riam nó iarum bid errd*a*rcu i cerdu cáintechta.

37 In tan boí for na spledaib[1] i tig P[h]ich*áin* meic
Moíl[e] Finde, conid ann as-bert Pichán secha, 'Cid mór
do muirn-si, a meic légind, ní-m dénann-sa subach di[2].'
'Cid [3]do-t-gní mif[r]ech[3]?' or Mac Con Glinne. 'Ná
555 fet*a*ra-su, a scolaige,' ol Pichán, '.i. Cathal mac Finguine co
maithib Muman do thidecht innocht, 7 cid doil*ig* lemm
mór-s[h]luag Muman, is annsa Cathal a aenur, 7 cid doil*ig*
e-ssium i n-a p[h]rím-chutig is doilge i n-a p[h]rím-airigid,
7 is doilgide a [fh]rith-airige doridisi? Fil trédi chondagur
560 icon [fh]rith-airigid-sin, .i. miach cuachán 7 miach fiad-
uball 7 miach min-aráin.'

38 'Cia lóg do-bértha dam-sa,' ar Mac Con Glinne, 'dia
ndingbaind dítt hé ón tráth-sa c*u*sin tráth ar a bárach, 7 ná
dignesta a aithe for da thuaith ná fort fén?' 'Do-s-béraind
565 fal*aig* n-óir 7 ech Bretnach duit,' ol Pichán. 'Do m'
debroth, fullfi fris[1],' ar Mac Con Glinne, 'in tan gébth*ar*!'
'Do-bér-sa beós,' ol Pichán, 'caera find cacha tige 7 cacha
trillsi ó Charnd co Corccaig.' 'Gébut-sa sin,' ar Mac Con

---

[2] B daidbir; *see Note.*   [3] B faichthi   [4] KM gab*ais, sed pr.*
[5] *See Note.*
37 [1] *sic* B; KM *emends to* splegaib, *sed pr.*   [2] *Interlinear.*
[3-3] B dosgní mifech
38 [1] B fr*ii*s

Glinne, 'acht co rab[at]² ríg 7 brug*aid*, filid 7 cáinte dam fri
taisec fhiach 7 dá comallad, co-nom t[h]orsit immlán; .i. ríg 570
do aithne na f*h*iach, briug*aid* do m' imfhulang³ do chaithem
bíd 7 lenda 7 lessaigthi [216a] leó céin beó ic tobach m'
fhiach. Dia f*h*ellt*ar* for m' fhiach*aib*, filid dia n-aír 7 [dia
n]gláim dícind⁴, cáinte dia sílad 7 dia ngabáil duit-siu 7 do
t' chloind 7 do t' c[h]ene*ól*, mina-m t[h]ísat mo fhéich.' 575
Ocus nadmis iarum for a chura.

39 Tánic Cathal mac Finguine co mbuidnib 7 marc-
shlóg f[h]er Muman, co ndessit*ar* for colbadu 7 imscinge 7
imdadu. Gabsat ingenai míne macdachta fosaic 7 fritháil*em*
do na slógaib 7 do na soch*ai*dib. Ní*con* dam Cathal mac 580
Finguine fria leth-éill a bróci do bein de in tan boí oc
tidnocul a beóil ó chechtar a dí lám do na h-ublaib bát*ar*
forsna sechedaib imme sechnón. Is and sin boí Mac Con
Glinne. Atn-aig oc blassachtaig isin leth aile don tig, 7
ní*con* ráthaig Cathal sin. Érgis Mac Con Glinne co díscir 585
déinmnetach diabulda i n-a ruathar bodbda 7 i n-a chéim
c[h]urata dar fiarlaít in rígthige, 7 buí rell d*er*máir 7 nert-lia
míled forsa n-indsmatís slega 7 semmunna 7 fria meltís
renda 7 faebra, 7 ba corthi curad in lecc-sin; 7 tócbais fri a
ais co h-áit a mboí remi for in c[h]olba, 7 indsmais in cend 590
n-uachtarach i n-a beólu di 7 araile for a glún, 7 f*o-r*óbairt ic
tomailt a [dé]t¹ frisin cloich. Is ed at-fiadut eólaig 7 senóire
7 libuir C[h]orccaige nát boí i f*h*occus in dúnaid ar medón
nó dianechtair ná cuala fuaim a dét frisin cloich boí i n-a
beólu, cia boí dia slemnu. 595

40 Tócbais Cathal ¹a chend¹ ar sin. 'Cid do-t-gní mer, a
meic légind?' or Cathal. 'Fil dá ní,' ar Mac Con Glinne, '.i.
Cathal mac fír-álaind Finguine, ard-rí² mór-Lethi Moga
N*uadat*, ard-c[h]osn*amaid*³ Érenn fria clanna *Cuinn Chét-
Chathaig*, fer ro h-oirdned ó Dia 7 ó Dúilem⁴, laech saer 600

---

² *See Note.*   ³ B doimfhulang; *see Note.*   ⁴ B ndícind
39 ¹ B dé *illegible.*
40 ¹⁻¹ *In l. h. margin.*   ² B ardrig   ³ B ardcosn*amaig*
⁴ B duilib; *see Note.*

socheneóil d' Eóganacht gríbda Glendamnach⁵ iar ceneól a
atharda, saeth lem-sa a acsin a aenur ic tomailt neich, 7 dia
mbet⁶ doíne a críchaib ciana istaig ic cuinch*id* áil nó aisc,
do-génut écnach cen m' ulchain-se ic comscísachtaig fria t'
605 ulchain-sea.'

41 'Is fír,' for Cathal, oc tabairt oen uba[i]ll dó, 7 ro
esairg a dó nó a trí i n-a beólu fén. Fri ré na trí leth-bli*adan*
boí in demun i mbrágait C[h]athail meic F[h]inguine, ní
derna doen*nacht* acht in t-aen uball fiadain út do Mac Con
610 Glinne iar n-a athc[h]uinch*id* co trén. 'Ferr déda hó oín i
nd-ecna,' ar Mac Con Glinne. Snedis aroli dó. 'Umir na
Trínóti,' or Mac Con Glinne. Cuiris oen dó. ¹'Ceth*air*
leba[i]r¹ in ts[h]os*céla* iar timna C[h]ríst.' Tidnais² oen
dó. 'Cóic lebair Moýsi³ iar *ndeich* timnai Rechta.' Cuiris
615 oen dó. 'Cétna airtecul ármide do-airis ó [a] rainde 7 ó [a]
chotib fadén, .i. in umir s[h]éda, acht is a trí a lleth, is a dó
a trian. Tabair dam in sess*ed*!' Snidis urch*ur* d' oen uball
dó. 'In *secht*⁴ do-rarngired do t' Dia i tal*main* .i. a
chompert, a gein, a bathis, *et* re*liqua*.' Tic oen dó. 'Ocht
620 mbiati in ts[h]os*céla*, a ruri ríg-brethaig!' B*er*is oen dó.
'Noí ngráid nime, a meic, a ríg-nia in betha!' Tidnacis oen
dó. 'Dechmad grád tal*man*, a chosn*amaid*⁵ in chóicid!' Tic
uball dó. 'Áirem anf*h*urbithi⁶ na n-asp*al* iar n-imorbus!'
Gnídis⁷ oen dó. 'Numir f[h]orpthi na n-asp*al* iar n-
625 imorbus cia do-rigset tairmthecht!' Ferais oen fair. 'Ba h-í
in buaid ós buadu 7 in umir f[h]orpthi, Críst for a asp*al*u.'

42 'Indeó,' or Cathal, 'dar Barre, no-m ísa dia-nom lena
ní as¹ mó!' Snedis Cathal in sechid co n-a h-ublaib dó, co ná
boí cúil nó frith*bac*² nó lár nó lepaid ná rístís na h-ublai, co
630 nár nessa do Mac Con Glinne inás do chách, 7 ba faide ó
Chathal iat. Gabaid feirg Cathal. Lingid ind ala súil dó i
n-a chend co ná tibred petta cuirre ass. Gab*aid* in súil n-aile

---

⁵ B gl*e*ndabrach; *see Index of Place-Names.*   ⁶ B bet*h*
41 ¹⁻¹ B ceth- lebar, H cethor leb-; KM ceth*ir* leba[i]r   ² *See
Note.*   ³ B mysi, H maoisi   ⁴ KM *sechte*   ⁵ B chosn*amaig*
⁶ B anfhurmithi   ⁷ B gnidis; *see Note.*
42 ¹ B as is   ² B frith-; *see Note.*

immach comba métith*ir* 7 og rerchirce hí i n-a chind, 7
bertais a druimm fria sliss in rígthige co ná fárcaib cleith nó
slait nó scolb nó dlaí nó uatni ná dic[h]sed as a inad; 7 saidis 635
'n-a s[h]uide³. 'Do chos 7 do gruad fót, a rí,' ar Mac Con
Glinne; 'ná tuc mallachtain dam 7 ná gat nem form!' 'Cid
do-t-rigne, a meic légind?' ol Cathal. 'So-dethbir dam,' ar
Mac Con Glinne; 'do-rala dam araír fri m*uintir* Corccaige 7
co tardsat a n-osnaid dam. Iss ed fo-t-ruair dam an-í-sin 640
frit-siu.' 'Luid dó, a Meic Con Glinne,' ol Cathal; 'dar
Imbliuch nIbair, diamad bés dam meic légind do marbad
. . .! Sech ní rísta, ní t[h]ísta.'

43 Aire trá ba luige dó-sam Imbliuch nIbair, ar is innte
fo-gebed a sháith min-aráin, 7 no bíd 7 bratt boinni odarda 645
imme, 7 a c[h]loidem ¹cruaid coilc-dírech¹ i n-a chlé-láim
ic tomeilt blog ó cech boith i n-aroli. Atn-aig and lá n-oen i
mboith aroli meic légind, 7 tic lán dó do blogaib. Figlis na
blogu. Figlis in mac légind in lethenach boí ar a bélaib.
Feib ro-siacht in lethenach do fhigl*ed*, sínis a thengaid d' 650
impód na duille. 'Cid do-t-rigne, a meic légind?' ol Cathal.
'Dethb*ir* mór accum,' or sé; 'in sluaiged co marbad immel
in tshaegail do thachur [216b] i lleth frim, .i. errand*us* do
chimais na bairgine do neoch t[h]echtas luaith 7 tene iar n-a
súgud do dethaig 7 do gaíth, co ná bí súg nó seag innte, cen 655
mír salle nó imme nó feóla, cen dig n*ach* cene*óil* acht deoch
do bodar-us*ce* na cuirre, co ra-m dígaib fo m' n*ert* 7 fo m'
t[h]racht; 7 in slógad ré cách 7 iar cách.' 'Indeó,' ar mac
Finguine .i. ar Cathal, 'dar Barre, céin bam beó-sa n*icon*
regu clérech i slógad lem-sa ó s[h]und immach;' 7 tégd*is* 660
clé*rig* Érenn slógud co sin fri ríg nÉrenn, conid e-ssium
benais in slógad do c[h]lérchib i tós riam. Fácbaid trá rath 7
bendachtu for deóradu Imblechu 7 ana min-aráin² i
nImbli[u]g; 7 is móu isin leth iarthar-descertaig³, ar is ann
do-línta hé beós. Etaraiss*néis* did*iu* sin remai[n]d.   665

---

³ KM B suuide, *sed pr.*
43 ¹⁻¹ B coilcdirech cruaid, *with transposition marks.*   ² B
m*h*inaráin   ³ KM B dercertaig, *sed pr.*

44 'Ar do ríge, ar do [fh]laith, ar th' innram, tabair
ascaid mbicc dam,' ar Mac Con Glinne, 'résiú imthiger.'
Do-garar dó Pichán isin tech. 'Atá in mac légind út,' or
Cathal, 'ic cuinch*id* ascada form.' 'A tabairt,' ol Pichán.
670 'Do-bérth*ar*,' or Cathal; 'abair frim,' ol Cathal, [1]'cid
c[h]ondigi.'[1] 'Ní*con* epér co rabat curu fri a c[h]omall.'
'Do-bérth*ar*,' ol Cathal. 'Do br*iathar*[2] f[h]latha ind?' ar
Mac Con Glinne. 'Do m' brét*hir*,' ol sé, 'do-géba; 7 sluind
in aiscid.' 'Is ed in so,' ar Mac Con Glinne, '.i. tochar
675 do-rala dam araír fri munntir Corccaige, co tardsat a
mallacht uli dam, 7 iss ed fo-d-era in comrorcu-sin dam i
lleth frit-sa. *Ocus* troscud cid duit-siu lem fri Dia innocht,
ar isat bráthair bunaid, do m' s[h]aerad for mallachtain
m*uin*tire Corccaige, iss ed c[h]ondaighim.'
680 **45** 'Ná h-apair, a meic légind,' ol Cathal; 'bó cach liss i
Mumain 7 uinge cach comaithig, la bratt cacha cille, 7 maer
dia tobach, 7 tú fodén i m' f[h]ail-sea ic p*ra*indiud oiret bé
ic tabach fhiach. *Ocus* do m' debroth,' or Cathal, 'is ferr
lemm ina fil ó iarthar co h-oirther 7 ó descert co tuaiscert
685 Muman duit oltás be[i]th adaig[1] cen biad.' 'Ba m' debroth,'
or Mac Con Glinne, 'ó ro-siacht do fhír flath*a* fris, 7 ná dlig
rí Caissil tidecht taris, dia tarta dam-sa ina fil i lLeth
[Moga] N*uadat*, ní*con* gébth*ar*. Fil trá, a ard-gaiscedaig 7 a
ríg-fhénnid Eórpa, a adbar accum cen co gabar coma uait,
690 ar ní fhil mo maín fén acht a nim nó i talmain nó[2] i n-ecna
nó i n-aircetal; 7 ní namá, ar is trumma cach ndédinach,
regut a n-iff*er*n cen crích, cen forcend mina-m s[h]aera for
mallachtain m*uin*tire Corccaige.' 'Do-bérth*ar* d*ù*it-siu
sin,' ol Cathal, '7 ní tuccad remi[3] ná i n-a diaid[4] co bruinde
695 brátha ní as lesciu lind oltás sin.' Troscis Cathal in oidche-
sin leis, 7 troscit a mboí and uli ol chena, 7 samaigis in mac
légind i tulg i taeb ursainde[5]; 7 iadais in tech.
46 In tan boí and i ndeód aidche, érgis s*uas* Pichán mac

44 [1-1] B *condigi cid, with transposition marks.*   [2] B br-ir
45 [1] B agaid   [2] KM *would emend to* .i., *but unnecessarily.*
[3] B rempi; *see Note.*   [4] B diaig   [5] [*]B nursainde; *see* § *ii.*

Mo[í]le Finne. 'Crét érg*ius* Pichán an inbuid-se?' or Mac
Con Glinne. 'Do dénam bíd do na slógaib-se,' ol Pichán, '7 700
ba ferr dún comad erlum ó 'né.' 'Níthó ám sin,' or Mac Con
Glinne; 'ro t[h]roscsium araír, p*r*ecept b*us* lind iarum i
mbárach i tossaig.' *Ocus* ansit co matain. Uathad sochaide a
mbátar, ní dechaid nech díb anund nó amach co tráth érgi
iar n-a bárach. At-racht Mac Con Glinne fessin ann-side 7 705
ro oslaic in tech. Ro indail a lámu 7 tuc a théig libair chucca
7 bertais a s[h]altair essi, 7 fo-rórbart p*r*ecept do na slógu. Is
ed at-fiadut senchaide 7 senóri 7 libair C[h]orccaige nát boí
do uasal nó d' ísel ná ro-s teilg trí frassa dér ic éstecht fri
p*r*ecept in scolaige. In tan tarnic in p[h]*r*ecept, do-gníth*er* 710
airnaigthi frisin ríg, co-na mbed fot saegail dó 7 co-na
mbeth maithius Muman fri a remes. Do-gníth*er* ernaigthi
frisna crích*a* 7 frisna cen*e*ól*a* 7 frisin cóiced ar chena, am*al*
is gnáth d' aithle p*r*eceptai.

47 'Maith,' ar Mac Con Glinne, 'cind*us* atáth*ar* ann-sin 715
indiú?' 'Daro m' debroth,' ol Cathal, 'ní bás remi riam ní is
messu, 7 ní beth*er* co bráth.' 'Cub*aid* ém,' or Mac Con
Glinne, 'do beth cu h-olc .i. demun 'cot' aidmill*ed* 7 'cot'
indrud fri ré trí leth-bl*iadan* indorsa, 7 ní ro t[h]roscis lá nó
aidche lat fén, 7 t*r*oscis fri p*er*saind tróig ndíscir nderóil mo 720
shamla-su.' 'Cid is maith de-sside, a meic légind?' ol
Cathal mac Finguine. 'Ní *h-annsa*. Ó ra t[h]roscis-[s]iu t'
aenur lium-sa araír, troiscem-ni uli, lín atáum, innocht, 7
troisc-siu fessin co f*h*agba cobair écin ó Dia.' 'Ná ráid ind
sin, a meic légind,' ol Cathal; 'cérba trom in toísech, i[s] 725
secht-truma in dédenach.' 'Ná ráid-siu ind sin,' or Mac
Con Glinne, 'acht calma do dénam and.' Troscis trá Cathal
in aidche-sin co n-a shlóg ó s[h]in co deód n-aidche.

48 Érgis Mac Con Glinne trá. 'In cotlad do P*h*ichán?' or
Mac Con Glinne. 'At-bér fír,' ol Pichán, 'dá rab Cathal co 730
bruinde mbrátha am*al* atá, ní choitél, ní thoimél, ní dingen
gen nó gáire.' 'Érig,' or Mac Con Glinne; 7 iarrais olar
sen-shaille 7 maeth bóshaille 7 lán-charna muilt 7 mil 'n-a
criathraib 7 salann Saxanach for teisc f[h]ír-álaind fhétta

E

735 f[h]ind-airgit, la cet[h]ri bera fír[217a]-dírge find-chuill
fóthib. Fo-gabur dó na biada ro thurim, 7 samaigis stacci
dí[fh]reccra deg-máru[1] forsna beraib. *Ocus* gab*aid*[2] iarum
lín-fhuathróicc [3]t[h]ís ime[3] 7 att leccda línaide ba c[h]léthi
a chend-mullaig, oc*us* atáid tenid caín cethar-drumnig
740 cethar-dorsig cethar-scoltig de[4] uindsinn[5] cen diaid, cen
chiaig, cen crithir. Sáidis bir cacha h-ordan díb, 7 ba
luathithir fria maing bá cét-laeg hé, nó fri h-eirb nó
fannaill nó fri gaíth n-imluim n-errchaide i mbolg-s[h]liss
Márta hé ma na beraib 7 ma na tenntib. Comlis in mil 7 in
745 salann in cach staic iar n-urd. Cia roba do mét na staci boí
frisin tenid, nícon tánic as na cet[h]ra[6] stacib sís co lár ní
no-s báided crithir chonnli, acht a mboí d' inmar intib, i n-a
medón fén do-chóid.

49 Ro faillsiged do P[h]ichán conid dó t[h]ánic in
750 scolaige, do thesarcain C[h]athail. *Ocus* in tan tarnac[t]ar
na staci-sin is ann at-bert Mac Con Glinne, 'Téta 7 refeda
dam!' 'Cid is áil díb-side?' ol Pichán; 7 rop iarfaige[1] dar
cubais dó-sum sin, uair ro faillsiged dó remi. Conid
[d]e-sin atá in senbriathar[2] .i. fiarfaige dar cub*ais*. At-agur
755 téta 7 refeda dó, 7 do neoch ba calma don laechraid. Furmit
a láma tar Cathal, 7 ro cenglad fon samail-sin hé do shliss in
rígthige. Tic Mac Con Glinne iarum 7 indlis baic 7 corránu
ead imchian forsna tétaib-sin. *Ocus* feib tarnic sin, tic-sium
istech 7 a c[h]et[h]ri bera fri a ais i n-ard-gabáil 7 a lumman
760 f[h]ind f[h]ír-scaílti i n-a diaid 7 a dá beind imo brágait, co
h-airmm a mboí Cathal; 7 sáidis na bera isin leba i n-a
f[h]iadnaise, 7 saidis fodén i n-a shuide 7 a dí choiss
ima-sech. Bendais a scín dia chris 7 benais mír don staic ba
nessa dó. Tummais isin mil boí forsin teisc f[h]ind-argait
765 út. 'A thosach ar míl firend so,'[3] ar Mac Con Glinne, ic
tabairt in míre i n-a beól fodén. Is ó s[h]in ille lentar in

---

48 [1] KM *would emend as* dermáru, *unnecessarily.*   [2] KM gab*ais,*
sed pr.   [3-3] *Interlinear.*   [4] *Interlinear.*   [5] KM uindsin,
sed pr.   [6] KM *emends to* cethri, *but unnecessarily; see Note.*
49 [1] B iarfaide   [2] B senbr-ir   [3] *Cf. Note to l.* 765.

senbr*iathar*[4]. Benais mír don staic n-aile,[5] 7 t*u*mmais isin
mil, 7 at-aig tar beólu Cathail i n-a beól fodén. 'Tinme dún
in mbiad, a meic légind!' ol Cathal. 'Do-gén,' or Mac Con
Glinne. Benais mír don staic ba nessa dó 7 t*u*mais fo*n*n   770
samail cétna [7 at-aig][6] sech bél Cathail i n-a beólu fodén.
   50 'Cia fot lenfa de-sin, a meic légind?' ol Cathal. 'Nád
lenab ó shunn. Acht aen ní chena, ro thomlis-[s]iu immad
na mblog n-imarcide n-écsamail c*u*sin trát-sa; in mbec fil
sund, is mise do-s-méla, 7 bid biad ó beólu duit-siu seo.'   775
Ocus senbr*iath*ar sin ille. Búraid 7 béccid Cathal iar sin, 7
fócrais a marbad in scolaige. Ní dernad trá fair-sium in
ní-sin. 'Maith, a C[h]athail,' ar Mac Con Glinne, 'aislinge
do-m-árfas, 7 it-c[h]uala it mait[h]-siu oc br*eith* for
aisl*ing*i.' 'Do m' debroth,' ol Cathal, 'dia mberaind for   780
aisl*ing*i fer talman, ní béraind for th' aisl*ing*i-se.' 'For-t-
gill*im*,' or Mac Con Glinne, 'cen co ruca-su, indisfith*er* hí i
t' f[h]iadnaise.' Fóbrais trá a aisl*ing*i. Is amlaid di*diu* ro
indis 7 dá mír nó a trí sech bél Cathail i n-a beólu fodén.

   51 a   1. 'Aisl*ing*i it-chonnarc araír,   785
               mo dul for fecht dís nó triúr,
               co n-acca ¹in tech find¹ forlán
               i raba a lommnán do biúd.

          2. ²Co n-acca in loch lemnachta
               for lár muige find,   790
               co n-acca in tech lér-gníma
               iar n-a thugaid d' imm.

          3. ²Tan tánuc 'n-a mórthimchell
               do f[h]égad a uird,
               maróca ar n-a cét-berbad   795
               ba h-iat sin a scuilb.

          4. A dí³ ersaind bocai brechtáin,
               a léibend do gruth is d' imm,

---

[4] B senbr-ir   [5] *See* § *xxiii*.   [6] *See Note.*
51 a ¹⁻¹ *sic* H; B in findtech find   ² H *om. verses 2 and 3.*
³ H da

imdadai do blonaig bladaig,
800   scéith iumdai do thanaig thimm.

5. ⁴Fir fo sciathraigib na sciath-sin,⁴
do moethail buic mellaig⁵ mín,
fir cen tuicse gona Goedil,
goeí gruitne cech oenfhir díb.

805   6. Coire ra-mór lán do luabin⁶,
dar liumm ro lámus riss gleó;
braisech bruithe duillech dond-bán,
lestar lommnán lán do cheó.

7. Tech saille dá *fhich*et toebán,
810   coelach coelán, coimge⁷ c[h]lann;
da cech biúd bud maith la duine
dar lium bátar uile and.'

Ais*lingi* it-c[h]onn*arc*

51 b *Ocus* dixit beós:

815   1. 'Aislingthe¹ it-chondarc araír,
ba caín gébend;
ba balcc bríge co tárfas dam
ríge nÉr*end*.

2. Co n-accai in liss mbilech mbarrach²,
820   ba saill sondach;
caisel ³do min-scellcib, carrach,³
tanach torrach.

3. Cadlai⁴ mucc, is de do-rónta
a⁵ cholbai cadlai;
825   suairc in sonba ⁶*ocus* uaitne⁶,
onba⁷ amra.

---

⁴⁻⁴ H fír fo sciatr*a*ib inda sciethae sin   ⁵ H mellanaig   ⁶ H
millsen   ⁷ B coimgne, H comge
    51 b ¹ H aislingi   ² *sic* H; B mbairrach   ³⁻³ B carrach imme
do minscellcib, H carroch imme do minsceillcib   ⁴ H carna
⁵ *sic* B *and* H; *see Introduction, p. xvii.*   ⁶⁻⁶ H occus uaithne
⁷ *sic* H; B ongha

4. Amra in fhís [8]dam do-árfas[8]
   cind[9] mo thellaig;
   fidchell imme co n-a foirind
   bláith, bricc, bendaig.   830

5. Bendachad Dia mo labra,
   líth cen tassa[10];
   iar[11] techt dam hi Sliab nImme
   [12]ro láit[h]ea[12] gille fo mm' assai.'

                                              Aislingi   835

52 Incipit do[n] fhábull sísana budesta.

Cérba tromm in phian les-sium beth dí láa co n-aidche
cen biad, ba ro-mó leis do phéin tuirem na mbiad n-imda
n-imorcide n-écsamail i n-a f[h]iadnaise, 7 cen ní díb dó.
Iar sin dó i cend na fáible.   840

'In tan trá ro mbá ann araír i m' lepaid chaín
chumdachta[1] co n-a h-uatnib forórda, co n-a colbaib
créduma, co cuala ní .i. in guth frim, [2]"Eirc, a t[h]ruaig, a
Meic Con Glinne!"[2] [3]Ocus ní ro f[h]recrus-[s]a in ní-sin.
Deithbir dam—ro boí do c[h]lithmaire mo lepthai 7 do   845
shádaile mo chuirp 7 do thressi mo chotultai. Co n-ebert
aridisi,[3] "Fomna, fomna, a Meic Con Glinne, beóchail ná
ro-t báda", .i. faitches lat ná ro-t báde beóil. Atom-raracht
matain moch ar n-a bárach don tiprait do indmad mo lám,
co n-acca ní, in scál mór a m' dochumm. "Maith in sin," ol   850
sé frim. "Maith ém," ol smé friss. "Maith trá, a t[h]róig,"
ol in Scál; "messi t[h]idnuis[4] robud duit araír, ná ro-t báde
beóchail. Acht aen ní c[h]enai:

53 [217b.1] "Ba robad do t[h]roich, ba h-irchuitbed fri
foigdech, ba tusliud clochi fria crand, ba sanais fri bodar, ba 855
díbad for dubach, bid cor eptha i cléith, ba gat im gainem

---

[8]-[8] B tarfas dam, H tarfas damh   [9] B hi cind, H i cinn   [10] H
taisi   [11] H ria   [12]-[12] H ro laad; see Note.

52 [1] B chumdsa (without suspension-stroke over s).   [2]-[2] sic H; B
om.   [3]-[3] In B this section is in space between budesta (l. 836) and
Cérba (l. 837), with marks indicating its proper place in the text.   [4] B
tidnuis; KM tidnus, sed pr.; see Note to l. 613.

nó im gual, ba [h-]esorcu darach do dhornaib, ba deól mela
a mecnaib¹ ibair, ba cuinchid imme i llige chon, ba longad i
scellaib scibair, ba [h-]iarraid olla for gabur, ba saiget i
860 corthi, ba cosc lára do broimnig, ba cosc mná boíthe do
drúis, ba [h-]us*ce* for tóin créthir, ba taeb fri coin
fholmnig, ba salond for luach*air*, ba tinnsccra iar n-indsma,
ba rún fri mnaí mbaíth, ba ciall i n-óinmit, ba mórad
mogad, ba lind do baethaib, ba h-immthús fria ríg, ba
865 coland cen chend, ba cend cen chol*aind*, ba caillech fri clog,
ba h-athlaech i cath*air* n-esp*uic*², ba tuath cen ríg, ba
h-imram luinge cen laí, ba h-arbor i cliab toll, ba h-ass for
sechid, ba tigadus cen mhnaí, ba caera for gaimen, ba
taidbsi (.i. messa)³ do p[h]ecdachu, ba h-athis i n-inchuib,
870 ba h-aisec cen taisec, ba cur síl i ndroch-ith*ir*, ba tárcud do
dhroch-mnaí, ba fognam do dhroch-[fh]laith, ba leth-ard
cundartha, ba tomus lettromm, ba tidecht tar fuigell, ba
sárug*ud* sosc*él*a, ba forcetul Ancríst t' f[h]orcetul-sa im do
longad, a Meic Con Glinne!'' '

875   **54** 'At-biur mo debroth,' or Mac Con Glinne, 'is cruaid
codut in cosc.' 'Ced sin?' ol in Scál. 'Ní *h-annsa*,' or Mac
Con Glinne, 'ní fhet*ar* can ti*ce* nó cia thégi nó can deitt fén
fria t' imchomarc nó fri t' aisnés doridise.' 'Ní *h-annsa* ém,'
ol in Scál, '.i. ¹Buarannach mac Elc-[C]aib Essamain¹ a
880 Síth Longthe do-m-ánaic-sea.' 'Do-munim,' or Mac Con
Glinne, 'mása thú, fileat scéla móra lat, 7 did*iu* fiss scél ó
biúd 7 ó longad. In fil lat?' 'Fil trá,' ol in Scál, '7 má 'tá,
nírb [sh]ursan do charait beth a ndíchumci longthi fri
comriachtain friss.' 'Ced ón?' or Mac Con Glinne. 'Ní
885 *h-annsa* ém,' ol in Scál, '.i. cen broind coíc-duirn
comlethain cernaig cian-fhota ceth*ar*-láin ceth*ar*-ochair
acca, i tallfatis² na trí noí n-ithe 7 na secht n-óla imm ól
nó*n*buir cacha díb-side, 7 na secht tomaltais 7 na noí

---

53 ¹ *sic* H; B mecna; *see* § *xxiii.*   ² B nasp-; *see Note.*
³ *Interlinear gloss.*
    54 ¹ ¹ H bruchtsalach mac buarandaig de ciniud ulgaib esomain
² B tanfatis

ndíthata, 7 praind c[h]ét cacha h-ithe 7 cacha h-óla 7 cacha
longthi 7 cacha díthata díb-side fo leith.' 890

55 'Ór ná fil lem-sa in mbroind-sin,' or Mac Con
Glinne, 'tidnais[1] comarli dam, ar is acobrach[2] dam fritt.'
'Do-bér-sa ón comairle duit,' ol in Scál; 'eirg,' ol sé,
'doc[h]umm in díserta ó tudchad-sa, .i. dísert ind
F[h]áthlegai, 7 fo-géba ann hícc do mian [217b.2] do 895
cach biúd at accobar do c[h]raes 7 do chride, airm i
n-airlím[fa]thar do déta ó na biadu immda inganta ilerda
it-chótamar; i n-indraithfither do dulas; i lláife do chiall[3]
bidgu; i mbat[4] budig do beóil do shain-ól 7 do shain-ait, do
longad 7 do brondad cacha bíd buic blasta bláth-milis bhus 900
tol do t' chorp, 7 nába tocrád do t' anmain; acht co rís a
dochumm ind F[h]áthlega ocus Becnat Bélathi ingen meic
Baetáin Brass-Longthig, a ben ind F[h]áthlega.

56 'In láa ricfa-su dochum in dúnaid, is é in lá-sin
tóicébthar a pupall hítha immpu[1] for a crund-muigib 905
córaib cruithnechta—in dá Loan, in Lón-Loingén[2], 7 in dag-
mac[3] Lón-Chorén co n-a [cho]choll[4] do íthascaig imme[5].
Bid maith duit-siu in láa ricfa doc[h]umm in dúnaid-sin, a
Meic Con Glinne,' ol sé in Scál, '7 didiu conid hé sin láa
gairfither toísig Tuathi in Bíd dochumm in dúine.' 'Ocus[6] 910
cia a n-anmanna-sin?' or Mac Con Glinne. 'Ní h-annsa,' ol
in Scál, '.i. Áirnechán mac Saille Slemni súgmaire, 7
Bairgenach mac Toraid Tirm-Charna[7], 7 Fás-Taib mac
Lón-Longén, 7 Lachtmarán mac Blichtucán, 7 Lám-
Dóitech mac Lethir-Chind, 7 Óc-Mael Blongi mac Slessa 915
Sen-Shaille.' 'Ocus[6] cia h' ainm-siu fodén fri iarfaige
didiu[8]?'

---

55 [1] *See Note to l. 613.*   [2] B acomrach   [3] B cheill
[4] B inbat
56 [1] B immpe   [2] B lotloingen   [3] B dagmacu   [4] B choll
[5] B impu   [6] B Et   [7] KM charnna, *sed pr.*   [8] B dín; *see*
Note.

57 a 'Ní *h-annsa*,' ol in Scál:[1]

1. 'Cruithnechtán mac Lemnachtán
meic [2]Saille[2] súgmaire
[3]m' ainm-si fén;[3]
Brechtán fo Mil
comainm in f[h]ir
bís fo m' théig.

2. Hiar[sh]liss[4] Caerech
comainm mo chon,
cadla band;
Blonag mo ben,
[5]tibid a[5] gen
tar braisce barr.

3. Millsén m' ingen
imthét inber[6],
gile a[7] glond;
Bóshall mo mac,
taitnid [8]a brat
tar ethri[8] n-oll.

4. Ól[9] nOlar
comainm inalta mo mná;
matan[10] moch
tar[11] Loch Lemnachta ro-s lá[12].

5. Bó-Ger m' airech,
sall boc brainech
brogas scuir;
is dín saethra
sadall maethla
for a muin.

---

57 a [1] H *om. verses 5 and 6, and 1 and 2 of 57 b; see Introduction,*
p. xviii. [2-2] H saille slemne [3-3] H mo chomainmsi fadein (B
fodén) [4] H iarslis [5-5] H fris tibim [6] B, H ninber; *see*
Note. [7] H *om.* [8-8] H dar brat nítha [9] B olor, H olar
[10] H re matne [11] H for [12] H romla

6. In tan lécar
   i n-a diaid
   oirech maethla,
   luath a ruth,   950
   híth ar allaib¹³
   bíd ar asnaib
   sech cach cruth.
                          Cruth.

57 b   1. 'Mór-mhuince do mulchán mellach   955
   im a chúl,
   adastar *ocus* a ell*ach*
   d' imim úr.

2. A srian co n-a aradnu hítha
   in cach dú,   960
   inb*ert* inbe co n-a tibrecht
   d' inbib crú.

3. Ug-Adarc mo gilla gloma[i]r¹,
   nít[h]a² tuir
   ³ré ndul i ndáil báis dáig—ní bras—³   965
   ⁴tí⁵ do-t-cuir.⁴
                          C[ruth].

4. ⁶M' inar craíbechán imum-sa⁶, ⁷
   in cach dú,
   ⁸blonacc-thinbe oc*cus* inbe   970
   ná téit crú.⁸
                          C[ruth].

58 'Cosna biadaib oirerda ingantaib út duit festa, a Meic
Con Glinne!' ol in Scál, '.i.

---

¹³ B allaig
57 b ¹ B, H glomar   ² B níta, H blad ce*ch*   ³⁻³ H da gai
chruithnechta na deslaim   ⁴⁻⁴ H leis diernguin   ⁵ B do*n*ti
⁶⁻⁶ H etgud craeibechan im*m*um fadein   ⁷ B im*um*sa féin
⁸⁻⁸ *sic* H; B i*n*bert inbe *con*a tibrecht dinbid crú

975   ¹Biada ile inganta,
         staci cach bíd bélaide²,
         miassa donna derg-buide
         lomnána cen locht;
         aisle buana bóshaille,
980   blongi bláthi bélaide²,
         tarthra[i]nn³ troma torcc.

'Cusna Blongib duit festa [218a] 7 cusna Maethlaib!' ol in
Scál. 'Regut ém,' or Mac Con Glinne, '7 tabair soscéla
immum.' 'Do-bérthar,' ol in Scál, '.i. soscéla do thirm-
985 cháisi c[h]ethar-ochair c[h]utrumma, 7 gébthair mo
p[h]ater-sa fodén imut, 7 ní-s tadaill athgéri nó occuras
int-í ima ngabar hí.'
    Ut dixit: 'For foesam duit na saille slemni súgmaire, a
Meic Con Glinne,' ol in Scál; 'for foesam duit na crothi
990 cruadi cúl-budi, a Meic Con Glinne,' ol in Scál; 'for
⁴foesam duit⁴ in chori lá[i]n do c[h]raíbechán, a Meic Con
Glinne,' ⁵ol in Scál⁵; 'for ⁴foesam duit⁴ in aigin lá[i]n do
c[h]raíbechán, a Meic Con Glinne,' ⁶ol in Scál.⁶ 'Dar mo
debroth i fiadnaise in Dúileman,' ar Mac Con Glinne, 'ba
995 maith lium co rísaind a dochum in dúnaid-sin, dáig co
tormolaind mo lór do na lendaib senaib síthaltai so-millsi 7
do na biadaib inganta aidble út.' 'Mad maith lat-sa ém,' ol
in Scál, 'fo-géba sin, 7 eirg amal as-berim-si frit; acht namá
dia téis, ní-s téig a merachad.' 'Cid sin?' ol Mac Con
1000 Glinne. 'Ní h-annsa ém,' ol in Scál; 'acht fo-[t-]c[h]erd for
faesum 7 comarci na n-óc n-antem n-anamail .i. to[í]sig
Thuath Bíd, ná⁷ ra-t rodba beóchoil.' 'Ced ón,' ol Mac Con
Glinne, 'cia do t[h]o[í]sechaib Tuath Bíd is gératu comarci
ar trom-thondaib beóchla?' 'Ní h-annsa ém,' ol in Scál, '.i.
1005 cusna Blongib 7 cusna Maethlaib.'
    59 'Atom-regar dó iar sin,' or Mac Con Glinne, 'co
h-erard cend-fhaelid cos-lúthmar. In goeth no-s tic darsin

---

58 ¹ H *om. the poem.*   ² B belaige   ³ B tarthran*n*
⁴⁻⁴ B f.d.   ⁵⁻⁵ B ol-   ⁶⁻⁶ B ol-.3   ⁷ *Interlinear.*

tír-sin, dúthracur conáb seocham no t[h]éissed acht comad
a m' beólu. Ba dethbir ón; boí do thrumma in galair 7 do
therci in legis [7] do accobar na n-ícidi[1]. Atom-raracht co 1010
dian díscir dénmnetach, co mianach míchuirdech, co
slemda slithemda am*al* sinchán do leith[2] aegaire nó aithech
do s[h]leith banrígna nó fendóc doc[h]um [n]gairr nó ag
n-all*aid* do gebbad guirt gem-shecoil a mís Mitheman[3].
Acht c[h]ena, tócba[i]m-sa mo lénid ós mell*aib* mo lárac, 7 1015
médith*ir* lem ná tairissed cuil nó crebar nó corrmíl for m'
iarcomla, for a déni 7 athluime, co ránuc maige 7 feda 7
fásaige dochumm in lacha 7 in dúnaid-sin.

    60 'Co n-acca ní i purt in lacha for mo chind .i. ethar bec
beóchlaide bóshaille co n-a immchassal gered, co n-a 1020
shessaib grotha, co n-a braine blongi, co n-a er*us* imme, co
n-a sculmarib smera, co n-a rámaib slessai sen-tuirc fair.
Ba soccair trá in lestar i ndechumar. Iar sin trá imrásium
dar lethan-mhag Lacha Lemnachta, dar trethna tremunta,
tar inberaib meda, tar bolg-onfad bupt[h]aid bláithche, tar 1025
báitsech*aib* buana bélaide, sech caille drúcht-bela, tar
tibrén úscai olorda, a n-indsib moethal, tar cruad-chaircib
gered g*er*thide[1], tar srónaib sen-grothai, tar tráchta
tana[ch] tirmaide, co ro gaibsium calath comnart cutruma
et*er* Sliab nImme 7 Loch nAiss 7 Bend Grotha ar bélu 1030
belaig críche h*Ua* Moch-Longthi for dorus díserta ind
F[h]áthlega. Cach ráma do-b*er*mís i lLoch Lemnachta, co
tochrad a mur-grian millsén for uachtar.'

    61 Conid [1]ann at-bert[1] Mac Con Glinne in guth a
n-uachtar a chind, 'Abb, abb, abb! Ní-m t[h]át múir[2] nád 1035
gabind[3].' Conid ann sin at-bert in Fáthliaig fri a m*ui*ntir,
'Fail dáim n-annsa in b*ar* ndochum anocht, a m*ui*nter,' ol
in Fáthliaig, '.i. Aniér Mac Con Glinne do M*ui*mnechaib,

59 [1] B naicidi; *see Note.*   [2] B sleith   [3] B mithemain; *see*
Note.
  60 [1] B gerthige
  61 [1-1] B atb*er*t ann *with transposition marks.*   [2] B muir; *see Note.*
[3] B gaibend

gláim-gilla uasal[4] oirchetail, oirfitig áin; dáig ro cait*er*
1040 a deg-[fh]ritháilem, ór is dublathi díscir dian dremun
dénmnetach, [5]*is*s é[5] mianach moch-loingt[h]ech, [5]*is*s é[5]
ithamail anf*h*ial occurach, [5]*is*s é[5] sám-[fh]ind so-bocc[6]
so-f[h]orcutbide[7]; 7 is fer bret[h]i budi 7 oirbiri. Dethbir
ón, dáig ro-fhétand aír 7 molad for tellach taige trebar-
1045 gloin mín maisig medraig midchuartai.'

    62 'Ba h-amra trá in dísiurt i mbád*us* ann, .i. secht fichit
cét sonn sleman sen-shaille imme, 7 ba h-é cas-draigen boí
uas c[h]léthi c[h]end-mullaig cacha suind s[h]ír-fhota, .i.
blonoc brothrach bélathi t[h]uirc t[h]rebair t[h]aiscelta fria
1050 fomtin imbualta[1] fri Tuath*aib* Mescán 7 Maethal bát*ar* for
Loch Lemnachta i cocad frisin Fáthliaig. Comla gered friss
7 gerrcend maróci furri. Atom-c[h]uirethar su*as* dó as mo
ethar,' or Mac Con Glinne, 'co dorus erdaim imdorais in
dúnaid dianechtair; 7 gebim bulbing br*us*-garbán boí for
1055 mo láim dírig deiss fri h-imdorus in dúnaid anechtair, 7
ticimm bulli de frissin coml*aid* ng*er*iud boí co nglass
maróice f*ur*ri, 7 fo-s-cerdimm sechum for fut immdorais
imechtraig in dúnaid, co ruachtus in prím-c[h]ath*raig*
mór-glain m*edh*ónaig in dúnaid dímóir; 7 indsmaimm
1060 mo deich n-ingne corra corcar-glana isin coml*aid* slemain
sen-shaille co n-a gl*as*s maethla furri, 7 fo-s-cerdimm
sec[h]umm 7 *con*-ludimm sec[h]a.

    63 'Co n-acca trá in doirrseóir. Ba caín delb in óclaig-sin,
7 ba h-é a chomainm .i. Mael Saille mac Maíl Imme meic
1065 Blongi, co n-a assaib slemna sen-[sh]aille i*ma*[1] bunnu; co
n-a ochraib do biúd scaiblíne ima lurg[n]ib; co n-a hinar
bóshaille imme; co n-a c[h]riss do lethar f[h]írésc taris; co
n-a chochall di thascaid imme; co n-a s[h]echt cornib imme
i n-a chind (7 bát*ar* secht n-immaire do f[h]ír-chainnind in
1070 cach coraind díb-side fo leth); co n-a s[h]echt n-epislib do
chaelánu inbi[2] fo [a] brágait; co n-a s[h]echt mbille do

⁴ B uasail   ⁵⁻⁵ B 7se   ⁶ B sobucc   ⁷ B
sotorchutbide
62 ¹ B im imbualta
63 ¹ B i*na*   ² B íbid *with dot above and below* d; *see Note.*

blonaig bruithi for cind cacha h-episle díb-side; co n-a
chapall [218b] saille foe co n-a *chethri* cossa brechtáin, co
n-a c[h]et*hri* crú do garb-arán chorca fou, co n-a chluassaib
grotha, co n-a dá shúil mela i n-a chind, co n-a s[h]rothaib   1075
sen-chrothi³ i cechtar a dí s[h]rón, co n-a buindib brocóti
as a iarcomlaid siar sec[h]tair, co n-a scóib dhulisc fair dia
mbendais secht nglacca cach lathi aic*en*ta, co n-a s[h]adull
blongi ⁴(nó bós[h]ailli)⁴ buadaige fair, co n-a drechongdás
toíb s[h]amaisce fri a c[h]end, co n-a munci do dressán   1080
sen-muilt bá brágait, co n-a chlucín do maethail asin munci
co n-a thengaid do métail tig⁵ t[h]immthasta asin c[h]lucín
sís. Co n-a s[h]rogill i n-a láim in marcaig-sin (batir
ialla bátar indi⁶, .i. deich⁷ n-indrechtána finda fichet do
indrechtánu bó bán-méthi, 7 no bíd sáith sacairt fria   1085
leth-bairgin in cach bainde beóchlaide no thuited a cind
cach indrechtáin díb-side fria lár); co n-a bachaill buic
bruthi bundraisse i n-a láim, co mbíd lán secht ndabach
cacha bainde beóchlaide no sceed tar a cuirr in tan no-s
fuirmed fri lár.'   1090

64 'Osslaict*her* dún in dísert,' ol Mac Con Glinne.
'A thróig ém,' or in doirrseóir, 'tair amuig.' 'Co n-acca
trá, iar ndul anund,' ol Mac Con Glinne, 'for mo láim
c[h]líi, .i. mogaid in F[h]áthlega co n-a mbroth*ar*-lumnib
brothracháin, co n-a mbroth*ar*-c[h]ertib boc-brechtáin, co   1095
n-a sluastib tur-aráin i n-a lámu, ic fochartad in ottraig
ingerta boí forsin [ch]loch-drochat¹ brechtáin óthá imm-
dorus in tige móir co h-imdorus in dúine inechtair. Co
n-acca trá do m' láim deiss, .i. in Fáthliaig co n-a dí lámaind
do lón-charna lán-mhéith bá lámaib ic lér-gním in taige   1100
lán-immerta do chaelánu *im*be ó mullach co talmain.
Atn-aigim isin cuchtair, co n-acca trá .i. mac ind
F[h]áthlega co n-a dubán blongi i n-a láim, co n-a ruaimnig
do min-scomartaig oige all*aid* ass, .i. smir a lurgan, co n-a

---

³ B sencrochi   ⁴ ⁴ *Interlinear.*   ⁵ B tiag   ⁶ B inidi;
KM *footnote* inide, *sed pr.*   ⁷ B .i.x.; KM noi, *sed pr.*
64 ¹ H clochdrochat, B lochdrochat; *see Note.*

1105 s[h]lait co *trích*a[i]t f[h]er-lám do chaelánu inbe asin
ruaimnig-sin sís, oc dubánacht for loch n-úsca. Cumma no
bered tinne sen-shaille 7 lón-longén bós[h]aille ar loch úsca
cummascaig[th]e mela for tír ngrotha ²boí i n-a f[h]arrad
isin c[h]uchtair²; (7 isin loch-sin ro báided mac in
1110 F[h]áthlega dia ndernad in marbnaid erdraicc, .i.

"Mac Eógain, clú ³má raind³," *et reliqua*).

At-aigimm isin tech mór iarum. Am*al* tuc*us* mo choiss
darsin tairrsech istech, co n-acca ní, .i.⁴ in colcaid⁵ n-én-gil
n-imme, co sess*ar* fu*r*ri, co-nam t[h]arr*u*sar innte co barr
1115 mo dí chluas. In ochtar is calma boí isin rígthig, a n-opar
'com' tharraing esti for cléthib cend-mull*aig*.

65 'No-m c[h]urth*er* iar sin áitt a mboí in Fáthliaig
fodessin. "Oráit, oráit!" ol mé friss. "I n-an*m*am maethla," or
sé frim, "is olc in féthán féth-s[h]nais fil for h' agaid," or in
1120 Fáthliaig; "uchán! is féth galair. At buide do láma, at brecca
do beóil, at liatha do shúile. Ro f[h]annaigsetar th' f[h]éthi,
at-rachtatar ós t' [sh]úli¹ 7 ós t' f[h]eóil 7 ós t' altaib 7
ós t' ingnib. Ro-[t] tairb*ir*setar *trí*² mná—uatha 7 éca 7
gorta—.i. do gobaib gorta galbigi. Ro-[t] táraill súil ná-t
1125 athbendach, ro-[t] táraill tám trom-galair. So-dethbir trá;
ní féth laíg lilicca lachtmair lessaigthi latt fo lámu dag-
choca, n[í] féth luirc³ fola lessaigt[h]i latt acht is féth meic
mí-altromma fo muich mí-lessaigt[h]i.'" 'So-dethbir ón,' ol
Mac Con Glinne, 'atá do thruime mo galair, do therci in
1130 legis, do accobar na h-ícce.'

66 'Asnéid dam do galar, a laích,' or in Fáthliaig.
'Asnédfit ém,' ol Mac Con Glinne, 'indrud mo c[h]redba 7
a ndo-m-gní miffrech mí-gnímach .i. carthain caemna,
miscais mí-chaemna, mian moch-longthi, min-chirrad m'
1135 il-blass, cnám carna, bronnud bánbíd. Géri 7 gorti,
ítmaire 7 ithemraige lemm mo chuit fodéin, co ná gaib

---

²⁻² *Interlinear*.　　³⁻³ B marind　　⁴ *Interlinear*.　　⁵ B colcaig
65 ¹ B tuli (i *infralinear*; KM *om., sed pr.*).　　² B iii; KM *teora, but
the contraction for that in AMC is* iiia.　　³ B luric; *see Note*.

*gre*im nó gabáil ina tomlim; doichell 7 dochta, diúltad 7
díchonnercli immon ní is leamm fodén, conadam lista
liumm fodén 7 na*ch*am inmain fris nach aen. Gorta co n-a
cethri fodlaib[1] fichet air-sin anuas .i. dogaillsi, díbe, dál fria   1140
h-essamna lem ré cách i cend cach bíd, inriud cach bíd
frim. Ba h-ed mo mian, biada ilarda immda inganta in
betha i comair mo c[h]raís do dénam mo tholi, do línad mo
shanti. Uch, trá, is mór in saeth-sin do neoch ná-dos-fagaib
uli.' 'At-biur mo bré*th*ir,' or in Fáthliaig, 'is olc ind accidit,   1145
is margócán dia-nos tarla, 7 níba fota foel*u*star. Ar is 'cot'
uide[c]ht duit do m' dísiurt-sa 7 do m' dúnad don chur-sa,
béra midchuine latt do [t'] tig d' ícc do galair, 7 bid[at][2] slán
c[h]aidche de.'

67 'Cade-side?' ol Mac Con Glinne. 'Ní *h-annsa* ém,' or   1150
in Fáthliaig; 'dia téis do [t'] tig innocht, eirg don tiprait d'
innmad do lám; *con*-melfi[1] dorni fri détu, 7 tochosaig[2] cach
finda fiar foltnide[3] iar n-a chóir do t' fhult. Iar sin, no-t gor
fri tenid trichemruaid do daroich d*eir*g dírig, nó do ocht
slisnib[4] uindsend fhásus i *f*hail airshlébi dú i caccut   1155
min-gelbuind, hi tellach thirmaide irard airísel, co ra-t gori
a gr*í*ss, ná ro-t losci a lassar, ná ro-t b*e*na a dé. Scarth*ar*
gemen findach fír-gamna fót[5] fria tenid anair-t[h]uaid[6] 7 do
s[h]liss fri colba f*i*nd-gel ferna saindrud; 7 toirb*ir*ed ben
dian dóit-gel imchialla fhorbáilid 's í sochla so-acallma[7],   1160
[219a] 's í bél-chorccra banamail, 's í so-beóil socheneó*i*l, 's
í m*uin*cech[8] bratach bretn*u*sach, co mbruach ndub[9] et*er* dá
ó[10] a bruit, ná ro fhera[11] brón f*u*rri. Teóra muime a h-ordan
f*u*rri; teóra h-aíble s*er*cci 7 áne[12] for a h-inch*aib*, cen fír
doichle i n-a h-étan. Écosc suairc so-chóir lee; bratt corccra   1165
coíc-diab*ulta* impe; eó ór-d*er*g i n-a brut; agaid ch*a*ín
f[h]orlethan lé; rosc glass caín i n-a cind. Dá brá doíle

---

66 [1] *Interlinear.*   [2] *See Note.*
67 [1] KM comelfi   [2] B tochosail; *see Note.*   [3] B foltnige
[4] B slisnig   [5] B fhót   [6] B anairtuaig   [7] B soacmallma
[8] B m-cach   [9] *sic* B; *see* § *iv.*   [10] B lo; *see Note.*
[11] B ros hera (*the* s *at end of line; see Note*).   [12] B ana

dub-gorma ós na rosca-sin; gruade corccra comarda lé.
Beóil deirg t[h]anaide; déta gela glanide i n-a cind, amal
1170 betís némaind. Rigthi boca bláth-gela; dí thaeb s[h]lemna
shnechtaide; sliasta ségda sebcaide; colptha córa cutruma;
traigthe tana tonn-gela; méra seta sith-alta; ingne áille[13]
iuchanta; corab álaind 7 corab gasta a fochéim 7 a
foímmt[h]echt na h-inghene-sin; corab tét-bind téth-milis
1175 a mín-chomrád 7 a mín-acallam; co ná roib locht nó on nó
anim risi mbenfa nach aicsed féig furachair óthá a h-ind co
a bond.

68 'Tabrad in ingen-sin duit do t[h]rí noí mírend, a Meic
Con Glinne, corab médithir fri h-og rerc[h]irci cach mír.
1180 Fo-dos-ceirdi for lua[i]sc luamnig i t' beólu na mírenda, co
ru-s impóat do shúile i t' chloiceand oca n-ithe. Na h-ocht
n-orbaind, ní-dos coicéla, a Meic Con Glinne, cia bali a
dochrat duit: secul, seruán, maelán, ruadán, cruithnec[h]t,
eórna, fidbach, corca. Ocht mbairgena cacha[1] h-orbaind[2]
1185 díb-side 7 ocht n-andlaind cacha bargine, 7 [ocht] torsnu
fria cach n-andland; 7 médithir fri h-og curri cach mír
fo-s-cerdi i t' beólu díb.

69 [219a.1] 'Cosna corénaib míne millsén duit festa, a
Meic Con Glinne! Co mucca úra; co lúna hítha; co lúnu
1190 messi [1].i. muilt bruithi[1]; cosin tuicsenach so-acallmach
c[h]osnait na slóig .i. cosin lón-longín bós[h]aille[2]; cosin
sercoll socheneóil, co mid; co leiges in chliab-galair .i. sean
sen-shaille[3]; co tothlugud mbrothc[h]áin [1].i. sen-gruth[1];
co mian ban aentuma .i. lemnacht[4]; co briscén mbanrígna[5]
1195 .i. cerrbacán[6]; co h-eill fir c[h]élide .i. cuirm; co cunnid
corgais .i. coilech circe; co h-étan briste .i. brechtán; co
lám-ar-cách .i. tur-arán; co torrach tellaig .i. tanach; cosin
mbrúchtaig mbolgaig .i. [7]nua corma[7]; co mian na sacart .i.

---

[13] B áidble; *see Note.*
68 [1] *Interlinear.*   [2] B horba *with* ind *suprascript.*
69 [1-1] *Interlinear.*   [2] B bo *at end of line with* saille *suprascript.*
[3] B sean *at end of line with* senshaille *suprascript.*   [4] B lem *at end of line with* nacht *suprascript.*   [5] B mbandrigna, H righnae
[6] *Interlinear.*   [7-7] *Interlinear.*

braisech bélaide[6]; cosin maín is míne 7 is millse da
[7]cach biúd .i. find-litte[7]; co h-ingur [8]cícarais cúigir[8] 1200
.i. craíbechán[9]; cosna lúb-diabulta emnaigib [7].i. caelánu
caerech[7]; co fiachu fraiged .i. cliathánu; co h-én crossi .i.
saland; co h-imdorus aenaig .i. ubla cumra; co némannu
tigi teglaig .i. uga cercc[6]; co brafud nochta .i. etneda.'

70 'Feib no-s turim dam na h-il-biadu, iar sin ordaigis 1205
dam mo deog mbolgaim: "Metríne bec bec nát ro-mór,
cet[h]ri fichit fer-bolcumm deit, a Meic Con Glinne, for na
biadaib-sin anuas, d' ass ro-thécht, d' ass nát ro-thécht, d'
ass lebar-thécht, d' ass eter dá thécht, d' ass buide bolcach
fo-loing in slucud-chocnum, don lomum da-ní in slaim- 1210
[m]egil[1] rethi[2] oc dul darsin mbrágait sís, co n-aprai[3] in
bolcum toísech frisin mbolcum ndédenach, 'For-t-gillim,
a charr-matraid, i fiadnaise in Dúilemun, cia thís anuas
regut-sa suas, ar ní thalla ar mataidecht ar ndís isin
istad-luc-sa.' In galar no-t gébad de-sin, a Meic Con 1215
Glinne, cenmothá aen-ghalar, is misse no-t ícfa, .i. galar
sruthi 7 dag-daíne, in galar is f[h]err cach ngalar, in galar is
f[h]iú slánti suthain, .i. in buar fodessin."''

Ind Aislingthi ind sin anuas, et reliqua.

71 [219a.2] Fri h-airerdacht na h-indisen 7 fri tuirem na 1220
mbiad n-imda n-écsamail n-oirerda i fiadnaise in ríg, in
t-anmunna indligthech ro aittrebastar a n-indib inmedónachaib Cathail meic Fhinguine tánic co mboí oc immlige a
bél[1] fri a chend anechtair. Is amlaid boí in mac légind co
tenid móir occa istaig. Do-berthí cach staic iar n-urd do na 1225
stacib frisin tenid, 7 do-s-bertís iar n-urd co beólu in ríg.
Tan ann tuccad staic díb co beólu in ríg, 7 lingis in mac
mallachtan[2] cor sháid a dí chrob isin staic boí i lláim in
me[i]c légind, 7 beris leis dar tellach anund 7 atn-aig fon

8-8 B cuigir cicharan, H om.; see Note. 9 B cra at end of line with
ibechan suprascript.
70 1 H sraindmeigil 2 B rethid, H ind reithe frangcaig
3 sic B; H apra
71 1 B abel abel 2 B mallachtain

F

1230 coire boí fri tenid anall, 7 impáith*er* in coire fair. Conid de
as-b*e*rair³ 'lón-choire'⁴ .i. don c[h]raes-lon boí i mbrága
C[h]athail meic Fhinguine do beith foí. Nocon ead at-⸳
fíadut scélaige,acht is ambrágait gilla in tshacairt do-chóid,
co ro báidead in gilla i llind mulind Dúine Caín for bélu
1235 puirt P[h]ich*áin* meic Moíle Finde hi Feraib Féni. Nocon
ed sin fil i llebruib Corccaige, acht conid isin coire tucad
o*cus* conid foe ro losced. 'Fri Dia 7 fri Brigit berma a
atlugud,' ol Mac Con Glinne, ic tabairt a bossi dessi fri a
gin fodén 7 a chlé-boss fria gin Cathail; 7 atn-agur
1240 lín-scóti bá chend Cathail 7 berair hé immach.

72 'Cid is nesam¹ dún,' or Pichán, 'i festa?' 'Iss asu [a]
chách lind,' ol Mac Con Glinne, 'berair na slóig 7 na
sochaide, ríg 7 rígna 7 m*uin*tera, éte 7 alma 7 indile 7 a uli
indmassa óir 7 argait in dúnaid, dar dún immach.' *Ocus*
1245 at-berait eólaig co nár fárcbad luag cossi [219b] cenbair do
nach innmas i ríg-imscing móir medónaig in dúnaid acht in
cori boí imm chend in luin. *Ocus* iatar in tech fair
indechtair 7 adáith*er* cet[h]*ri* tendti dermára sain-chan isin
tech. In tan boí in tech i n-a thuir t[h]richemruaid 7 i n-a
1250 briaid adbul-móir, lingis in demun i féic in rígthige s*ua*s, 7
nír choem in tene ní dó; 7 saidis forsin taig ba nessa dó.

73 'Maith trá, a f[h]iru Muman,' ol Mac Con Glinne, 'fil
sund út bar cara; 7 iadaid bar mbeóla, co r*u-s* acailler-sa in
manach n-oibéil¹ ndermitnech út. Maith, a thróig,' ol Mac
1255 Con Glinne, 'déna umalóit dún.' 'Do-gén-sa ón,' or diabul,
'ór ní chumgam cen a dénam; uair at fer co rath Dé, co
n-imma[d] ecnai, co ng*é*ri inntlechta, co lléri umalóti,
co mian cach maith*iusa*, co rath in Spir*uta sech*taig.
Am demon-sa aicenta co n-adb*ar* nem-brisc, 7 indisfet
1260 mo thindram det-siu. Atám teóra leth-bl*iadn*a hi ngin
C[h]athail oc admill*ed* Muman 7 L*eth*e Moga N*uadat* ol
chena, 7 dia mbeind teóra leth-bl*iadn*a ele, no millfind

---

³ *sic* B.   ⁴ *See Note.*
72 ¹ B nesem
73 ¹ B noibell

Ér*inn* uli. Mina beth dia n-uaisle 7 dia n-ecnaidecht,
dia n-ógi 7 dia n-indrac*us* 7 d' immad a n-esp*oc* 7
a n-an[m]charut m*uin*tire Corccaige móire Muman ó   1265
tudchad-su do m' shaigid-sea, 7 do indrac*us* a gotha 7 a
bréthri 7 enig 7 anmma in ríg uasail oirmitnig dia tánac
tesarcain; 7 di*diu* mina beth do t' uaisle-siu 7 t' indrac*us* 7 t'
ógi 7 t' ecnaide, d' immbud t' fhessa 7 t' airchetail, is i t'[2]
brág*ait* fén no ragaind, co ngabdaís coin-téill 7 slipre 7   1270
echl*a*sca duit sechnón Érenn, 7 comad hé galar no-t bérad,
gorta.'

74 'Airde na crochi coimdetta uam-sa i t' agaid!' ol Mac
Con Glinne, 7 atn-aig trí tomaid don tshosc*é*la friss; 7
at-bert in demun, 'Minbad in mbáin mbic a Cuirrech   1275
Liffe,[1] do m' debroth fia Dia, a C[h]athail meic Fhinguine,
do-s-béraind do chorp i tal*main* 7 t' animm a n-iffernn ré
nómaide anocht.' *Ocus* foluamnigis i n-ethiar iar sin la
m*uin*tir iffirnn.

'Cid do-géntar ann hi festa, a Meic Con Glinne?' or   1280
Pichán. 'Ní *h-annsa*,' ol Mac Con Glinne, 'lemnacht 7 imm
úr, a comberbad tria mhil 7 a n-ól do nua-dhig don ríg.'
Do-rigned samlaid. Tuccad cori [2]cét chombruthi[2] do
loimm lán-berbthi dia shain-ól don ríg, conid hí sáith mór
dédenach do thomail Cathal iarsan lun in tsáith-sin.   1285
Déraigth*er* iar sin don ríg for colcid clúm-dérai[g]thi, 7 aes
ciúil 7 airfitig ó etart[h]ráth co h-etrud. Fesiss in rí[3] i n-a
shuan-torthim chodulta. Fessaiter in rígrad um Pichán feib
is aíbne 7 is anórdha bátar riam remi. Cáttu mór 7 anóir for
in scolaige leó in adaig-sin[4]. At-berut eólaig (.i. scélaige)[5]   1290
co mboí in rí teóra láa 7 teóra [h]-aidche isi[n] aen
chodlad-sin. At-berat lib*air* C[h]orccaige ná boí acht ón
tráth co 'raile.

75 At-raig in rí[1] iar n-a bárach 7 tig a láim dar [a] agaid, 7

---

[2] it inserted *between* s *of* is *and* b *of* brag*ait by* B.
74 [1] *See Note.*   [2-2] B chombruthi cét *with transposition marks.*
[3] B ríg   [4] B agaidsin   [5] *Interlinear.*
75 [1] B ríg

1295 níba luga oltá uball féta fír-chumra cach banna drúchta
dond-c[h]orccra boí tria n-[a] agaid. 'C' áit hi fil Mac Con
Glinne?' ol Cathal. 'Atá sund,' ol sé. 'Indis in t-aisl*ingi*[2]
dún i fecht-sa.' 'Do-géntar,' ol Mac Con Glinne. 'Cé fota
bé 'ca h-indissi indiú, ní fota lemm,' ol Cathal, 'ní h-inand
1300 7 indé.' Fácbais Cathal rath 7 bendachtu for cach n-oen
no-t légfa[d] 7 no-t lessaigfed. 'Maith,' ol in rígrad, 'do
dénam for Mac Con Glinne.' 'Do-géntar,' ol Cathal; 'bó
cach liss hi Mumain-tír dó, 7 uinge cach comathig, brat hó
cach cill 7 caera[3] cach thige ó Charn cu Corccaig fri a
1305 thaeb-sin. Do-bérth*ar* trá in sét is f[h]err oltás sin uile .i.
cocholl Manchíne.'[4]

76 Is ann trá tánic Roennu Ressamnach isin tech 7
Cruit-Fhiach a mac 7 Mael Chiar a ingen, conid ind
do-s-gní na rundu-sa:

1310   1. 'Do-lluid Manchín, monar nglé,
        d' accra for Mac Con Glinne;
        is é Manchín melltais[1] de[2]
        [3]don chochlín bec[3] boí imme.'[4]

        2. 'Nírb uróil do Chomgán glan'(.i. ar mac in drúith)[5]
1315   '(cen co bad[6] uann a bunad[7])
        in cocholl it-chiú co mblad
        cémad fhiú trí secht cumal,
        cia no beth fo dathaib[8] bran,
        ó Chathal, ó ríg Muman.'

1320   3. '[9]Nírb oróil[9] lemm uaimm fodén
        gémad [10]ór i n-a t[h]airmchéill[10],
        [11]am*al* no berad fri a[11] réir
        is[12] it-berad tria glan-chéill,

---

    [2] *On* int *see Note.*   [3] B bó; *see Note.*   [4] *On the word order in*
ll. 1302–1306 see Note.
    76 [1] H tarras   [2] *sic* H; B *om.*   [3-3] H man cochall ro
[4] H *adds a couplet :* cochall Mancin cid maith se / ni ro do mac conglinne.
[5] B *interlinear;* H *om.*   [6] B coba, H cubad   [7] *sic* H; B buanad
[8] *sic* H; B tathaib   [9-9] H nibad mor   [10-10] H dor andorrumcheill
[11-11] H 7 aicc ris dia   [12] H mar

¹³is do¹³ C[h]athal i[s] slán céill¹⁴

¹⁵in t-erriud¹⁵ do-ll*uid* Manchéin¹⁶.'   1325

Dolluid M.

Tecar ann sin bó cach liss, uinge cach comathig, bratt cach
cille, fail óir ⁊ ech Bretnach, caeru fhind cach t[h]ige ó
Charnn co Corccaig. Dá t[h]rian immpide (⁊ trian d'
f[h]eraib Érenn ol chenai), ⁊ leth-lám C[h]athail do grés. 1330
At-agur dó sin uli, feib ro ráidsium.

77 Tidnocul cacha cluaisi ⁊ cach thengad tuicsinche di
araile, feib at-c[h]ódutar sruthi ⁊ senóri ⁊ senchaide, feib
légait[h]*er* ⁊ scríbth*ar* i¹ liub*ar* Chorccaige, feib ro ordaig
aingel Dé do Mac Con Glinne, feib ro shluind Mac Con 1335
Glinne do Chathal mac Fhinguine ⁊ do f[h]eraib Muman ol
chena. Ní closti ní bes dogra; bat c[h]omga bl*iadn*a da cach
aen at-chuala. At*át* deich prím-ratha fichet forsin sceól-sa,
⁊ is lór uath*ad* díb for desmb*er*echt. In lánomain dia
n-ind[is]fith*er* i cét-adaig² ní scérat cen comorba; ní bet i 1340
terca bíd nó étaig. In tech nua do chét-sceól, ní bérth*ar*
marb ass, níba terc mbíd nó étaig, ní loisc tene. In rí³
dia n-aisnéth*er* ré cath nó comrac, a mbuaid laiss. Oc
taisselb*ad* lenda, oc biath*ad* f[h]l*ath*a, oc gab*áil* orbai ⁊
athardha, in scél-sa do aiss*néis*. Is é lóg aisnéssi in 1345
sceóil-sea, bó brecc-f[h]ind hó-derg, léne do nua-lín, brat
longain lómair co n-a delg, ó ríg ⁊ ó rígain, hó lánamnaib, ó
maeraib, ó fhlathib, dont-í chui*m*gess⁴ a fhaiss*néis* ⁊ a
indisse dóib.

FINIT   1350

¹³ ¹³ H uair is   ¹⁴ H cell   ¹⁵ ¹⁵ H don tir*us*   ¹⁶ H
mancen
77 ¹ B *om.*   ² B cetagaid   ³ B rig   ⁴ B chui*n*gess; *see*
Note.

NOTES

3 This formulaic introduction often occurs in religious and historical works from at least the 8th century on. A striking ex. is that prefixed to Fél. 2, p. 2, and cf. e.g. ACL III, 3. Originally a Latin rhetorical device to establish credibility in legal evidence, perhaps adopted in Irish from Boethius; see Flower, Ériu VIII, 150 ff. P. Ó Néill discusses it in early Irish Biblical commentaries, Ériu XXX, 150 ff.

cuintesta is for OI *cuintechtai*, gerundive of *con-diaig*, influenced by the *s*-subjunctive; cf. GOI p. 444 on *comitesti*.

6 *Anér* (*Aniér, Anéra*, see Index of Persons), name of Mac Con Glinne (Stokes, Fél. 2, p. 400, 'an alias'). It appears to be very rare, and its form unclear; *Anéra*, and its 'etymology' from negative *an-* and *éra* 'refusal, rejection', are probably both inventions. In the probably 11th-century notes to Fél. 2, p. 208, where AMC § 8, v. 4 is quoted (see Introd. p. xxxix), the form is *Aindiar*; the variant in Fél. 1, p. cxlv is *Aindiairr*. The commentator perhaps took it as related to *aindiar(r)aid* 'wrathful, fierce', which is hardly supported by the forms in AMC.

7 *Cathal*, king of Munster 721–742, like his father Finguine (d. 696) and his grandfather Cú cen Máthair (d. 665), was of the Eóganacht dynasty of Glennamain (cf. Index of Places), and his son was the last king of Munster of this branch of the Eóganacht. Cú cen Gairm belonged to a different family, and the Compiler was mistaken here. In 721–722 Cathal was at war with Fergal son of Mael Dúin, king of the Northern Uí Néill. Fergal attacked in 722, and was killed at the battle of Allen. The poem in § 4, a prophetic argument referring to an expected raid by Fergal, is no doubt from some lost story about these hostilities, but it does not occur in the extant tale about the battle of Allen ('Cath Almaine', most recently edited by P. Ó Riain, Dublin, 1978; refer to its pp. xii ff. for more details).

meic. Almost always abbreviated, in AMC, in sg. voc. and gen. and pl. nom. as *m-c* or *m-*. Doubts whether to expand this as *maic, meic*, or *mic* are solved by sg. gen. *mec* 392, 1229 and pl. nom. *meicc* and *mecc* 195, all written in full. Hence AMC uses the usual MI *meic*, and KM's frequent *mic*, without indication of contractions, is incorrect.

9 *lon crais* (cf. § 7). This refers to the well-known popular belief about tape-worms and the cure for them; see Introd. p. xxvi f. The tale in various forms is international; see ST 2, B 784. 2.1.1 and 2.2; very few references are given. In Irish folk-lore, where the story is common (S. Ó Súilleabháin and R. Christiansen, *The Types of the Irish Folktale*, Helsinki, 1963, no. 286B*, give references to 66 modern Irish versions), the creature is called *earc, airc*, or *alp luachra*, and is regarded as a newt or lizard; see DIL E 164. 36 ff. *Lon crais*, 'demon of gluttony', shows the beast was thought of as a devil in early Irish, but the only other early use of this phrase I know is in LBr. 143a4 ff., about Herod's *lon crais* which deprived him of his food (cf. DIL L 197. 70 f.).

14 f. *ag teóra ferglacc*, 'a bullock of three "hands"', i.e. not much more than a foot high. Read *teóra ferglacc ndéc*? But cf. SG 21.11, *agh trí nglac;* and particularly DIL G 88. 35–37 where the phrase is glossed (unconvincingly) as

referring to the size of its horns, hoofs, and tail. It looks like a traditional expression of large size.

17 f. *prim-airaigid . . . frith-airaigid . . . mór-fheiss*; cf. l. 558 f. *Mór-fheiss* is presumably dinner; for *airaigid* and *cutig* see DIL A 1. 212. 83 ff. and C 3. 604. 86 ff. KM's renderings are unsatisfactory. Perhaps 'first choice portion' for the first, 'second choice portion' for the second, and 'first dish' for *prím-chutig* in 558?

18 *feiss* is treated in DIL F 1. 67. 32, tentatively, as a f. *ā*-stem, with sg. gen. *feisse* (and *fessa*), but *dáig in mór-fheiss* suggests a variant m̊. *o*-stem *fess*.

21 f. KM takes *boí . . . sercus . . . dó fria Lígaig* as meaning C. fell in love with L. ('love felt *by* X', and *fri* 'towards'), but the context in ll. 35 f. and 51 f. rather suggests the converse was the case. *Boí serc do X* can mean 'there was love felt for X'; and *fri* used of a subjective mental state felt *by* someone see DIL F 2. 420. 43–55, notably the exx. PH 4299 and 7178. Translate here, then, 'L. fell in love, for the first time, with him, never having met him.'? But admittedly the converse is more natural idiomatically. This motif, called *serc écmaise* in Irish, is an international one; see ST 2.11.1, falling in love with someone never met, because of wonderful tales heard about him/her. Cf. DIL E 43. 4 ff. and Celtica I, 345 ff. and III, 179.

25 f. The two hags or witches are not identified, though the northern one is a partisan of Fergal and the southern of Cathal; see Note to l. 7. *Achad Úr* is Freshford in Co. Kilkenny.

27 On the infixed pronoun see § xxxiii.

30 *aineba*, rhyming with *ailechu*, must be an ex. of the MI fut. in short *-ab-/-eb-* which continues the OI *f*-fut. without syncope. Cf. PH 3633 *terbabaid* and Celtica XI, 95. See next Note.

32 *érnaba* must be a further example. The form with short *-a-* is supported by IGT III, § 11, *ternafaid* and *do-ernafa* as alternatives to *térnábaid*, and sg. 1 *térnafad*, and other exx. of the fut. of *do-érnai* given in DIL D 3. 256. See further Celtica XI, 95. If *érnaba* is fut., however, *dia* should mean 'when' here rather than 'if', since 'if' requires the subjunct.; but this may be an early ex. of fut. used for subjunct. 'He *will* stay, and he will be thankful when he escapes' is presumably defensible.

34 B reads *dia*nus *táir Cath*al *nisberaba*, which should mean something like 'If C. overtakes him [i.e. F.] he will not carry them off', with sg. 3 fem. infixed pronoun for masc. But this is hypermetric by one syllable, and the second verb-form is difficult. The first can be met by dropping the *-nus* and taking *do-áirret* (see **tárraid**) here in its intransitive sense 'comes up, arrives'; and the second by reading *béraba* as required by the rhyme, and treating it as an unparalleled fusion of the regular *é*-fut. of *beir-* with the non-syncopated type of *f*-fut. seen in *aineba* and *érnaba*, perhaps coined under their influence. For similar MI fusions see §§ lxxxvii (2) passive and lxxxviii (3) passive. So, 'if C. arrives, he [F.] will not carry them off [i.e. the cows]'. Cf. Celtica XI, 96 f.; where I would now drop *ní-s béra, ba* because of the extreme badness of such a rhyme, if not also the rather unexpected *ba* for *bú* at this date.

38 *do-mbert bennachtain*. On the proleptic infixed pronoun sg. 3 masc. (but *bennachtain* fem.) see §§ xxxiii and xxxiv sg. 3 fem.

44 For *do-foichell / do-ruachell* see DIL D 3. 351. 45 ff. and 352. 3 ff. The present form suits *di-fo-gell-* (or *-chell-*) better than *di-od-gell-*.

50 f. After the words *nem 7 talam lá* there is a lacuna to the end of B 213a61 with room for 9 or 10 letters. It is evident that the exemplar must have had the 7 *adaig* usual in this formula after *lá*. But this makes 8 'universal things', not 7 (B *sechta*); the repeated pairs linked by *ocus* but lacking it before *lá* show this. The copyist B must have failed to read the missing words, and left a blank in which to supply the deficiency later, as he did with the lacuna in l. 55. No doubt his source read *uiīa*, i.e. *ochta*, 'eight things', but as he knew only seven of them his literal mind made him write *uiīa*. 7 *adaig* would take 6 spaces, but a short phrase to the effect that the messengers urged C., in the name of the 8 'elements', to eat the apples is needed after it. Since *na n-uball* is genitive a vn. is required before it, and I suggest *im ithe*, four spaces, making exactly 10 in all. Cf. Glossary sv. **guidid** and DIL G 173. 45 ff.; and on *for* for *ar* in l. 49 see the same sv. 1 **for**, and DIL A 2. 366. 60.

The passage is an imitation of the well-known early Irish motif of a person taking the sun, moon etc. as his guarantors for the due performance of a vow, and being punished by them afterwards for breaking his oath; which is modelled on the practice in ancient Irish law of taking oaths of future conduct guaranteed by sureties. See EIHM p. 298, and D. Binchy, IE and IE p. 357. On *coitchend* here see Glossary.

55 At the beginning of B 213a65 there is a further lacuna, of about 16 or 17 letters. The emendation offered in the text expresses the idea probably omitted, and its 16 spaces exactly fill the lacuna; but it is of course conjectural.

61 B reads here the MI pl. pass. past ind. *ro canait*, but this must be due to confusion, since *in laíd* is of course singular.

§ 8 On this poem see Introd. p. xxxix f. It describes a collection of strange characters. Little is known of Dub Dá Thuath and nothing of Donnfhiach, but the others were a prophetic half-wit, a cunning trickster, a supernatural hag, two Wild Men of the Woods, and Mac Con Glinne. Was he himself originally something similar, a kind of Panurge or even a Puck? It looks as if the poem is simply a collection of oddities. They are all said to have been 'in Armagh', which has led to the improbable idea that the poem celebrates them as fellow students at the monastic school there (even the Hag of Beare ?); but except for MC himself, 'from the Bann' (l. 75), none of them seem to have connections with the North-East, several belong to Munster, and almost none seem likely monastic students. The sole reason for introducing Armagh may be because of MC's links. But apart from Donnfhiach, of whom nothing is known, all were reputed to be poets; perhaps the poem is really 'Eight Eccentrics who were Poets'.

The passage in the MI commentary on the Félire of Oengus referred to in the Note to l. 6 above quotes an obviously related verse naming three of the present eight, and in the same order: *Cridan ainm maic Rustaing rain, | Garb Daire ainm Maic Samhain, | Aindiar ar Mac Con Glinne, | mór do laídib do-rinne* (Fél. 2, p. 208), where MC's quality as a poet is emphasised.

Comgán = Mac Dá Cherda, a legendary Munster character; see S. Ó Coileáin, Ériu XXV, 91 ff. Mentally unstable, sometimes a prophet of sound judgement, sometimes 'the chief fool of Ireland', and a sort of Lord of Wild Creatures (cf. Ériu V, 20 f.). His by-name was taken in the developed tradition to mean 'Son of Two Crafts/Occupations' (cf. DIL C 1. 139. 70 ff.), and explained by his alternations between frenzy and sanity. But this is rather artificial, and there is early evidence for the old form Moccu-Cerda which, as Ó Coileáin notes (op. cit. p. 104 f.), suggests he was of the Cerdraige of West Cork. An old verse attributed to him as Moccu-Cerda occurs in Cormac's Glossary (see ECNP pp. 14, 39, 117). 'He was renowned in following the quarry', l. 67, may refer to his aspect as a Lord of Wild Creatures.

Crítán = Mac Rustaing. The verse from the notes to the Félire quoted above is preceded in both editions by a note that Mac Rustaing was uterine brother of [St.] Coemán Brecc of Russagh in Co. Westmeath (d. 615), and that no woman could see Mac Rustaing's grave without farting or giving a loud silly laugh. Both also quote a verse about the woman to the same effect. This suggests that Mac R. had some sexual/humorous connotation (KM, p. 131, thinks he was a jester). There can be little doubt that he was the same person as the Scottish Mac a' Rusgaich. In Sc. G. St. I, 210, Watson gives the name as Mac Rùslaing, Mac Cruislig, or Mac a' Rùsgaich, and quotes Highland sources for him as a 'wild character', a clever twister, a bogey etc., quoting Boswell's Hebridean journal, September 8th, on Mc Cruslick, 'which it seems was the designation of a kind of *wild man*' [my italics]. J. F. Campbell's West Highland Tales, second ed., II, 318 ff., shows Mac a' Rùsgaich as the wily servant tricking the farmer or stupid giant of various folk-tales, some of them international.

Dub Dá Thuath, 'The Black One of the Two Tribes', unidentified. There are nine men of this name in O'Brien's Corp. Gen. p. 600, but none is son of a Stéléne. KM suggests, p. 131, that he was the abbot of Rahugh who d. 783, and in his later PIM p. 37, identifies him with the Dub Dá Thuath who is given in some MSS as author of the poem 'Diambad messe bad rí réil', edited Ériu IX, 43 ff., for the date of which see K. Hughes, 'The Church in Early Irish Society', p. 163. This may suggest that our Dub Dá Thuath was a poet, but not necessarily that he was this poet.

Donn-Fhiach, 'Dusky Raven', unidentified. KM's *punctum delens* under the MS f is imaginary. On his p. 131 he took this as the name of the Hag of Beare, followed by DIL D 3. 350. 13, but her name appears to have been Buí (EIL pp. 75 and 305, and Binchy, 'Scéla Cano' [Dublin, 1963], p. xxiv). Treating D.-F. and the C.B. as the same person reduces the 'eight people' of l. 62 to seven, and there is no necessity anyway for the two names to refer to one person just because they occur in the same line.

Caillech Bérre, 'the Old Woman/Hag/Witch of Beare' (SW. of Cos. Kerry and Cork). There is a considerable body of commentary on this figure, familiar in literature and folk-lore; apparently a mythological personage, ancestress of the Corcu Loígde of that region (see Binchy, loc. cit. above). See KM 131 ff. and 208 ff.; Murphy, EIL pp. 75 ff. and 206 ff.; S. Ó Coileáin, Ériu XXV, 137 ff.; Carney (with whom I cannot always agree), Éigse XIII, 236 ff.; and the same, in Medium Aevum XXXVIII, 245 ff.

Garb Daire for Mac Samán, 'M. S. was called the Rough One of the (Oak) Wood', i.e. the Wild Man of the Woods; cf. the verse quoted above from the Félire of Oengus. Cormac's Glossary sv. *aitend* (Anecd. IV, 6) gives an OI verse attributed to Mac Samáin or Mael Odráin (the second probably a Wild Man comparable to Mac Dá Cherda), saying of a wood that 'its leaves wound me, its thicket does not shelter me'. This is strongly reminiscent of the Wild Man Suibne Geilt; cf. ECNP p. 113 n. 1. The List A of early Irish tales in LL includes 'The Killing of Mac Samáin' (see P. Mac Cana, 'The Learned Tales of Medieval Ireland', p. 44), but nothing is known of this, and though a personal name Samán does sometimes occur, none of its bearers known to me is likely to suit the poem. The Mac S. in Cog. p. 186 seems to belong to 'mythology' and heroic tradition. A possible clue may lie in the Sc. G. *samhanach*, a wild folk-tale creature, an ogre (see TGSI XXXIV, 2; partly vitiated by etymological speculation etc.). Compare 'Eochu in Samanach', 'E. the *samanach*', in a

Leinster genealogy in Corp. Gen. p. 63, though DIL gives no such noun for Irish. The idea suits Garb Daire well enough.

Becán, Becnait, 'Little Small (Man), Little Small (Woman)'. These are genuine names, but cf. the suggestion in Ériu XXV, 104 that here they were 'selected for their humorous content and so as to make fun of Marbán himself'.

Marbán, 'Little Corpse'. Familiar elsewhere in early literature, e.g. in the poem 'King and Hermit' in EIL p. 10 ff. (where he is called *díthrubach*, 'dweller in the wilderness'), the tale 'Tromdámh Guaire', etc. The idea that he was a religious is found in 'King and Hermit' only, and in other sources he is more a Wild Man of the Woods, a prophet and poet like Mac Dá Cherda and Suibne Geilt, which fits well here. There was a constant tendency to confuse Wild Men and hermits; cf. ECNP pp. 121 ff., and my note in N. K. Chadwick (ed.), 'Studies in the Early British Church' (Cambridge, 1958), p. 355; also S. Ó Coileáin, Ériu XXV, 104. For a possible explanation of his name see P. Mac Cana, BBCS XIX, 1 ff.

70 *ba togairm nglé*. See §viii.

76 *bolg don ár*, a cheville, with very little meaning, as so often; lit. 'a bag/bellows/quiver for the slaughter/battle', meaning perhaps either that B. and B. incited warriors to slaughter or metaphorically provided arrows for it.

77 *sceó* 'and' is a normally very early conjunction, but may survive rarely later as an archaism. See §xliii.

78 f. *nime náir*; B *nais*. Sg. gen. masc. of DIL's adj. 1 **nas(s)** would give no sense. KM's emendation *náir* must be right, since *nár* 'glorious' is a common epithet with *nem* and *rí nime*; see DIL N 13. 84 f. and 14. 9 ff. B's *buad nais* could well mean 'victory over death' (see DIL N 14. 76, 80); or one could read *buad n-áis*, 'victory/gift of fruitfulness', cf. DIL A 2. 421. 64 ff.; but the rhyme -*r:-s* is very bad. Prof. B. Ó Cuív suggests the *buad n-áir*, 'victory in battle', adopted in the text. Scribal misreading of *r* as *s* may be easy.

80 B *Muire*, but see next Note. *Mod nát bá* (B notba). KM's 'Thine the way' is desperate. Hull emends as *nat ba* (ZCP XXIX, 330, n. 3), and renders 'a way that does not die' (cf. DIL B 7. 5), but it is hardly clear that *báid* can be used thus metaphorically. I follow the emendation, hesitatingly, but it would suit the interpretation of *buad náir* given above if we take *mod nát bá* as a (nasal) rel. clause, lit. 'in the way that one does not die', i.e. 'so that one does not perish', referring to ll. 78 f. But note that *báid* seems to have been archaic, early; cf. Ériu XVI, 154 n. 2. Taking *nát bá* as a cheville, 'which is not an advantage', (cf. DIL B 6. 75 ff.) would give even worse sense in the context than is usual with chevilles.

81 KM reads *comur ngáire*, 'a confluence of cries', which is unusually meaningless even for a cheville. Read rather *gaire* (there is no length-mark in the MS), 'proximity, nearness', and translate lit. 'a meeting of closeness', i.e. 'a close gathering', referring to the 'eight people . . . in Armagh'. If we read *Maire* in l. 80, the older form of B's *Muire*, we get internal rhyme, which supports it.

92 *cuairt fhilidechta*, the professional visitation by a high-class qualified poet to a succession of noble patrons. Used here ironically of MC's trip.

93 *cuairt ríg*, a similar regular circuit by a king round his noble dependents from one court to another.

95 On *bánbiad* see Lucas, Gwerin III, ii, 15.

97 f. *aidche Sathairn*, Friday night, the *eve* of Saturday.

101 *i n-a théig libair.* AMC fluctuates between forms in *leb-* and *li(u)b-*.

105 I follow DIL M 95. 55 and 96. 56–59 here and in ll. 540 and 1015 in expanding the contraction *mell-* as *mell*aib, which is more usual and probable than KM's *mell*ach.

106 *mílech . . . uasu,* lit. 'a brooch above him', i.e. on him. 'Above them, on them', i.e. the *léne* and *lumman,* would be possible, taking *uasu* as the uncommon pl. 3 seen in TBC II R 4538, *bruitt uane; blae bána . . . uasu,* 'green mantles [with] white overmantles above them', i.e. over the mantles.

110 f. A copy of the Gospels was hung round his neck as a protective charm; cf. ll. 482 and 984.

112 ff. Setting out from Roscommon in the centre of Ireland, MC passes through the southern part of the county and the SE of Co. Galway to the Slieve Aughty range on its border with Co. Clare, which he crosses, arrives at Limerick, and finally reaches Cork—a journey of nearly 120 miles in a single day. From Limerick to Cork his route is described in greater detail, and it doubtless represents that in general use in the Composer's time, of which he had local knowledge. I am much indebted to Dr. Breandán Ó Cíobháin (see Preface) for his kind help with the place-names Carn Feradaig and Berna Trí Carpat, and for confirming, with details, Hogan's identifications of the others. The usual identification of the first with Cahernarry, 4 miles SE of Limerick seemed doubtful because of the *-he-,* but Dr. Ó Cíobháin's list of forms from 626 to 1937 shows that it remained Carn F(h)eradaig or Carnarry (in various spellings) till the middle of the 17th century, when the first element became conflated with *cathair* 'city' etc. For Berna Trí Carpat, Dr. Ó Cíobháin suggests convincingly that the *berna,* 'gap, pass', is the 'long narrow defile immediately to the south of Carnarry through which the Limerick to Kilmallock road runs for three quarters of a mile'. Sliab Caín is Slieve Reagh on the borders of Cos. Limerick and Cork, 'now the Ballyhoura Hills'. The *'tír Fer Fhéni* called Fermoy today' (l. 114 f.) is in fact the Barony of Fermoy north of Cork; and Móin Mór is the mountain stretching E and W south of Mallow (presumably here the part of it called Nagles Mountains in that barony).

116 *sel becc,* dative of time, 'at a little time', cf. *indlis . . . corránu ead imchian,* 757 f., of extent, and see § xvi. Accusative would need nasalised adjectives.
Chorcaige; the lenition, if not an error, is unexpected.

117 See Note to l. 97 f.

118 ff. MC's shabby reception at the guest-house is derived from the old tale 'The Second Battle of Moytura'; see RC XII, 68 ff. Bres, king of the Tuatha Dé Danann, who was notoriously mean as a host to chiefs and poets, is visited by the poet Coirpre. The guest-house is described as 'a little narrow house, dark and dim, where there was neither fire nor furniture nor made bed. Three little dry loaves were brought him on a small dish. He got up next day, then, and he was not grateful'. As he was crossing the courtyard he composed a verse satire on Bres's meanness, condemning him to similar privations. This anecdote also exists separately, and is verbally almost identical, in a MS at Trinity College Dublin, discussed and edited thence by Hull in ZCP XVIII, 63 ff., who traces it back to the 9th century at latest. It is clear that the Composer knew and used it, though MC's satire is quite different.

122 'The royal palace', referring to the beggarly guest-house, is ironical.
Sétigi, word not given in DIL S. The quality of the *t,* the gender, and the meaning all seem unknown, but KM's guess 'blanket' suits the context well.

127 The 'stones' would be heated and put into the bath water to warm it; see Lucas, JRSAI XCV, 76 ff.

128 f. *fosaic*, see Lucas, op. cit. p. 84 ff.; and for *aithindlat*, 89 f.

130 f. *for a luirg*; KM 'on the peg' (recte 'its peg'), but whether *lorg* can mean 'peg' seems doubtful. 'Its peg' i.e. a peg for satchels etc. BÓC suggests 'his satchel [which was hanging] on his staff against the wall'.

131 *teclumaid a lámu laiss*, lit. 'collects his arms with him', i.e. tucks them up.

133 B's *drithrenna* may be a scribal error rather than a genuine variant form; cf. DIL D 3. 399. 85 ff.

138 and 591 *fo-róbairt* is the old *t*-perfect sg. 3, with *ro*, of the verb which was pres. ind. sg. 3 **fo-opair*, *fópair* in OI, becoming *fópraid* in MI. In *fo-rórbart* 707, and the later form *fo-rórbairt* in 348 and 546 a second *ro* was inserted before the verb stem, by confusion with the verb *for-beir*. See DIL F 2. 315. 86 and 448. 35 ff., and for an analogy, GOI p. 513. *Fóbrais* in 783 is a case of *t*-pret. becoming *s*-pret.; see §lxxxix.

140 *son a gotha in scolaige*. This, with both nouns definite instead of the usual second only, is not rare in early Irish.

141 f. *diapsalmaib 7 sinsalmaib*. See KM in Hib. Min. p. 30.

158 The usage of *cuachán* 'little bowl' and *corc(c)a* 'oats' in AMC is not quite clear. In l. 158 *cuachán .i. corcca do medg-usce* can be rendered 'a little porridge bowl of whey-water', but in 185 f. (and in H, KM 115. 18 f.) whey-water is not mentioned, and one might translate either as 'Cork's little bowl of oatmeal porridge', with a difference over the contents, or perhaps better simply 'Cork's little porridge bowl', with the whey-water understood. The real difficulty is in 560, where *miach cuachán* cannot be 'a bushel of little (porridge-)bowls'. DIL C 3. 569. 16 f. appears to invent a meaning 'oats' for *cuachán* here. Could we suppose, rather, that the scribe had ll. 158 f. and 185 f. in mind in writing 560, and wrote *cuachán* by error for *corca*?
On whey-water see Lucas, Gwerin III, ii, 21.

162 B *nícon fhetar*. Sg. 3 -*fitir* seems required, but it would be rather drastic to emend so. It is not clear whether two servants or only one brought MC his food; two are evident in 151 f. and 193 f., justifying pl. verb in 162, though the context favours sg. The 'two' implied by *in dala n-aeí* in 163 could be either two servants or one and MC. The regular pl. 3 is -*fetatar*, but an isolated -*fetar*, with syncope, does occur in OI (DIL R 87. 38), which may make emendation unnecessary.

165 *thac*ar, B *thach-*. *Tachor* 'returning' etc. gives no sense, and *tacar* 'collecting', here 'provisioning', suits better. For occasional confusion between the two see DIL svv. **tacar, tathchor,** and **tochar.**

167 B *erg*, 'go'. But the sense, and *nocon érus* in 170, suggest it is an error for *érig* 'get up'. Cf. the Note to l. 843.

168 *mo debroth* is probably 'by my God's doom!' i.e. Doomsday, rather than the interpretation given in DIL D 1. 180. 43. On the quantity of the -*e*- see loc. cit. l. 39 ff.

169 B's *fesser*, sg. 2, must be a mistake for sg. 1 *fessur* or *fessar*.

172 f. *ind oíbill*. But perhaps we should read *in d[í] oíbill*, 'the two sparks'.

174 *ut dixit MC*, Latin, 'as MC said'. Poems are often introduced in MSS by this or *cecinit* 'sang'.

180 f. *goirt* here = 'hungry, starved', and *grian* = 'earth, ground, soil'; hence '[even] its sand is starved [and] its soil is sandy'.

184 *acht minu-s tecma*. The object pronoun *-s* refers either to Cork, which is fem., or to 'them' (so KM), the men of Cork. MC will not eat the wretched food supplied by the monastery unless famine overtakes *it* or *them*—and himself too, as their guest. I do not understand the application of Hull's Note 4, ZCP XXIX, 357.

190 *Scolóc* was originally, and generally remained, a fem. *ā*-stem; hence vocat. *scolóc* in 150 and 175. But it refers to a man, and its pronoun may be masc., so that it may sometimes be treated as an *o*-stem (see IGT II, § 12, l. 25 f.). Hence vocat. *scolóic* here, proved by rhyme.

195 B *atmait meicc mí-fhoccuil*. It is not clear how KM got his 'The ill word will tell you the boy', or what he supposed this to mean. It refers obviously to 'little boys will sing those verses', and looks like a proverbial saying. Hull suggests *at maith* etc., 'evil worded boys are proficient' (ZCP XXIX, 330, n. 5), but this is no better, and there is no evidence in AMC for pl. copula with sg. adj. predicate (§ xxvii). The late Myles Dillon suggested to me the simple emendation adopted in the text, giving 'evil words are the materials/contrivances of a boy', i.e. are just the stuff boys delight in inventing and spreading.
gébdait, see § lxxxvii (2), pl. 3.

196 *Cid fil lat-su?* 'What [intention] have you?'

201 *bodar-sháith d' usce. Bodar-usce* (215, 657) is 'stagnant/muddy water'. Here it seems *bodar* is transferred from *usce* to *sáith*; 'his fill of the muddy water', lit. 'his muddy fill of the water'.

204 KM takes *fessid* as impv. sg. 3, which, as a spelling for *fessed*, is possible, but it is more likely pres. ind. sg. 3, part of the parenthesis beginning *Ocus ní boí*.

214 B *f-a a*. KM emends as *fair, a*, ignoring the second *a*, apparently taking the whole as lit. 'so that something was put on him, his fill' etc. But *f-* is the regular contraction for *for*, not *fair*. P. Henry, expanding it as *for*, translates lit. 'thing beyond his fill', i.e. 'more than enough', which is better (ZCP XXVIII, 43). The second *a*, which begins the next line, is a mere case of scribal dittography.

217 *matain moch (matan* masc./fem.). Either (acc./dat.) fem. *matain muich* or masc. *matan moch* would be expected; cf. ll. 357 f., 939. But the same again occurs in l. 849 and in e.g. SCC 589 f. and LMU l. 144. Dillon, SCC p. 78, takes *moch* here as sg. dat. masc. used adverbially; cf. DIL M 153. 4. But *matain* points to an acc./dat. of time. Perhaps a confusion due to the ambiguous gender.

219 Sg. acc. *tech* may be used here for dat. (see § xxiii), but could be defended as referring to *ro tinólit*, 'were gathered together *into* the house'.

221 *aréir*. There are four examples of this form in the text (the last at 505) and eight of *araír* (the first at 639).

229 *p-cept* = *precept*. The second and third letters are always expressed by a suspension in AMC, which could mean the common alternative *procept*.

On *bocht* in the sense of 'culdee' see BÓC, Celtica XVIII, 105 ff.

234 *bess* is subjunct. for fut., as are several other forms of the 'future' in AMC; see §xcviii and Glossary sv. **atá**; and Ériu II, 46 ff.

235 B's *tuccar . . . crochar* are spellings for *tuccthar* and *crochthar*. Cf. *tucar*, IGT III, §14.

247 f. It is not easy to distinguish *con-daig-* (*con-dig-*) from *connaigid* (*connigid*), because B does not distinguish *nd* from *nn*; see DIL C 2. 433. 47. All exx. of *cond-*, *conn-* in this verb in AMC are relative, therefore absolute; and since two of the five where the *c-* is lenitable (519 must be nasalised and 559 is passive) are written lenited by B, the others must be so as well, and are emended so here. It follows they are not deutero. *con-d-* but 'simple proto.', properly *conn-*. These then must be cases of DIL's *connaigid/connigid*. Vn. *cuinchid* and gerundive *cuintesta* continue closely OI *-cuin(t)ch-* / *-cuin(t)g-*, *-cuin(d)g-*, whence in MI the new 'simple prototonics' *cuinn(t)chid, cuind(i)gid, cuingid, cuinnid*, the third of which occurs in AMC 328 as pres. subjunct. sg. 1 *cuinger*. Cf. §§lxix ff. and lxxvii sv. *condaigid*.

249 ff. For the legal terms in this passage see Binchy, IE and IE p. 355 ff.

255 On sg. acc. *téig* for nom. *tiag* here see §xxii.

257 MC solemnly offers the monks tithes of his miserable gallows-meal. On this see Introd. pp. xxv and xxxiii.

262 *an ro boí* or *an roboi*, see §cviii.

265 *in dechmad*. On the asyntactical use of the nom. here see DIL R 91. 70. *oldá-su* must be corrupt, since sg. 1 is needed. The correct *oldú-sa* is restored in the Text.

272 The noun *fír* was originally neut., and this is preserved here and in 346 in archaic legal phrases; cf. §vii.

280 B *cométaig*. KM emends as *cométaid*, but there is no such word with this genitive. Emendation as *cométa* is possible, and is strongly supported by l. 287, but a (verbal) noun form *cométach* is warranted by DIL C 2. 302. 26, and emendation seems unnecessary. However, EGQ suggests the scribe might have added *-ig* under the influence of *cuimrig*.

282 *ro mben*. On the nasalisation see Note to l. 38. The situation here is the same, including the fact that the object *lumain* is fem.; see §xxxiv, sg. 3 fem.

283 f. 'Under the slope of his back' seems to mean that when he lay supine his book-satchel came under his shoulders and hence caused his back to slope. But EGQ suggests *fo leirg* means simply 'under' here, referring to DIL L 112. 47 ff.

284 'The ring of his brooch' is the penannular ring of the Celtic brooch round which the pin swivelled.

285 ff. For the motif of spinning out a respite from death see AT 2. 1199–1199 B.

290 *ina-m thoirched*, 'that which used to come to me', i.e. whatever I used to get. OI *a ndo-dam-roiched* or *a ndo-m-roiched*; see §cviii.

297 *co ndigset*. Depending on how we take *for-t-gellaimm*, the subjunct. may be used as fut. here; cf. Ériu XXIX, 21.

302 *luath-chomarc*, 'an impromptu agreement'; see DIL C 2. 353. 29.

304 *timchill*id looks like an unattested agent-noun in *-id*, 'one who surrounds; a guard' (so BÓC).

co ndiged. KM emends as *digsed*, but asigmatic forms of the subjunct. of *téit*, later generalised, were already appearing about this time. So, pres. subjunct. sg. 1 -*dech*, PH 1823; past sg. 1 -*dechaind*, TBC II R 1917; sg. 2 -*digthea*, PH 2419; sg. 3 -*dighed*, TTr. 1, 1291 etc. (but LL text -*digsed*). Hence the emendation is not required. Contrast the regular -*dichsed* in l. 635.

305 *ro crochtha;* B *ro croch*-, on the face of it, means *ro crochad*, past ind. pass. sg. But this does not suit the context, past subjunct. pass. sg. being needed, and KM translated it so, while inconsistently reading *ro croch*ad. Hull would take it as active, 'so that he might hang' (ZCP XXIX, 336, n. 3), but intransitive 'hang', meaning 'be hanged', is an Anglicism. The contraction mark must be B's favourite suspension, which has a variety of meanings, e.g. his *ro sást*- in 314 f., which must represent *ro sásta*.

306 *matroga* looks like a compound of *matra* 'cur' and *roga* 'choice, decision', giving *matroga* by haplology, and was so taken by the glossator. KM renders 'a sentence of curs', but gives it in his glossary as *mát-roga*, 'a swinish choice', with an archaic *mátt*, 'pig'. That is as may be, but the glossator did not take it so, and there is no length-mark in the MS—for what that is worth. Apparently unsolved.

308 *ro-chóid* for *do-chóid* is a case of the later MI confusion of certain preverbs, as in CCath. 3236, *ro-cóid*, a feature probably not earlier than the 11 th cent.; cf. Ériu XXVIII, 23 and 24, and see § l.

319 B has .*M*., which is the usual abbreviation for *Manchín*, but the sense requires *Mac Con Glinne*.

327 On the nasalisation by *maithem* see § viii.

328 *cuinger* is no doubt pres. subjunct. sg. 1 active, rather than pass. sg. with KM. Here the old *s*-subjunct., which still survived in MI in this verb, gives place to the *ā*-subjunct., see §§ lxxvi sv. *condaigid* and lxxxv (1) sg. 1; also Note to l. 247 f.

ní-s tá dam, lit. 'there is not to me' = 'I have not'. The infix is meaningless here (cf. § xxxiv and Ériu I, 170) but OI would have had *ní-m thá*, without *dam*, and perhaps the need for an infix was still obscurely felt in spite of *dam*, since *ní tá* would have been a solecism; and since -*s*- could be meaningless in MI it would have been the obvious one to use. Hull would take it as proleptic (ZCP XXIX, 357, n. 5), but it anticipates nothing. The difficulty made by Hull about the gender of *maithem* is irrelevant, since -*s*- had become common gender (§ xxxiii).

332 DIL C 1. 243. 35 takes *clith* here as the adj., suggesting its noun may be lost before it. Certainly a noun is needed, and *clith* itself is also a noun; and *clith . . . do étach* must be 'a covering of clothing', i.e. a suit of clothes.

335 B's length-mark in his *fúidbe* is an ex. of the secondary lengthenings in speech not accepted in the Classical language but used by B here and elsewhere (e.g. in his PH), and common with other late scribes.

337 (and 340, 774). On the survival of neuter gender in sg. nom. *bec* see § §vii f. The fut. pass. *cengelt*- of the MS needs a sg. 2 pronoun subject. Hull would add *tú* (ZCP XXIX, 340, n. 2), but independent pronouns being rare as subjects of passives in AMC (§xxx), I emend rather *no-t c[h]engéltar*; but Hull may be right, of course.

342 On dependent (conj.) *tiagat* for independent (abs.) *tiagait* see § lxvi.

343 On *ro lécsit* for *ro lécset* see § lxviii.

344 f. *do Dia 7 don Choimdid* is an ex., not of heresy but of the common use of *X ocus Y* where X and Y are the same person or thing. Cf. l. 600 Note.

346 B *noch- damad*. This can mean *nocho damad* or *nocho ndamad* (*nochon damad* is less likely); see § li.

350 *ro-the*, see DIL T 1. 93. 62 ff. The quantity varies, *te/té*. There is no proof it is not long here; in 388 the aicill with *Láirce* shows it is short there. The variant *téith* seems to be, or usually to be, long and is so marked in B in 1174. For omission of *no-*, specially common in the verb *téit*, see.§ xlv.

so-fhulaing consists of *so-* (qv.) with *i*-stem adj. formed from *o*-stem vn. (GOI p. 219); but see Ériu XII, 229. Cf. *so-óil* sv. 1 **ól**.

353 For *cennphort* see DIL C 1. 131. 51; the 'introduction' is to the main body of the Vision tale, which begins at l. 430. *Cennphurt* here seems a case of dat. for acc. (§ xxiv); the nasalisation and construction both show it is used for acc. (§ xix).

354 *bid* must be past subjunct. sg. 3 rel., 'which might be'. The normal rel. is *bed*, *bad*, or in late MSS *bud;* and in OI *bid* is confined to the use with *amal*. In MI its use is wider; see DIL I 2. 314. 67 ff., and cf. l. 550 below.

ro fhaillsiged, the *f* having the lenition dot above it, meaning here perhaps [*b*]*f* = /v/ (see Introd. p. xii f.), i.e. a nasalising rel. clause with *amal;* see § cvii. If not, it would be a leniting relative clause, since lenition with passives when rel. was still possible; see § i.

355 *at-aig*, generally *atn-aig* in MI with fossilised infixed pronoun, as in e.g. *at-beir*. Cf. DIL A 1. 28. 76 ff., and Hull ZCP XXIX, 357, n. 2.

On the phrase *do léri* see DIL L 91. 31 and 90. 17 ff.

360 Nasalisation of pl. gen. after *in cumair* is probably an ex. of the 'inorganic' type common in TBC St. (see COR's ed. p. xlii), e.g. its *cuid bfer* l. 455. Or it could possibly be due to nominalisation of an adj. as a neut. noun, cf. §§ vii (5) and viii (5); or an ex. of acc. for nom., see § xxii.

361 *do-m-árfaid*, 'which appeared to me', with infixed pron. in dat. sense; cf. DIL D 2. 180. 75 ff.

371 *comgne*, see DIL C 2. 303. 67 ff. and P. Mac Cana, 'The Learned Tales of Medieval Ireland' (Dublin 1980), pp. 123 ff.

372 Here *bolc* 'bag, bladder, belly' may refer to a bag-like vessel of the leather bottle type; hence 'Honey-bag, Bottle of Honey'.

373 Sg. nom. *beóil* but gen. *bela*, proved here by rhyme (see DIL B 80. 86 and cf. **bélaide**) seems unlikely. EGQ kindly suggests, by letter, that the nom. may once have been disyllabic *beöil*, later contracted, which solves the difficulty.

388 The meaning of *loingén*, and of 2 **long** of which it seems to be a diminutive (see Glossary), and also the bearing of 2 **lón** (ibid.) when compounded with it, appears obscure; but some edible part of an animal's belly is evidently meant, and 'cartilage' and 'tube' are both suggested by some of the exx., see DIL L 198. 74 ff. and 200. 68 ff. *Long bronn* in some of these, and in l. 391 below gen. *Loinge Brond*, as well perhaps as *langánach* in DIL L 51. 52, suggest the diaphragm or peritoneum; and *long/loingén brágat* perhaps the gullet, windpipe (cf. DIL L 198. 80 f. *lonloingen* 'flute, recorder'). But diaphragms, peritonea, and gullets are hardly dainties. If *lón-* here is the word meaning 'haunch' or 'rump', 'rump-cartilage' does not give good sense, but 'rump-pipe' might well suggest chitterlings or sausages, which last could suit *Lón-Loingén láin-te*

G

('stuffed and hot'? but more likely 'very hot'; DIL L 49. 26 ff.) in l. 388, and *lón-longén/-ín bóshaille* in 1107 and 1191 could be 'corned beef sausage'?

394 On *tremanta*, 'whey made of buttermilk and sweet milk', see DIL T 2. 295. 47 ff. and Gwerin III, ii, 22.

396 *Inber Indsén*, 'The River-mouth of the Little Island', is tentatively identified in Hogan, Onom. p. 458 with Little Island near Cork, but this cannot be more than a guess. Dr. Ó Cíobháin (see Preface) tells me he cannot identify it as a place.

408 f. 'Gruel . . . with its purple berries' would seem to be something like blackberries stewed in gruel—an unusual and unappetising dish.

412 KM's 'bone-nourishing' for *cnáim-fhéil* is unconvincing; rather, 'generous in providing gnawing' (*cnám*)?

417 A final sarcastic reference to Manchín's crozier, which annoys him.

422 For *dignestar* see § lxxxvii (2), passive.

424 f. B's *nimcubaid* is taken by KM, p. 35, as *n' imcubaid*, which he says in his footnote and implies in his translation may be emended as *is imchubaid* 'it is fitting'. But this is rather violent. *N' imc[h]ubaid* is impossible anyway, since *ní* 'is not' cannot be elided before *V*- since it prefixes *h*- to vowels. The absence of *-i h*- may well be a mere slip. The sense 'it is not unfitting' would suit well, and by treating the contraction for *m* as a mistake for the similar one for *n* we get exactly that, *ní h-inc[h]ubaid*, thus keeping closer to the reading of B. For the negative prefix *in*- see GOI p. 544, where Thurneysen notes that it mostly takes the form *an*- before *c*-; but *in*- here could be a MI confusion. For this see DIL A 2. 314 I ff.

430 Here we reach at last the voyage to the Earthly Paradise and perhaps the popular motif of the Land of Cockayne.

442 *amal mil* presumably refers to the colour of the gravel.

457 On the omission of *no* before *serndais* see § xlv.

466 B *doroí*, H *dorroi*. DIL D 3. 363. 11 suggests that it is fut. sg. 3 of *do-roich*, therefore 'will arrive, come'. But fut. is semantically impossible here, and a fut. sg. 3 for this verb is ill-attested. It also proposes queryingly (but inconsistently; ibid. 376. 66) that it is perf. of *do-soí* 'turns', rendering 'has flowed', but it is difficult to get this out of a verb meaning 'turns'. The knot is cut here by an emendation; 'comes across its midst'. The MS agreement is not a serious objection, since their verse texts are generally close enough to suggest a near common exemplar (see Introd. p. xxx f.), in which *-ch* could well have been dropped by scribal error. The few other verbs in § 33 are imperfects, but present here makes for vividness.

476 *fírlossa*, perhaps onions or garlic; see Lucas, Gwerin III, ii, 27. But perhaps 476 f. means 'a very tall thicket of fresh vegetables, [i.e.] leeks and carrots'.

479 B *inichin* (H *inicin*), unknown, see DIL I 2. 268. 31. The emendation *inchinni* is attributive sg. gen. of *inchinn*, 'brains, intelligence', cf. DIL I 2. 207. 11; 'a generous, intelligent company'.

482 *epistle* were charms or spells for protection, written out like 'letters', and hung round the neck as amulets. See DIL E 157. 6, and cf. ll. 110 f. and 983 f. here.

488 *luchtaire.* Here something like 'head-waiter' (*lucht* 'household') would fit the context better than 'cook' (DIL L 234. 40 ff.).

490 *ahél* (B *aéhel*, H *ael*). DIL A 1. 77. 40 'perhaps originally disyllabic'. But Sc. G. *athal, adhal* shows it *must* have been so, and B's spelling (an attempt to indicate the hiatus, like the Sc. G.) and the scansion in both MSS, as well as some of the passages quoted by DIL, strongly suggest it could remain disyllabic quite late. On monosyllabic *ri a* here and in l. 496 see **fri** in Glossary.

493 *fó fer* plus a rel. clause seems a traditional phrase meaning something like 'he is satisfied [who] . . .', at any rate in early texts; cf. Binchy, IC p. 35, n. 1. Here perhaps 'happy is the man [who] . . .'? Otherwise, '(Cathal) is a good man', which is feeble in the context.

494 B's *bind* can hardly stand, since pl. *binde* would be needed, which would be hypermetric. H's *bid* (= *bíd*) gives the monosyllable and suits perfectly; 'famous tales of food'. B may have added the *n*-contraction mechanically, *bind* being an appropriate adj. for *airscél.*

502 On the gender of *in aislingi* see Note on l. 1297.

509 *ató* appears to be a metathesis of *ótá* or *óthá* 'from'; cf. DIL O 167. 30.

513 *cia* 'though' normally takes indep. construction, but sometimes dep. in MI, as here; see Ériu XII, 207 f.

518 B *nit.* Hull (ZCP XXIX, 352 f.) would emend as *nát*, rel. and 'responsive' pres. ind. sg. 3. DIL I 2. 306. 19 f. keeps the MS reading and takes it as pl. 3 (which does not fit sg. *cochall*), presumably altering *mór* to *móra.* The simplest solution is to read *ní* for *nit*, but rel. *nát* would be possible ('it is [something] which is not great').

520 *ro éraid* must surely be an ex. of the MI past ind. pass. pl. in *ro . . . -(a)it* (see §lxii), hence lit. 'about which the clergy were refused'. KM takes it ditto active sg. 3, 'which he refused', which is impossible. DIL E 160. 3 renders it 'which was refused', without comment.

bár throiscset, 'to obtain which they fasted' (*bár = ima ro*); see **troiscid**. On the custom of 'fasting against' someone to obtain a concession see Introd. p. xxxv above.

521 B's *fiadsu* is ungrammatical, though quoted without comment in DIL F 2. 110. 80. One might emend as *fiad tú*, since *fiad* seems to have been dying out in late MI (it appears not to occur in Classical Irish), and forms with suffixed pronouns may have been going out of date. But the contrast with *fiadum-sa* seems to point to reading *fiadut-su* here.

526 *in Cathal,* def. art. with personal name. This construction, known elsewhere, with virtually meaningless article, is perhaps a stereotype of an archaic usage when it had a trace of its old demonstrative force—'this Cathal'.

528 Hull's doubts (ZCP XXIX, 339) about *-tibar*, with compendium for *ar*, are unnecessary. The form *-tibar*, common in EMod. I, occurs at least as early as AS 7317 (and cf. sg. 3 *-tibrea*, op. cit. 6040). In AMC, *-tibar* is either a still earlier ex. or is due to the scribe. See §lxxxvii (2), sg. 1.

535 f. The *Uí Echach Muman* were a royal kindred whose territory reached from Mizen Head in the west (see Note to l. 568), in SW. Co. Cork, to Cork in the east, and whose king in AMC is Pichán (unidentified). The *Corcu Loígde* were another royal kindred, whose country was the later diocese of Ross to the south of the Uí Echach, stretching eastwards along the coast from Clear Island to

Courtmacsherry. Hence Dún Coba (unidentified) must have been somewhere close to the southern boundary of the Uí Echach. I am grateful to Dr. B. Ó Cíobháin for help with the identification of these boundaries; cf. Preface.

538 B's *daidbir*, 'poor, feeble', does not suit the context at all well. I emend as *dedbirech* 'hasty' (cf. KM); cf. ll. 152, 585 f., 1011.

544 On *-bádus* see § xcix.

545 f. *girru cach n-uachtarach* etc., 'each becoming shorter [going] upwards . . . and longer [going] downwards'. *Cach* plus nominalised neut. adj. is a survival seen elsewhere in this construction; cf. *is trumma cach ndédinach*, 'everything that is last is most grievous', l. 691. For neut. *cach* in MI see DIL C 1. 2. 66 ff., and for the phrase cf. the same in MU 2 (LL), 626.

549 The context suggests that *duana* here implies scurrilous poems, though the word itself has no such implication. *Filidecht*, the art of high class poetry, is contrasted with it.

co ro h-asblad hé. The meaning of *asblad* is unknown (cf. DIL A 2. 427. 15). KM would emend to *asbrad*, and translates 'it has been said', but this is impossible for the past ind. pass. depend. sg. of *as-beir*, and no part of its perf./past ind. ever took *ro* before it at any period. Pret. *co n-abrad* or past ind. *co n-érbrad* is required. The use of a subject *hé* with the passive of this verb is also extremely unlikely stylistically. Hull's suggestion in ZCP XXIX, 347, n. 2 *omnino silentio praeterire satis habeo*. All that can safely be said is that *co n-abrad*, without *hé*, would fit very well.

550 *bid* is an ex. of a rel. verb without antecedent expressed. See GOI p. 315 f.; VGK II, 183; Celtica III, 174; EIL pp. 210, 264.

For *i cerdu = i cerdaib* see § xxiii.

551 f. In *in tan boí . . . i tig Phícháin . . ., conid ann as-bert*, the *conid* for *is* might seem ungrammatical, but main clauses introduced by *co* after temporal clauses are a common idiom.

as-bert . . . secha. The prep. pronoun has little or no force; see DIL S 123. 46 ff.

568 *ó Charnd co Corccaig* here, and in 1304 and 1329, is a phrase describing the W.–E. extent of the kingdom of Uí Echach; see Note to 535 f. Dr. Ó Cíobháin tells me that Carnd is Carn Uí Néid, Mizen Head.

569 B *corab*, but the substantive verb is required.

On the duties of the *briugu* see DIL B 194. 17 ff. Professor Binchy kindly comments that in Cathal's time kings would never have contemplated enforcing private debts; see further Note to ll. 249 ff., and Introd. p. xxxiv.

570 On *torsit* see § lxvi.

571 B's *do imfhulang* makes no sense in the context. Prof. Binchy suggests the emendation adopted here; MC was to be supported while levying his dues.

573 f. On *dia n-áir 7 gláim ndícind* (B) see § ii. On *glám dícind* see DIL D 3. 73. 5 ff. and Ériu XIII, 140.

587 On *rell*, a 'hapax legomenon', see DIL R 40. 30. 'Block' is a plausible guess.

594 f. *i n-a beólu*, for *bélaib*, see § xxxiii.

599 *clanna Cuinn*, see Index of Names of Persons.

600 *ó Dia 7 ó Dúilem*, 'by God the Creator'. B *duilib* (cf. DIL D 3. 437. 75), which KM translates 'of God and the elements'; cf. l. 344 f. Note.

601 *Eóganacht . . . Glendamnach*, see Note to l. 7.

602 f. Beggars and petitioners will scoff that C. gormandizes and gives no food to MC; that is, that he is mean, one of the worst vices a prince could be charged with.

§ 41, see Introd. p. xxxiii.

612 B *ceth-*, which is not its normal suspension for either *cethri* or *cethra* but which would be natural for *cethair*, adopted here *pace* DIL C 1. 157. 59 and 67.

613 B's *tidnais* must be a form of the *s*-pret. sg. 3 of *tidnaicid* (itself probably a denominative from the vn. *tidnacol*), 'bestows' etc., of which the expected form *tidna[i]cis* actually occurs in l. 621 in what is in fact the same phrase as in 613. But *tidnais* can hardly be an error for this, as DIL D 3. 315. 14 implies it is, since the same occurs, as *tidnu*is, in 852, with the contraction which can mean *uis* as well as *us*. KM read *tidnus* without indicating the contraction, and so misled DIL, and Hull in ZCP XXIX, 342, into taking it as sg. 1, which the syntax here forbids. Besides, it also occurs, as impv. sg. 2 *tidnais* written in full, in l. 892. Hull treats this last as jussive *s*-subjunct., op. cit. 335 n. 6; but it seems unclear that the jussive survived so late in *positive* clauses. Perhaps the best solution, not impossible in view of the chaotic state of the MI verb, is to suppose that in MI a by-form pres. ind. *tidnaisid could exist side by side with *tidnaicid* (both being 'simple prototonics' type 1 (b), see § lxx), derived from the subjunct. and fut. *s*-stems of the non-denominative OI verb *do-i(n)dnaig. Tidnais* in 892 would then be sg. 2 impv. of this, and the pret. sg. 3 *tidnais*/*-uis* as in ll. 613 and 852, a 'simple prototonic' type 1 (a), see loc. cit. Or, a haplology of 1 (b) *tidnaisis*, whether genuine or a scribal error, would be an easy alternative. Hull's 'slanting stroke' in *tidnais* in l. 892 is not a suspension but a length-mark by the scribe, indicating the EMod. I lengthening of vowels before certain consonant groups, due to the LBr. scribe who often writes it.

614 The 'Five Books of Moses'—Genesis, Exodus, Leviticus, Numbers, and Deuteronomy.

timnai and *rainde*, 615, are exx. of pl. acc. for dat.; § xxiii. On *rainde* for *randa* see DIL R 10. 68–70. What MC is trying to say here is that 6 is the first number, counting from 1, which is divisible by three numbers, i.e. by 2, 3, and 6.

618 KM *sechte*, but B has *uii*, not *uiie*; cf. DIL S 133. 62 ff., especially 65. The 'Seven Things which were prophesied' are given elsewhere in LBr. (p. 74 c. 9-12) as the Conception, the Birth, the Crucifixion, the Entombment, the Resurrection, the Ascension, the Seat on the right hand of God, and the Last Judgement, which makes eight, not seven, even though the Baptism mentioned in AMC is omitted. Fr. P. Ó Fiannachta (see Preface) kindly draws my attention to the variant of the LBr. text from Brussels MS 4190–4200, f. 214 b in Otia Merseiana II, 97, 38, which has the Birth, Baptism, Crucifixion, Entombment, Resurrection, Ascension, and Descent for the Last Judgement. There seems to have been some hesitation in the sources about what constituted the Seven Things.

619 f. The eight Beatitudes, Matthew V, 3-10.

621 The Nine Orders of Angels.

622 The Tenth Order, of Earth, is evidently Mankind, as Fr. Ó Fiannachta suggests; mediaeval angelology regarded Mankind as having been created to fill the gap caused by the Fall.

623 *aspal* is an early ex. of a form of *apstal* with metathesis. The sin in question is that of Judas.

624 *gnidis*, B. This must be pret. sg. 3 *gniis*, with -*d*- marking hiatus, as in other hiatus verbs such as *sréidis*.

629 B *frith*-. The - is presumably a suspension, and the only word this can be seems to be *frithbac*, of rather uncertain meaning but perhaps 'angle, corner, recess' (DIL F 2. 436. 8).

631 ff. An imitation of part of Cú Chulainn's 'distortions'. For this see e.g. TBC I R ll. 430–32 with translation p. 137; and a very full version in TBC II R ll. 2262 ff. (specially 2273–76), with translation p. 201. Also T. P. Cross, 'Motif-Index of Early Irish Literature' (Bloomington, Indiana), p. 281, no. F 541. 5*.

634 *bertais*, mixed pret. of *beirid*, sg. 3; see DIL B 86. 69 f. and 55. 48 f.; also § lxxxix.

636 *Do chos 7 do gruad fót*. According to Fr. P. O'Leary this was a traditional phrase expressing submission, implying the inferior lays his head on the ground under the foot of the superior (Gaelic Journal VIII, 137); but his attempts to explain *do* seem self-contradictory and unconvincing, and he does not show the phrase ever existed outside AMC.

§ 43 An apocryphal explanation of how the clergy became exempt from military service, something which did apparently happen in the lifetime of Cathal. See P. Mac Cana, Celtica XI, 126–28, and Introd. p. xxxvi. The expression is obscure, and KM does little to disentangle it (translation pp. 52.33–54.9). It seems the student has received a call-up notice for 'an expedition to the border' (cf. D. Binchy, 'Críth Gablach' p. 106), which he describes as 'to the edge of the world', and dreads the prospect of the shocking bad rations he will receive—a share of the crust of a loaf with no nourishment in it, baked in smoky ashes, without a scrap of food or drink, the only drink available being pond-water; and the awful idea has driven him into a depression.

652 f. *in sluaiged co marbad immel in tshaegail*, 'the hosting for the killing of [the men of] the borders of the world'. *in sluaiged…do thachur i lleth frim* presumably means lit. '[a summons to] the hosting…has been sent relative to me'.

654 *do neoch*, with partitive *di/do*, lit. 'of whatever (has)', as relative pronominal antecedent, is not to be confused with *do neoch* 'to/for whoever' in ll. 755 and 1144.

663 f. *Imbliuch* is an old neut. *u*-stem (hence the nom. nasalises, l. 644), and the gen. *Imblechu* (-*u* = -*o* or -*a*) is correct. B's dat *Imblig* must stand for *Imbliug*.

667 *résiú imthiger*, 'before I die [of the monks' curse]', one of the meanings of *imthigid*, as also of its simplex *téit*. KM 'before I go', but 'die' suits better MC's wheedling, self-pitying attitude to Cathal.

673 *do-géba* is an ex. of the development of *fo-gaib* to *do-gaib*, for which see § l.

681 *uinge cach comaithig la bratt cacha cille*, exx. of the common distributive genitive; 'an ounce for each fellow-tenant', etc.

682 *oiret bé*. KM seems to take this for sg. 3, but that would need *bes(s)* in MI, and sg. 3 dependent -*bé* would be impossible in such a clause. *Bé* here must be dependent sg. 2 (lenited; OI *no mbé*). Translate 'while you be levying the dues' (through the agency of the *maer*). Cf. l. 1298 f., *cé fota bé*, 'however long you may be'.

691 *is trumma cach ndédinach*, see Note to l. 545 f.

694 B's *rempi*, prep. pron. sg. 3 fem., must be a mistake for masc. *remi* in its adverbial sense 'before'.

697 For B's *nursainde* see §ii.

707 *bertais*, see Note to l. 634.

716 *daro m'*, for *dar m'*, with epenthetic vowel.

730 For pres. subjunct. perfective sg. 3 *-rab* see PH p. 899a ll. 9 ff.

731 For *-dingen* see §lxxxvii (2), sg. 3.

734 Salt was imported to Ireland in the Middle Ages and later.

746 *cethra*. KM's emendation *cethri* is unnecessary; see DIL C 1. 157. 67.

750 B *tarnacar*, past ind. deponent dep. sg. 3 with pl. subj. Pl. verb is more likely at this date, hence the emendation.

752 f. *dar cubais*. The noun is a *u*-stem, so that sg. acc. (and dat.) is normally *cubus*, but for confusion with the *i*-stem *cobais* see DIL C 3. 580. 75. *Iarfaige dar cubais*, 'a question on/by [one's] conscience'; cf. KM, Contrib. sv. *cuibsigim* (reference kindly given by EGQ). The point of the 'saying' seems to be that the reply to a question which must be answered on one's conscience is incapable of absolute proof, and therefore it is useless to ask it.

758 For *ead imchian* see Note to l. 116.

763 *bendais*, see §lxxxix.

765 *A thosach ar mil firend*, apparently a traditional saying, the application of which is unclear. See ll. 754 and 775 f.

768 *tinme*, for older *tinbe*, from OI *do-inben-* with nasal assimilation. DIL D 3. 313. 56 takes this as jussive subjunct., but its alternative, impv. of derivative denominative *tinmid*, seems preferable.

771 The words in square brackets seem required.

775 f. Another unidentified proverb or 'saying'; cf. Introd. p. xxxviii.

§51 b On this poem and the emendations in it see Introd. p. xvii f.

818 *ríge nÉrend*, see §viii (3).

826 *onba* (H), evidently some kind of food, has already occurred in l. 401. B has *ongha* here, which might mean a fire or hearth (DIL O 146. 78) and would suit a house well, but a food seems needed here as in 401.

829 If *fidchell* is chess, *bendach* could refer to the caps of the pawns, the mitres of the bishops, etc. But it is not certain that it is chess at all, though clearly some board-game with two opposed sets of 'men' (*foirend*).

834 *ro láithea* is pl. pass., and *gille* pl. nom.; 'servants were set under (= to remove) my shoes'. For *gille* plural see §xiii. H has substituted *ro laad*, sg., the later use (§lix), perhaps thinking one servant was enough for the purpose; but *two* would be an index of the host's lavishness. MC's shoes were taken off and his feet washed, a familiar attention when a traveller arrived. KM mentions the ceremony in an ecclesiastical context (his p. 143), but his idea that the present passage is a 'skit' on Irish church custom is quite unnecessary. Hull's picture of MC being carried on a litter is not convincing (ZCP XXIX, 348, n. 1).

836 Punctuation of §§52-70—in particular the insertion of quotation-marks—has been determined by interpreting the 'fábull' as being shared by two narrators, Mac Con Glinne and the author, alternating as follows: MC

841-74; Auth. 875-1005; M 1006-33; A 1034-45; M 1046-90; A 1091-2; M 1092-1128; A 1128-1204; M 1205-18. (P. Ó Macháin.)

841 Note the nasalising rel. clause; see § cvii.

843 *eirc* 'go' and *éirig* 'get up' were liable to confusion; cf. the Note on l. 167. For H's *eirc* we should probably read *érig* here.

851 In *ol smé* for *ol mé* the *s-* is an accretion on the analogy of *ol sé*. See GOI p. 255 and EGQ, Celtica V, 101, n. 1.

852 For *tidnuis* see Note to 613.

§ 53 Only six out of this great list of Useless or Futile Actions or Ideas occur in H (= KM p. 125), in a different order from B's and with no variants of interest. H gives thirteen not found in B; and all begin with *is*, not *ba*. An oral stage is obvious here, as elsewhere (Introd. p. xxxi). The motif is widespread in international folklore and literature. As a folktale see ST 2. H 1010-1049. 4, specially 1023. 2 ff. (filling a leaky vessel with water, Q 512.1, or baling water out with one, and making ropes of sand, H 1021. 1, are particularly common). Some Irish literary exx., noting only those Actions also in AMC, are (1) The early Triads, no. 83, p. 11 (*robud do throich, airchisecht fri faigdech, cosc mná baíthe do drúis*). (2) 'Airec Menman Uraird', Anecd. II, 72 (*esarguin darach do dorn, saighet a gcartha, buain mhela a mecnaib iobhair, cuingi ime a lighe chon,* where a common source with AMC is evident). (3) Cog. p. 162 (*esargain darach du dorndaib, gat im gainem nó im grian*). (4) CRR 2. pp. 90, 92 (*esargain darach do dhoirnibh*). (5) Dánta Gr. no. 32, l. 53 f. (*cur gaid um ghainimh*). In Sc. G., TGSI XIV, 240 (ropes of sand); Celtic Review V, 168 f. (ditto etc.); etc. In England, Ben Jonson, 'The Devil is an Ass', Act V, Sc. 2, eleven Actions, one being making ropes of sand. E. S. Hartland, 'English Fairy and other Folk Tales', p. 158, the well-known Cornish tale of wicked Tregeagle's soul condemned for ever to bale out Dozmary Pool with a punctured limpet shell, make sheaves of sand bound with ropes of sand, etc.

854 f. 'Making excuses to a beggar' (for giving him nothing) is futile. See DIL A 1. 176. 72 ff., specially 177. 4, where it is not made clear that KM's 'mocking' is mistaken.

857 KM emends *gual* as *grian*, 'gravel, sand', but charcoal would be just as difficult to tie with a withy.

esorcu The OI form of this noun is *esorcon*, an *ā*-stem. A later form *esorcud* also occurs of which the earliest example, cited in DIL E 202. 5, is sg. gen. *esorcthe* (TBC I U). The only instance of *esorcu* in DIL is taken from AMC. It is therefore probable that, by mistake, the *n*-stroke over the final -*u* was omitted by the scribe and that we should read *esorcun* here. Alternatively, it is possible that a final -*d* has been assimilated into the following word *darach* and that the later form *esorcud* should be read.

865 The motif of the supernatural *colann gan cheann*, the headless body, well-known in Irish and Scottish Gaelic folklore.

866 On the acc. in *i cathaír n-espuic* see § xxiii.

868 'Berries on a hide' seems a traditional phrase for something ineffectual; see Ériu VII, 242.

869 I.e. it is a hopeless task to try to make amends for having insulted someone, merely by repeating the insult.

870 B *ith-* = ith*ir*; DIL I 2. 327. 64 f., and BÓC; 'corn-land, arable'.

NOTES 63

877 *ní fhetar can tice* etc., a phrase addressed to visitors from the Otherworld in Irish narrative tradition; see Ériu XXVI, 39.

879 *Elcab* is obscure, and so is H's *Ulgab*; see DIL U 78. 34-42, and C 3. 613. 53-79. A comic name is needed; possibly a compound of the rare *elc* 'mischievous, bad' (DIL E 107. 7) and *cab* 'mouth' (C 1. 1. 23); *Elc-[c]ab* 'Bad-Mouth'?

880 *do-m-ánaic*, old perf. of *do-icc* (see **ticc**) with infixed pron. sg. 1, lit. 'has come to me' = 'I am'. A MI development of the analogous OI *atom-chomnaic*, 'has happened to me', with same meaning. See GOI p. 480; JS, Ériu I, 160; Vendryes, Celtica III, 195.

887 B's *tanfatís* gives no sense, but KM's suggested *tallfatís* suits well; *n* for *ll* is a fairly easy scribal error. Hull's *tenfatís* 'could be squeezed' (for *tennfatís*, ZCP XXIX, 339, n. 1) is less likely.

888 *cacha díb-side* must be a pronominal construction, probably representing *cach ae díb-side*, where *cach ae* is secondarily stressed and reduced before *díb-side*. Cf. GOI, p. 280. (I wish to thank Mr. J. Uhlich for this suggestion.)

894 The Fáthliaig's *dísert* is rendered by KM throughout as 'hermitage', its common meaning, but the story in AMC shows it was a fort, not a religious foundation, and the alternative and more original meaning, 'a retreat in the wilds', is obviously right in the tale.

898 On *dulas* see DIL D 3. 447. 35.

906 f. MS 7 *in dagmacu lonchoren* cona *choll . . . impu*. This seems to be corrupt. KM emends, rightly, as *dagmac*, and also *cona cochull*, taking the context as plural, 'the two Loins, the Gullet, and the worthy Son of Fat-kettle, with their mantles of . . . about them'. But 'mantles' requires *cochlaib* in that case. I would read *co n-a [cho]choll...imme*, and take the phrase as singular, referring to the last of the three names only; *[cho]choll* is much closer to *choll*, and the dropping of *cho* was easy, whereas *cochlaib* is very improbable; *impu > imme* is not a very objectionable emendation, as *cochlaib* is as source of *choll*. *Impu* may have been influenced by MS *immpe* in l. 905. 'The two Fatties (and) the Sausage, and the good son of Food Potlet with his cowl...on him.'

907 *íthascach* seems to be a hapax legomenon (cf. DIL I 2. 326. 3), but is presumably a derivative of *íth* 'fat'; therefore 'suet' here?

914 f. *Lám-Dóitech*. The precise meaning of the phrase *lám doe* is unclear (see DIL D 3. 243. 44-47), but perhaps interpreted by story-tellers as 'right-handed' or 'right-armed'. But since *doe* means primarily the upper arm, it might have been taken to mean 'having an arm (*lám*) particularly notable ('thick'?) in the upper part'? But EGQ suggests a dvandva comp., 'lower-and-upper-arm', and his comparison with 'hip and thigh' is apt.

917 B's *dín* seems difficult, semantically ('of/from us'?). But B's exemplar may have been *dī*, the regular abbreviation for *didiu*, and he may have expanded this as *din*, and then added the length-mark which should properly belong with *dín(n)*. I emend it as *didiu*.

932 f. *imthét*, lit. 'goes round'. Rather obscure, but perhaps 'busies herself with'? Cf. DIL I 1. 156. 62. But EGQ suggests, queryingly, 'the brilliance of her exploits pervades the cooking-spit'; where 'pervades' is an ingenious and in the context a probable interpretation of *imthét*. On B H *ninber* see §ii.

937 The line in both MSS being a syllable too long, I emend to *Ól nOlar*, 'a Vat of Creams'; see DIL O 132. 5, and §viii.

944 The sg. gen. of *saethar* is *saethair*; *saethra* here looks like an ad hoc declension change made for the sake of rhyme.

947 *lécar*; on the stem *léc-* see DIL L 75. 56 and 62 ff.

948 *diaid* scans as two syllables here (cf. DIL D 1. 171. 23 ff.), which is an archaism. So Marstrander, RC XXXVII, 218, 'In poetry the disyllabic form was occasionally introduced even in 12th century poetry to suit the metre', and cf. McE in PBA LXXVIII, 125.

951 B *allaig*, evidently some part of a horse or its harness. The emendation in the text, *allaib* 'reins', seems probable; cf. DIL A 1. 286. 5 ff., especially 10–12. (EGQ suggests a possible sg. dat. of a collective **allach*.)

961 f. I would render this rather unclear couplet as 'A saddle-bag of tripe with its overspill of bloody tripes' (sg. gen. of *crú*, indeclinable; DIL C 3. 553. 55).

963 Rather obscure. 'Egg-Horn' seems improbable, but taking *adarc* as DIL 2 **adarc** (A 1. 34. 83), 'destruction(?)', it could be 'Egg-Destroyer', i.e. 'Egg-Guzzler'? Or, H calls the Fáthliaig's manservant Ug-Adart, 'Egg-Pillow' (KM 121. 39), and though this gives worse sense, and the two are not the same people, perhaps this should be read in l. 963.

964 ff. Hull's *nítha* for *níta* gives sense (ZCP XXIX, 344, n. 2), as does his *i ndáil...bras* 'in a meeting of certain death, a quick thing' (id., 352, n. 2), though this is not entirely convincing. On the omission of B's *don* at the beginning of 966 see Introd. p. xix, and cf. DIL I 1. 10. 33 ff. with its three exx. already in SR. I translate 964–6 as 'a pillar in conflict, before going to a meeting with the certain death (a sudden thing) which summons him'. Or, with EGQ's suggestion, '...with death—for it is not violent—', which seems more natural for *dáig*, but perhaps does not improve the sense.

970 f. B repeats l. 961 f. almost unchanged, which is surely a scribal error, probably induced by the preceding *in cach dú* in both verses. The reading of H is therefore adopted here, and I translate 'A slice of suet, and tripe which does not bleed (lit. 'does not go to blood')'. KM's 'of uncooked food' for B's *dínbid crú* is unlikely, because the sg. dat. of *biad* is *biúd* throughout AMC, and is never *bíd* at any period.
For a discussion of some metrical cruxes in this poem see Introd. p. xix f.

973 and 982 *cosna/cusna* should take acc., not dat.; see § xxiv.

981 B's *tarthrann* is desperate as it stands; DIL T 1. 87. 55 can offer no explanation, merely quoting KM's guess 'flitches' without explaining how it can be plural. It seems clear that *-rann* must be the word meaning 'share, portion' etc., the pl. nom. of which is *ranna*, which would not scan; but in later MI it is sometimes a masc. *o*-stem (DIL R 10. 67), hence the emendation *-rainn*. But *tarth* still seems hopeless. *Tarath* (= *torad*, 'fruit' etc.) would be hypermetric. At any rate, 'heavy portions of boars' gives good sense, whatever the meaning of *tarth*.

990 The common *cúl-buide*, referring to hair at the back of the head (*cúl*), 'yellow-haired', can scarcely apply to cream or curds: and KM's 'yellow-skinned', is too remote. Comparing the analogous use of *craebach* 'branchy, tressed', of liquids streaming into branches, and Sc. G. poetic *craobhach* (lit. 'bushy') of blood etc. flowing in rills branching outwards, one might suggest here something like 'yellow-oozing'. *Cruaid* applied to *croth* 'cream' in this passage must mean 'thick, clotted'.

999 *ní-s téig* is not impv., which would require *ná*, but must be negative jussive subjunct., an early ex. of the way the *s*-subjunct. adopted the indic. stem *téig-/tiag-*, which becomes common in EMod. I; see §lxxvi sv. *téit*. JS takes the infix here as meaningless (Ériu I, 170), but it is surely proleptic neuter, 'don't go to it', i.e. 'there', i.e. 'astray'. Cf. Note to 1007.

1000 *fo-t-cherd*, 'put yourself'. See Hull, ZCP XXIX, 332.

1002 There appears to be no simple finite verb *rodbaid* other than this ex., but there is a compound, *do-rodba* 'destroys, wipes out; injures' (DIL D 3. 362. 28 ff.) and a simple vn. *rodbad* 'subduing, overpowering' (DIL R 85. 4 ff.). See ZCP XXII, 32 ff.

1006 *Atom-regar*. The preservation of *-reg-* for *-rag-* is notable, and so is the deponent flexion. A false archaism?

1006 f. *co...cend-fhaelid*, lit. 'head-joyfully'; 'joyfully with head held high, jauntily'.

1007 *no-s tic*. Earlier, 'which comes' was *do-icc*, but 'simple prototonic' *tic(c)* largely took over, and AMC has only one ex. of the old compound (see Glossary). Hence the pronoun is infixed by *no*, instead of *do-s-icc*. On the function of *-s-* here see l. 999 Note.

1007 ff. If MC kept straight into the wind it would guide him in the right direction.

1009 The 'disease' is hunger.

1010 B's *aicidi* is defended by Marstrander (Lochlann II, 201), but his evidence for 'contagious disease, sickness' is very late and scanty. The context calls for a word meaning 'healer', and KM's comparison with *na h-ícce* in the parallel passage in l. 1129 f. is apt.

1012 *do leith*, 'avoiding, slinking past'; see DIL L 126. 72.

1013 *nó fendóc...nó ag n-allaid*. For nom. *fendóc* and on *ag n-allaid* see § xxi.

1014 Sg. gen. *Mitheman* would be expected, but DIL M 150. 18 suggests B's dat. here is appositional to *mís*. Hardly probable, and emendation is simpler.

1015 *Acht c[h]ena*. The first letter looks very like *f* with the suprascript– over it, i.e. the usual contraction for *for* (confusion for *ol* or *ar*, see Glossary, 1 **for** and **chena**). The short horizontal against the right of the shank of *f* in B appears to me to be clear enough; therefore *for* (*c[h]ena*) 'moreover' or 'besides'. This seems a perfectly possible formation, but DIL (C 1. 114. 77) gives only *archena* and *olchena*. BÓC describes the horizontal as 'a slight shadow or mark on the shank . . . either . . . from the recto or is a smudge, I think', and prefers to take the letter, therefore, as *s* with the suprascript contraction–over it, i.e. *acht* (*c[h]ena*); which may very well be right, and is adopted in the Text.

1016 B's *médithir* 'as big as' looks like a slip, and KM's *midithir* 'it is (= was) thought' would be right. The verb was deponent in OI, with pres. ind. pass. sg. abs. therefore *mittir*, which is not happily dealt with by JS in TPhS 1894, 532. *Midithir* here would be simply the passive of the MI active *midid*. But as EGQ points out, *midithir lem* is odd for 'I think', and he suggests convincingly that the phrase in B is a MI distortion of (*ba*) *méite lem* 'I thought it likely' with equative ending, as if 'likely to the point of certainty'.

1026 DIL B 22. 22 treats *báitsechaib* as a hapax legomenon, but it must be *báistech* (earlier *báitsech*) 'rain', in spite of the fact that that word seems very poorly recorded in MI. It is evident that the -*a*- must have been long, though not so marked in AMC and other early sources. The sense in 1026 is 'showers of rain'. See L. Mac Mathúna in Ériu XXIX, 49.

1030 For *Bend* instead of sg. acc. *Beind* see DIL B 74. 57; but the lack of nasalisation suggests it is really sg. nom. here; for which see §§ xvi or xxi. Even *Loch nAiss* may be nom., since the old neut. sg. nom. in place-names nasalises very late (§ vii).

ar bélu for *ar bélaib*, see § xxiii.

1031 *for dorus*, cf. *i n-a dorus*, l. 120. The second phrase is popularly taken to mean 'in front of', but where it refers to things which actually have a door(way), as it generally does, it is quite gratuitous to reject the obvious literal meaning 'in/at the door(way)'. Would *i ndorus in fhir* mean 'in front of the man'?

1035 *Abb!* Greene takes this as a cry of surprise (Ériu XXII, 167), but this does not suit the context, and KM rightly took it as a defiance (his p. 156).

Ní-m thát múir nád gabind (B *nimtat muir nad gaibend*). KM 'these are not the seas that I would not take'. Hull rightly emends B's *gaibend* but treats it as imperf., which cannot suit the context; it requires past subjunct. *gab(a)ind*. Op. cit. p. 349, n. 1, he notes the first verb requires pl. subject, which *muir* 'sea' is not (and add that 'sea' is improbable anyway, since MC has already overcome it), and suggests *múir* 'walls', but without explaining this. Simply, MC has arrived at the *dísert*, noted its fortifications, and shouts defiantly, 'Ho, ho, ho! There are no walls that I could not capture!' (lit. 'I have no walls . . .', the idiom of dependent -*tá* with infixed pronoun, 'there is to X' = 'X has'; see DIL A 2. 473. 3 ff.).

1039 *ro caiter*, see DIL C 1. 56. 16. The *ro* is correct, and is not an ex. of the MI use of *ro* for *no*.

1043 B's *sotorchutbide* is difficult because of the -*tor*-. On *so*- see the Glossary; *cutbide* must be from *con-tibi* 'mocks'; cf. DIL C 3. 607. 1–4, *cuitbide* 'jester'. Reading -*for*- for -*tor*- (cf. DIL F 2. 237. 27 f., *forcuitbid* 'jester'), we could get *forcutbide* on the analogy of *cuitbide*. The -*tor*- could be saved if there were any evidence for **to-for-con-tib-*; the parallel w. *so-bocc* here suggests *so*- must be the adj. prefix *so*-.

1044 *ro-fhétand*. For *fétaid* compounded with *ro*- (later *do*-) in deuterotonic position cf. DIL F 2. 100. 21–26, and see IGT III, 60. Analogy of *ro-fitir*:-*fitir*?

1049 *brothrach*. KM 'fried', which DIL B 206. 9 f. repeats without comment except for '?'. KM may have had *brothach* 'boiling' in mind, but if so the -*r*- is unexplained. Emend, and translate 'boiled suet'? Cf. the 'seals of boiled [*bruithi*] suet' in l. 1072?

1052 *Atom-chuirethar* is formally sg. 3, 'it removes me', but must be impersonal here, meaning 'I betook myself'; cf. DIL A 1. 47. 70.

1053 On the meanings of *erdam* and *imdorus* cf. McE in the North Munster Antiquarian Journal XX (1978), 54 f. See Glossary.

1062 *con-ludimm* (see Glossary) is a fusion of *con-luí* 'goes' (DIL C 3. 449. 1 ff.) and MI *luidid* 'goes' (DIL T 1. 127. 74 ff.), a generalised formation from the older *pret.* stem *lud*-, the impv. sg. 2 of which occurs in AMC l. 641.

1068 *tascaid*, apparently a hapax; meaning uncertain. KM took his 'flummery' from Hennessy, not a sound source (KM pp. viii and 196); O'Clery's 'fat heifer-beef' seems more likely.

1069 f. *secht n-immaire do fhír-chainnind in cach coraind díb*, '[the produce of] seven rows of fresh leeks [had gone] into each circlet of them'. See Lucas, Gwerin III, ii, 25 f.

1071 KM's foot-note 2 on his p. 89 is unnecessary, since the *d* has a punctum delens above and below it.

1072 *blonaig bruithi*; see Note to l. 1049.

1079 *drechongdás*, queried in DIL D 3. 391. 24 and O 147. 32. A heifer's hide means made of leather. Probably *drech* 'face, front'. *Ongdás* recalls *ongaid* 'afflicts' and *ong* 'distress'; the basic meaning may have been 'squeeze', (Vendryes, LEIA O-24). But what is *dás* (the length-mark may of course be without significance, see Introd. p. xiii)? The whole may be '(brow-)band', the horse-harness strap across the forehead just in front of the ears.

1084 B's *.i. x nindrechtana* is perfectly clear; 'that is, ten sausages'. KM misread *.i. x* as *ix*.

1088 *bundraisse*. According to KM p. 163 'an edible seaweed', which he Anglicises as 'bundrish', followed by Dinneen's 'Foclóir'. This seems to be a guess of KM's; Dr. Michael Guiry of the Department of Botany at Univ. Coll., Galway, kindly assures me that there is no such seaweed known. DIL B 244. 50 quotes only AMC and KM's rendering (in inverted commas), but suggests a compound of *bun* ('base' etc.) and *dris* ('briar'). Perhaps, then, '(wood) of the briar-root'? which would suit a staff. But in that case *bona drisse* or *b. dressa*, sg. gen., would be necessary.

1092 Here *tair amuig* clearly means 'come (in) *from* outside'; cf. O'Brien, Celtica IV, 100, and PH 76, *in fer tanic amuig*.

1095 *brothrachán*, from 1 **brothrach**, i.e. '(a dress) like a blanket'? Or direct from *brothar*, i.e. '(a dress) of shaggy cloth'?

1097 *ingerta*, 'suitable for manure'. See DIL I 2. 193. 76.

cloch-drochat H; B *lochdrochat*. Evidently a stone causeway crossing the mud and cattle-dung in the bailey between the outer wall and that of the main house or keep inside. Cf. McE, the North Munster Antiquarian Journal XX (1978), 56.

1101 *lán-immerta do chaelánu imbe. Immerta*, pass. partcp. of *imrid* in the sense 'applied' or 'covered', see DIL I 1. 133. 31; therefore 'fully covered with chitterlings round it'. The *imbe* of the MS is emended by KM to *inbe*, 'tripe', but 'round it' can very well stand. The form with *-mb-* survived quite late, e.g. in PH.

1104 *min-scomartach* seems to mean 'small fragments'; see DF III, 298 f. 'Small fragments of deer' as constituents of a fishing-line is odd, and the scribal gloss 'marrow of its shanks' is not helpful.

1106 *dubánacht for loch n-úsca*. Dat. *loch úsca* would be expected, see § xxiii, but acc. can be defended by assuming that throwing the hook out on to the water is implied. However, as EGQ points out, the nasalisation by the dat. can represent a generalisation of the old nom. *loch*^{N} (see § viii).

The 'loch' in the kitchen must have been a pool of running water for live fish, a *vivarium* such as were found in large mediaeval kitchens.

1111 On *rann* 'fate' see DIL R 11. 43. In copying tales, scribes often omitted the poems with which they were decorated, quoting only the first words or first line followed by *et reliqua* to indicate the omission. The present ex. is no doubt a 'spoof' on this practice.

1114 In *co-nam tharrusar*, 'so that I stuck', the infixed pron. is meaningless, since the verb is not transitive. Cf. JS, Ériu I, 160.

1118 On *anmam* see § xvi.

1123 *ben* 'woman' is sometimes used pejoratively as 'witch' etc.; cf. the verse on the drowning of Conaing in 622 (RC XVII, 175; a variant in Met. Ds. IV, 244.45).

1127 *luirc.* B has *luric*, and KM would connect this with *lúirech* 'corselet', followed hesitatingly by DIL L 242. 74. This makes no sense, and simple metathesis gives the sg. gen. of *lurc*, apparently 'pigling'; on which see DIL L 246. 58 and *lorcán* 206. 40. This gives a good parallel with *ní féth laíg* in l. 1126. Translate 'it is not the look of a young pig of well cared-for blood'.

1132 On *credb* see Marstrander in ZCP VII, 399.

1134 f. *min-chirrad m' il-blass. Blas* 'taste' seems not used as '[having] a taste [*for* something]', though 'sense of taste' (DIL B 115. 17; late sources only) comes near it. MC has frustrated fantasies of food; perhaps 'mulling in detail over my many hankerings for food' would serve.

1140 *co n-a iiii fodlaib xxet*, but only four 'subdivisions' are mentioned. B perhaps did not know the other twenty, or did not trouble to include them.

dál fria h-essamna etc. *Dál* must be DIL's 2 **dál**, D 1. 43. 10, which takes *fri* governing the thing met with. The meaning is not clear; KM's translation is obscure. DIL E 181. 24 queryingly 'a tryst with boldness', which seems not to make good sense here. A phrase describing one of the four miseries of starvation is needed. I suggest, very literally 'an encounter, through me, with [over-]confidence, [going] before everyone else towards the food'; i.e., to paraphrase, 'forcing myself to be met with arrogance in trying to get at the food before everyone else'. MC expresses revulsion at being obliged, as a desperate beggar, to jump the queue when food is handed out in charity?

1141 The 'harm' (*indriud*) done him by the food must be because he bolts it on a starving stomach?

1146 The addition of the (commonly affectionate) suffix *-ócán* may be paralleled by the current colloquial 'poor dears'.

1148 B *bid slán. Bid* cannot be sg. 2 of the copula (cf. Hull, ZCP XXIX, 354 n. 3). The MI sg. 2 *bidat* is needed.

1152 KM's *dochosail* (pp. 95. 21 and 173) is unknown, though his translation 'comb' (p. 94) is a reasonable guess. An impv. sg. 2 is needed, but KM's *d-* is, rather, a *t-*, which suggests connection with *tochasaid* 'scratches' (DIL T 2. 204. 36), Mod. I (Dinneen) *tochasaim* and *tochsuighim* 'scratch, scrape'. Emend therefore *tochosaig* impv. sg. 2, 'scrape every single hair'. The *-l* could be preserved by postulating a verb **toch(o)sáilid*, of the formation treated by BÓC in Celtica XIII, 125 ff. But it is doubtful that this (quite unrecorded) verb would have developed so early. (I wish to thank Prof. W. Gillies for putting me on to this line of thought.)

1154 f. B *ocht slisnig uindsend*. KM treats this as *ochts[h]lisnig*, as if sg. dat. fem. of an adj. *ocht-shlisnech* 'eight-sided', and translates 'of octagonal ash'. But if so, the adj. would, rather improbably, precede its noun, and sg. gen. *uindsend* would have to be a spelling or mistake for sg. dat. *uindsind*. DIL S 277. 77 accepts the existence of an adj. *slisnech*, without translating, as a derivative of *slisiu* 'shavings, splinters', and calls it a substantive in this passage (to accommodate gen. *uindsend*?), which is its sole example, but is coy about its exact meaning, while evidently rejecting *slisne* 'side'. The problem is solved by reading *slisnib* (*slisnig* being a case of spelling confusion of final voiced spirants found elsewhere in B),

NOTES 69

pl. dat. of *slisne* 'a chip' (DIL S 277. 74), here a chunk of wood. Cf. some of the meanings of *slisiu*, ibid. ll. 59 ff. Translate 'of eight chunks of ash'.

1159 *toirbired* evidently means 'serve [you]' here, but no object is expressed.

1162 *muincech*. B's *m-cach* is odd, perhaps a slip; *muincech* 'wearing a necklace' suits the context well. But EGQ suggests *mongach* 'long-haired' (because of the -*a*-), which would suit just as well, except that -*nc*- for -*ng*- is scarcely expected. *co mbruach ndub*. On the nasalisation see §iv.

1163 *dá ó* (B *lo*). See F. Shaw, Ériu XVI, 200 ff. He suggests B's *l* is a misreading of the tall *e*, and that the original *eó* of the exemplar arose by confusion of *ó* 'corner' with *eó* 'point'. Pace Shaw, the 'two corners' are probably the two points of a shawl where, it having been folded in a triangle, they hang down in front.
B *ná ros hera*. KM (p. 147) would emend as *ná ro-s fhera*, presumably with *fh-* = nasalised *f-* after the sg. 3 fem. infix -*s*ᴺ- referring to fem. *brón*. He translates 'that sorrow may not come upon her', one supposes from *feraid*; lit. 'that sorrow may not inflict itself upon her' or the like? Hull follows, ZCP XXIX, 356, and so does DIL F 1. 86. 75, reading *ros[f]hera*. But the infixed object pronoun never nasalises in AMC, and of course it cannot lenite; and it would be simpler to take the *s* as an easy scribal error for *f*, therefore *ná ro fhera*, with lenition by *ro*, treating the verb either as impersonal with *brón* as object, 'that it may not inflict sorrow on her', or as intransitive with *brón* as subject, 'that sorrow may not have effect on her' (in both, 'on her' = *furri*).
Teóra muime a h-ordan furri, 'three nurses of her [own] rank in addition to her[self]'. On pl. gen. *ordan* see DIL O 157. 9-12, particularly 11, *muime ordan*.

1164 *teóra h-aíble sercci ⁊ áne*. 'Three sparks of love and sportiveness'. B's *ana*, 'wealth, riches, prosperity', is much less likely in the context, and the emendation seems justified.

1169 B *beoil d-g*, see §xxv.

1172 *sith-alta*, see DIL S 252. 12, and Glossary sv. **alta**.
B *ingne áidble iuchanta*, 'vast pink nails'. 'Vast' is grossly incongruous. Compare the analogous and obviously related description of Étaín in IT I (1880), p. 119, §4, specially p. 120 l. 3, *ingni ailli iuchanda*, 'beautiful pink nails'. B's *áidble* must be another error for *áille*.

1183 *dochrat* has *d-* representing nasalised *t-*, normally spelt *t-*.

1188 ff. This list of foods is about as long as H's version, KM p. 127, but only eleven of those in H are more or less the same as B's, so that H has very few useful variants.

1189 *lúna/lúnu*. These must be pl. acc. of the OI disyllabic sg. nom. *lo-on*, *lo-an*, 'fat, food; provisions; feast', which contracted to *lón* in late OI or EMI; see DIL L 197. 76 ff. In Pr.I the pl. acc. *luwunūh would develop to *lúnu* OI, *lúna* MI; but the history of early hiatus, specially in relation to syncope, is not yet systematically worked out. The *lúnu* of 1189 is not likely to be DIL's 2 **lón, luan,** 'buttock', since this was not a hiatus word, and had *ua* from *ó*, not *ó* from *o-o*; though as EGQ points out the sense suits the context rather better.

1190 *lúnu messi* is apparently lit. 'feasts of rams' (see DIL M 115. 20), and is glossed 'that is, of boiled mutton'.

1194 *briscén* is the tansy or wild carrot, which used to be eaten in the Hebrides (Sc. G. *brisgean*). 'A queen's wild carrot' would be, presumably, the garden carrot.

1196 *coilech circe*, lit. 'hen's cock', means the common domestic cock as distinct from a cock-bird of other species.

1200 B's *cuigir cicharan* is at first sight desperate, but something may be made of it. First, KM's *cingir* is incorrect, pace the Facsimile which was his source for AMC; the first minim in '*in*' does not descend below the line, and *cuigir* is at least as likely as *cingir*. This must be *cúigir*, 'of five men', where *úi* for earlier and contemporary *ói* is as early as SR (ll. 742–43). Prof. Binchy makes the ingenious suggestion (by letter) that *cúiger* here has its legal sense of a *gelfine*, the family group of three generations (cf. DIL C 2. 294. 55 and G 60. 35), adding that by the time of the author of AMC the *gelfine* had become the normal family unit in law. Therefore here, *cúigir* = 'of a family'. The real difficulty is *cicharan*; see DIL C 1. 184. 1. *Cícaras* 'greed' would suit the context very well, and if we read *co h-ingur cícarais cúigir*, 'to the restraint (lit. 'anchor') of the greed of a family' (i.e., a good feed of porridge would appease the hunger of a whole family), we should get sense out of this crux at the expense of an emendation involving a scribal metathesis of two words, and two minor scribal errors—taking an accidental spot for the lenition mark, and mistaking *is* for *n* which is not difficult if the *s* is unclear.

1202 'The legal dues of a wall/walls' seems obscure, but for customary seating against the walls of a banqueting hall see DIL F 2. 400. 38 ff. A question of rights to precedence in seating?
'The bird of a cross' is likewise obscure. Possibly 'cross' in the sense of 'hindrance, prohibition' (DIL C 3. 549. 30 ff.)?

1204 Of itself, *brafud*, which means 'moment', has nothing to do with the eye except in the phrase *brafud súla*; cf. Greene, Ériu XXI, 27. Hence KM's 'glance' will not do. *Brafud nochta* would mean 'a moment of nakedness'; *b. n-ochta* would be 'a moment of eight things' (*ochta*) or 'of a breast' (*ucht*), all three pretty senseless though hardly more so than some of the others in this list.

1210 For the sg. dat. *lomum* cf. DIL L 187. 41.

1211 For *co n-aprai* (H *-apra*, better sp.) one would expect indic., *co n-apair* 'with the result that it says'. But *-apra* is subjunct., and since it can hardly be a final clause it must be a hypothetical consecutive, 'with the result that it may say'.

1217 *is f[h]err cach ngalar*, 'which is better than any disease', see §xxviii (b).

1219 The end of the Vision proper, which really began at l. 785.

1230 f. An absurd attempt at an etymology for *lón-choire*, 'food-cauldron', as if 'demon-cauldron'. B does not mark the *o* long, but that means nothing.

1234 *Dún Caín*, 'opposite Pichán's fort in the land of the Fir Fhéni'. Unidentified. Dr. B. Ó Cíobháin kindly suggests that it was somewhere in the land of the Uí Bhéice in Fermoy barony, since the Cenél mBéice was the dominant sept of the Uí Echach, Pichán's kindred, in the 11th and 12th centuries.

1237 On *berma* see §lxxxii pl. 1.

1239 7 *a chlé-boss*, sg. nom., 'his left palm being . . .'.

1242 *berair*, impv. pass. sg. On the termination see §lviii, and on the pl. subject §lix.

1254 B's *oibell* cannot be for *oíbell* 'heat' or 'spark', which would make no sense here. I emend as *oibéil*, taking *ll* as a very simple error. Sp. for *aibéil* 'quick'; here 'spry, industrious [at wickedness], busy, meddlesome'? Cf. DIL A 1. 162.

62 ff. DIL D 2. 69. 2 suggests *dibell* 'worn out, old', with *o* an error for *d*, but this does not suit the demon.

1256 *cumgam*, and *atám* in 1260, are probably exx. of the 'editorial we', a usage common in MI and EMod.I. KM's *chumga[i]m* and Hull's treatment of *atám* as sg. 1 (ZCP XXIX, 349) are both unnecessary, specially since the MI sg. 1 of the second is usually *atú*.

1274 The declension of *tomad* seems ambiguous; see DIL T 2. 243. 20. It is a *u*-stem (though originally apparently an *á*-stem), of which the pl. acc. in MI is *toimthe*. But in DIL loc. cit. l. 23, *re tresi in tomaid*, it is treated as an *o*-stem. If so, *atn-aig trí tomaid* here can be explained as pl. nom. used for acc. (§§ xviii, xx).

1275 'The little fair woman from the Curragh of the Liffey' is St. Bridget.

1285 On *do thomail* for *ro thomail* see § l.

1297 *aisling(th)e* is sometimes masc. (DIL A 1. 247. 70), as in l. 502; here the def. art. *in t-* is masc., and also sg. nom. for acc. (§§ vi and xviii).

1301 *no-t légfad ⁊ no-t lessaigfed*. According to JS, Ériu I, 172, n. 1, this looks like a traditional formula. The pronouns refer to *aislinge*; see § xxxvi.

1304 KM's emendation *caera* for *bó* is justified, because a cow has just been mentioned, and what MC actually gets in l. 1328 is a sheep.

1305 In B, *do-berthar...oltás sin uile* comes after *hó cach cill* and before *⁊ bó cach thige...i. cocholl Manchíne*, and there seem to be no transposition marks. The emendation made silently by KM must surely be right.

1307 *ressamnach* seems a hapax; perhaps from *ressad* 'act of satirising (?)'; hence 'R. the Satirist'? This suits the context.

1309 Notwithstanding the sg. verb *do-s-gní*, the three verses seem to be sung by Roennu, his son, and his daughter respectively.

1310 ff. This poem on the lawsuit involving Manchín, Mac Con Glinne, and Cathal (cf. H, KM p. 128, ll. 23-34) is partly obscure, including the reference to 'Comgán' (hardly the C. of Text l. 66; possibly the bishop of Cork of l. 529?).

1311 *d' accra*. This would seem to refer to l. 240, *atn-aig M. oc taccra fris*; but H p. 128 ll. 23 ff. (KM) explains its presence here much better.

1315 *cen co bad uann a bunad*. Sic H, B *buanad*. H makes better sense; 'though his ancestry were not from ours'. But *buanad* could be kept if we render it 'though it were not our business to perpetuate his memory'; cf. DIL B 228. 44, and O 74. 44 ff. on *ó* in this sense.

1321 *i n-a t[h]airmchéill*. The sg. dat. should be *tairmchell*, and *-chéill* here must be purely metri gratia, like similar rhymes in SR.

1329 f. 'Two thirds of the rights to intercession [were granted to MC], the [other] third [belongs] to the men of Ireland'. On these profitable 'rights' see DIL I 2. 164. 10 ff.

1340 On the form *-bet* for fut. pl. 3 of the substantive verb see § xcviii.

1342 *terc mbíd nó étaig*. *Bíd* and *étaig* are gens. of respect (cf. DIL T 1. 150. 81 ff.). For nasalisation in this construction see § v.

1343 *a mbuaid*. Not likely to be the neut. def. art. here, which never occurs anywhere else in AMC (see § vi), though *buaid* was an old neut.; rather, possessive adj. pl. 3 'their', 'victory over them', i.e. the *cath* and *comrac*; cf. e.g. Ml. 115 d 9, *buaid inna mBabelóndae*, 'victory over the Babylonians'.

H

1348 B's *chuingess*. The context obviously requires the pres. ind. rel. of the 'simple prototonic' *cuimgid/cumgaid* 'is able'; OI *con-icc* (see DIL C 2. 446. 8); not of *condaigid* with Hull, ZCP, XXIX, 329, n. 3. Hence I emend as *chuimgess*, a simple matter of easily confused contraction marks, though indeed CCath. 2409 *-cuingebtais* 'would be able' supports the possibility of *-ng-* for *-mg-* in this verb.

APPENDIX: THE LANGUAGE

THE INITIAL MUTATIONS[1]

LENITION AND PREFIXING OF H-

§ i Simple and prototonic active verbs after the preverbs *no, ro, ni*
etc., and the tonic part of deuterotonics when non-relative (as well as
when relative) must have been generally lenited in MI or at any rate
later MI, though scribes were often remiss in marking it (cf. TTr.1, §§
278 ff.). I have inserted the *h* in square brackets where B omits it, e.g.
at-c[h]uala l. 62 but *at-chuala* l. 94; he writes lenition often enough to
show it should be restored everywhere. I have not inserted it with
passive verbs when relative, since there is fluctuation here to a late
period. Lenition of initial of noun object after a transitive verb is
always absent in AMC, as is very often the case in MI, which falls
below the standard of the Bardic schools in this regard.

Where prefixed pre-vocalic *h-* is missing I have restored this too.

NASALISATION[2]

§ ii As the neut. gender died out, as the acc. as a case separate from
the nom. became obscured, and as the difference between prepositions
taking the acc. and those taking the dat. began to be confused, various
types of incorrect nasalisation appeared in MI and EMod.I. A few of
these, not constituting regularly recognisable and obviously accepted
'irregularities' but probably mere scribal blunders, are emended in the
text with the MS readings in the apparatus criticus. Thus *imthét inber*,
l. 932, for the *ninber* of both MSS. *Dia n-aír 7 gláim ndícind*, 'to satirise
and lampoon them extempore', is an error, presumably scribal, for *dia
n-aír 7 [dia] ngláim dícind*, and is so emended. On the other hand the
apparently incorrect *co mbátar .... .i. isin tech n-oíged* may be
defended on the ground that the parenthetical *.i.* clause picks up the
preceding *ro tinólit*, 'they were gathered *into* ....', and it is not
emended here. The same defence cannot apply to *samaigis....i taeb
n-ursainde*, which is presumably a case of acc. for dat., and it is emended
here.

---

[1] The following discussions of the language of AMC are not intended to be a
complete grammar, but an account of the main MI features with special
reference to questions of date where possible.
  Line reference numbers are often omitted in the Appendix, to save space;
references are readily identified in the complete Glossary.
[2] See also §§ vi, vii, and xvii ff.

§iii Other instances of nasalisation are of a type known in MSS, called here above 'accepted "irregularities"', and these are not emended. The phrase *co mian ban aentuma*, 'to the craving of unmarried women', should be *co mian mban n-aentuma*, since *ban* is pl. genitive (for *mian* as nom. here see §xxi). But nasalisation by genitives pl. was disappearing in MI, though it survives in parts of Munster (IDPP p. 214; cf. CMT 2, p. 14 and Ériu XV, 164); and *ban aentuma* is an ex. of this. On the other hand, pl. genitives may themselves sometimes be wrongly nasalised, presumably by anticipation (cf. TBC St. p. xlii), and the nasalisation in *in cumair* (nom.) *mbriathar*, l. 360, may be a case; see Note.

§iv Again, *co mbruach ndub*, 'with a black hem', has nasalisation of the adj. where lenition would be correct, since co^N 'with' governs the dat., not the acc. But nasalisation after co^N plus noun is not uncommon in MI and EMod.I; so PH 852 *co ngeim nderscaigthe* and others (cf. PH p. 588a, bottom;DF III, 279; Éigse III, 55 n.;DIL C 2. 273. 60–62, and Bergin, TSh. p. 434 sv. 1 **go**). For other preps. acting similarly see § xxiii, but co^N seems to behave like this unusually often, and in texts where these others do not do so; it appears to be a special case.

§v Nasalisation in phrases of copula plus adj. plus genitive of respect is not any kind of irregularity. The gen. is regularly nasalised in Classical verse; cf. TD I, pp. lxviii, lxix, and civ. There are two exx. in AMC; *ba so-accobrach mbánbíd*, lit. 'he was very avid in respect of white meat', and *níba terc mbíd*, lit. 'will not be scanty in respect of food'. Cf. TBC II R, 1590, *is lór n-árgigi* etc. But contrast AMC l. 927, *cadla band*, not *mband*; etc.

THE DEFINITE ARTICLE[3]

§vi The chief differences from the OI paradigm are (1) the fact that *inna*[H] has become everywhere *na*[H], with two exceptions, i.e. sg. gen. f. *ina h-* 210 and pl. acc. m. ditto 48; and (2), the OI pl. dat. -(s)n(a)ib is everywhere replaced by -(s)na[H]. Of these, (1) *na*[H] was already beginning to appear in late OI, and the almost exclusive *na*[H] of AMC does not help to date the text; the two exceptions may be merely exx. of scribal habit rather than archaisms. (2), the last ex. of -(s)n(a)ib in AU is in 892 A.D., and -(s)na, which occurs (very rarely) in the Glosses, has completely driven out -(s)n(a)ib in SR. The one ex. in TTr.1 is regarded by McE (p. 202) as evidence for his hypothetical original text older than SR.

[3] See the Glossary for collection.

The neut. sg. nom./acc. a^N is dead in AMC, replaced by the m. or f. according to the fate of the old neut. noun with which it occurs; the neut. article was pretty well extinct by about the year 1000 (cf. Ériu I, 163 n. and MID p. 208).

The pl. nom. m. ind^L (in^L, int^L) was already falling together with pl. nom. f. *inna* in OI, and this was completed later by the last evolving to *na* along with all other *inna*; there are no survivals of the old pl. m. in AMC, though there are a very few *in(d)* in PH, for which see p. 764b, bottom, two at least of which must be archaisms. Note the spelling of pl. nom. m. as *ina* in AMC 48.

Sg. gen. m. and nom. f. ind^L, as well as dat. sg. m./f. $-(s)ind^L$ suffixed to prepositions, are *in* and $-(s)in$ respectively in AMC, apart from a few remnants with *-nd* before *V-* and *fh-*; sg. dat. *fonn* 770 for *fon* is probably a mere matter of spelling. This is a MI development, but preservation of the *-d* is not rare in MI, for instance in PH. The OI sg. acc. m./f. in^N, and when suffixed to prepositions $-(s)in^N$, remain; the few spellings *ind* before *V-*(e.g. H 485), familiar in PH, are no doubt for $inn = in^N$. In fact, sg. acc. *in* does not always nasalise, specially masc. nouns, and occasionally fem. ones whose sg. acc. form is the same as the nom. and hence the whole may be nom. for acc. (§ xx). Note *indis in t-aislingi* 1297, with article nom. instead of acc.; see Note, and cf. PH 765a, top and TBC St. xli bottom. In *an-i-sin* 640, in the three exx. of the sg. dat. (f.) of time, *an inbuid*, and in the sg. dat. (m.) *iarsan lun*, 1285, where the *a* for older *i* recognises the long established reduction of the vowel to /ə/, this may be due to B, though it is quite common in PH.

The dual form of nom./acc./ gen. of both genders in AMC (there are no datives) is *in*, as in OI (nom. 906, acc. 26,172, gen. 25). This began to be replaced by the pl. *na* in the 10th century, was already well on its way in SR, and was apparently regular in MI texts in LU, but *in* still survived to some extent; PH has about as many *na* as *in*. JS finds what he calls a 'reversion' to *in* in late MI texts (MID pp. 240 ff.), but much of his evidence is from very late sources. The very small evidence of four *in* and no *na* in AMC is not adequate for dating it late or early, and cf. JS's own words, op. cit. p. 242, ll. 12–14.

THE NOUN

GENDER: THE SURVIVAL OF THE NEUTER

§ vii The absorption of the OI neuter gender of the noun into the masc. or fem., or in some cases to common gender ('m./f.'), led to complications.

This breakdown was beginning faintly in OI and was quite well advanced by the time of SR, where m. or f. nouns are quite often

treated as neut. The last neut. noun nasalising its adj. in AU occurs in
998 A.D.; five of JS's eight exx. in MI texts in LU are stereotyped
phrases (MID p. 208); and there appear to be not more than three non-
stereotyped ones at most in PH (see p. 809b §c, plus *airdhe mbróin*
3160). This means that the neut. disappeared as a living gender in the
11th century. But in certain types of word or phrase it survived later, in
some cases much later, as a fossil. These, which constitute the least
unequivocal evidence for the neut., consist of a noun in the sg. nom.,
plus an adj. or qualifying genitive,[4] where the noun nasalises the
epithet; which can only happen grammatically in the sg. nom. when
the noun is neut. Petrified phrases may be classed as follows:- (1)
place-names, which have an inherent tendency to remain fixed in
obsolete form (cf. Anglo-Irish Lough Neagh for Irish Loch
nEachach). (2) family or kindred names beginning with old neuter
$Síl^N$, $Ceinél^N$ and the like. (3) legal and analogous formulae, which of
course also tend to be stereotyped. (4) chevilles, brief traditional
phrases used for filling up a line of verse. (5) OI (*a m)becc^N*, (*a m)mór^N*,
nominalised neut. adj. plus genitive, with or without preceding neuter
article, '(the) small/large (quantity) of . . . .', where in MI the masc.
article *in* replaced neut. a^N but could itself still nasalise and the adj.
always nasalised the noun. This continued throughout EMod.I. (6)
certain less easily classified phrases such as *tech n-óla* 'drinking hall',
tech n-oíged 'guesthouse' etc. See further MID p. 208.

§viii   There seem to be no exx. of the non-stereotyped neut. in
AMC, but almost all the above six types are represented. (1) *Imbliuch
nIbair* and perhaps *Loch nAiss* (1030; see Note) are the only ones, but
possibly *loch n-úsca* 1106 is a further ex.; see Note. (2) *Síl nÁdaim*, 'the
Seed of Adam', i.e. mankind 363, a traditional term which retained its
nasalisation into Mod.I, Sc. G, and Manx (*sheelnaue*). (3) the legal
phrases *fír ndligid* (but *fír dligid* 273) and *fír n-indligid*, respectively lit.
'justice of legality' and 'justice of illegality', i.e. justice and injustice. In
these phrases sg. nom. *fír* continued to nasalise to a very late period.
Ríge nÉrend 'the kingdom/sovereignty of Ireland' (in verse; cf. TBC
St. p. xli) is similar. On *maithem n-anocuil*, 'granting of quarter' see
DIL M 45. 66, where it is suggested that nasalisation by this fem. noun
(later also masc.) spread from the acc. to the nom. This seems rather
unlikely (parallels?), and the legal look of the phrase seems a more
probable cause. (4) the following two are familiar MI chevilles in
AMC:- *togairm nglé* and *monar nglé*; and *buaid mbainde* (cf. Éigse III,
66) is evidently an analogical coining preserving the old neut. gender
of *buaid* (cf. MID p. 208). (5) *in mbec* 774, and without the article but

---

[4] These two are described in this book under the one title of 'epithets', for
brevity.

with nasalisation of the epithet, *do/a bec n-étaig* 337, 340. Whether *in cumair mbriathar*, lit. 'the short [amount] of words', i.e. the summary, can be taken as another instance is less clear; see Note to 360. (6) There seem to be no certain exx. in AMC, but this is probably pure chance; e.g. sg. dat. *taig aíged* occurs but nom. *tech n-aíged* (*or tech aíged*) does not. However, *ag n-allaid* 1013 f. may be a case, but see § xxi. The comic name *Ól n-Olar*, 'vat of creams', with *ól* an old neut., may probably be included here.

§ix   The OI pl. nom. of neut. *o*-stems had a long form in $-C^w a$ beside the more ancient short one in $-C^w$. When these stems adopted masc. gender, the masc. $-C^j$ replaced the short neut. in some words, but in others the long $-C^w a$ survived. Exx. of this in AMC are *biada*, *míla*, *óla*, *scéla*, *ubla*. The pl. acc. *rosca* of the old *o*-stem neut. *rosc* looks like another survival, since if masc. it should have been *ruscu* or *rusca* with *u*-affection like the other masc. *o*-stem pl. accs. in AMC. But it could be a modernisation by the late scribe.

§x   The neut. pronoun *ed* 'it' was replaced early by m. or f. in some constructions, but in others remained much later, in some even to the present day. The only certain ex. of the first type in AMC, one where *ed* refers directly to (an old) neuter noun, is *ba h-ed mo mian*. In AMC *ba h-é* would be expected. Another, apparent, case is *is ed siút a cennphort*, but this noun was always masc., and the *ed* must presumably be a mistake, similar to some of the confusions in SR (cf. MID p. 210) arising out of uncertainty as to which was correct. The only exx. of neut. nasalisation after a pronominal are seen in *girru cach n-uachtarach* etc., 545 f. (see Note), *trumma cach ndédinach* 691, and *is ferr cach ngalar* 1217 (§ xxviii (b)). For the neut. article see § vi.

NUMBER: THE DUAL

§xi   Of the thirty-one exx. of nouns in the dual number in AMC, almost all are perfectly normal. There are only three of the dat., all fem. *ā*-stems; *for dá bairgin, co n-a dá shúil*, and *co n-a dí lámaind*. In OI these would have been preposition plus *díb mbairgenaib, díb súilib*, and *díb lámannaib* (see § xxxix), but nom. dual has already replaced the dat. here. In MID p. 240 JS quotes a few MI exx. of this, including two each from SR and PH. Note sg. nom. for sg. dual in a cons. stem, *dá mír* (cf. MID p. 239 f.), but contrast *dí ersaind*.

CHANGES IN STEMS

§xii   During the MI period and later there was a tendency for nouns to change their declension. JS gives lists of such nouns in MID

82   APPENDIX

pp. 212, 221 f., 224 f., 226, 231, 233 f., 235, and 239, and see also
Greene in Ériu XXV, 190 ff. This applied particularly, at first, to the
jo/jā-stems (GOI pp. 179, 185), which in the MI period lost all
distinctions of number and case, except in the pl. dat., through
phonetic falling together of OI *-e* with *-i* and *-ae* with *-ai*. These
adopted the endings of the OI *th-* and spirant *d*-stems (GOI p. 205),
beginning with the pl. nom./acc. (with the old acc. ending *-ada/-eda* in
the MI nom. as well as the acc., instead of the old nom. *-aid/-id*). They
were commoner as pl. endings than as sg. at first, though even as late as
the EMod.I classical verse language, where they are frequent, they
were still optional; cf. IGT II, §§ 1 and 2. This development is very
little found before PH, which has many exx., largely of pl. nom./acc.
-ada/-eda (pl. nom. *trachtaireda*, LU 2405, is in hand H), and is
common in LL, where *-ada/-eda* is regular. According to Greene (op.
cit. p. 196) there are no examples in texts which might with some
confidence be dated to the 11th century, though they are plentiful in
12th cent. ones; but 'with some confidence' is an ambiguous term, and
he admits this is very surprising. The fact that it is rare in AMC and
common in PH shows that it would be much too strong to date the
former 12th century on these grounds.

§ xiii   This development in old *-jo/-jā* stems is found in only two
nouns in AMC. *Colba* has pl. acc. *for colbadu* 578 (but pl. nom. *colbai*
824); dat. *for colbadaib* 220 (but *fo cholbaib* 121, *co n-a colbaib* 842).
The pl. nom. of *etne* is *etneda* 1204.

§ xiv   Nouns of other declensions were also joining the dental stems
in MI, and AMC offers two or three. The *i*-stem *fraig* has sg. dat. *isin
fraigid* 131, and sg. or pl. gen. *fraiged* 1202.[5] The pl. nom. and gen. of
the *u*-stem *mug* in AMC are respectively *mogaid* 1094 and *mogad* 864,
which appears in SR 7427 as pl. nom. *mogaid*. On the other hand, the
irregular *i*-stem *caill* has pl. acc. *caille* in AMC 1026, whereas dental
stem pl. dat. *cailltib* is found already in SR 6269. The *i*-stem *móin* has
also joined the dental stems in AMC; ll. 160 and 172.

§ xv   AMC seems to have no other very notable examples of other
types of MI stem changes (e.g. none of its *r*-stems show any *ch* forms);
but note *i*-stem *fail* with sg. dat. *falaig*, and *i*-stem *ail* with pl. acc.
ailechu—but this last had gone over to the *ch*-stems early. The old *nt*-
stem (OI /d/) *coeca* became an *o*-stem on its old base *coecat-*, hence sg.
gen. *coecait* 143. Other stems, see Glossary svv. **bliadain, comrorcu,
dair**, and **eclais** (MID pp. 225, 211, 233, and 226 respectively).

The above developments are hardly adequate to suggest that AMC
cannot be any older than the 12th century.

[5] LU has several exx. of dental case-endings in this word, in MDúin, SCC,
and FB.

CASE: (I) MI FEATURES

§xvi

Singular Nominative

The usage mentioned in BST §70b whereby one or more noun objects, co-ordinated by *ocus* with a preceding noun in the accusative, may stand in the nominative is exemplified in AMC by e.g. *do neoch thechtas luaith ⁊ tene*; and *co ránuc maige ⁊ feda*, where pl. nom. *feda* is used, not acc. *ḟidu* or *fida*. See Note to 1030. Cf. SR 313, *do-rigne aear n-uar ⁊ tene*, but see DIL T 1. 116. 10 f. However, any of these could be explained as exx. of §xviii. In the Classical language, when an infixed pronoun anticipates a following object noun, the noun is or may be in the nominative (BST p. 249 (g)); but in AMC, which has 16 examples of such prolepsis, the nouns are in the accusative when their form is able to show this; the rest are ambiguous but may be regarded as accusative too.

Singular Accusative

Note the prepositionless accusatives of time *deód n-aidche* 353 (see §xxiv); *lá n-oen* 647; also *aidche Sathairn* 97 f., *fessid ind aidche-sin* 204 f., *troiscset in aen aidchi* 520, *troscis in oidche-sin* 695, and *ro throscis lá nó aidche* 719 f.; and in the plural, *boí.... teóra láa ⁊ teóra h-aidche isin aen chodlad* 1291. For others, with nom. for acc., see §xxi.

Singular Genitive

O-stem nouns in *-án* and *-én* make their sg. gen. almost always without palatalisation in AMC; cf. GOI p. 677 n. 58 and LAU pp. 23 and 24; and for the same in the pl. nom. see Ériu XVIII, 10, v. 5 c and p. 33. But with sg. gen. *-áin* note *indrechtáin* 382, 1087, *garbáin* 407 (but *brus-garbán* 1054).

Singular Dative

The 'short' dat. of OI consonant stems (GOI p. 200) survives to some extent in MI (cf. MID p. 232 f.), but in the old neut. *n*-stems, where this seems a MI development, they are commoner than others (op. cit. p. 235). In AMC we have very few, namely *i mbrága* for *i mbrágait* and two exx. of *imm* 'butter' (old neut. *n*-stem) beside one of the long dat. *imim*. *Anmam* (old neut. *n*-stem) 1118 is a form of the long dat. *anmaim*, found also in LU 2336 and 3193, both H; in TBC II R, 911; and ten times in PH beside about the same numbers of the expected long form and of the short form *ainm*. Long dat. *lomum*, AMC 1210 beside short *loimm* is also noteworthy. *Mumai* 'Munster' and *gleó* in AMC (long datives *Mumain* and *gliaid*), both functioning as accusatives, could be either nom. for acc. (§xviii f.) or short dat. for ditto (§xxiv). McE regards the short dat. as one of his early MI features not later than the 11th cent. (Ériu XXVIII, 22 f. and 24).

Prepositionless datives of time and extent, *co ndessid sel bec* 'at a little time' (cf. *sel becc* in PH 498, 593, 3036), *bet nómaide* 'I shall be for three days', *do-lluid deód n-aidche* 'went at the end of the night' (see §xxiv), and *indlis . . . . ead imchian* 'arranged . . . . a long way . . . .'.

Plural Nominative and Accusative

The pl. nom./acc. ending of OI neut. *n*-stems was *-an(n)* or *-en(n)*; hence that of *ainm* was *anman(n)*. JS found *-ann/-enn* 'usual' in his early MI sources, but *-nna*, not occurring in LU, appeared in later MI; e.g. PH with *anmand* etc. 'but usually *anmanna*' etc. (MID p. 235 f.). AMC has *nadmand* and *sesbémend* but *anmanna* and *mírenda*.

CASE: (2) CONFUSIONS IN USAGE

§xvii Confusion in the uses of the nominative, accusative, and dative cases began to set in in MI. This arose partly because in some declensions the sg. nom. and acc. forms were the same; in some the same was true in the pl.; and in some the sg. acc. and dat. were identical; not to mention the collapse of the *-jo/-jā* stems (§xii). Further, the fact that some simple prepositions took the accusative in one sense and the dative in the other, a distinction which was beginning to be blurred in MI, also played a part in causing the breakdown of the clear-cut OI case system. With prepositions this was more marked in the pl. than the sg., though the teaching of the Schools tried to preserve the difference. In the following discussions, as elsewhere in this book, recourse is had to the codified doctrine of the Schools where this is helpful, which was strictly speaking later than the composition of AMC; but in many respects it carries on essentially the language of the MI period.

Nominative for Accusative as Object of Verbs

§xviii The nom. for acc. was already not very rare in SR (cf. MID pp. 211, 216 and n. 5, and 233), but in non-H MI forms in LU cited by JS ibidd. it seems, oddly, extremely rare.[6] By PH it seems fairly well-established; by AS, common; by the 13th–14th centuries the acc. was rare in ordinary prose, and in Mandeville (year 1475) there are none. In verse, however, the acc. had lasted long enough to be regarded as correct for objects of verbs in nouns of either gender which had an acc. different from the nom., though the nom. was an

---

[6] Note that here and elsewhere JS's collections in MID were not always necessarily complete.

acceptable alternative (Éigse III, 55 ff. and BST p. 287); and under this influence it could survive occasionally in classical EMod.I prose as late as e.g. EU l. 3225.

§ xix   In AMC the position is as follows:- the 'correct' original form of the noun complex is well maintained. The article, if present, nasalises the noun, which itself takes its separate acc. form if there is one (otherwise its nom./acc.), and nasalises any epithet, and when this last is an adj., causes it to take its accusative if it has a separate one. So, e.g. with verb and o-stem noun nom./acc. and nasalised epithet, *comur ngaire ro-chuala*; with verb plus i-stem fem. noun nom./acc., plus acc. adj. fem., *tabair ascaid mbic*; with verb plus ā-stem noun acc. plus acc. adj., *fail dáim n-annsa*; with verb plus consonant-stem noun acc. fem. plus gen. epithet, *do-s-béraind falaig n-óir* (nom. *fail*); verb plus def. art. acc. plus o-stem noun nom./acc., *geb-si in n-arán* (cf. 193, 768 f.); verb plus def. art. acc. plus ā-stem noun acc., *sétis ind oíbill* (*ind* sp. for *in n-*, § vi; nom. *oíbell*); with verb plus def. art. acc. plus cons.-stem fem. noun acc., *fil lem-sa in mbroind* (nom. *brú*); verb plus o-stem noun nom./acc. plus nasalised adj. acc., *cumaid cennphurt mbec* (cf. 590 f.); with verb plus def. art. acc. plus o-stem noun nom./acc. plus nasalised epithets, *co n-accai in liss ndermitnech mbarrach*; ditto but i-stem noun nom./acc., *co n-acca in colcaid n-éngil n-imme* (cf. 632).

§ xx   The only divergences from these, the OI patterns, in AMC are almost all exx. of the alternative with nom. for acc. accepted by the Classical grammarians (provided the nom. and acc. forms are identical), as indicated by the nom. form of the noun, and/or the nom. or non-nasalising form of the article, and/or the non-nasalisation of the epithet when the noun is masc. and lenition of it when the noun is fem. The exx. of this in AMC are *ná caithium in Domnach* (cf. Éigse III, 55, and l. 315 here); *indis in t-aislingi* 1297 (see Note); *co fhagba cobair écin*; *no-s báided crithir chonnli*; *at-bert .... in guth*; *co n-acca in doirrseóir*. In the pl. of o-stems, *indlis baic, brogas scuir*, and *atn-aig trí tomaid* 1274 (see Note) would also be allowed (Éigse III, 59, l. 28). There are few exx. which fall below these standards; note *ná tibratis dál* 364 and the almost identical phrase in 427, the objection being that *dál* is nom. and its acc. is different, *dáil*; and *fo-d-era in comrorcu* 676. On *ro gab Mumai* and *ro lámus gleó* see § xvi, sg. dat.

Nominative for Accusative as Object of Prepositions

§ xxi   With preps. which take the acc., AMC generally has the acc. (made visible by nasalisation, with nouns, whether definite or indefinite, whose nom. and acc. are the same). So, with indef. nouns, *cen mether n-étaig* 202; cf. 730 f., 936, 1013 f., 1193, 1194. With def. art., *frisin tech n-óbela n-oslacthi n-imdorcha* 161 f.; cf. 202, 1212. With fem. nouns, indef., having nom. and acc. different, *cen mbroind cóic-duirn comlethain cernaig* 885 f.; cf. 224, 323, 487, 720, 742 f., 863. The same with def. art., *frisin comlaid ngeriud* 1056; cf. 1197 f., 1211, 1275. In *eter Sliab nImme* .... 7 *Bend Grotha* the reason the second name is nom. is because it follows *ocus* (§ xvi). Instances of the same type as those discussed in § xx are *dar in dorus aile*; *cen fír doichle*; *co mian ban*; and cf. 694 f., 1025, 1191, 1196, 1202. However, there are a few cases of preps. which should take the acc. being actually followed by the nom. forms of nouns when their accs. are different. These are *co lám* 1196 f.; *co torrach* 1197; *fri Brigit* 1237 (but apart from *adaig*, the sg. acc. forms of *ī*-stems were almost dead in MI, cf. MID p. 225 f.; and cf. nom. for dat. in AMC 291 *i n-oen adaig* and 1340 *i cét-adaig*). In *amal sinchán* .... *nó fendóc* .... *nó ag n-allaid* the nom. *fendóc* may be another instance or may be due to the long separation from *amal*, but *ag n-allaid* is accusative again unless the nasalisation is because *ag* was an old neuter. With the prepositionless acc. of time note nom. for acc. in *in adaig-sin* 102 f. etc., and *beith adaig cen biad* 685. None of the exx. in AMC are in the pl.; cf. Bergin in Ériu XI, 138, who notes that the pl. is not found in literary MI.

In MID p. 243, JS quotes a number of exx. of the allowable nominative alternative; three in LU (1418, 2026, 2164; 3090 is H) and six in PH. His exx. in LU 138 and PH 328, 1740, 2008, 2050, 2780, and 2951 are all instances of nouns whose sg. nom. and acc. differ, and all of which therefore would be rejected by the rules of the Classical grammarians; as also would be AMC's *co lám* etc. above.

Accusative for Nominative as Subject of Verbs

§ xxii This is discussed by JS in MID pp. 211, 216, 232 f., and 237 f. Unluckily his collections are often incomplete, sometimes very much so. Thus, on *ā*-stems he comments 'I have no extensive collections ...', I must be content to give some I have noted from earlier [MI] texts' (p. 211), and the same seems to apply to other stems. In fact, the *words* he actually gives, both for the sg. and the pl., in SR and (nòn-H) LU, omitting some non-applicable exx., can be counted on the fingers of one hand; and the case is little better with PH or even the 12th cent. Irish Aeneid, though there the numbers of *occurrences*, particularly in the pl., (27), chiefly of consonant stems, are becoming greater. BÓC comments on the 'noteworthy' tendency [in the Classical verse language] to use the acc. for the nom. in the pl. of consonant stems, quoting e.g. EMod.I *cathracha, cionta, teinte, aithre*, and *goibne*, and classing these among forms in general use about 1200 adopted to the exclusion or near exclusion of the older use (Celtica X, 132).

AMC has only two apparent exx. of *words* in the sg.:- one in an *ā*-stem, *do-berar a théig dó* 255, and two *occurrences* of one *word* in a consonant stem, acc. *ulidetaid* for nom. *ulidetu* 213, 271. All could be cases of the sporadic MI and EMod.I use of the acc. for nom. as the subjects of passives (cf. DF III, cxviii n. 1 and Desid. p. 247), but the nom. in the sentence preceding *a théig*, namely *tucthar mo thiag*, also with passive verb, may suggest rather that here the acc. may be a mere inadvertence.

In the pl. AMC has only six *words* (and *occurrences*):- in *o*-stems, *curu, indrechtána* and *torsnu*, and in cons. stems *rigthi, traigthe*, and *tendti*. On *etneda* see § xiii.

The above evidence scarcely demands a 12th century date for AMC.

Accusative for Dative as Object of Prepositions[7]

§ xxiii Since the dative is almost always governed by a preposition, instances where the noun is not the object of one are rare; but see § xvi. Acc. for dat. is specially common when the prep. is one which can take acc. or dat. according to sense; see BST p. 107 f. for some rather subtle distinctions, in the teaching of the Classical bardic schools, between the uses of such prepositions. Examples in MI are SR 6529 *for clainn n-íraig nIsrahel*; PH 202 *ro-s dermait hí . . . . isin tegdais mbic*. With other prepositions, e.g. SR 5890 *ria nDauid ndian* and LU M (BDD) 6965 *iar fuinud ngréne*. For six further exx. in SR and one further one in PH see MID p. 243.

In the singular, AMC has only two exx. where the form of the noun is that of the accusative when the sense demands the dative; *co mbátar . . . . isin tech n-oíged* 218 f. and *adáither . . . . isin tech* 1248 f.; both for dat. *taig* or *tig*. Instances where the fact that the object of the prep. is (wrongly) accusative is betrayed only by the nasalisation of its epithet instead of the correct lenition are quite familiar in MI. JS gives a list of such phrases from SR (six exx.) and other MI texts (9 exx.), MID p. 243. For *co*[N] in this connection, where wrong nasalisation seems particularly common, see § iv. In AMC we have only *don staic n-aile, athlaech i cathaír n-espuic*, and *oc dubánacht for loch n-úsca*. The last two might be defended if we could take them respectively as '(seating himself) on to a bishop's throne' instead of '(sitting in)' ditto, which seems unlikely, and 'throwing his hook out on to a lake' (see Note to l. 1106).

In the pl. JS notes that this rarely appears in early MI (SR and LU) but is more frequent later (MID p. 243 f.), but it would be more accurate to say that it is quite frequent in e.g. PH, which JS seems to regard (mistakenly for the most part, in my view), as very late MI; cf.

[7] Cf. § xvii.

the glossary to PH svv. *as, de, do, fiad, iar, ré*. It is very rare in SR and in non-H MI texts in LU; only four exx. in SR, and only one of JS's four exx. in LU on his p. 245 is in fact valid, *forsna crunnu*, l. 2053 (FA).

In AMC it is much commoner in the pl. than in the sg., as is the case also with the converse, pl. dat. for acc., §xxiv, and as with MI prose in general. The exx. are *co n-a aradnu*; *for a h-aspalu*; *ar bélu* 1030; *for bélu* 1234; *i n-a beólu* 594 f.; *ó beólu* 775 (in 1030 and 1234 the *é* is correct for the dat., and there is confusion in the endings only; in 594 f. and 775 the *eó* is incorrect for the dat. as well as the *-u*); *ó na biadu*; *co n-a bille*; *ós buadu*; *do chaelánu* (3 exx.); *i cerdu*; *ó a chnámu*; *co n-a chethri cossa* ('with'); *co n-a chethri crú* (ditto); *for colbadaib* 7 *immdadu* (the first being correct dat.); *do indrechtánu*; *fo lámu*; *i n-a lámu*; *a mecna* 858 B; *do phecdachu*; *ó a rainde*; *ós na rosca* (w. *o* proper to the dat.); *do na slógu*; *ós t' shúli*; and *iar deich timnai*.

Dative for Accusative as Object of Prepositions

§xxiv   This seems very rare in the sg. For the situation where the *form* of the noun is that proper to the dat. JS quotes one ex. from SR 3572, one from LU 250, and four from PH 126, 1322, 6295, and 7225 (MID p. 242), in the first four of which the *-u-* of the *o*-stems indicates they are dat., and in the last two the *ëi* of the *s*-stem. With lenition of the epithet showing the noun is dat., PH 2607 *tria guth challaire*.

There are three cases in AMC where the sg. dat. is shown by the form of the noun; *ic tabairt in míre i n-a beól* (for acc. *bél*); *at-aig ... i n-a beól* (ditto) and *saidis forsin taig* (for acc. *tech*). Also prepositionless *deód n-* 353, where the form is dat. but the nasalisation implies acc. (§xvi).

As noted above, it is much commoner in the pl. than in the sg. in MI, including in AMC. There was occasional confusion already in OI, and JS quotes 13 exx. of this with *ar, cen, dar, for, fri, im, la*, and *tre* (MID p. 243 n. 3), saying that preps. originally taking acc. commonly take dat. in MI, and gives 24 exx. from SR and 30 from non-H MI texts in LU with *co*[H], *eter, for, fri, i, la*, and *tri* (p. 244 f.).

AMC has *isna h-il-blassaib* 45, 47, *tria rúnaib* 140, *fri m' lámaib* 295, *cosna biadaib* 973, *cusna Blongib* .... 7 *cusna Maethlaib* 982, 1005; *tar inberaib* ... , *tar báitsechaib*, ... *a n-indsib*, ... *tar cruad-chaircib*, ... *tar srónaib* ...., 1025–8 (in a sentence with three other prepositions taking the correct acc. pl.); *ma na beraib* 7 *ma na tenntib* 744, *fri Tuathaib Mescán* 1050, *ima lurgnib* 1066, *cosna corénaib* 1188, and *cosna lúb-diabulta emnaigib* 1201.

THE ADJECTIVE

ATTRIBUTIVE ADJECTIVES

§xxv   In the pl. noms. of masc. *o*-stems the ending in OI was *C^j*, e.g. *mairb* pl. of *marb*, whereas in fem. *ā*-stems and the 'long' pls. of neut. *o*-stems it was -*C^w a*, e.g. *marba*. In MI the fem./neut. was replacing the masc. Cf. JS in MID pp. 217 ff., and in Dillon ZCP XVI, 343, whose discussion however needs some critical re-assessment, particularly the date of PH. He argued that the *mairb* type vanished *c.* 1150 (i.e. PH), but showed that the -(*a*)*ig* pls. of the -*ach*/-*ech* sgs. remained longer in MI. The old *mairb* was beginning to die out in very early MI; later it survived only rarely and sporadically, chiefly in texts derived in part from OI sources such as TBC II, and in petrified 'runs' etc.

There is only one example of the *mairb* type in AMC, *beóil deirg thanaide* 1169 in a long traditional decorative passage in which all the other attributive *o*-stem nom. pls. are in -*C^w a*; in such a context the type *mairb* is still occasionally possible at this time. Cf. the obviously related passage in IT I (1880) p. 120 l. 1, *peoil deirg tanuighe*.

§xxvi   The dative plural of all declensions ended in -(*a*)*ib* in OI. In MI they lost the -*b*, leaving -*a*/-*e*, the same as the nom. and acc.; so *marbaib, maithib* became *marba, maithe*. See MID p. 246. SR still has about twice as many with -*b* as without (cf. McE., ZCP XXXIX, 10). According to JS the -*b* form is normal in the MI texts which he used in LU; he gives only four exx. of -*a*/-*e*, but two of them are in H (MID p. 246).

The pl. dat. in -*ib* is rare in AMC. There are five exx., two of which are mixed; *d'ócaib dercaib tenn-shádchib*; *for a crund-maigib córaib*; *a n-indib inmedónachaib*; and with a mixture, *cosna biadaib oirerda ingantaib* and *dona lendaib senaib síthaltai so-millsi*. Contrast e.g. *ó na biadu* (acc. for dat.) *immda inganta ilerda* and at least six others (409, 473, 603, 842, 997, 1026). This does not suggest a late date for AMC.

PREDICATIVE ADJECTIVES

§xxvii   The development of the pl. nom. predicative of masc. *o*-stem adjs. in original -*C^j* to subsequent -*C^w a* with the pl. copula was broadly the same as that of the attributive, but there are certain differences, specially chronological ones. The -(*a*)*ig* pl. of *o*-stem adjs., e.g. *toirsig* pl. of *toirsech*, is a special case. For a discussion see JS, MID 217 ff., and Dillon, ZCP XVI, 313 ff., specially 322–346 (with the same caveat as in §xxv); the latter deals only with those cases where the predicative is an adjective. The types *it mairb* and *it toirsig* remained common in very early MI, and *it marba*, which was beginning faintly in OI, was still rather rare. Later, *it marba* took over completely until it was superseded by the sg. impersonal construction *is marb* (see § ci), but the type *it toirsig* reached the sg. *is toirsech* almost without passing through *it toirsecha*. In very late MI *it mairb* is already obsolete, *it marba* is dying, and *is marb* and *is toirsech* are taking over, as they had fully in Classical verse practice though not in theory (Celtica X, 135 and BST pp. 127 ff.).

The position in AMC is that there are no exx. of the *mairb* type and only one of the *toirsig*, namely *i mbat budig do beóil* 899, and contrast *at brecca do beóil* 1120 f. *Ba faide . . . iat* 630 f. is ambiguous in the adj., though *ba* is sg. and *iat* of course pl. The evidence in AMC is thus so meagre that little can be deduced from it about the date.

COMPARISON OF ADJECTIVES

§ xxviii   (a) The equative. The *-ithir/-idir* equative went out of normal use at the end of OI, replaced by the construction of *com-* plus the positive grade of the adjective plus *fri* or other preposition. But it lingered sporadically in traditional prose narrative, particularly in the heroic style, and later almost solely in the rhetorical decorative passages of ancient inspiration, even as late as the 16th–17th century Eachtra Uilliam (see EU p. xxii, etc.). In OI it had taken the acc. form of the thing compared, and this can still be found in MI, but *ocus* plus the nom. or *fri* or some other suitable preposition was usual. In late sources the form of the equative itself becomes corrupted in various ways.

AMC has five certain exx. of the equative, all more or less echoes of the heroic style: *lilithir drúcht* 204, with the OI direct accusative; *métithir 7 og* 633; *liridir fri gainem . . . . nó fri drithlenna . . . . nó fri drúcht* 133 f.; and *métithir/médithir fri h-og* 1179, 1186 (for *médithir* in 1016 see the Note). AMC has no exx. of the construction with *com-*. *Lilithir* has assimilation for the older *lirithir*, and both are neologisms for the original irregular equative form *lir*.

(b) The comparative. In OI the something to which something else is compared stands in the independent dative, or in the nom. after *oldáas* etc. In MI, sporadic exx. of *cach*[N] plus noun look like acc., but are more likely to be cases of the spread of *cach*[N] mentioned in DIL C 1. 2. 66 ff. Cf. FA, LU 2133, *do-lleci in n-osnaid as trummu cach n-osnaid*, and PH 6405, *is uaisle cech n-oentaid*, etc. In AMC, *is ferr cach ngalar* 1217.

(c) The superlative. The OI superlative grade of the adj. ending in *-am/-em* went out of use in MI apart from some occasional and sporadic survivals, and was replaced by the comparative in the construction 'the X which is more Y'; cf. French 'le plus grand'. In AMC there are two exx. of the old superlat. ending, *nes(s)am* 227 f. and 1241 (beside four of the newer comparat. in this word, *ba nessa* 144, 763 f., 770, 1251).

THE NUMERALS[8]

§ xxix   In OI the cardinal numeral adjs. 'two', 'three' and 'four' had different forms for the masc./neut. and the fem.; that is, nom. masc. and neut. *dá* 'two', *trí* 'three', and *cethair* 'four', as distinct from fem. *dí*, *téoir/téora*, and *cethéoir/cethéora*. For full paradigms see GOI p. 242. However, the distinction was breaking down (and moreover the dat. of all three numerals in -*b* lost the -*b*), and the fem. may be used for the masc. and vice versa. The confusion in the genders in 'two' and 'three' is very thoroughgoing in AMC; for the wrong use of masc. *cethri* etc. for fem. *cetheóir* (fem. for masc. does not occur in AMC) see Glossary. The OI gen. for 'two' was *dá* in all genders, and the dat. was *díb*, but in AMC the gen. fem. *dí* for *dá* is influenced by the nom. and acc.; and its fem. *dá* rather than *dí* for older *díb* is due to the increasing preponderance of all-purpose *dá* in MI. For 'four' *cethair*, if correct, is the OI nom. masc., which is normally replaced in MI by the acc. *cethri*; see Note to l. 612. On *cethra* 746 see Note.

THE PRONOUN

SUBJECT AND PREDICATE PRONOUNS

§ xxx   In AMC these are sg. 1 *mé*, *mise*; 2 *tú*, *thú*; 3 m. (*h*)*é*, *essium*, *e-s(s)ide*; f. (*h*)*í*; neut. *ed*. Pl. 3 *iat*. The earlier forms of the pl. 3 *é* and *eat* do not occur in AMC. The third persons do not take *s*-, i.e. *sé* etc., except as subjects of *ol* 'said', as in OI. *Issé*, 7 *sé* or *ocussé* 'and he' occur four times (123, 1041 (2), 1042), but these stand no doubt for *iss é* etc., not for *is sé* etc., and are so treated in the Text above. The same is true with the copula in *issed* 'it is it', treated as *iss ed*, 'it is it'. The occasional *ba sé* etc. in MI is probably an analogical extension, not found in AMC. Note the 'absolute' use *mé fén*, *nícon tibér*, '[as for] myself, I shall not give' 364 f., and *tú fodén i m' fhail*, 'you yourself [being] in my company' 682.

There are no examples in AMC of these pronouns as subjects of non-copula active verbs, a MI development hardly older than the 12th

---

[8] See further details in Glossary.

century. As subjects of passives there are eight exx., or nine if we read *cengélt*air *tú* in 337 f. (see Note); six of them in sg. 3 m., 214, 280, 549, 665, 756, 1240; two f. 782, 987; no pls.; and perhaps the sg. 2 *cengélt*air [*tú*]. Pronoun subjects of passives seem to appear first in LU hand M, where they are rare. This evidence hardly suggests that AMC must be late MI.

§xxxi   As subjects of the copula, the type is *is X é*, where X is a noun or adj. The exx. in AMC are sg. 3 m. *ba luathithir fria maing .... hé nó fri gaíth ....hé*; *cid doilig essium*; *ba cosnamaid e-sside*; *ba mílach .... e-side*. With copula understood, *araile laech-míl ....e-sside*; *scolaigi .... e-sside*; sg. 3 f. *comba métithir 7 og ....hí*. Pl. 3, *ba faide ....iat*.

SR has only two exx. of this construction, both with the copula *understood*, 3493 and 5517. Seven cases with the copula and two without it do not necessarily imply a specially late MI date for AMC. Note that of the total of nine exx. just quoted (two without the copula and seven with it), five are forms with the enclitic 'emphasising' particle -*sium* or the anaphoric -*side*. The construction with the copula expressed probably began in the very early 11th century; while that with absence of the enclitics seems to have arisen a little later, in the first half of the same century.

As predicates of the copula, the type *is é (essium, é so/é sin) X* where X is a noun, or a relative clause, or both, goes back to OI. The neut. pron. *ed* occurs in AMC for this construction almost exclusively as a genderless referend of a relative clause; type 'it is this that he said' = 'this is what he said', etc. If so, it may stand in apposition to a verbal noun, lit. e.g. 'it is this that I shall do, putting it ....' = 'what I shall do is to put it ....' and the like. When it has direct reference to a noun, not to a clause, it should logically be used only when the noun is a neuter, but in this use the neuter is archaic in AMC, and there is only one, or at most two examples in AMC (for this and the exx. see §x).

§xxxii   The examples are:- Sg. 1, *is mé choilles*; with 'emphatic' suffix, *is mise do-s-méla*; *is misse no-t ícfa*, and with omission of the copula *missi thidnuis*. Sg. 2, *mása thú* 'if it is you'. Sg. 3 m. *is hé .... fáth airicc*; *ba h-é ainm* 71; *níba h-é cét ní aicéras*; *conid é cét mír ad-uaid*; *bid hé lá a phennati*; *is é in lá-sin tóicebthar*; *ba h-é cas-draigen boí...*; *ba h-é a chomainm*; *comad hé galar no-t bérad*; *is é Manchín melltais*; *is é lóg aisnéssi in sceóil-sea*. With *essium* or demonstrative, *conid essium benais in slógad*; *cen cop é so a deriud*; *conid hé sin fáth*; *conid hé sin láa gairfither*. Sg. 3 f., *is í proind ruccad*; *ba h-í in buaid*; *conid hí sáith .... do thomail*. With demonstrative, *ba h-í in sin a phrím-airaigid*. Sg. 3 neut., the following are the exx. in AMC of *ed* as a genderless referend of a relative clause, not directly qualifying a noun (contrast §x):- *iss ed as cuintesta, loc* 7 *persu*; *iss/nocon ed ad-fiadat* with a noun subject 138, 592, 707 f., 1232; *iss ed ro imfhulaing, in chomrargu*; *is ed is nessam, sailm do ghabháil*; *ní h-ead chondaigimm*; *iss ed chondaigim*; *iss ed do-gnínd...*, *a taiscid*; *iss ed tuccad, bendacht*; *cid ed bess de*; *iss ed fo-t-ruair dam, an-í-sin*; *is ed in so, tochar*; *iss ed fo-d-era, in comrorcu-sin*; *nocon ed sin fil i llebruib.* Pl. 1 and 2, no exx.; pl. 3, *is iat mo scéla*; with a demonstrative, *ba h-iat sin a scuilb.*

OBJECT PRONOUNS

The Infixed Pronouns

§xxxiii   The OI distinction of three Classes, A, B, and C, is evidently obsolescent or obsolete in AMC, and the *-d-* forms of Class C survive almost solely in the use after *co*[N] 'that' and *dia*[N] 'if'. Non-nasalising *-s-* seems to have become a general-purpose infix for all 3rd persons. The proleptic use of infixes, whereby the pronoun still has force in anticipating the noun object (or with *fil*, subject) of the same number and person (never pronoun in AMC) which follows and picks it up, occurs fifteen times.

On the *case* of the noun see §xvi. This prolepsis is a characteristic of MI (cf. the very long list in PH p. 856 f.), but began already in OI; cf. GOI p. 266 and Celtica XII p. 90 f., and see this last reference for sg. 3 infixes as objects of intransitive verbs of coming and going. Prolepsis is marked here below by commas before the nouns etc. AMC uses *-s-* as a relative marker or as totally meaningless only twice and three times respectively; it is incorrect to take these pronouns as commonly meaningless or as features of very late MI only, cf. §xxxvii.

§xxxiv   The infixes in AMC are as follows:-

Class A, Sg. 1: *ra-m fhuirged*; *do-m-ratad*; *ro-m fhorrgi*; *ní-m dénann*; *mina-m thísat*; *no-m ísa*; *co ra-m dígaib*; *mina-m shaera*; *ní-m thát* 1035; *no-m churther*; plus the emendation *no-m bered* for *no bered* 292. With the use of Class A for C (perfectly normal in OI in first and second persons), *ina-m thoirched*; *do-m-árfaid*; cf. *do-m-árfas* 424, 430, 779; *a ndo-m-gní.* Plus an irregular use of A for B, *do-m-ánaic* for *atom-ánaic* 880. Total 18.

Sg. 2: *-t-* in *ná ro-t báda* 847 f., *ná ro-t báde* 848, 852; *ná ra-t rodba*; *ro-[t] tairbisetar*; *ro-[t] táraill* 1124, 1125; *no-t gor*; *co ra-t gori* 1156; *ná ro-t losci*; *ná ro-t bena*; plus emendations *fo-t-cherd* for *fo-cerd* and perhaps *no-t chengéltar* for B's *cengelt-* (see Note to l. 337). With the use of Class A for C (cf. sv. Sg. 1), *cid do-t-rigne*; *súil ná-t athbendach*; *in galar no-t gébad*; *is misse no-t ícfa*; *galar no-t bérad*; *cid do-t-gní.* Total 18 (*no-t chengéltar* too uncertain to be counted).

Sg. 3 masc./neut.: There is no -(a)^N- or -(a)^L- (but see Sg. 3 f. below), only -s- (never -s^N-), properly the fem. *Ní-s tánic; ro-s gab; ro-s léic; ro-s torsig; no-s imarchuir; ní-s tadaill.* Irregular use of Class A for C in a 3rd person, *is mise do-s-méla.* Proleptic, *do-s-fil ...*, *mac Moíle Dúin* (see Note 27); *ní-s fagbad, a grianad; ní-s téig, a merachad; in goeth no-s tic, darsin tír,*[9] 'which comes, there', i.e. 'across the land' (with A for C, see Note to l. 999); *co ru-s acailler-sa, in manach; do-s-béraind, do chorp.* Meaningless, *ní-s tá dam* (see Note to l. 328). Total 13, plus one meaningless = 14.

Sg. 3 fem.: -s- (never -s^N- in AMC), but masc. -(a)^N- is twice used for the fem. *Minu-s tecma; ní-s dligthi; do-s-rat* 282; *ro-s lá; fo-s cerdimm* 1057, 1061. Irregular use of A for C, *is mairg do-s-méla; ní no-s báided, crithir* (proleptic); *in tan no-s fuirmed; do-s-béraind, falaig* (proleptic). Expressing mere relativity (and A for C), *cach mír fo-s cerdi.* With masc. (a)^N for fem. -s-, both proleptic, *do-mbert, bennachtain; ro mben, a lumain* (but JS doubts whether these had any real meaning, Ériu I, 162). Total 12, plus 1 expressing only relativity, = 13.

Pl. 1 and 2, no examples.

Pl. 3: -s- (never -s^N- in AMC). *Ní-s béraba; coru-s impóat; do-s bertís.* Irregular A for C in 3rd persons (both proleptic), *ná ro-s teilg, trí frassa; feib no-s turim, biadu.* Regular and proleptic, *ro-s bensum, clucu, do-s-gní, na rundu,* and *do-s-rat, sin.* Total 8.

§ xxxv Class B, sg. 1 only, *atom-* (-*t*- = /d/), consisting of *ad-* preposition and -*tom-* (= /dom/), infix sg. 1. I do not include verbs with meaningless petrified sg. 3 neut. infix -t^L- throughout the verb such as *at-beir* or *for-t-gella.* None of the exx. is relative. There is a total of three in AMC: *atom-raracht, atom-regar,* and *atom-chuirethar.*

§ xxxvi Class C. This falls into two types: (a) true relative clauses, and (b) subordinate clauses where the infix is introduced by *co*^{N} 'that' or *dia*^{N} 'if'. In the type (b) the nasalised *d-*, properly *nd-*, is often represented in MI by *n-*, as usually in AMC.

Sg. 1, -*dom-*, -*dam-*. (a) Irregular C for A, *ní-dam chrochthar*; (b) *co-nom thorsit; dia-nom lena;* in *co-nam tharrusar* the infix is apparently meaningless (cf. Ériu I, 160). Total 3, plus one meaningless, = 4.

Sg. 2, no examples.

Sg. 3, masc. The forms in AMC are -*t*- = /d/, and -*da*-. (a) *tí do-t cuir* 966 'which summons him'; *is misse no-t ícfa* 'who will cure it'; irregular C for A, and proleptic, *ro-t gab, a throstán* 108. The -*t* in *no-t*

---

[9] JS takes this as an ex. of the relative use, Ériu I, 169, which is possible but perhaps less likely.

légfad 7 *no-t lessaigfed*, l. 1301, refers to the *aislingi* in l. 1297, normally a fem. noun, but in ll. 504 and 1297 it is masc., hence -*t*- here, not fem. -*s*-. (b) *co-nda gaib; co-na mbed; co-na mbeth*. In *nach tibre* ..., *in cochall* it is unclear whether this is a case of prolepsis ('who does not give it, the cowl') or simply a case of MI *nach* ('which .... not') for older *nád*; see § liii (1). Total 8 plus a doubtful instance.

Sg. 3 fem. The form in AMC is -*dos*-. (a) *dia-nos tarla*, lit. 'to whom it put itself', 1146. Total 1.

Pl. 1 and 2, no exx.

Pl. 3. The form is -*dos*- in AMC. (a) *do neoch ná-dos fagaib*. Irregular C for A, *ní dos coicéla; fo-dos-ceirdi* ..., *na mírenda* is proleptic. Total 3.

There is thus a total of 91 infixed pronouns of various kinds in AMC, including a few in proleptic construction and a mere five of relative markers and apparently meaningless ones. For a discussion of dating see § xxxviii.

(N.B. 'Irregular' in §§ xxxiv and xxxv means 'irregular in *Old* Irish'.)

§ xxxvii   The system of the infixed pronouns was breaking down in MI. The clear-cut distinctions between Classes A, B, and C were becoming increasingly blurred, hence the irregular uses of A for C and C for A in the above list; and Class B became very rare except in survivals of the OI idiom *ata-comnaic*. The three exx. of B *atom*- in AMC are certainly not indications of lateness. The new MI -*das*- and -*dos*- for Class C sg. 3 f. and pl. 3 -*da*- are already common in early MI, and hence appear above. One of the chief marks of the MI infixed pronoun is the great spread of sg. 3 f. and pl. 3 -$s^{(N)}$- into the sg. 3 m. in place of OI $(a)^N$. This may have been beginning in SR, though the two exx. there are both doubtful (Ériu I, 165); it increased in the subsequent period, and is very common in e.g. PH. It does not nasalise in AMC, though it still did so sometimes in SR (but almost exclusively before *V*-), and later. The use of -*s*-, both as a mere relative particle and apparently without any meaning at all, is largely a feature of the later MI period (cf. § xxxviii), likewise common in PH; and their rarity in AMC suggests again a comparatively early date for AMC.

The Independent Object Pronouns; and the Proportional Figures of Independent and Infixed Pronouns

§ xxxviii   In later MI the personal pronouns which had acted previously as predicates and subjects with the copula only began to replace the infixed pronouns as objects of verbs; thus *do-s-beir* 'it gives them' gives place to *do-beir iat* in the same meaning. There are only three of these independent pronoun objects in AMC; *do-bér hé* 528, *dia ndingbaind dítt hé* 563, and *oslaicis hí* 255.

This means that in AMC, with 3 independent and a total of 91 infixed object pronouns, the proportion is 1:30, whereas in TTr.1 it is 1:9.5 (6 independent and 57 infixes, see TTr.1 pp. 191–193). Thus the proportion of independent object pronouns to infixed ones is much larger in TTr.1 than it is in AMC, which would certainly suggest that AMC is clearly older than TTr.1. Here the 'statistical sample' in these two longish texts is surely adequate to validate the 'proportional method'. The earliest exx. of independent objects in MI are found in LU hands A and M, but though they were rare before about 1100 (cf. Ériu XVIII, 110), they had become almost universal by about 1200, subsequent archaisms in verse and in high-flown prose apart (cf. Celtica X, 129 and 135). The fact that there is no trace of infixed pronouns in Sc.G. and Manx must presumably mean that they were quite dead in the ordinary spoken languages by at least the 13th century (cf. PBA XXXVII, 71 ff.). Dillon calculated the proportion of independents to infixes in TBC II as 1:2 (ZCP XVI, 330). GM's remark in DF III, cviii, that independent pronouns seem commoner than infixed by 1150 can hardly be accurate if 'by 1150' he meant 'in PH', which text he dated at that time without distinctions, which I consider misleading (see PSIC p. 6 f.). He mentions the 'degenerate' uses of the infixes (proleptic, relative, and meaningless) as being commonest about the middle of the 12th century—but in AMC there are scarcely any exx. of the two last, and the first is irrelevant (§xxxiii). According to McE the infixes were 'almost completely ousted' by the independents by the mid-12th century (PBA LXVIII, 135), which seems to me a little too early (cf. DTL § 30 (b)). Prof. Ó Concheanainn sees the infixes as breaking down in the 11th century (cf. the notes on the pronouns in his article in Éigse XV, 277 ff.), and finds this date supported in texts in LU and 11th century authors; but his arguments are inconclusive and depend on his novel dating of the scribe H of LU as being contemporary with A and M, which I cannot accept (see PSIC p. 3 f.). In view of the great preponderance of infixes compared with independents in PH it is impossible to credit this; nor can I believe that the elaborate system of infixes in AMC is only about fifty years older than the very reduced one, a simple fusion of Class A with the vowel of Class C (e.g. A -*m*- with C -*dam*-), taught in the Bardic Schools but little used in practice. The upshot of all the above is that on the grounds of independent versus infixed pronouns AMC seems to be *older* than TTr.1; but this is the only feature in the tale which suggests this.

For prepositional pronouns see §xl.

PRONOMINALS

§ xxxix   Few of the OI pronominals listed in GOI pp. 305–312 call for comment in their MI forms in AMC.

Cach, pronominal adjective, 'each, every'. The form *cech* occurs in AMC only three times, all in verse, two of them in a single poem. It is indeclinable except for the sg. gen. f. *cacha*[H], but in MI this distinction between sg. gen. m. and f. was dying out and there was considerable confusion between these forms, as appears in the Glossary; cf. DIL C 1. 2. 78 ff. and Éigse III, 184. Hence out of 22 exx. in AMC where sg. gen. m. *cach/cech* is required grammatically 8 are *cacha*, and of 10 where the fem. *cacha* is needed two take the masc. form *cach*. There is nothing to show in AMC whether *cach* nasalises its noun when this is object of a verb, but as object of a prep. note *fria cach n-andland* 1186 and *for cach n-oen* 1300; cf. BST p. 194. On the nasalisation with the sg. acc. in *girru cach n-uachtarach* etc. and *is trumma cach ndédinach* see Note to 545 f.; on that in *is fherr cach ngalar* see Note to 1217.

Fén, fodén/fadén, fessin, fodessin/fadessin, budessin, 'self'. Forms with initial *c*- do not occur in AMC; final *-én* is in all cases a sp. for *-éin*.

The extraordinary variety of these is remarkable; cf. Greene in Ériu XXI, 93 f. In AMC the order of frequency is *fodén* 16 exx., *fén* 15, *fessin* 5, *fadessin* 2, and *fadén, fodessin*, and *budessin* 1 each. This order agrees pretty well with that in PH (see DIL F 1. 4. 68 ff.). In EMod.I all but *féin* were in process of disappearing except as archaisms, till *féin* became invariable.

PREPOSITIONS AND PREPOSITIONAL PRONOUNS

(Forms which are entirely unremarkable are not mentioned. Note that there is no case of a prepositional pronoun used as a simple preposition; cf. PBA LXVIII, 111.)

§ xl   (a) *a* 'from' etc. Seven exx., all *a*. Sg. 3 f., several *e(i)ssi*, one *esti* 1116, which is a late form, rare in non-H LU but occurring in LL and particularly in YBL; and probably scribal here.

(b) *acht* 'except', with acc. obj. once 224, but also nom. once 609, which is regular according to Classical verse usage; cf. IGT I, § 109.

(c) *amal* 'like'. Four exx., none of *immar* or *mar*.

(d) *ar* 'for' etc. No exx. of the the later *air* or *er* in AMC, agreeing with all but the latest part of PH (XXXIV; cf. PH p. 681b). See *for* below, and the Glossary sv. for the confusion between them.

(e) *ató* 'from', apparently very rare; see 509 Note.

(f) *co* 'to'; sometimes *cu*, never *go*, *gu* in AMC. Prep. prons. always with *ch*-. Sg. 3 m. *chuc(c)a* (OI *cuc(c)i*, *cuccai*) four times, *chuice/chuci* once each. PH normally *chuice*, only 6 *chuca(i)*. CEMod.I verse *chuga* and *chuige*.

(g) *co* 'with'. No exx. of *cu*, which is rare in OI and MI.

(h) *dar* 'across' etc.; less often *tar*. W. def. art. *darsin*, *dar in* (cf. *darin*, TBC I Y 2893).

(i) *di/de* 'from' etc.; see Glossary. As simple prep. it has fallen together almost entirely with *do*; but spelt twice *di* and once *de*. The -*V* is fairly often elided before *V*- and *fhV*-. Otherwise, distinct from *do* in the prep. prons. only; which forms of (i) need no comment here.

(j) *do* 'to' etc. Nothing notable except *dá* 'to their' once for what in all third persons is otherwise *dia*; only a few exx. of elision, e.g. 39, 650. Prep. pron. pl. 1 *dún* not *dúin(n)*.

(k) *fiad* 'in the presence of', obsolete by the very late MI period. Often written *fia* before *d*- (so in AMC 264, 1276). The sg. 2 *fiad-su* is probably a late error for *fiadut*, and is emended so in the text, 521.

(l) *fo* 'under' etc.; once *ba* 685 = /və/, but not *fa* or other MI forms, in AMC. The rare *ba* is found in late parts of PH, notably XXXIV; the one case here may probably be due to the scribe B. For contamination with *im(m)* see (q) below. Of prep. prons., the late MI sg. 3 m. *foa*, *fua* does not occur, unless *fou* 1074 is to be taken so. There is only one ex. of the intrusive -*th*-, in the pl. 3 dat. *fóthib* 736, not an early form (three *fúthib* in late parts of PH).

(m) *for* 'on' etc. The MI *bar* = /vər/, common in LL, is not found in AMC. With the def. art. there is the alternation *fors-/for-* which goes back to OI, but with the rel. particle *forsa*, neg. *forsná* only. There are no exx. of *fhor-* or *or*- (ZCP XXXIX, 18 n.). Confusion of *for* and *ar* and of their meanings is well established in AMC (see DIL A 2. 369. 4 ff. and F 2. 302. 8 ff.). This is at least as old as LU (the exx. in SR may be scribal). For the pronominal forms, there is only one ex. of sg. 3 m. *air* 1140, beside numerous cases of *fair*. Note sg. 3 f. *fu(i)rre* (no equivalent of OI *forrae*), pl. 2 *foraib* (not *foirib*), 3 *forru*. The chiefly late MI -*rth*- forms of sg. 3 f. and pl. 3 do not occur in AMC, nor do those in *fho-*, *fhu-*, *o*-, or *u*- (already sg. 2 *ort* in TBC U 6097 M).

(n) *fri* 'towards' etc. *Fri* or the common MI *fria* are the norms for the simple prep. in AMC.[10] *Re* and *ra* but not *ri* or *ro* also occur, but are not nearly so common (one each) as in some MI sources; cf. DIL F 2. 413. 71. With def. art., *resin* once, and with possessives and

---

[10] P. Henry, 'The Early English and Celtic Lyric' (London, 1966, p. 223) mentions *frie* in a poem ostensibly of the beginning of the 10th century (and also two exx. of *ar* for *for*); but the MS is not contemporary.

contracted ditto *ri a* (monosyllabic) twice and contracted *ré* once; and
with the rel. particle **-a**, *risi* and *fria* once each. The *f-* was beginning
to be lost early in MI and was already obsolete in the Classical verse
language, though it survived as a sporadic archaism in prose.
Pronominal forms; the only one worth noting is the single case of sg.
3 m. *riss* 806 beside 8 exx. of *fris(s)*. There are only 2 cases of the use of
fri for *la* which was already beginning in the 12th century.

(o) *i* 'in, into'. Passim, but there are 19 exx. of the common MI *a*,
too many to be taken as being due purely to B. With the def. art. sg.,
always *isin(d)*, pl. *isna*; never the EMod.I and Mod.I *insan*, pl. *insna* in
AMC, but already found in the very late PH XXXIV with *a-*. 'In
which' is *i* or *a*, not yet the EMod.I *ina*; cf. BST p. 161. Prep. prons.:-
sg. 3 m. *ind*/*and*, f. *inde*/*innte*; these pairs, respectively acc. and dat. in
both, are now used in AMC without distinction, though in Classical
verse and even prose such distinctions could still be made (see BST
p. 7, '*inn* is correct in the sense of motion', and see op. cit. p. 116, and
Desid. p. 360). The pl. 3 is *intib* (one ex. in AMC), which is a fusion of
the old acc. *intiu* with dat. *indib*; but *indib* itself, and MI *inta* from OI
intiu, do not occur in AMC. The same seems the case in PH.

(p) *iar* 'after' etc., passim. This began to fall together with 5 **ar** and
1 **for** in MI at least as early as LU 3605 M, though this new *ar*
continued to nasalise. Apart from the phrase *ar n-a bárach*, there is only
one ex. of this *ar* in AMC, 596. PH has six, all in late or relatively late
parts, beside numerous exx. of *iar*. These, and the one in AMC, may be
due to the scribe B. There are no pronominal forms of *iar* in AMC.

(q) *im(m)* 'round' etc., passim. There is one ex. each of *ba* = /və/ (cf.
fo above) and *um*, and with the def. art. pl. two exx. of *ma na*;
contracted w. possessives, *má* twice, *bá* four times; and with preverb
ro, once *bár*. Most of these rare forms in AMC, occurring also in PH,
are likely to be due to the scribe B (TBC II R has four *ma*, one *má*, and
one *moa*, all 'about which', in op. cit. ll. 90, 200, 678, 2442, 3014, and
3043). W. prepositional prons., sg. m. *im(m)e* is the norm in AMC, but
imbe occurs once; this OI-looking form survives quite late in MI, and
is not to be regarded as evidence of OI date. In AMC there are no exx.
of *um-* or *uim-*, whereas PH has some.

(r) *la* 'with' etc. The simple prep. is almost always *la*; there is no ex.
of the later *le* in AMC. PH has *la* passim, and apparently only five *le*
outside the late section XXXIV; this seems a late MI development, cf.
DIL L 1. 30. In PH it is likely to be due to B. Similarly there are no
exx. of the prep. pron. sg. 2 *let(t)* but only *lat(t)*, though *le(i)s(s)* occurs
in AMC almost exactly as often as *lais(s)*. In PH there are apparently
three times as many *lat* as *let*, and nearly twice as many *lais* as *leis*. Sg.
3 f. *lee* is twice contracted to *lé* in AMC. There are no cases of *la* for *fri*:
see (n) above.

(s) *mar* (and *immar*) see *amal*, (c) above.

(t) *ó* 'from' (no exx. of *ua*). With prepositional prons. the MI sg. 1 *uam* is found once in AMC beside the older *uaimm* once, and apparently twice in PH. There are no cases of the sg. 3 f. *uaithe* or pl. 3 *uatha*; but one *uadaib*.

(u) *oc, ic* 'at, by' etc. *Ic* seems almost confined in AMC to the use with verbal nouns or the equivalent, where it is much commoner than *oc. Ac* and *ag* do not occur as simple preps. there (unlike PH, which has five exx. of simple *ac*, with demonstratives, outside the late section XXXIV, where *ac* and *ag* are both found). With def. art., *icon*. With possessive prons. the vowel is dropped in sg. 1 *'com*, 2 *'cot*, and 3 *'ca*, but pl. 3 *oca*, and with the rel. particle -a, *'ga* 209, the only ex. with *-g-* in AMC. With suffixed prons., there is *a-* in sg. 1 *accum* and 3 m. *acca*, twice each, beside *occum* and *occa*, but f. *aicce* (OI *occai/-ae*). Pl. 1 *occaind* and 3 *occu*, but in OI *occunn* and particularly **occaib*. The *ac-* forms of the prep. prons. appear in LU; and *occu* was probably already current for *occaib* c. 1000 (McE, Ériu XXVIII, 23; cf. XXXI, 117). The pl. 3 *ocaib* is still found in LU. There are no *-th-* forms in AMC parallel to the MI *octhaib* in Ériu IV, 144, 1 (cf. DIL O 82. 54). In PH, *-g-* forms are rare and practically confined to the very late section XXXIV, and almost all the sg. 1 and 2 *ac-* and *ag-* forms of the prep. prons. are seen in XXXIV only, though sg. 3 f. *aic(c)e* and pl. *ac(c)-* (but not *ag-*) occur outside it. In the Classical verse language *a(i)g-* is generalised outside the sg. 3 f. and pl. 3.

(v) *ré, ria* 'before' etc. Both forms are found in MI and in Classical verse; the MI simple prep. forms *reim* and *roim* are not seen in AMC. In the prep. prons., forms without *-m-* were giving way in EMod.I to sg. 1 *remum*, 2 *remut*, pl. 1 *remaind*, 2 *remaib*; and OI pl. 3 *remib* was being replaced by *rempu*. Sg. 3 m./n. *riam* became adverbial and was supplanted by *reme* as prep. pron.; while the f. *remi* gave place to *rempe*. Of these, AMC has adopted the new ones in sg. 3 m. and pl. 1 and 3; but in sg. 1, *romum* 422 shows the later MI stage *rom-/roim-* (cf. DIL R 21. 68). Classical verse has two complete sets, in *remh-/remp-* and *romh-/romp-*. *Rom-* is seen in TBC II L, CRR, CCath., the Banshenchus, and the late parts of PH; the single ex. in AMC could be due to the scribe B.

(w) *sech* 'past'. The EMod.I *seoch* is not seen in AMC as simple prep., and in the prep. prons. the *-eo-* is lacking except for sg. 1 *seocham* 1008, beside two *sechum(m)* and sg. 3 m. *secha* twice; this last functioning adverbially. *Seoch(-)* seems not to occur in PH or TBC II etc., and its single occurrence in AMC may be scribal.

Apart from some isolated late forms, which may be due to the scribe B, the above evidence on prepositions in §xl does not suggest a distinctly late date for AMC.

NOMINAL PREPOSITIONS WITH
THE GENITIVE

§ xli   Of the many Irish prepositions so constructed only the following call for note in AMC.

Cind, prepositionless dat. of *cend*, 'at the end of . . . .', 828, seems uncommon in late MI.

Dáig, 'as to'; only one ex., and none of the compounds like *ar dáig*, *fo dáig*, etc. appear in AMC.

Deód, *i ndeód* 'at the end of . . . .', and *co deód* 'till the end of . . .', plus *aidche* 'night' are apparently petrified phrases by this time, having given place otherwise to the later sg. dat. *diaid*.

CONJUNCTIONS

§ xlii   Most of the rather few compound nominal conjunctions which arose during the MI period, notably the beginnings of the later numerous ones in *co*, and of the much more numerous ones belonging to EMod.I, are lacking in AMC; e.g. there are none of the several different compounds of *bíth(in)* etc., which grew up in MI.

WITH MAIN CLAUSES

§ xliii   *Sceó* 'and'. This, regarded as primarily Archaic and Old Irish, mostly in retorics and early legal contexts etc., does occur later in verse, where it is an obvious poetic archaism. This is clearly so with the one ex. in AMC, one of the very few such deliberate archaisms in the text. It can hardly date the poem back to OI, since nothing else indicates that it is so early. In early sources it takes the genitive (see DIL S 88. 15 ff., and Binchy, Celtica V, 77); later, less often the accusative or dative, but also the nominative. In l. 77 the contracted obj. *m-r* conceals the case, but I have expanded it as *máthair*, which may be equally sg. nom., acc., or dat.

sech ní . . . . ní . . . ., 'neither . . . . nor . . . .'. This seems not to be a late MI feature; cf. McE, Ériu XXVIII, 23, who classes it (p. 24) as one which survived till about the 11th century, and describes it as apparently limited to OI and early MI.

WITH SUBORDINATE CLAUSES

§ xliv   *acht co/ná* 'provided that (not)' developed in very late OI and was superseding the simple *acht* in this sense in the course of MI.; cf. B. Ó Buachalla, Ériu XXIII, 144 f. Its presence in three exx. in AMC provides no narrow indication of date.

amal 'as'. There are eight examples. *Mar* (*immar*) does not occur; it is found in SR (190), but is not common in LU.

ar 'because'. Note that of the six exx. of the negative all are *ar ní*, none being *ar ná*; the latter appears in LL (cf. Celtica IX, 121 f.).

cia, cé, gé 'though', negative *cen co*. There is only one *cé* (1298) in AMC, apart from one *cérba* and one each of *cémad* and *gémad* in the copula, in the poem § 76. *Cé* and *gé* seem late in MI and do not become common till EMod.I where *gé* is general, though *cia* and *gia* do survive. The *g-* forms are sporadic in MI; there are a few in PH, mostly in late texts. The one ex., i.e. *gémad* beside *cémad* in AMC may be due to the scribe. The -*m*- (for -*mb*-) in *cémad/gémad* is a post-OI development seen already in SR, LU, etc. There are no exx. in AMC of the use of *cid* ('though it is/be') for *cia*, which is typically EMod.I though it is found sometimes in MI; nor are there any of the OI and early MI negative *ceni/cani*, only the normal MI *ce(i)n co* (with pres. subjunct. of copula *cen cop*, past *cen co bad*). Used in the sense of 'that', introducing noun clauses, there are three exx. of this OI and MI construction.

dáig 'because' occurs three times in AMC, and one ex. each of *dáig co* 'so that' and *ar dáig ná* 'so that not', but none of the other compound conjuncts. such as *dáig ar, fo dáig(in), óir dóig*, etc.

dia 'if, when'. The later *dá* is found sporadically in late MI. There are two cases of this in AMC in the sense of 'if' (*dá* 730 and *dámad*, with copula, 523), beside 18 *dia* and one *diamad*; and three in PH of which one is in the very late section XXXIV. In both texts *dá* is likely to be due to the scribe of LBr.

feib 'as, how, as if; when'. In the sense 'when' there are half as many exx. as of the sense 'as' etc. 'When' seems to be found first in LL texts (MU and CRR).

(*in*) *tan* 'when' is found in the sense of 'before' only once in AMC; this seems very late OI at earliest.

uair 'for'; there are no exx. of *uaire/óre, ó(i)r*, or *in uair* etc. in AMC.

THE VERB

PREVERBAL PARTICLES

No

§ xlv   This was employed in OI, with simple verbs only, in three ways; (a) prefixed to secondary tenses when the construction was independent; (b) with any other tenses to infix a pronoun; and (c) in relative clauses where the primary simple verb form was not one of those with the special rel. endings. In MI, (a) and (b) remained in regular use, but the use of *no* in (c) began to die out (there are almost

none in SR), and only the lenition of the verb indicated that it was
relative. There is, however, an instance of its survival in TTr.1, *no
maíde*, see McE p. 179. The above is the situation in AMC.

No is omitted sporadically in (a)-type clauses with the imperf.,
particularly pl. 3, and also when the verb is *téit* (cf. Celtica II, 350,
Ériu XI, 88 and XII, 204) and of course when it is relative, (c). There
are 13 cases of this in SR; in TBC II L it is 'very often dropped' (VST
3403). In AMC there are four exx., of which three are relative (*téged*
350, *serndais* 457, *tégdís* 660, and *melltais* 1312, three of which are pl. 3
and two belong to *téit*; 457 and 1312 being in verse). Omission of *no* is
regarded by McE as an early feature in MI and apparently as specially
characteristic of verse; Ériu XXVIII, 23 and 24. *No* was of course not
used before compound verbs in OI, since the first prep. of the deutero.
compound verb functioned in its place, but as the development of the
new 'simple prototonics' began in MI (on which see §lxix), *no*
naturally came to be prefixed to them in type (a) and (b) clauses. There
are already eight exx. of this in SR; JS collected 30 non-H and 10 H
ones in LU (ZCP II, 491 f.); there seem to be 16 in the verbal index in
TTr.1, and it is common later. In AMC there are six; *no thisad*, *no
rissed*, *no-s imarchair*, *no-s tic*, *no-s fuirmed*, and *no-s turim*. In OI these
would have been *do-ísed* etc.

AMC has no examples of the common late MI and early EMod.I
confusion whereby *ro* (§xlvi) came to be used for *no* (cf. DIL R 78.
23–28; which is however a quite inadequate treatment). This is not
found in TTr.1 (McE p. 179) but is relatively frequent in TBC II L (at
least 12 exx., VST 3345 ff.), PH, CCath. (23 exx., RC XXXVI, 35 f.),
AS, and later. This supports a relatively early date for AMC. Nor has
AMC (nor TTr.1, it seems) any cases of *do* for *no*; CCath. has 10, and
do is common in AS. In the Classical language it became of course the
norm, and remains to the present, but both *no* and *ro* are occasionally
found in a relatively late EMod.I prose text like St. Erc., an obvious
archaism.

Ro

§ xlvi This originally perfective particle was used chiefly to
perfectivise the subjunctive and the preterite, making the latter a
perfect. The former survived in MI as a mere formal expression of the
subjunct., not differing from the non-perfectivised subjunct. The
latter became a sign of the general past tense, no longer a perfect, called
in this book 'past indicative' (cf. the Glossary, introductory note 1) to
distinguish these *forms* from those of the obsolescent preterite.

In OI, *ro*, prefixed to simple verbs, was normally infixed into the
deutero. prepositional-compound verb; thus *to-mel-* made the

preterite sg. 3 *do-melt* but perfect *do-romalt*. But already in OI it could, rarely, be prefixed instead, giving a type *ro tomalt*, and this development went ahead at an accelerating rate during MI, hence *ro thomail* in AMC, until in EMod.I only a very few 'irregular' verbs retained infixation. In the figures which follow, whether for AMC or other texts, a small group like *at-rubairt, do-rigne* etc. is ignored because *ro* lasted in these well into the EMod.I period, and in a few to the present day. The following are otherwise lists of the relevant verb-forms in AMC. The interest here centres on the existence of the *forms*, not on the numbers of their separate *occurrences*.

§xlvii (a) Infixed after the second preposition. *Do-m-árfaid, tuarcaib.* (b) Infixed after the first preposition. *Atom-raracht, do-rairngired, do-s-rat, do-rala, do-romel, do-ruachell, fo-t-ruair, fo-róbairt* (and *fo-rórbairt*).

Tuarcaib is an instance of the deutero. becoming a 'simple proto.', but retaining the infixation of *ro*. (To list (a) one may add the examples in AMC of infixed *ro* in prototonic forms after conjunct particles: *co tarsat, co tárfas, dia no-s tarla, co tormolaind* (perfective subjunct.), *co ná fárcaib*. But these, whose root forms all belong to those just listed in (a) and (b), do not add to the total, which makes nine.)

§xlviii The following compound-verb forms represent the *ro thomail* type, where *ro* has shifted to the head of the verbal complex: *ro h-aithned, ro aittrebastar, ro esairg, ro fácbad, ó ra-m fhuirged, ro fuirmed, ro imfhulaing, ro h-imred, ro indail, ro oslaic, ro-t tairbirsetar, ro-t táraill, ro thomlis, ro thurim*. The same type in dependent construction after conjunct particles may be mentioned: *co ru-s acailler, nír choem, co ra-m dígaib, ná ro élád, cor érfhuirged, co ro etarscara, ní ro fhrecrus, co ru-s impóat, ná ro-s teilg*. However, this last group is hardly relevant to the numbers, since this is the OI 'moveable *ro*' (GOI p. 339).

§xlix Thus the total of compound verbs in independent construction which still preserved forms with infixed *ro* (§xlvii (a) and (b)) in AMC is 9, and of the same which had transferred it to initial position is 14; a proportion of 1 to just over 1.5.

According to Ó Máille the change to prefixation 'did not become general [in the Annals of Ulster] till after the middle of the 10th century' (LAU p. 169); but 'general' is something of an exaggeration. In TTr.1 there are 21 verbs of the first type, exclusive of *at-rubairt, do-rigne* etc., which infix *ro*, and 64 which prefix it in independent construction (cf. McE, TTr.1 p. 177); that is to say, a proportion of 1 : 3. While such proportional calculations may be of limited value (cf. PSIC p. 5 f.), these do not suggest at any rate that AMC is later than TTr.1, but rather the reverse.

§1 The apocope in *ro* just seen in the type *nír choem, cor érfhuirged* (for *ní ro, co ro*) is rare in AMC, some half dozen exx. (see Glossary sv. 2 **ro**); it is slightly less common in TTr.1, only three exx. (McE p. 177) in a text approaching twice the length of AMC. Curiously, it is 'already frequent' in SR (VSR p. 10), but this may well be *metri gratia*; the figures suggest that good prose writers were sparing with it.

None of the above statistical comparisons would of themselves show that AMC is as late as the 12th century.

As regards confusion of preverbs, AMC has only one case of *ro* for *do*, in *ro-chóid* 308 (see Note), and only one of *do* for *ro, do thomail* 1285. The second can scarcely be a mere confusion comparable to the late MI confusions of various preverbs so common in e.g. TBC II L (cf. VST 3437 ff.). *Do* for *ro* in the past indic. became the norm in EMod.I. SR appears to have only four exx. (VSR p. 29), TTr.1 has three (McE p. 178), but TBC II L has 14 (VST 3425 ff.), and CCath. 19. The common confusions of other preverbs just mentioned are almost unknown in AMC, which has only *at-* for *ro-* or *do-* in a few verbs where this became fixed early and regularly; and once *do-géba* for *fo-géba* 673. This last, *do-ga(i)b-* for *fo-ga(i)b-*, is found already in PH 13 times, but 11 of them are in the very late, EMod.I, section XXXIV, and the other two are no doubt due to the late scribe B, as also in the present ex. in AMC. In fact, *do-ga(i)b-* seems to be an EMod.I development.

Negative Particles

§li With most main clauses the chief negative has always been *ní*, as is true in AMC, and requires no comment.

OI also had *nícon*, which was a dying form in early MI; PH has 11, but only two are in late texts. In AMC there are 9, which may be significant considering how very much shorter than PH it is. Seven of the nine are not followed by visibly lenitable consonants, but ll. 128 and 162 both stand before *f-* which I emend as *fh-*.

In later MI the word became *noc(h)o(n)*, and AMC has 4 exx. with non-copula verbs (170, 183, both *nocon* ¯; 182 *nocon f-*, emended here *fh-*; and *nocho d-* 346, B *noch-* with contraction, see Note); and three with the copula (419, 1232, 1235, all with ¯). The form in *-ch-* is later than that in *-c-*; the latest stage of all, *nocha*, does not occur in AMC. In OI the form for *nícon* in subordinate clauses was *nadc(h)on*. This survived in MI only rarely and does not occur in AMC.

The above evidence does not suggest that AMC is a late MI text.

ná, nád/nát, nach. These are the OI forms of the negative particles
introducing subordinate clauses[11] and some types of logically main
clauses which took or in MI came to take subordinate construction; cf.
GOI p. 539 f. These forms and their constructions are very
complicated, and the complication is compounded by occasional exx.
of 'wrong' forms used. This state was being simplified during MI,
partly by the gradual replacement of *nád/nát* by *ná*, and partly by *ná*
and *nach* increasingly taking over and *nach* encroaching on the sphere
of *ná*, though *ná* still remained commoner than *nach* in MI; in
CEMod.I verse, however, the reverse became the case. Hence in
EMod.I the language was left (apart from archaisms, including false
ones) with *ná*—whether original or from *nád*—and *nach*. These were
apparently interchangeable with non-copula verbs except in the
imperative, where *ná* is invariable. In the copula the old situation
remained, i.e. that the pres. ind. is *nach* and the rest is *ná* plus the
copula form.

§ lii   In AMC the simplification has advanced fairly far in the
direction of Mod.I, but there are some survivals of earlier usages. The
position is as follows (for references see Glossary sv. 1 **ná** and 1 **is**):-
   (A) In logically main clauses:-
   (1) The 'responsive' *nád* occurs only once in AMC. The latest exx.
of this survival known to me are in TBC II L and CRR. Nothing about
date can be safely inferred from this single case in AMC.
   (2) The interrogative is found once with a non-copula verb in AMC
and once with the copula, being *ná?* (= OI *nád?*) and *nach?*
respectively. *Nach?* in non-copula clauses seems fairly late in MI.
   (3) The OI *nach* before a (neut.) infixed pron. may perhaps be
present in AMC (525), but only once. But this ex. is perhaps to be
explained, rather, as representing the fact that the construction is
relative (see § lii B 1).
   (4) The imperative without infixed pron. takes *ná* only, as remains
the rule to the present.
   (5) With the jussive subjunct. the OI main-clause negative particle
ní with non-perfective verbs, which continued sporadically in MI (*ní-
dam chrochthar* is an ex. in AMC 237), began to be replaced early in MI
by *ná* and dependent construction, commonly with the perfective; this
last perhaps under the influence of the optative (perfective subjunct.
with *ní* in OI). The use of *ná*, which began in the optative about the
same time, was presumably due to the model of the imperative. In
effect, the OI jussive subjunct. and optative fell together early in MI.
Jussive *ní* plus *ro* is found already in SR; and it survived, side by side

---

[11] I omit *nant, nan(d)*, as they are not relevant to AMC.

with *ná ro* (also recorded already in SR) into very early EMod.I, presumably as an archaism. The only instance in AMC seems to be *ná ro brister* 200.

§liii (B) In logically subordinate clauses:-

(1) In direct rel. clauses the OI *nád* (which survived for a while in MI, chiefly in the sagas) is found in AMC only once, in a non-copula clause, *nád gabind* (= OI *nád ngabainn*). Otherwise, there are only the now normal *ná* or the past indic. *ná ro*, in seven instances. Of these, three take infixed prons., *ná-t, ná-dos*, and *ná ro-s* 709. They would have had *nach* in OI, and for the second cf. *nach-dot romarbus* in SR 1908. Further, there is *mairg nach tibre .... in cochall* 525, where *nach*, rather than being a case of the new relative *nach* encroaching on *ná*, perhaps represents *nach*ᴺ, the form with the sg. 3 m. infixed pron., referring proleptically to *in cochall*; cf. *ná ro-s teilg, trí frassa* 709; see §§ xxxiv pl. 3 and lii A (3). With the copula, OI *nát*, by-form of *nád*, is found twice in ll. 1206 and 1208, and in past tenses *ná* in *nárba*. In early MI, *nach* already occurs with the direct relative, but not in AMC.

(2) There is one indirect rel. clause after a prep., i.e. *dar ná dlegar* 225 (OI *tar ná/nád*); and two after conjuncts., both with *ná*, OI *nád*. One of these, *ó* 'because' 686, took main clause construction in OI; but *ná* here can be explained from the idiom whereby a second, coordinate main clause when negative could be introduced by *ná* rather than by the logical *ní* (cf. VGK II, 254). *Ná* remained in these types in MI till ousted by *nach*, which was beginning here already in SR.

As to OI noun clauses with *nád*ᴺ, there are eleven non-copula instances of their MI descendants in AMC, two of them with (non-nasalising) *nát*, the representative of the OI *nád*ᴺ/*nát*ᴺ, six with *ná* from *nád*ᴺ, and three continuing the rare OI *co ná/co nár* introducing negative statements, which was spreading in MI. There is further one copula ex., *co náb*. There is no case in AMC of the OI and MI alternative noun clause type constructed as a main clause introduced by *ní*, and here AMC is later than TTr.1 (McE p. 185 f.).

(3) In consecutive and final clauses. There are six non-copula consecutive exx. introduced by *co ná* (120, 628, 632, 634, 655, 1136) and one copula one with *co nár* (629 f.). Note also with the copula sg. 1 *nacham* 1139 (OI *náda*), a MI formation on which see § cii. Here *co* is omitted because the clause is coordinate with a preceding positive one in *co*, a common syntactical feature.

In negative non-copula *final* clauses there is one in *co ná* in AMC, 1175, and seven in *ná* without *co* (333, 847, 848, 852, 1002, 1157 (2)), all of which seven have infixed prons., the two in 1157 being coordinate with a preceding positive with *co*. In MI there are also *co nach* and *nach* in consecutive and final clauses even without infixes, and this becomes common in EMod.I. PH has many *co ná* and even more simple *ná*, and also sometimes *co nach*. The OI and MI *ar ná* or *ar nach*, equivalent to *co ná*, is not found in AMC.

§liv   It is striking that apart from the one possible case in l. 525, AMC has no exx. of non-copula *nach*, whether with an infixed pron. or not. On the other hand, it has no fewer than ten cases of *ná* [12] or *ná ro* [13] plus infix (where OI would have had *nach* and *nach ro* plus infix) to set against 525; and this is the more remarkable since the OI construction continued sporadically in MI as long as the infixed prons. lasted; chiefly however in late MSS of saga texts, though also in e.g. PH. Meanwhile, *nach* without infixes was beginning to spread over almost the whole range of the dependent negative. In the past indic., whether with non-copula verbs or particularly with the copula, it appears as *nachar*, and in the copula also as *nacharb*, forms which do not occur in AMC.

§lv   The evidence of all the above on date is rather conflicting. AMC has resisted the encroachment of *nach* and *nachar* into the sphere of *ná*, which might be an indication of earliness, and so might be the survivals of *nád/nát*. It is worth noting that VT 2 has four cases of *nád* in direct relat. clauses and seven in noun clauses, while SR has respectively four and one; TTr.1 appears to have only one in a noun clause, one in a copula relat. clause, and none in direct relat. clauses, respectively pp. 186, 152, and 183 f. On the other hand, AMC's preference for *ná* as against older *nach* before infixed prons. is secondary and perhaps is an indication of comparative lateness. How far the modern geographically defined preferences for *nach* versus *ná* have any significance here it is impossible to assess, but see p. xxxix f. of the Introduction above on the probability that the composer of AMC was a Munster man.

VOICE

The Deponent

§lvi   Apart from a small handful of deponents which lasted in MI, including *ro-fitir* which survives to the present in the forms -*feadar*

[12] 1124, 1144.
[13] 333, 709, 847, 848, 852, 1002, 1157 (2).

etc., the OI deponent verb was replaced by the active in MI. Only five old deponents still show some deponent forms in SR other than *ro-fitir* etc. and the suffixed prets. with their new sg. deponents, sg. 3 *ro domair* (for *ro dámair*), and *tarrasair* three times. In TTr.1 the deponent system as such is almost dead; indeed, outside *ro-fitir* and the suffixless pret. the only deponent which remains there is two exx. of *at-águr* (TTr.1, p. 180 ff., McE). One may fairly say that the deponential system collapsed almost completely in the 10th century, and the active flexion took its place; the process had already begun in OI (see JS, TPhS 1894, pp. 444 ff.).

The only old, visibly deponent forms, i.e. with the distinctive *-r* endings, which still survive in AMC are pres. ind. sg. 3 *atom-chuirethar*; the preterito-pres. sg. 1 *dúthracur*; several parts of *ro-fitir*; and the suffixless pret. sg. 1 *-sessar* (OI *-siasar*) and *-tarrusar*, both of which are found in other MI texts. Pres. ind. sg. 1 *atom-regar* is however an ex. of a *new* early MI formation in which the old active verb *at-raig* took on the deponent *-ar*. As for the preterito-pres. *ro-fitir*, the forms call for no remark in AMC except pres. ind. sg. 2 *-fetara* (cf. PH 719 *-fetura*), which has a new MI sg. 2 ending, formed out of the old deponent sg. 2 *-fetar* with the old active *-a* added to distinguish it clearly from the sg. 1. Thus one may say that AMC is at much the same stage as TTr.1 in respect of the deponent verb.

For *médithir* 1016 see Note.

For the *new* 'deponent' *s*-prets. of active verbs see § xcii *ad fin.*

For the forms of the deponent and passive *-r* endings see next section.

The Passive

§ lvii   In OI the primary *-r* endings of the deponent and passive,[14] sg. and pl. 3 in simple verbs were in $/-r^{\text{J}}/$ in the non-relative absolute forms, that is, sg. *-(th)(a)ir* and pl. *-t(a)ir*; and in $/-r^{\text{w}}/$ in the relative and conjunct forms and in the imperative, that is, sg. *-(th)ar/-(th)er* and pl. *-tar/-ter*. In compound verbs they were the same endings as the second set. In MI, a process of eliminating the absolute endings in favour of the conjunct was beginning faintly in SR and in TTr.1, accelerated no doubt by the fact that the new 'simple prototonics' (§ lxix) could tend to retain their original conjunct endings even in independent construction. For a time there was confusion both ways, e.g. in PH, TBC II L, and CCath., but it settled down eventually in the EMod.I period through the exclusive adoption of the old sg. conj. endings (the pl. being obsolete, see § lix), though survivals of the old

---

[14] The discussion of the *-r* endings in this § applies equally to both.

abs. are found in Classical verse. It is difficult to make out the precise situation in MI because these endings were so often contracted in MSS, the contractions used are frequently ambiguous, and because in any case many editors do not italicise when they expand contractions. In the case of AMC, B sometimes writes the endings in full or is using a contraction about which there can be no ambiguity, in which case I do not italicise; but he often uses the highly ambiguous suspension-mark for which the choice of expansion is quite uncertain. However, since B's non-ambiguous endings agree with the OI forms three or four times as often as they disagree (see below), I have adopted the OI forms in expanding contractions, italicising of course.

§lviii   The evidence in B's case seems as follows:-
Written in full or with unambiguous contraction. (i) 'Correct' by OI standards:[15] pres. ind. of original simple verbs, independent -air 244, 280, 1240; relative -ar 947; dependent -ar 225, 254, 987. 'Simple prototonics', independent -ar 1327; -er 219; relative -ur 559. Deuterotonic forms, -ar/-ur 110, 230, 237, 239, 240, 250, 255, 668, 736, 754, 1331. (ii) 'Incorrect' by OI standards: original simple verbs, independent -ar 157, 766, 1247; relative -air 319; deuterotonic forms, -air 320, 1231.

Impv. (i) 'Correct': original simple verbs, -ar 237; 'simple prototonics', -ar 206. (ii) 'Incorrect': original simple, -air 1242.

Pres. subjunct. (i) 'Correct': original simple verbs dependent, -ar 237, -er 360.

Future. (i) 'Correct': 'simple prototonic' dependent -ar 897; relative, -ar 1146; deuterotonic, -ar 1280, 1298, 1302. (ii) 'Incorrect': original simple -er 337.

Thus there are 30 'correct' passive r-forms and only 8 'incorrect', and hence the situation in AMC might suggest that the process towards complete confusion between the original 'correct' and 'incorrect' forms in B was comparatively rather little advanced; but any conclusion is made very hazardous by the fact that in more than 40 instances B uses the ambiguous suspension.

Of the old deponents the 3rd person pl. -fetar is the only ex. which is written in full (see Note 162), and is 'correct'. All but one of the new 'deponent' s-prets. and past indicatives of active verbs sg. 3 and pl. 3 (§xcii ad fin.) are written in full, with 'correct' non-palatalised -r. This one, l. 91, has the suspension, which may safely be expanded as -ar.

[15] OI is irrelevant directly, but it gives a standard as a basis for discussion. Here I treat the 'simple prototonics' as if they were still OI deuterotonics for practical purposes.

The plural passive

§ lix   The OI pl. pass. forms were dying out during the MI period. In the primary tenses the old endings -tair/-tar and -tir/-ter disappeared, and their place was taken by the singular, -(th)air/-(th)ar and -(th)ir/-(th)er, with plural subjects when these were expressed. The sg./pl. distinction is still kept up in SR, but sg. for pl. is beginning in LU; TBC II L still has a number of pls., and so has CCath., but in some MSS (notably in the late ones which contain CCath.) the fact that -t-, not -th- is sometimes written with plural subjects may be misleading, a mere scribal omission of the lenition-mark, or perhaps an early ex. of the later common delenition in the sg., regular in Mod.I (e.g. cuirtear); and archaism must be reckoned with as well. The only possible ex. of a pl. pass. in a primary tense in AMC is ná ro brister a chnámu, 'let not his bones be broken', 200. But the lack of any other pls. makes it probable that this is really the singular brister, with the normal sandhi in *bris-ther; see § lx.

§ lx   In the secondary tenses the OI pl. endings, i.e. the imperf., past subjunct., and condit. -t(a)is, gave place similarly to the singular -t(h)a/-t(h)ea, -t(h)e/-t(h)i in MI (an example in AMC is ro sásta 342 f.). Survival of the OI pls., with the -(a)i- sometimes lengthened (see § lxxxi), seem pretty rare in MI. CCath. has several, but most of these are in a long decorative passage. AMC has five (see §§ lxxxiii, lxxxvi). In the past indic. (there are no pret. pl. passives in AMC) the OI conjunct perf. pl. in -t(h)a, -t(h)ea, or -ssa lasted on in MI to some extent, the -a or -ea being sometimes lengthened. These endings are fairly common in MI, and are well evidenced still in TTr.1 (20 exx.), TBC II L (12 exx.), CRR I (13 exx.), and CCath. (at least 18 exx.), and there is even a couple in AS. It is notable, though, that in the wholly non-archaising language of AI the last instance is in 997. AMC has three, one in prose, ro sásta 314 f., the -a being a contraction, and two in a single poem, do-rónta 823 (short -a proved by rhyme) and láithea 834; all three pl. past indic.

It is rather unexpected that AMC is so sparing of the old pl. pass. It could be a sign of lateness, but it may indicate rather that the Composer was less given to archaisms than some of the writers of this period—which indeed other evidence suggests was the case.

§ lxi   The loss of the pl. pass. was compensated for in two ways; the use of the singular pass. with pl. subjects, and the creation of a new form for the pl. pass. There are the following exx. of the former in AMC:- in primary tenses, probably ro brister a chnámu, as above; atn-agar rátha; fo-gabur na biada; at-agur téta; -airlímfathar do déta;

gairfither toísig; berair na slóig. In *do-bérthar* 670 and 672 the sg. could be explained differently, since there is no explicit subject, and though the referends are plural the implied subjects in both could be 'it' or 'that thing'. In the past subjunct., *co ro sásta boicht*, and in the past indic., *uair* .... *tuccad* .... 51 f., referring to *na n-uball*, the explanation for 670 and 672 is perhaps less likely to apply.

§ lxii   The old pl. endings of the pret. and past indic. passive mentioned above (§ lx) had already become ambiguous in late OI owing to phonetic changes; and eventually a new, more marked form was created. The perfective *ro* (by now a mere sign of the past indic.) was prefixed to the *pres.* indic. plural 3 *active* ending in -(*a*)*it*, unless the verb was already perfective by nature, in which case *ro* was omitted. So, *ro canait* 'they were sung' (but *tuccait* 'they were brought', *tucc-* being perfective by nature). This development is not yet found in SR (cf. Stud. Hib. XIX, 197), and the first exx. in the non-archaising language of the Annals are in AI 1013 and AU 1014. However, in the literary language of MI the form appears sporadically earlier, in the non-H texts in LU; there are 19 -(*a*)*it* in TTr.1 versus 20 of the older -*tha* etc. in the same; in TBC II L the proportion is 5 : 2; in CRR I there are 13 of each; in CCath. (VST p. 139), a proportion of about 6 : 1; and there are still some -*tha* etc. in AS. An obvious archaism is *tinóilte* c. 1330; Éigse VIII, 30 f. The new pl. in -(*a*)*it* is regular, side by side with exx. of the singular, in Classical verse, and lingered in CEMod.I prose narrative as an artificial archaism down to the 17th century.

In AMC there are only five exx. of the new pl. in -(*a*)*it*:- *ro tidnacit*, *ro collit* (2), *ro tinólit*, and *ro éraid*; *ro canait* 61 must be emended to sg. *ro canad*. This seems very few, but so are the four old -*tha* etc. plurals in AMC. To offer a proportion when the figures are so meagre is idle, but one might think they suggest, for what they are worth, a late 11th cent. date, specially in view of the figures for TBC II L and CCath.

§ lxiii   There are no pret. passives used as actives in AMC; cf. J. Corthals, ZCP XXXVII, 203 ff. On the question of the occasional use of the accusative noun as 'subject' of passives in (chiefly) MI see e.g. GM in DF III, cxvii ff. *Ro benad ulidetaid* .... *de* 212 f., 270 f. might be an instance (cf. DIL U 66.3), and so might acc. *téig* for nom. *tiag* in 255. But it is just as likely that these are examples of the use of the accusative for the nominative in other circumstances (see § xxii), which may be the true explanation of the use with the passive.

ABSOLUTE AND CONJUNCT

§ lxiv   The OI system of two parallel sets of verbal terminations, 'absolute' and 'conjunct', was beginning to break down in MI. This happened progressively over the following centuries by the generalisation of conj. for abs. in some forms and vice-versa in others, so that the final result in current Irish is that the functioning distinction has vanished, and there is only one set of endings. One or two of the innovations occur already in SR, others in non-H LU, others in PH or TBC II L or CCath., still others not till EMod.I, even quite late; and periods of confusion precede their completion. A factor in encouraging this would have been the development of the 'simple prototonics' (see §lxix).

§lxv There are a few exx. of this phenomenon in AMC, as follows:- (1) Pres. ind. pl. 2 -*dligthi*, with abs. for conj. -*dligid*. There is -*facthi* in non-H LU 1471, -*tabaerthi* once in TTr.1, and *at-berthe/at-berthai* in TBC II LU as against four cases of conj. -(*a*)*id*; PH has -*indsaigthi* 985 and -*cretithi* 2303; while CCath. has 10 exx. of the former ending as against one of the latter. It may survive, i.e. -(*a*)*id*, in Classical verse, but the abs. for old conj. is the norm. With the *ā*-subjunct., SR already has abs. *at-chethi* 2627 for the conj.; similarly *do-gnethi* in LU 6869 M; TTr.1 has 3 exx. of abs. for conj.; and in TBC II L there are some. After PH, the pres. abs. becomes pretty universal, but the intrusion of the new form seems comparatively late in the future; see §lxxxi.

§lxvi (2) Pres. ind. and *s*-subjunct. pl. 3. In the former, abs. *at-berait* AMC 1245 is for conj. *at-berat*, and per contra, conj. *tiagat* 342 is for abs. *tiagait*. This is not in SR or TTr.1, but -(*a*)*it* for -*at/-et* is coming in rarely in PH, e.g. *cretit* 1752, and is almost wholly established in AS; thereafter the abs. -(*a*)*it* is fully established apart from sporadic conj. -*at/-et* exceptions. The situation is much the same in the *ā*-subjunct. In the *s*-subjunct. there is -*torsit* AMC 570 for -*torset*.

§lxvii (3) In the *s*-pret. the old abs. endings of the sg. and pl. 1 and 2 did not outlast OI, the conj. endings being substituted; hence AMC 1023 *imrásium*. In the pl. 3, however, abs. -*sait/-sit* survived for a time in MI side by side w. conj. -*sat/-set* used for abs. In SR there are 7 cases of the former in indep. construction, e.g. *dolbsait* 3852, against 11 already of the latter, e.g. *scarsat* 3953. Quiggin quotes 28 cases of correct abs. -*s(a)it* in LU (Ériu IV, 207), but they are all in texts of OI or very early MI origin; cf. the 12 exx. of -*sat/-set* for -*s(a)it* in LU quoted by Quiggin, op. cit. p. 196, though 7 of them are in LU H. In TTr.1 there are no absolutes, and TBC II L has only one; after that there are sporadic exx., e.g. a few in PH etc. (i.e. -*s(a)it* where this is historically correct, though -*s(a)it* may also spread into the conj.;

otherwise the conj. -sat/-set takes over). There are 2 exx. of pret. abs. -sit in indep. constr. where historically correct, ansit and timoircsit (the second a 'simple proto.') in AMC; and only one pret. conj. used historically incorrectly for abs., gabsat; see §xci.

§ lxviii   In the old perf., later 'past indic.', the ro form of course took the conj., but in AMC there is one case of abs., ro lécsit. One might take this as an ex. of the scribal spelling of unstressed e as i (cf. § lxxxvii (1)), but for the fact that there seems to have been a short-lived fashion in the 11th–12th cents. for using the abs. ending pl. 3 for the conj. in the ro past indic., beginning in PH (ro chretsit 1082; ro lécsit 704, 3286; ro trecsit 4020), and last recorded, so far as I know, in CCath. (6 exx., RC XXXVI, 334). It looks as if the MI abs./conj. confusion began particularly early in the pret.

For the -r passive of primary verbs see § lvii f.

DEUTEROTONICS GIVING PLACE TO 'SIMPLE PROTOTONICS' IN INDEPENDENT CONSTRUCTIONS

§ lxix   'Simple prototonic' means original prototonic compound-verb forms which have come to be used in independent construction instead of their corresponding deuterotonics, and in due course take over the abs. endings where appropriate, thus becoming new simple verbs. Here and in the Glossary I have assumed, of any given compound verb which is known to have become a simple prototonic, that if no deuterotonic forms appear in AMC it has already developed into a simple one, considering the probable date of the text; and I have treated the headwords as such in the Glossary.

§ lxx   This began very early in OI, apparently at first only in verbs compounded in to-, ro- (ro-icc), de-/di-, and some traces already in later OI with fo- (cf. ZCP XVI, 73 n., and Thes. II 240, 14, 15), in all cases before verbal and prepositional V- or lenited f-; thus in e.g. to-icc-, fo-ad-gaib- etc. The result was a form identical with the prototonic one, but the deuterotonic was naturally preserved where there was an infix (and this continued in use, to a decreasing extent, as long as infixes survived). I call this Type (1). At first the verbal endings remained conjunct (Type (1 a)), which survived very late in a few verbs, e.g. ticc 'comes' (not abs. ticcid until very late), but in general they quickly fell into line with the old simple verbs and took the abs. endings, e.g. pres. ind. pl. 3 tecait for tecat. However, note fut. pl. 3 ticfait in SR 1164 etc. but still the older ticfat 8037; and in AMC tidnacis 621, perhaps beside older tidnais 613 (see Note), 852. This type, (1 b), first appears in the earlier ninth century.

§lxxi   The pattern was now set for the other compound verbs, those where elision of the final vowel of the proclitic preposition in compounds was not possible, either because the following element began with a C- or because the proclitic prep. ended with a -C, or both. This is Type (2), either the very rare (2 a) where the endings remain conj., and the verb therefore identical with its prototonic form in OI, or the very common (2 b) where they have become assimilated to the simple verbs by adopting the absolute endings. So (2 a) indep. fut. sg. 3 *cumgéba*, SR 8091, 8107, where the (2 b) would have been *cumgébaid*. In SR there are three exx. of (2 b); 1008, 2429, and 8246. In (2) types there is normally syncope of the root vowel where applicable, the preverbal element being now stressed.

The developments in §§ xlv and xlvi above, whereby compound verbs came to prefix *no* to their prototonics instead of using their deuterotonics, and to prefix *ro* before their prototonics in place of infixing it in their deuterotonics, were no doubt also part of the same general movement towards simplifying the compound verb.

§lxxii   The following lists of deuteros. and 'simple protos.' in independent position in AMC omit the group of deuteros. such as *at-beir*, *do-gní* etc. which survived as such too late to be relevant to the present statistics. Denominative verbs derived from vns. are also excluded, since they were always treated as weak verbs and never had deutero. forms. Only *one* relevant ex. is given for each verb, because what counts here is the *verbs* and not their total *occurrences*. Where there is no evidence for abs. endings the verb is ignored.

§lxxiii   The surviving deuteros. in AMC (exclusive of the small group of old compounds which retained its deutero. forms very late) are the following:- *at(n)-aig, atom-chuirethar, at-fiadat, at-raig, ad-uaid, con-ludimm, con-melfi, do-adbat, do-airis, do-t-cuir, do-chummlai, do-s-fil, do-garar* 668 etc., *do-m-ánic, do-airngir, do-línta, do-lluid, do-s-méla, do-munim, do-roich* (emendation, 446), *fo-t-cherd, fo-d-era, fo-loing, for-t-gillim*; a total of 24. To these we must add the eight verbs with *ro* in § xlvii above (*tuarcaib* being excluded because already simple proto., and *atom-raracht* because of *at-raig* above), which makes a total of 32. Note that disregarding the verbs which have 'petrified' infixes, *at(n)-aig, at-fiadat, at-raig, fo-d-era*, and *for-t-gillim*, there are only six where the survival of the deutero. in AMC contexts may be due to the presence of their infixed pronouns.

To set against these, we have the following instances of the simple protos.:-

(1a) *ricfa, ruc, tuarcaib, tairnic, ticc* (but *do-m-ánic* above), *tucc*.

(1b) *fácbaid, fóbrais, fócrais, taisselbait, taitnid, tecbaid, tidnacis* (see Note 613), *timoircsit, tócbaid.*

(1 a/b) ambiguous, because the ending does not distinguish abs. and conj., or in the case of deponents and passives because the distinction is confused in MI (see §lvii f.); *dúthracur, foelustar* (from proximate **fo-ilostar*).

(2 a) *imrásium, imthét.*

(2 b) *aicéras, asnédfit, atáid* 'kindles', *atlaigis, comlis, connaigimm, cosnait, cuimgess, érgius, furmit, imnaiscis, indlais, oslaicis.*

(2 a/b) ambiguous, *auroslaicther, impáither, imthiger.*

§ lxxiv This makes a total of 31 (excluding the ambiguous group), and by contrast with the above 32 deuteros. it follows that the proportion of deuteros. to simple protos. in AMC is about 1:1. The corresponding figure in SR (excluding the small group of deuteros. which survived very late) seems to be about 132:56, i.e. c. 1:0.4; in TTr.1, c. 37:31, = 1:0.8. Thus the proportion of deuteros. to simple protos. decreased from SR to TTr.1 and from TTr.1 to AMC. This evidence, for what it is worth, might suggest that AMC is at any rate later than TTr.1. One may add that in CCath. there are about 24 deuteros. and 44 simple protos., giving a proportion of about 1:1.8, which, again for what it is worth, would show that AMC is earlier than CCath. But these statistics are very inconclusive, because the differences are so very small.

VERB STEMS

§ lxxv The OI system of weak and strong verbs is set out in GOI pp. 352 ff. The weak verbs were very regular throughout, with stems in original *ā* and *ī*, but the strong verbs with presential stem-syllables of *e/o* alternating (thematic stems), *i*, and *na*, and a couple of others not relevant to MI, were more complicated. The weak verbs took the *ā*-subjunct., the *f*-fut., and the *s*-pret.; the strong verbs, many of which had *s*-subjuncts. and the rest *ā*-subjuncts., had a variety of fut. and pret. stems. In the process of simplifying the verb typical of MI and EMod.I this remarkable variety was being much reduced. The strong verbs gradually assimilated their presential stem-syllables to the weak system. The result in Mod.I, the few remaining irregular verbs apart, is that all now have presential stems in either *-a-* or *-i-*; subjuncts. representing the old *ā*-subjunct.; and past indics. descended from the *s*-pret. in the sg. and from the suffixless pret. in the pl. Most futs. are from the old *f*-fut., but beginning in early MI the old *ē*-fut. extended itself in various ways and evolved variously in late MI and EMod.I; see Celtica XI, 101 ff. There is no trace of these secondary developments of the ē-fut. in AMC except for the first stages where it began to spread in early MI from verbs with OI -él-, -ér-, -én- etc. to disyllabic verb-stems, weak or strong, in liquids, nasals, voiced spirants, and occasionally -g- and -s-. On this see Celtica XI, 100 f. The only ex. of this in AMC is -coitél, ē-fut. of the simple proto. cotlaid, which formerly took f-fut. On the futs. -aineba, -érnaba, and -béraba see Notes 30, 32, and 34; these forms in AMC can all be early MI. The simple protos. came to be treated as weak verbs, and I do not mention these below unless they offer features of real interest.

Thematic stems

§ lxxvi   The reflexes of the e/o alternation remain unchanged in the presential stem of beir-/ber- and in its compounds at-beir and do-beir; the beir- grade was not yet generalised, as it became later. The sg. 3 t-pret. birt is replaced in AMC by weak s-pret. beris, and by bertais which is a mixture of the two (cf. TBC II L bertis, -bertsat, and pass. -bertad, VST p. 98 f.), but otherwise the past tense stem in AMC is the old perfect rucc-, generalised in PH, CCath., AS, and thereafter except for occasional survivals of the s-stem preterite. The compound fóbraid retains its strong t-pret. in six of the seven AMC exx., but in fóbrais the seventh has adopted the weak s-pret. The first ex. of this in DIL is fo-rópair LU 3922 (SCC, in the probably 11th cent. part).

Canaid was partly thematic and partly a weak ā-stem in OI; in AMC, cf. the weak past indic. pass. sg. ro canad (61), emendation. SR still has strong pret. for this form, -rochet 7533.

Fo-ceird. The pres. ind. sg. 2 fo-cherdi (AMC) has the -i/-e ending of the OI i-stems and ī-stems attracted to it, a MI development; cf. at-beire SR 1268, PH 98 etc., TBC II R 1411; IGT III § 14 l. 15 do-bire, do-bere, but adir (from at-bir), op. cit. §6, p. 176, ex. 83, thematic. Impv. sg. 2 fo-ceirdi for fo-cerd (AMC) is unexpected.

Cingid had strong reduplicated pret. cechaing in OI, but AMC gives the weak s-pret. cingis; cf. TBC II R 1702, 1704.

Dligid. This retains the thematic presential e/o reflexes late. In AMC, pres. ind. sg. 3 -dlig, pass. -dlegar; cf. PH dligid 3598, -dlig 2817, pl. 3 -dlegat 1505 etc., pass. sg. dlegar 239 etc. In IGT III § 35 the stem has mostly become generalised as dlig-, but there are a few dleag- forms.

At-fét. There are no exx. of the e-grade in AMC, but at-fiadat preserves the o-grade.

Do-gní. The deutero. lost its g- in the course of MI, presumably generalised from forms with lenition, where the fricative would easily be lost in /ɟnʲ/. The oldest exx. I know are two do-ní in LU 9869 f. M, where both had rel. lenition. TTr.1 has do-níthear once, but in PH the *gn-* spelling is still very common except in mostly late sections. The only ex. of *do-n-* in AMC is in l. 1210. In the imperative AMC twice has the MI sg. 2 *déna* for older *déine*; PH overwhelmingly *déna*, w. only once *déine*. The old fut. proto. stem *-dig(e)n-* is still seen in AMC in the fut. pass. sg. *-dignestar* and condit. ditto *-dignesta*, conflated w. the fut. *s*-stem, for older *-digentar* and *-digenta*; see Note to l. 422. AMC has no exx. of the later *-ding(e)n-*. In the past indic. active deutero. OI *do-rig(é)n-* but pass. *do-rón-*, AMC keeps the old active sg. 3 *do-rigne* and pass. *do-rónad*, pl. *do-rónta*; but it also takes a new pass. sg. *do-rigned*, from the active stem. However, it does not use the active stem for the pass., as MI often does. The act. sg. 2 *do-rindis* 231 (= *do-rinnis*) from *do-rignis*, with post-tonic intervocal /jnʲ/ giving /nʲ:/, is another common MI feature, the source of Mod.I dialect *do-rinn-*, which occurs as early as SR. The apparent freak pl. 3 *do-rigset* 302 and 625, presumably from **do-rignset*, occurs already six times in SR. McE suggests it was a dialect form; IMN 1961, p. 44.

Con-icc gives simple proto. pres. ind. sg. 3 *cumcaid/cuimcid*, hence the pres. ind. relative *cuimgess* in 1348, but the past indic. sg. 3 *-r choem*, a late and uncommon by-form, is a trace of the OI suffixless pret. *-coemnacair* (later *s*-pret. *-caemnaic*) e.g. TBC II R 646, 1486; cf. BNnE *for-caomhsat*, unnecessarily called 'a spurious form' in DIL F 2. 327.40.

Ticc (*do-icc*) preserved the thematic present throughout MI and beyond; so AMC simple proto. pres. ind. sg. 3 *ticc* beside sg. pass. *tecar*, and cf. IGT III § 5 sg. 3 *tig*, pl. 1 *-tegam*, pass. *tegar*. AMC still keeps *s*-subjunct. *tís-*; so also CEMod.I; the substitution of *ā*-subjunct. *tig-* is apparently later than MI.

Ithid. The OI perf. *do-fuaid* still occurs in SR, but later became mostly *ad-uaid* w. change of preverb, as in AMC (cf. VGK II, 558), PH, IGT III § 31, p. 200 l. 10, etc., side by side with simple *s*-pret. form *do ith*. But *do-fhuaid* lasted into EMod.I (cf. IGT III § 31) and survives in some spoken dialects.

Lingid. The OI suffixless pret. *leblaing* survived in some forms into EMod.I, but appears as ordinary *s*-pret. *lingis* in AMC; PH has the *s*-pret. only.

Fo-loing. The AMC forms *fo-loing* and *fo-loingtis* have not yet adopted the simple proto. inflexion *fuilngid* which is already generalised in PH and TBC II L. However, *foelustar* is a simple proto., but keeps its OI reduplicated *s*-fut. inflexion (deutero. *fo-lilastar*).

Con-meil. In AMC fut. *con-melfi* the OI *ē*-fut. *con-mél-* has gone over to the *f*-fut., and in *comlis* the *t*-pret. (OI *con-melt*) joined the *s*-pret. as a simple proto.

Do-meil keeps its deutero. inflexion in the *ē*-fut. *do-méla* etc. in AMC, but its old *t*-pret. is now the *s*-pret. simple proto. *-toimless, do* *thomail* etc.; *do-romel* however is still deuterotonic, and w. infixed *ro*. Cf. PH *ro thomail* but *do-romailt*.

At-raig. Atom-regar preserves the old form of the thematic *o*-grade, but see Note l. 1006. The old *s*-fut. remains in *-érus*; and the deutero. *t*-pret. in *at-racht* etc. But the simple proto. pres. ind. rel. and the *s*-pret. sg. 3 have taken over in *érgius* and *érgis* respectively. The impv. sg. 2 *eirc* 843 is used for *érig* by confusion with the verb *téit*.

Ro-saig. Past ind. sg. 1 *-ruachtus* is the old *t*-pret. having adopted the *s*-pret. ending while preserving its *-t(-)*; see § xciii.

Condaigid, simple proto. (OI *con-diaig*), see Note to l. 247 f. SR 3095, deutero. pres. ind. sg. 2 *con-daige*; PH simple proto. pres. ind. sg. 3 *cuindigid, cuingid, cuinchid*; TBC II L *cungid, cuinnid*; CCath. simple proto. pres. ind. sg. 2 *connaige* 3342. Hence pres. subjunct. sg. 1 *cuinger* AMC 328 is a normal MI form, beside those in *connaig-*; see Note to l. 247 f.

Téit. The thematic *e/o* grades are preserved in pres. ind. sg. 2 *tégi*, pl. 3 *tiagat*; *s*-subjunct. sg. 1 *-tias*, sg. 2 *téis*; and suffixless pret. sg. 3 *luid*, pl. 1 *lodmar*; but generalisation of *téig-* was appearing in late MI and was largely accepted in the Classical literary language beside the less usual *tiag-*. In *-téig* 999 the *s*-subjunct. has given place to the indic. stem, in general an EMod.I development of which this seems an early ex.; cf. PH 410 *ná tiaga*. The perfective past subjunct. sg. 3 *-diged* AMC 304 for *-digsed* is an analogous instance. This was already appearing in TTr.1, PH, and TBC II L; see Notes to 304 and 999. The quite different suppletive fut. stem keeps the OI *reg-* form in AMC with one exception, *rag-* in *no ragaind*; this appears, beside *reg-*, already in SR, TBC I U, TTr.1, and PH, but TBC II L, CCath., and IGT have *rag-* or *rach-* only.

i-stems

§ lxxvii The *i*-stems mostly became weak ī-stems in the MI reorganisation of the verb.

Damaid (OI *daimid*). In OI this took the deponent suffixless pret., sg. 3 *dámair*; cf. PH 4893 *(ro) damair* (*a* for *á*). But AMC has adopted the active *s*-pret., sg. 3 *-dam*, pass. *(ro) damad*.

Gabaid. OI had presential ind. *gaib-*, subjunct. *gab-*, fut. *géb-*, and *s*-pret. *gab-*. In MI, *gab-* was being generalised as the pres. stem, but *gaib-* still remained as alternative, particularly in pres. ind. and pret. sg. 3 dep. *-gaib*. Also a new MI presential stem *geib-*, beginning in SR, is found beside *gaib-/gab-* all through MI and into the IGT, after which it becomes rare; in the 12th century it occasionally penetrated to the pret. In AMC *-gaib* occurs once each in the pres. ind. sg. 3 and pret. ditto, plus past indic. pl. 1 *ro gaibsium*; and *geib-* in pres. ind. sg. 1

K

gebim and impv. sg. 2 *geb*. Otherwise the stem in AMC is *gab*- in all cases except in the fut. *géb*-.

Fo-gaib, compound of *gaib*-. The forms of interest in AMC are pres. ind. sg. 3 *-fagaib*, imperf. sg. 3 *fo-gebed*, past subjunct. sg. 2 *-fagtha*, fut. sg. 2 *-fuigbe* (see Note 335), past ind. sg. 1 *-fuarus*, and past ind. pass. sg. *-fríth*. The *-fa-* for *-fo-* in proto. forms is normal in MI from SR on, though *-fo-* occurs sporadically as late as CEMod.I. Deutero. *fo-geib-* for older *fo-gaib-* in the presential stem is found in SR, LU, PH, AS etc.; and in EMod.I, including IGT, it is pretty well generalised as *do-gheibh-*. In the proto., *-fagV-* for older *-fagbV-* is a late MI development seen in PH, TBC II L, CRR I, CCath., and once in TBC I U (H) 6155 pres. subjunct. pass. sg. *-fagthar*, after which it becomes general; but AMC has only one ex. of this, past subjunct. sg. 2 *-fagtha*. The MI proto. fut. stem *-fuigb-* (older *-foigb-*) occurs in MI in LU, PH, TBC II L, etc., and in the Classical language; AMC has sg. 2 *-fuigbe*, but no exx. of the later *-foigV-* or *-fuigV-*. B's length-mark in his *fúidbe* 335 is a case of the late secondary lengthening in the early Mod.I spoken language not accepted in Classical verse. The old suffixless pret. sg. 1 and 2 *-fuar* was beginning to be replaced early in MI by a new *s*-pret. form *-fuarus*, *-fuarais* respectively, seen in SR (seven exx.), hence AMC sg. 1 *fuarus*; but the old passive *-fríth* lasted to the end of the EMod.I period, and hence occurs in AMC.

Fácbaid, compound of *gaib-* from deutero. *fo-ácaib*, became the simple proto. form in MI, as in AMC; but still had infixed *-ro-* instead of prefixing it in its perfective subjunct. and past indic. stems, cf. AMC past indic. sg. 3 *-fárcaib* and pass. sg. *-fárcbad*. Note already SR *-fargsat* 6495, with *-rcbs-* simplified to *-rcs-* (*-rgs-*). This development took place very early in the *s*-pret. and resulted in the whole verb *fácbaid* appearing as *fácaid* later (not in AMC), though apparently little accepted in the Bardic schools except in the *f*-fut. (IGT III § 85, where pres. ind. pl. 1 *fágmuid* is grudgingly allowed as a current usage), and hence not common in elevated CEMod.I prose.

Gairid took the *é*-fut. in early MI, which survived in e.g. TBC II R 2808 sg. 3 *-géra* (in verse), but had gone over to the *f*-fut. in PH and CRR I, as also in AMC pass. sg. rel. *gairfither*.

Guidid. AMC pl. 3 *ro gáidetar* keeps the old long-vowel suffixless pret. (= past indic.)—though the *-/dʲ/-* is presumably influenced by the sg. 3 *gáid*—and so does SR throughout; but the *s*-pret. appears already in TBC I U 6688 M pass. sg. *ro guded* (= TBC I Y *ro guided*). TTr.1 *ro gaid*; PH has the *s*-pret. only, with numerous exx.

Lamaid. The OI deponent suffixless perf. sg. 1 *ro-lámar* has become active *s*-pret. (= past ind.) in AMC *ro lámus*. The sg. 3 is seen already in e.g. TBC I U *-ro láim* 4774 M.

Maidid. This took *s*-subjunct. in OI; so sg. 3 -*má*. But in AMC it has joined the *ā*-subjunct., hence -*muide* (later form of -*maide*; cf. TBC I Y 4043 -*maidi*).

Saidid. AMC retains the OI reduplicated suffixless pret. sg. 1 -*siasar* in the evolved -*sessar* (see GOI p. 427; cf. sg. 3 *siasur* for *siasair* in CMT 1, RC XII, 79, §71), and the perfect sg. 3 -*dessid*, pl. 3 -*dessitar*; but it also has the new *s*-pret. sg. 3 *saidis* three times. SR preserves several *dessid* and -*dessid*, but seems to have no pl.; TTr.1 has more than one *deisid*; PH fifteen *dessid* and one *desitar*, all apparently early; and CCath. *do* (= *ro*) *deisidh* 4751.

na-stems

§ lxxviii   The *na*-stems fell together with the weak *ā*-stems in MI, conjugated on the presential stem all through the verb, but with occasional traces of their strong inflexions.

Benaid. All the AMC exx. are weak, hence *f*-fut. pass. *benfaider* for old suffixless *bethir*; but pret. sg. 3 *bendais* for normal *benais* has intrusion of the *t*-pret. stem; see Note to 763. The weak stem is generalised in PH, but TBC II L retains a few strong forms like fut. sg. 3 -*bia*, perfect *ro bí*, -*ruba*, no doubt from the early sources of TBC II.

Lenaid. The same generalisation of weak *ā* took place with *len*-, with no exceptions in AMC. The same is true of PH except for past ind. sg. 3 -*r lil* 6538, and of TBC II (L) R pret. sg. 3 *lilis* 1359, 1757, 3806 and past ind. ditto *ro lil* 912; cf. *ro bí* just above.

Weak stems

§ lxxix   There is little to say, but note the following:- Long *ā*-stems: *Scaraid* was regular in OI, hence *f*-fut., but its compounds took *é*-fut., e.g. *con-scéra*. This influenced the simple verb early, as in TTr.1 *no scéra*, and in AMC, pl. 3 -*scérat*. Long *ī*-stems: *Léicid* naturally has stem *léic*-, but there is a post-OI variant as an *ā*-stem, *léc*-. This is found in AMC in the pres. ind. pass. *lécar* (with strong verb pass. termination -*ar* for weak -*thar*). The OI -*i* ending of the pres. ind. conj. sg. 3 was commonly lost in MI, hence -*loisc* for -*loisci* in AMC 1342.

VERBAL FORMS AND TERMINATIONS

§ lxxx   It is unnecessary to give a complete collection, as this has already been done by Vernam Hull in ZCP XXIX, 325 ff. (here 'Hull'), though I cannot always agree with his interpretations (these being noted in all cases).

The following list concentrates on forms of special interest, particularly those bearing on matters of date. They are set out thus:- (a) simple verbs, including 'simple prototonics', in independent construction; (b) the same in dependent construction; (c) compound verbs independent; (d) compound verbs dependent. Group (a) normally has the old abs. endings, and the rest the old conj., subject to the developments in §§ lxv ff. They are listed in the alphabetical order of the Glossary, and where it is unnecessary to quote forms, line-numbers only may be given; 'etc.' after a line-number means 'consult the Glossary for more exx. of the same'. Minor spelling differences irrelevant to the terminations are ignored. For the meaning of 'past indicative' see the introduction to the Glossary.

Lengthened endings

§ lxxxi   The vowels of certain terminations could be lengthened in MI; see Introduction p. xiii. The evidence for this in MI is complex. There is great variety as between texts, and inconsistency within any one text, as well as within any one part of the verb. This must often depend not on the date of the text but rather on the date and individual practice of the scribes; and in any event in most parts of the verb concerned the evidence of Mod.I suggests it was a matter of dialect, as it still is.

The situation in AMC is as follows:- In the pres. ind. the only form occurring where lengthening would take place is active pl. 2, and the only ex., -*dligthi*, is not marked long in B. Imperf. acts. not written long in pl. 3 are *fo-loingtis*, *melltais*, *serndais*, *tégdis*; long, pl. 1 *do-bermís*, 3 *do-s-bertís*; pass. not long, sg., *at-bertha*, *do-línta*, -*fétta*, pl. -*bendais*, *do-bertís*; long, sg. *do-berthí*, pl. -*indsmatís*, *meltís*. Pres. subjunct., no exx. Past *ā*-subjunct. act., not long, sg. 2 -*tarta*, -*fagtha*, pass. not long, sg. *ro crocht*ha 305 (-tha a contraction); long, -*crochthá* 243; pl. not long, *ro sásta* (-a a contraction); long, -*betís* (substantive verb and copula); -*gabdaís*. Past *s*-subjunct. act. not long, sg. 2, -*rísta*, -*tísta*, pl. 1 -*fesmais*; long, pl. 3 -*rístís*; pass. not long, sg. -*festa*; no pl. Fut. of *téit*, act. not long. pl. 1. -*regmait*. *F*-condit. act. not long, none; long, pl. 3 -*tallfatís*. *S*-condit. act. not long, none; pass. not long, -*dignesta*; long, none. The *é*-condit. act. not long, sg. 2 *do-bértha*, pl. 1 *do-bérmais*, 3 -*tabratis*; long, none. Past ind. pass. pl. not long *do-rónta* (short -*a* proved by metre), *ro sásta* 314 f. (-a a contraction), *ro láithea*; no longs.

There are thus about three times as many cases of non-lengthenings as of lengthenings in AMC. Lengthening is found, rarely and sporadically, in LU M (e.g. nine active -*tís* in ll. 1684-1695) and in TBC II L, but quite often in PH and AS.

Present Indicative

§ lxxxii   Active sg. 1 Always -(*a*)*im*(*m*) except (c) *at-biur* (but *as-berim* 998, *at-berim* 326; *as-* and *at-* vary freely in this verb in MI), *do-biur, it-chiú*, and *-tú/-tó* in the substantive verb, see § xcvi. Generalisation of -(*a*)*im* began already in OI. *At-biur* and *do-biur* still occur not rarely in MI texts beside *at-berim* (already in SR), and later *do-berim*; *do-chiú* and *-tú* occur as late as the 17th century.

Sg. 2 -*e*/-*i* in (a) 877 (2) and (c) 252, 518, 671, 1187. This is the OI -*i*, and lasted, along with -*a*, all through MI and beyond. The new -(*a*)*ir*, beginning to appear occasionally in late MI, is not found in AMC either here or in the other primary tenses; cf. § lxxxv (1), sg. 2.

Sg. 3 (a) OI -(*a*)*id* remains unchanged in MI. *Téit* always lacked this termination, and some 'simple protos.' type (1a) did not adopt it during MI; e.g. *ticc*. In (b), endless -C^u/-C^j of strong verbs remains in AMC, e.g. *-ben, -dlig*, but weak verbs lost their final -*V*, so *-loisc* (OI *-loisci*), the only ex. in simple verbs in AMC, cf. § lxxix. (c) The final endless -*C* of strong verbs continues here too, as it did throughout MI and beyond, e.g. *at-raig*, except in verbs with radical -*V* like *do-gní* 554 etc. (where in any case the -*V* is not a termination); *fo-d-era* is a petrified form, an old compound weak *ā*-verb. (d) The same here; *-fagaib, -taet*, and with radical endingless -*V*, *-talla*. However, the new MI conj. sg. 3 ending -*ann*/(-*enn*) is seen in (c) *ro-fhétand* 1044, and (d) *-dénann* 553. This conj. ending appears as an alternative near the end of the 10th century and is already not very rare in LU A and M; cf. Thurneysen, ZCP I, 343 f. (op. cit. p. 345; a text containing -*ann*/-*enn* cannot be older than the 11th cent.), and JS, ZCP II, 481, who gives a score of exx. in MI texts in LU. M O Daly notes in VST ll. 3737 ff. that the -*ann*/-*enn* ending is less common in TBC II L than in CCath., the former text having 32 cases of the old endings versus only 9 of the new one, and CCath. having 26 versus 18 respectively.

Pl. 1 (a) The only ex. (*berma* 1237) directly continuing OI non-rel. *bermai* or rel. *bermae* (§ cvi) is one of the only two (a) pls. 1 in AMC; for the other, fut. *regmait*, see § lxxxvii (4). The pres. ind. -*mai*/-*mae* was replaced early by -*m*(*a*)*it*, beginning in SR, and the older ending is very rare in MI. There are none of the latter in SR or TTr.1, both having -*m*(*a*)*it* only. There are three exx. of -*ma*(*i*) in TBC I U, therefore probably OI; on the petrified *ailme* in VT and PH see DTL p. 34. TBC II R has two, *berma* 374 and *lodma* 1567, the former in verse (the TBC I U version reads *tiagmai*), the latter in prose and not in LU; both in TBC II L are probably from an old source. TBC II R 511 has fut. *ragma* (in prose), but this is the same in the corresponding passage in the LU version, TBC I U 4767 *regmai*. (*Regmai* in various spellings occurs often enough in MI MSS of OI or very early MI texts to suggest it is a special case. But *berma* in AMC can hardly be taken as evidence of a very early date.) In (c) and (d) the OI conj. ending, *-am/ -em*, is found in AMC in *at-beram* and *-dénum*, and also in (c) the substantive verb *atá(u)m*, on which see § xcvi (1). There is no ex. of the growing use in MI of abs. pres. ind. *-m(a)it* for conj. *-am/-em* in AMC.

Pl. 2 There is only (b) *-dligthi*, with the abs. ending for the conj. *-id*; whether the *-i* should be marked long it is impossible to say (§ lxxxi). On the date see § lxv.

Pl. 3 In (a) the expected abs. *-(a)it* is preserved in AMC, in *cosnait*, *taisselbait* (both simple proto.), *-troscit* etc., and in (b), (c), and (d) the old conj. *-at/-et*, so (b) *-impóat*, *-caccut* etc.; (c) *at-berat*, *atn-agut*, *at- fiadat*, etc.; (d) *-dochrat*.

With conj. for abs., (a) *tiagat* 342, and abs. for conj., (c) *at-berait* 1245; see § lxvi.

Pres. ind. relat. (a), and simple proto. (a), *brogas, fásus, techtas, coilles; cuimgess, éirgius*.

Deponent. See § lvi. For sg. 1 *-fetar* and sg. 2 *-fetara* see Glossary.

Passive sg. See § lvii f. Forms with 'incorrect' endings are bracketed. (a) *berair (berar*; rel. *berair), bentair, (iatar)*, rel. *légaither, lécar, lentar, scríbthar*. Simple protos. *adáither, auroslaicther, déraigther, impáither, (tecar)*. (b) *-caiter, -curther, -dlegar, -gabar, -ráiter*. Simple protos. *-aisnéthar, -condagur*. (c) *(as-berair), at(n)-agar, do-berar (do-berair), do-garar, do-gníther, fo-gabar*.

In the pass., the old strong verbs *ben-* and *len-* have acquired the *-th-* of weak verbs (*bentair, lentar*, just above), and the weak verb *léic-* has lost its *-th-* under the influence of the strong (*lécar*); but *-gabar* with strong ending would have been *-gaibther* in OI, and the same would probably have applied to *fo-gabar*.

There are no plural passives.

Imperfect

§ lxxxiii The secondary endings are the same as those of the past subjunct. and essentially the same as those of the condit.; see §§ lxxxvi and lxxxviii. On lengthenings see § lxxxi.

Active sg. 1 (b) *-caithind*; (c) *do-gnínd* (on B's *gaibend* see Note to l. 1035). No sg. 2. Sg. 3, always *-ad/-ed*; see Hull p. 333. Pl. 1 (c) *do- bermís*. No pl. 2. Pl. 3 (a) *melltais, serndais, tegdís*. (c) *do-s-bertis, fo- loingtis*.

Passive sg. (b) *-fétta*. (c) *at-bertha, do-berthí, do-línta*. Pl. (b) *-bendais, -indsmatís, -meltís*. (c) *do-bertis*.

Apart from *at-bertha* and *do-berthí*, all the imperf. endings in AMC continue the OI directly (*do-gnínd* with contraction). *At-bertha*, which

corresponds to OI *at-berthe* is identical in form with its past subjunct.
(OI *at-berthae*), and perhaps arose by confusion with it. There is the
same form in PH 5751, 5753 (cf. act. *at-berad* 5748 for *at-beired*), AS
adertha 6984. The *-thí* in *do-berthí* is familiar in CEMod.I (BST p. 4,
§191, ll. 8–11 seems to regard it as normal), but is apparently of late
MI origin (cf. Celtica X, 134).

There are no sg. passives in *-thea* or *-theá* in AMC.

Imperative

§lxxxiv   Active sg. 2 Allowing for minor variations of spelling,
almost all forms are direct continuations of the OI. For *geb* (= *geib*) see
§lxxvii, *gabaid*; on *eirc* see Note to l. 843; on *déna* see §lxxvii, *do-gní*;
note *fomna* in l. 847.

Sg. 3 *-ad/-ed* 831, 1159.

Pl. 1 *-em*, *-ium* (no *-am* in AMC) 315, 723, and pl. 2 *-aid* 1253 are all
normal OI and MI; there is no pl. 3.

Passive sg. (no pls. in AMC). Verbs in *-thar* 206, 237, *-ther* 1091,
and *-ar* 237 and 1327 keep the OI endings; on 'incorrect' *berair* for
berar see §lviii.

Present Subjunctive

§lxxxv   (1) The *ā*-stems.

Active sg. 1 (a) *cuinger*, *imthiger*. (b) *-acailler*, (all three are simple
protos., and the first two took *s*-subjunct. in OI). (d) *-dén*. Here *-ar/-er*
is the new 'deponent' ending which developed in MI, replacing the old
active abs. *-a/-ea* and conj. nil; the older endingless form survives in
-dén. This new ending spread to the act. because the other terminations
were insufficiently distinctive. It is first found in SR (4 or 5 exx.) and in
VT (2 or 3 exx., see DTL p. 35), and became common in MI in the
11th cent., beside the older endingless ones which virtually disappeared in regular verbs by EMod.I.

Sg. 2 There are no exx. of the old abs. endings in AMC, but the old
conj. *-a* is still the rule (no *-e* in AMC); so (b) *-ruca*, *-lena*, *-saera*, (d)
-fagba. The new 'deponent' *-air* is not found in either the *ā*- or the *s*-
subjunct.; it seems of very late MI origin (one late and four very late
exx. of the *ā*-subjunct. in PH; two exx. of the *-s(a)ir s*-subjunct. in LL,
tiasair 8570 and *tísir* 3467 are probably due to the scribe); and it was
not accepted in the Classical language of verse. Nor has AMC any exx.
of the new, rare late MI *-ea/-eá* (two in TBC II L, see VST 427-29;
one in PH 2472).

Sg. 3 No exx. of the abs. Conj. in *-a*, (b) 184 (*-tecma*, old *s*-subjunct.)
529, 848, 1002, 1157, 1163; (d) *-aprai* (sp. for *-abra*) 1211; in *-e/-i*, (b)

199 (*-muide*, old *s*-subjunct.), 333, 366, 852, 1156, 1157. These continue OI *-a* and *-ea* respectively.

Pl. and deponents, no exx.

Passive. The regular OI and MI conj. in weak verbs, *-t(h)ar* (b) 237; *-t(h)er* (b) 360. In the strong verbs, (c) *do-gnether.* (b) *-gabar* 987 for OI *-gabthar* is influenced by *-berar* etc. On *ro brister* see § lix.

(2) The pres. subjunct. *s*-stems (see sv. *ā*-stems for some notes). This was a dying form in the 10th cent., reduced in MI to some dozen irregular verbs such as *ricc-, ticc-, téig-, ro-saig* etc.

Active sg. 1 (b) *-tias* (contrast LU M abs. *tiasur* 7882).

Sg. 2 (a) *tís* (simple proto.). (b) *-rís, -téis.*

Sg. 3 (d) *-táir, -dig.*

Pl. 3 w. conj. *-sat/-set*, (a) *-tísat.* (d) *-digset, -torsit* (see § lxvi).

Deponent sg. 1 (b) *-fessur* (see Note to l. 169).

Passive, none

Past Subjunctive

§ lxxxvi W. the secondary endings of the OI and MI imperf., see §§ lxxxiii and lxxxviii.

(1) *ā*-stems

Active sg. 1 *-aind* 563, 780, 996, 1036.

Sg. 2 *-t(h)a* 224, 687.

Sg. 3 *-ad/-ed* 58 f., 92, 206 f., 1016, 1322.

No pl. actives, nor deponents.

Passive sg. (b) *-thá* 243 (*-tha* in 305 is an expanded contraction), *-ta* 314 f., 342.

Pl. pass. *-gabdaís* 1270.

(2) *s*-stems

Active sg. 1 (b) *-rísaind* 995.

Sg. 2 (b) *-rísta, -tísta.*

Sg. 3 *-sad/-sed.* (b) *-tísad, -ríssed, -téissed.* (d) *-dichsed.* On *-diged*, 304, see Note. The *-tísad* for OI *-tísed* (contrast *-téissed*) is an ex. of the MI tendency, already beginning in OI, to generalise *-s^w-* for *-s^j-* in *s*-subjuncts.; cf. Ériu XXIV, 126.

Pl. 3 (b) *-rístís.*

Deponent pl. 1 (b) *-fesmais.*

Passive sg. *-festa.*

Future

§ lxxxvii (1) The *f*-stem. The MI tendency to simplification in verbs caused assimilations in the other fut. stems to the mostly weak-verb *f*-fut. stem, though the reverse is occasionally found (see (2) below). The rise of the simple protos., which joined the weak stems, facilitated this. In AMC, *benfa* and *-lenab* were formerly reduplicated futs.; *gairfither* and *con-melfi* were *é*-futs., *asnédfit* an *s*-fut., and *indisfet*, *-indraithfither*, and *érnaba* are simple prototonics. For the contaminated *-béraba* and *-dignestar* see (2) below. Cf. §lxxv.

OI sg. 1 abs. *-fa/-fea* already developed a form *-f(a)it* in late OI which became *-fat/-fet* in the course of the 10th cent., as seen in SR with five such versus only one *-fi* (VSR 292 ff.); TTr.1 has none without *-t*. Cf. *gébut* and *regut* below. In AMC, *-fit* in 1132 is more likely to represent a sp. for *-fet* than an ancient survival, *curfit-sa* in TTr.1 l. 1452 and even *firfit-sea* in RC XII, 82, notwithstanding; cf. *-dessitar* for *-dessetar* AMC 578.' There are in any case no exx. of *-fa/ -fe* in AMC. Dependent *-lenab* continues OI *-ub*.

Active sg. 1 (a) *asnédfit, indisfet*. (b) *-lenab*.

Sg. 2 (a) *lenfa, ricfa; fullfi*. (c) *con-melfi*. These continue OI sg. 2 *-fa/-fe*; the newer 'deponent' *-f(a)ir* is a post-MI development.

Sg. 3 (a) *anfaid*. (b) *-aineba, -benfa, -érnaba, -ícfa, -láife*. These represent older abs. *-faid* and conj. *-fa/-fea*; on *-aineba* and *-érnaba* see Note to l. 30.

There are no plurals, or deponents.

Passive sg. (no pls.). The *-d-/-th-* alternation is without significance. (a) *benfaider* (*-er* is 'incorrect' for *-ir*), *indisfithir, lécfithir*, rel. *gairfither*. (b) *-airlímfathar* (emendation), *-indisfither, -indraithfither*.

(2) *ē*-stems. There is no trace of the *eó-, éch-*, or *eóch*- fut. of very late MI in AMC, nor in TBC II L either, but they are occasionally found in CCath. (see VST ll. 3756 ff.) and the later parts of PH. There are almost no AMC exx. of the spread of the *é*-fut. to stems which did not take it in OI; TBC II L has only three cases, and CCath. nine (op. cit. ll. 3752–56). There are two instances of contamination in AMC; *-béraba*, with *bér-* influenced by the *f*-fut., and *-dignestar* with *do-gén-* influenced by the *s*-fut.

Active sg. 1 (a) *gébut*. (b), (c), and (d) all repeat the endingless *-éC^w* of OI. (b) *-coitél*. (c) *at-bér, do-bér, do-gén*. (d) *-tibér, -tibar, -epér, -dingen*,[16] *toimél*. For *-tibar* and *-dingen* see sg. 3 and Notes 528 and 731.

The history of *-at* (*-ut*) in sg. 1 is the same as that of *-fat/(-fet)*.

Sg. 2 Abs. and conj. both *-éCa*, as in OI. (a) *béra*. (b) *-coicéla*. (c) *do-géba* 673, *fo-géba*. (d) *-fuigbe* 335 (see sg. 3 below).

On *do-* for *fo-* in 673 see Note; probably scribal. In 335, *-fuigéba* might have been expected, but *-fuigbe* is a form with syncope, also found in OI; cf. sg. 3. The *-(a)ir* sg. 2 is absent in AMC (see §§lxxxii

---

[16] *-dingen* w. *-ng-* for *-g-* is a MI by-form which later became usual (AMC otherwise *-g-*). Note already in TTr.1 p. 95, sg. 1 *-dingiun*.

sg. 2 and lxxxv (1) sg. 2), the oldest ex. I know being in the very late section of PH.

Sg. 3 The expected (a) *-éCaid* does not occur in AMC. (b) *béraba*, see Note 34. (c) *do-méla* is the normal conj. *-éCa*. (d) *-tibre* is another case of the by-form of OI *-tibéra* with syncope, first seen in very late OI and in SR; cf. §lxxxviii (2) and sg. 2 *-fuigbe*. In sg. 1 *-tibar* and *-dingen* the short second vowels are inferred from the syncope-forms *-tibr-* and *-dingn-*. Sg. 3 relative *aicéras* 274 is an ex. of the rel. sg. 3 *-as* termination, the only fut. one in AMC.

No pl. 1 or 2.

Pl. 3 The expected (a) *-éCait* does not occur in AMC, but (a) *gébdait* is a form for *gébait* plus meaningless suffixed pron., found sometimes in LU, PH, and TBC II L; see GOI p. 271, and Celtica XII, 91 f. on the general development. Conj. *-éCat* is seen in (b) *-scérat*, and in (c) *do-gébut*.

Passive sg. (no pls.) (a) *gébth*air, relat. *tóicébth*ar; (b) *-bérth*ar, *-cengélt*ar (or (a) *cengélt*air, see Note 337), *-gébth*ar; (c) *do-bérth*ar, *do-géntar* 1280, 1298, 1302. (d) *-dignes*tar is a contamination of the normal *é*-fut. *-digentar* w. the *s*-fut.; see §lxxxviii (3) passive, and JS's note on *faigbistar* in ZCP III, 479, n.2, 'a barbarous mixture' of the *s*- and *f*-futs.

(3) The *s*-stems. These were dying out rapidly in MI. SR has ten *s*-stems, including *fo-loing* and of course *ro-fitir*; they seem to be not rare in LU, but this is mostly true of the OI texts there only; TTr.1 has six, including *fo-loing*; PH has a couple (but Atkinson takes several others as being *s*-futs. when they are really *s*-subjuncts., without considering their syntax), and CCath. the same; but TBC II L has 15 (but one must remember that it both archaises and uses old sources). As for AMC, it has *s*-futs. from the verbs *at-raig*, *fo-loing*, *ro-fitir*, and *ithid* only; but if we discount TBC II L this is perfectly in line with MI texts from TTr.1 on.

Active sg. 1 (d) *-érus*.

Sg. 2 (b) *-ísa*.

Pass. sg. (no pls.) (a) relat. *foelustar* (*fo-loing*, simple proto.). (d) *-dignestar* (see *-digentar* above, *é*-fut. pass.). These endings continue the OI ones.

(4) The future of *téit*. This was made on the suppletive stem *reg-*, beside which *rag-* appears already in SR, LU, and TTr.1; *reg-* becomes more uncommon as MI proceeds, e.g. TBC II L and CCath. have *rag-* only (both w. the occasional variant *rach-*), whereas AMC has three exx. of *reg-* and only one of *rag-*; see §lxxxviii (4). Possibly this last is due to the scribe; certainly the state of *reg-/rag-* in AMC is no argument for a late date.

Sg. 1 (a) *regut* (on *-ut* for *-at* see § lxxxvii (2), sg. 1).

Sg. 3 (b) *-rega*.

Pl. 1 (a) *regmait*. Apart from *berma*, this is the only ex. in AMC of the abs. pl. 1 of a primary tense. The *-t* is of the same origin as that in post-OI abs. futs. sg. 1 above; see § lxxxii, pl. 1.

(5) The asigmatic reduplicated future. This died out almost entirely in early MI; there are however some ten exx. in TBC II L, the explanation of which must be the same as with the *s*-fut., (3) above, on the dying out of that fut., and the survivals in TBC II L, with the occasional *at-cichera* (from *at-cí*; a freak-form) and *íb-* (from *ibid*) lasting later. There are none in AMC.

The Conditional

§ lxxxviii Essentially the same secondary endings as in the imperf. and past subjunct., see §§ lxxiii and lxxxvi. Some of the comments on the stems under Future apply equally to the Conditional.

(1) The *f*-stem.

Active sg. 1 (a) *no millfind*.

Sg. 3 (a) *no légfad, no lessaigfed*.

Pl. 3 (b) *-tallfatís*.

No passives.

(2) The *ē*-stem.

Active sg. 1 (b) *-béraind*. (c) *do-béraind*.

Sg. 2 (c) *do-bértha* 562.

Sg. 3 (a) *no gébad*. (c) *do-bérad*. (d) *-tibred*.

Pl. 1 (c) *do-bérmais*.

Pl. 3 (d) *-tibratis*.

No passives.

In *-tibred* and *-tibratis* there is the same syncope as in the fut. (OI *-tibérad, -tibértais* without syncope; see § lxxxvii (2), sg. 3). The depalatalisation seen in *-tibratis*, accepted beside *-tibr*[j]- in the Classical language (IGT III, 185, l. 20) seems a late MI feature (cf. CCath. 3454 *-tibratais*) which eventually drove out *-tibr*[j]- in EMod.I.

(3) The *s*-stem.

Active sg. 1 (b) *-ísaind*.

Passive of deponent, sg. (b) *-festa*.

Passive sg. (d) *-dignesta*, w. the same contamination as in § lxxxvii (2), passive.

(4) The conditional of *téit*.

Active sg. 1 (a) *no ragaind*.

(5) No conditionals.

Past Tenses of the Indicative

§lxxxix The OI categories of *s*-preterites (weak verbs and a few strong ones), *t*-prets. (strong verbs in -*l*, -*r*, and some in -*g* and -*m*), and suffixless prets. (the other strong verbs) remained in MI; but as an aspect of the simplification of the verb and clarification of the endings typical of MI the second and third groups were beginning to join the *s*-prets., usually by suffixing *s*-endings to the presential stem, but sometimes to the *t*-pret. or suffixless stems. The last two of the three were not uncommon in SR and non-H texts in LU, but this was soon overtaken by the *s*-endings, and the others probably barely outlasted the MI period apart from a small group of the modern 'irregular' verbs; cf. §lxxv. The simple prototonics and the denominatives from verbal nouns also took the *s*-pret., in their quality as weak verbs.

In AMC the following recruits to the *s*-prets. may be noted (ignoring simple strong verbs now wholly weak, simple protos. w. no deutero. forms found in AMC, and denominatives; see these in Hull pp. 342–345).

(A) *t*-prets.: *érgis, beris, comlis, do-romel, fóbrais*; with the *t*-stem preserved but plus -*s*(-), *bertais, -ruachtus*.

(B) Suffixless prets.: *benais*, past ind. -*r choem* (the normal simple proto. is *cumcais*), *fuarus, -fuair*, past ind. *ro lámus, saidis*. Formerly suffixless (but now with presential stem), contaminated w. *t*-pret., *bendais*.

Set beside the number of *t*-prets. and suffixless prets. which did still survive in AMC, this total is unimpressive, and the evidence hardly suggests a specially late date for AMC.

The question of the new MI pret. and past ind. 'deponent' endings of active verbs in the *s*-pret. sg. 3 -*astar*/-*estar*, pl. 1 -*samar*/-*semar*, and pl. 3 -*satar*/-*setar*, and their statistical and chronological relation to the old active terminations is a very complicated one, and need not be discussed here beyond noting that the active terminations are much commoner than the newer 'deponent' ones in AMC. This agrees well enough with the general situation in non-saga texts of the latter part of the MI period. Cf. McE, TTr.1, p. 195 and IMN 1961, p. 41 f.

The *s*-Preterite

§xc There are no survivals of the OI absolute endings in MI except in the 3rd persons; in the 1st and 2nd persons their places were taken by the corresponding conjuncts. Hence both the abs. and conj. sg. 1 *us*(-*as*)/-*es*(-*ius*); 2 -*ais*/-*is*; pl. 1 -*sam*/-*sem* (-*sium*); 2 -*said*/-*sid*.

In the sg. 3 the abs. -*ais*/-*is*, which is infrequent in SR (18 exx., VSR 524 ff.) and TTr.1 (6 exx., p. 102) and considering its size, in PH, is very common in TBC II L (144 exx.), which McE loc. cit. attributes to its archaising tendencies; but was pretty uncommon again in CCath. (24 exx., RC XXXVI, 324). However, it seems to have regained some popularity in literary circles as a 'high-class' form in EMod.I (cf. Celtica X, 135)—strikingly so in Keating. The very numerous cases in AMC are hardly expected in a text of this character and probable date. The sg. 3 conj. pret. has no ending, cf. below, and this remains to the present day in the past indic.

In the pl. 3 the absolute OI pret. ending was -*sait*/-*sit*. There are seven in SR (VSR 753–54), and LU has 28, but these are almost all in OI texts. TTr.1 has none, TBC II L only one, and CCath. none. It died out in MI, its place in independ. constr. being taken by conj. -*sat*/-*set*, of which there are already 11 exx. in SR (VSR 748–51). AMC has two abs. -*sit* (*ansit* and *timoircsit*); and only one conj. pret. form for abs. construction, *gabsat*. Cf. § lxvii f.

§ xci Active sg. 1 The only exx. are (a) *fuarus*; (b) -*fuarus*. Both are cases of suffixless prets. taking *s*-pret. endings.

Sg. 2 (a) *troscis*.

Sg. 3 There is a very considerable number of independent forms, (a), -(*a*)*is*, e.g. *iadais*, *sínis*. These include old simple strong verbs having become wholly weak, like *benais*, *cingis*; simple protos. like *atlaigis*, *fácbais*, *tócbais*; and denominatives like *naidmis*. On *tidnais* see Note to l. 613. For a complete list see Hull p. 342 f. The (endingless) dependent form is much rarer, since here the past indicative largely took over; the total is only eight:- (a) *no-s imarchuir*, *no-s turim*; (b) -*ben*, -*dam*, -*gaib*, -*fuair*, -*ráthaig*, -*tadaill*.

Pl. 1 (a) *imrásium*.

Pl. 3 (a) *ansit*, *timoircsit*; *gabsat*, w. conj. ending for abs., see § lxvii.

The new deponent endings in active sense (see § xcii *ad fin*.).

Pl. 3 (a) *fessaiter*.

Passive, see § xcv.

The *s*-Past Indicative

§ xcii All forms are those of the corresponding *s*-pret. conjunct, with infixed or preceding *ro* (or being in origin *ro*-less perfectives, e.g. *tucc*), and in (b) and (d) with initial preverb.

Active sg. 1 (a) *tucus*, *ro lámus*; (b) *ní ro chaithes*, *ní ro fhrecrus*; (d) -*tardus*, -*r thoimles*, -*ruachtus*.

Sg 2 (b) *ní ro throscis*; (c) *do-rindis*, *ro thomlis*; (d) -*derndais*.

Sg. 3 Hull (p. 343 f., q.v.) gives a sizeable list (some of them however are pres. ind.), all with the expected endingless -C^w/-C^j, or rarely -V. A selection is as follows:- (a) with infixed *ro*, *tuarcaib*; w. prefixed *ro, ro ben, ro lá, ro fhaillsig, ro gab, ro esairg, ro oslaic*; *ro*-less perfective, *tuc(c)*; (b) *-r choem, co ra-m dígaib, -r sháid, ná ro-s teilg*; (c) w. infixed *ro, do-rat, do-rala, do-ruachell, do-rigne, fo-t-ruair, do-romel*; (d) w. infixed *ro, -tarla, -derna*.

Pl. 1 (a) with prefixed *ro, ro bensum, ro ráidsium, ro throscsium*; (b) *ní ro-s bensum, -r bensumm, co ro gaibsium*; (d) w. infixed *ro, -dernsamm*.

Pl. 3 (a) *ro lécsit*; (b) *-r throiscset*; (c) w. infixed *ro, do-rigset*, and with prefixed, *ro thomailset*; (d) w. infixed *ro, -tardsat, -dernsat*.

On *-sit* for *-set* in *ro lécsit* see § lxviii.

The new deponent endings in active sense, the only exx. in AMC.

Sg. 3 (a) *ro aittrebastar, ro scrútustar*.

Pl. 3 (a) *ro fhannaigsetar, ro-t tairbirsetar*.

Compare the pret. pl. 3 *fessaiter*, § xci.

The *t*-Preterite and Past Indicative

§ xciii   This was a dying category in MI, in process of joining the *s*-pret. (§ lxxxix), either in the contaminated form e.g. sg. 1 *at-rachtus*, or in the regular *s*-pret. manner on the presential (and simple proto.) stem, e.g. *ro éirgius*. Only a few verbs still kept the *-t-* by the beginning of EMod.I (*at-bert, at-racht, ro-siacht*, and *do-riacht/do-ruacht*, which last itself soon disappeared as a verb). SR has 28 verbs with *t*-prets., but even in TTr.1 (p. 110 f.) there are only seven, i.e. the above 4 plus *ad-anacht, at-bailt*, and *do-airngert*, while CCath. has eight, i.e. the same 4 above plus *do-bert, for-congart, fris-gart*, and *do-comort*. TBC II L is odd man out in having considerably more, but its great length and the factor mentioned in Introduction p. xxi probably account for this. Thus the *t*-pret. seems to have undergone a catastrophic collapse between the late 10th century and the middle of the 11th. There are only five in AMC, *at-bert, do-bert, fo-róbairt, at-racht*, and *ro-siacht*.

In OI the sg. 3 ending was $-C^w t^w$, but in final unstressed syllables this was already beginning to become $-C^j t^j$ in the 9th century, except in *-cht*, which remained. There is a case of $-C^w t^w$ in AMC in *fo-rórbart* 707 beside *fo-rórbairt* 348 etc.

The pl. 1 and 3 were deponent in form in OI, and continued so throughout; they and the corresponding forms in the suffixless pret. have given the equivalent modern endings of all verbs past indic., *-(e)amar, -(e)adar*.

In AMC, pret. active sg. 3 (c) *as-bert/at-bert, at-racht, do-bert, ro-siacht*; (d) *-epert, -roacht*.

Pl. 3 (c) *at-rachtatar*.

Past Indicative Active (with infixed *ro*)

Sg. 1 (c) *atom-raracht*.

Sg. 3 (c) *fo-róbairt (fo-rórbart, fo-rórbairt)*.

The Suffixless Preterite

§ xciv   The OI sub-categories of reduplicated and long-vowel prets. have no significance as to the endings by now and are ignored here. Most of the verbs in the AMC list below are old perfects or preterito-perfects. Here the verb endings were added directly to the final root-consonant without an intervening stem-consonant. The endings are active in the singular, except of course in deponent verbs, and deponent in the pl. 1 and 3. Most of the forms under Past Indic. were originally inherently perfect or preterito-perfect, so that their original perfectivity is not clearly apparent except in *ro-gáidetar*. For the preterito-present see § lvi.

It happens that several of these preterites belong to common verbs with basic meanings like 'see, hear, know, come, get, reach' etc., and these have survived to the present day among the 'irregular' verbs. The rest were absorbed into the *s*-prets. at various times in MI and EMod.I. SR has about 50 actives and deponents, TTr.1 about 35, CCath. about 20. In AMC there are 19, which shows a considerable drop from TTr.1 (which is however nearly twice the length of AMC), but agrees well with CCath. Apart from the substantive verb (see § xcix) there are not, in AMC, any exx. of the intrusive *-d-* and final *-d* which appear in the sg. persons of a few suffixless prets. such as *-cualaid* in CCath.

The Preterite

Active sg. 1 (c) *fuarus* (joined *s*-pret.); (d) *-fuarus* (ditto).

Sg. 3 (a) *luid*; (c) *do-lluid*; (d) *-fuair*.

Pl. 1 (a) *lodmar*.

Deponent sg. 1 (b) *-sessar*; (d) *-tarrusar*.

Pl. 3 (b) *-fetar* 162 (see Note).

Past Indicative

Active sg. 1 (a) *tánuc*; (b) *-ránuc*; (c) *at-chonnarc, ro-chuala* (*at-chuala*); (d) *-acca, -cuala, -tudchad, -dechad.*

Sg. 2 (b) *-tánac*; (d) *-tudchad.*

Sg. 3 (a) *tairnic, táinic*; (b) *-tánic*; (c) *at-chuala, do-m-árfaid, ad-uaid, do-chóid* (*ro-chóid*), *do-m-ánaic*; (d) *-cuala, -dechaid, -dessid.*

Pl. 1 (a) *ráncumar*; (c) *it-chótamar*; (d) *-dechumar.*

Pl. 3 (a) *ro gáidetar, tarnactar, táncatar*; (c) *at-chódutar, -dessitar.*

Preterite and Past Indicative Passive

§ xcv   Singular. There are no exx. of the old abs. forms, which died out by MI. Most OI past tense passives were assimilated to the endings of the weak verbs and to some strong verbs, i.e. *-ad/-ed*. For a long list of these in AMC see Hull, p. 347 f. As they offer no features of interest they may be omitted here, except to mention that the inherited perfect pass. *do-rónad* of l. 8 etc. has been replaced by the new coining on the active stem *do-rigned* in l. 211 etc. Of surviving strong verbs, there are no exx. of the endings *-cht*, *-lt*, *-rt*, and *-ét*, and the only instances are the *-s* of dental stems in *do-árfas*, *-tárfas* 817 (*-closs* 139, already established in SR, being the only ex. of the characteristic MI spread of the *-s* to an old *-th* passive, OI *-cloth*), and the *-th* of vowel-stems in *-fríth*.

Plural. OI *-tha/-thea*. In AMC there are one *-thea* and two *-ta* (*-sta* and *-nta*), see § lx. For the passive in *-(a)it* see § lxii.

THE VERB 'TO BE'[17]

The Substantive Verb

Present Indicative

§ xcvi Sg. 1 For (d) *-tú*, *-tó* see § lxxxii.

Pl. 1 (c) *atám* (*atáum* 723 is a sp. for *atáam*); (d) *-támm*.

Pl. 3 (c) *atát* (*atáut*, cf. *atáum*; for these *-áa-* cf. TTr.1, p. 127 f.).

These sps. are all normal in MI, and the forms w. abs. endings *atámait* and *atáit* do not appear till late MI (but see just below), though the conj. endings in *atám*, *atát* lingered much later. *Atám* in 1260 is not pl. 1 in sense, but an ex. of the 'royal *we*', i.e. 'I'.

The nasalising relat. constr. *oltás*, 'than (which is ...)' occurs five times in AMC; sg. 1 *oldú* (B *oldá*) once and sg. 3 *oltá* three times. The common alternative with *in-* for *ol-* is found once in AMC, rel. *inás* (for older *indás*). See TTr.1, p. 126 f. The abs. pl. 3 ending mentioned above, in *atáit*, appears once in TTr.1 *andáit*, and *-dáit* is commoner than *-dát* in PH.

The relative *fil* is almost wholly indeclinable and impersonal in AMC, and *fail*, already found in OI, occurs only once, 1037; there is no instance of *file*. There are however three cases of personal forms, all non-relative pl. 3 (-)*file(a)t*. This was beginning in SR, once in pl. 1 *-failmet* 6320, and otherwise solely in pl. 3 (cf. TTr.1 p. 129); and is still the case in TBC II L.

The 'passive' (impersonal) *filter* 359, relat., seems to be rare at any period, presumably because *atá* took over the rel. function in MI, see § c, paragr. (C), and 'passive' (*a*)*táthar* was familiar from OI on. For the uses of *fil* see the Glossary and § c.

---

[17] Full collections are given in the Glossary, and only matters of special interest are discussed here.

Present Subjunctive, non-perfective

§xcvii This was being replaced, already in MI, by the perfective.
Sg. 1 *beó*, not yet *beór* with the late MI deponent ending of this
person, found already in LL and MD; cf. §lxxxv, sg. 1.
Sg. 2 *-bé* 682, 1299. Probably the OI conj. *-bé* in these two temporal
clauses, where OI would have had *no mbé*.
The other non-perfective forms in AMC all have the expected *be*(-)
(cf. next §).

Future

§ xcviii Sg. 1 *biat* is the OI abs. *bia* plus the new *-t* attached to sg. 1,
see § lxxxvii (1) and (2), sg. 1. But sg. 1 *bet* in 293, 294, and 516, relat.
bess 234, and pl. 3 *-bet* all have the *be-* of the pres. subjunct. where OI
had respectively *bia*, *bias*, and *-biat* (but impers. sg. *-bether* 717 is good
OI). These are exx. of the confusion between the pres. subjunct. and
the fut. which was beginning in OI in the substantive verb and
expressing itself in the sporadic use of the former for and beside the
latter.

Preterite

§ xcix The forms are unremarkable except for sg. 1 *-bádus* and
impers. ('passive') *-bádus*, for OI and MI suffixless pret. act. *-bá* (cf. *ro
bá* 289, 841) and MI 'passive' *-bás* (OI *-both*) respectively. The
development to *-bás*, 'passive' (cf. l. 716), is analogous to that of pass.
-cloth becoming *-clos* (§xcv), and, like it, is already the form in SR and
thereafter. The sg. 1, active, is an ex. of a suffixless pret. going over to
the *s*-pret. (§xciii). The *-d-* is a neologism which became common in
late MI and thereafter in the sg. persons of a few suffixless prets. which
had joined the *s*-prets. (§xciv), as seen in e.g. OI and MI sg. 2 *-cuala*
becoming late MI *-cualadais* (cf. Bergin, Ériu I, 140 ff.; the two exx. he
mentions in SR seem isolated so early). It appears, well established, in
past indic. sg. 1 *ro bádus* and sg. 2 *ro bádais* in PH (chiefly the late parts)
and in CCath. 553 sg. 2 *ro bádhais*.

Some usages of the Substantive Verb

§ c (A) In OI the 'subject' of the impersonal *fil*, when a noun, was
in the accusative. This was becoming replaced in MI by the more
logical nominative, though the acc. still occurs as a survival in Classical
verse. In AMC, noun subjects are mostly either nom., as in *fil sund út
bar cara* 1252 f., or ambiguous, i.e. those whose nom. and acc. were the
same, as in *fil in popul* 336, or where the spelling is ambiguous, or where

L

nasalisation by the article or noun could not be shown. *In filet aígid* 150 has nom. because *fil* is here personalised. Still, there are five or six exx. of the accusative:- *i fil cluca* (in verse) 179; *fil liumm* .... *ulidetaid a étaig do bein de* 197 f. (but this could be a case of acc. for nom., § xxii); *fil dechmaid sund* 258; *ór ná fil lem-sa in mbroind-sin* 891; and *fail dáim n-annsa in bar ndochum* 1037.

Both usages occur in SR; TTr.1 (p. 129) has no visible accusatives; TBC II L has only one probable acc. and one clear nom., the rest being ambiguous (VST ll. 1916–22). In the large number in PH, glossary, there are no certain accusatives and only five certain noms., the rest being ambiguous. In CCath. Sommerfelt's exx. (RC XXXVIII, 41) are all ambiguous, *fil gné n-aill* being an ex. of stereotyped ambiguous neuter. The Bardic schools still inculcated acc. subj. when the noun was indefinite (BST § 214, 25 f. and p. 155), and hence it may be found in CEMod.I prose as late as the 17th cent. The above evidence on AMC is scanty, but hardly suggests a late date.

(B) Use of *fil* for -*tá* introduced by a prep. in a relat. clause.

Here OI had -*tá* etc., e.g. *forsa tá* 'on which it is', but *fil* began to be substituted in MI. AMC has three exx. of (*h*)*i fil*, 'in which it is' 179, 534, 1296, beside others of the older type such as *'ga tá*, *'ca tú*, *hi támm*, *i tát*. There are two cases of this in VT 2 (MSS E and R), *i fail* 1242 and *hi fil* 2000, the second however in a Preface; see DTL § 27. SR apparently has four (591, 636, 6135, 6137), the last three being (*h*)*i fail*. It seems absent in TTr.1, and on the contrary note *hi táat* there, l. 911; but PH and CCath. have both constructions. It is notable that *i fil* 'in which (it) is' seems particularly common.

(C) Use of *atá* for *fil* in direct relat. clauses.

OI had *fil(e)* in these, but *atá* was faintly beginning to take its place in SR, in 7708 *is hé atá*, and 7948 *cia dath atá . . .?* In TTr.1 note only *in lucht atáat* (p. 127), but in PH it has become common. AMC has 12 exx. of *fil* and one of impersonal *filter*, but only two of *atá* and one of *atáum* in the constr. in question. Here again there is nothing to suggest that AMC is particularly late in MI.

(D) *Fil, fail* introducing statements in the sense 'there is/are' are common in SR but absent in TTr.1 (p. 129). AMC has nine sg. exx. (one of them *Fail* . . . .), and one pl.

The Copula

§ci Among the OI parts of the copula there were too many which caused ambiguity because their forms were too similar to each other or were insufficiently 'marked'. This led in early MI to a new set of 'personalised' forms, almost all using sg. 3 *is, ba* etc. with the addition of appropriate personal endings. Hence e.g. pres. ind. sg. 1 *isam*, 2 *condat*; pres. subjunctive sg. 1 *bam*; fut. sg. 2 and pl. 3 *bidat*; pret. pl. 3 *bat*, etc. etc., respectively for OI *am*, *conda*, *ba*, *be*, *bit*, *batir* etc. etc. This was beginning in late OI (Fél. 2, Sept. 8th, pres. ind. sg. 2 negat. *nít*), and had become common by SR, which has 29 exx. totalling 23 different forms. It occurs, not rarely, in e.g. 11th cent. texts in LU (note *conidam* 'so that I am', still later in LU (10285 H), cf. *conadam* AMC 1138); and is familiar e.g. in PH, TBC II L (for a list see VST pp. 89 ff.) and CCath. However, it seems to have died out very early in EMod.I apart from Classical doctrine and sporadic survivals. The Bardic language rarely uses them, e.g. *ó 'sam*, IGT II, p. 56, ex. 376; *robam*, IGT III, 63, ex. 537; Ó Bruad. II, xviii, 3 [*i*]*sam* and II, xx, 14 *ním*, both in Classical metres. Normally, they were killed off by the constr. of impers. sg. 3 plus noun or pron. sg. or pl., e.g. *is mé*, *ba h-iad*, which was beginning faintly in SR and more in the 11th cent. (see TTr.1, pp. 169 ff.), and is now universal.

§ cii   There are five personalised forms in AMC; the sg. 1 *conadam*, and *nacham* 'so that I am not'; 2 *isat*; pres. subjunct. sg. 1 *bam*; and fut. sg. 2 *bidat* (but this is an emendation). In TTr.1 there seem to be 7 forms (11 occurrences). It is hazardous to conclude anything from this, TTr.1 being nearly twice the length of AMC, and the figures so small. At least it can hardly prove that AMC is much later than TTr.1.

Side by side with the new personalised forms, some of the original OI ones still survived all the time into MI, with the usual sporadic archaising occurrences later, chiefly in and due to CEMod.I verse usage (see Celtica X, 129 n.). Indeed, the old set of forms seems rather commoner in late MI than the personalised ones. The chief are pres. ind. sg. 1 *am*, 2 *at/it*, pl. 3 *at/it*; past subjunct. pl. 3 (-)*betis/-btis*; pret. *batar/-btar*; and past indic. *robtar/-rbtar*. *Betis* occurs notably after *amal*, a usage which lasted late in MI.

The following *original* OI-type personal forms, i.e. exclusive of sg. 3, survive in AMC:- Pres. ind. sg. 1 *am*; 2 *at* (*it* 779); pl. 3 *at*, rel. *at*, non-rel. negat. *nidat*; past subjunct. *betís*; fut. pl. 3 -*bat*; pret. *batir*. Note that the late spellings past subjunct. sg. 3 *dámad* 523 and *gémad* 1321 for *diamad* 642 and *cémad* 1317 could well be due to the scribe.

§ ciii   The impersonal use of the sg. 3 copula for pl. w. pl. noun or pronoun, mentioned in § ci, is found only three times in AMC, in 190, 630 f., and 796; there are seven or eight in TTr.1 (p. 169 f.). The distinction between pres. ind. non-relat. *is* and relat. *as*^L disappeared when their unstressed vowels both became /ə/, and confusion set in in their spelling, though the word could continue to lenite when relative.

In AMC the former is regularly *is* and the latter is *as* six times and *us* (contraction) once, but the relative is also written *is* 18 times, showing that the pronunciation of both was identical.

§civ   The OI pres. ind. sg. 3 *conid* 'so that it is' and *dianid* 'to which it is' continued to be common all through MI, but reductions to *conad*, *dianad* and other forms were appearing. AMC has numerous *conid*, but only once *conad*, in the personal form sg. 1 *conadam*, and two *dianad* but no *dianid* or other form. In TTr.1 (p. 151) there are some 20 *conid* versus only one *conad*, and three *dianid* but none of the reduced forms. PH and CCath. have both *conid* and *conad*, PH almost exclusively *conid* but mostly *dianad*. *Corab/corob/corup*, perfective pres. subjunct. sg. 3, is found 6 times in AMC; in 334 and 338 it introduces final clauses, but in 1173 (2), 1174, and 1179 they appear to be optative (cf. EIL pp. 193 and 255), a development not necessarily quite so late as GM there suggests.

§cv   In the independent perfect, OI *ropo*^{L} began to lose *-o* in MI (by elision) before *V-*, *fh-*, and *sh-*, but not before *C-*. This seems rare early (SR has none, and it is apparently very rare in LU also), but commoner in later MI. TTr.1 has both, and in PH and later texts elision is the rule. AMC has no exx. of *robo* and only three of *rop/rob* 41, 223, 752. In the depend. forms, where OI has *-rbo*^{L}, elision of *-o* was frequent in MI, hence *nírb*^{L} etc. In SR there are some dozen exx. of *-rb* before *V-*, *fh-*, and *sh-*, and in CEMod.I, and to the present day it was and is common. So in AMC, *nírb V-* in 1314, 1320 and *nírb sh-* in 883, though elision is absent in *nírbo fherr* 221 f. TTr.1, pp. 165–168 seems to have only one ex. of *-rb V-* versus seven of *-rbo*. The further stage *-r*^{L} in these contexts, occurring twice in SR (3038, 6903), is rare in MI and EMod.I. TTr.1 appears to have only one (*nachar fhécen*, l. 1403) and AMC has none, though in the Classical verse language it is accepted as a variant of *-rbh* before *V-* and *fh-* (BST p. 162). Before conss., however, the MI *-rbo/-rba* usually remained (regularly so in SR), but could be simplified first to *-rb* (4 exx. in SR; apparently none in TTr.1); but the resulting clumsy *-/rvC(C)/-* was further simplified to *-/rC(C)/-* (only one in SR, 3304). The process seems to have been slow. So, TTr.1 has no exx. of *-rb C(C)-* and only one of *-r C-* (? *nár mó* l. 73) as against about 18 of *-rbo C(C)-*. AMC has three *-rba C-* (548, 725, 837) and two *-r C-* (*nír b-* 223 and *nár n-* 630).

The copula forms in *-rbs-* and particularly *-rs-*, found not only in the past indic. but also in pres. ind. and pres. subjunct., occur already in SR (*órsam* 'since I am' 1786, *nárbsat* 'that you were not' 1387), and still in late EMod.I prose, their greatest popularity having been apparently

in the 12th and very early 13th cents. It may be significant that they are
not found in AMC nor apparently in TTr.1.

§ cvi   The special forms of the simple and simple prototonic verbs
in primary tenses in relative clauses were all obsolete long before the
probable date of AMC except for the sg. 3 in *-as/-es*, which has
survived to the present day. AMC has the following:- pres. ind. *brogas,
coilles, fásus, techtas, cuimgess*, and *érgius*; and é-fut. *aicéras*. Whether
the pres. ind. pl. 1 *berma*, in a clause which is syntactically relat. in MI
but non-relat. in OI, is a form representing the OI relat. or non-relat.
is a moot point (cf. § lxxxii, pl. 1).

The OI construction of direct relat. clauses in which other tenses,
moods, numbers and persons took *no-* prefixed to all simple non-relat.
forms lacking any other conjunct particle to make them relat., whether
leniting or nasalising according to the type of clause, died out in MI
through the dropping of *no-* in this function. The exx. of *no-* in AMC
all introduce either secondary tenses or infixed pronouns (§ xlv), and
are not present merely because the verb is relative; there are no AMC
cases of *no-* due purely to verbal relativity alone.

§ cvii   Indirect relat. clauses of the type called 'cleft' sentences
where the antecedent in the introductory copula-clause is not in
apposition to 'who, whom, which' but is an adverb or prepositional
phrase (that is to say, the sentence is e.g. of the type 'it is *thus* that he
did it') are not normally treated as relative clauses at all in OI (see GOI
p. 320). In MI, however, relat. constr. became regular in such
sentences, though it is not universal, e.g. in TTr.1; thus see there
p. 186. It seems normal in AMC.

On the type of OI indirect rel. clause where the verb is nasalised see
GOI pp. 316–319 (omitting § 501, which is the direct relative). This
survived to some extent into early MI, particularly in temporal
clauses, and sporadically as an archaism later, but was normally
replaced in early MI by the leniting type of relative constr. (cf. TTr.1,
p. 184 ff.). I know only four exx. of the nasalising type in SR (1400,
1477, 4030, and 7564), and TTr.1 has only three (TTr.1 p. 185). In
PH I know only 3725 ff. *in tan .... ro mbá-sa* and 6614 *cindus ro
mbábair*, both in probably early sections. There are three instances in
AMC, of which two are uncertain. In temporal clauses, *in tan ro mbá*
841 'when I was' is certain; B's *céin bam beó* 659, 'as long as I may be
alive' could be read as *ba mbeó*, as in OI, but *bam beó* w. personalised
copula seems more likely; cf. § ci. In a comparative clause *amal ro*

fhaillsiged 354 is ambiguous, since the punctum delens over the *f* may represent either nasalisation or lenition; see Note to l. 354. Otherwise, constructions where OI would have had nasalisation lack it in AMC; see ll. 285, 289, 572 (*céin beó*), 682, all temporal, and *crét érgius* 699 'why does he get up?' In the first four the relative lenition of *b-* is of course not written but must have existed.

§ cviii   The demonstrative particle a^N/an, '(all) those (who), (all) that (which)', functioning as antecedent relative pronoun, occurs seven times in AMC, and the later ina^N four times (the alternatives i^N and ana^N are lacking there). See Glossary 4 $\mathbf{a}^N$ and $\mathbf{ina}^N$.

The early form, as in OI, is a^N/an; i^N and ana^N/ina^N are later (i^N is specially common in PH, but $(i)na^N$ (with dependent verb-form) seems limited to late sections there). *An* normally occurs only before *ro*; but note also e.g. *an condigim* in AMC 519; cf. SR 1874 *an con-dn-íis* and VT 2. 365 *an fo-gebed* (but in MS E only). The first exx. of ana^N/ina^N that I know are SR 336 '*na fail* and 3394 '*na fuair*, and cf. LU 4253 M *ina ndéni*; cf. VT 2. 3098 MSS E and R *inna nderna* in a Peroration. The last two of these take the dependent verb-form. Ana^N/ina^N seem scarcely to have outlived MI, and they were apparently not accepted in Classical grammatical teaching, the use of a^N being normal there (BST p. 273). Later exx. of ana^N/ina^N are archaisms, no doubt.

As regards the constructions taken by these words, in OI and usually in early MI the verb-form is the independent, mostly with a^N/an, but in MI the dependent form was overtaking it. In TTr.1 (p. 187) both verb-forms are found, regardless of whether the word is a^N etc. or ina^N etc.; cf. a^N with both verb-forms in PH. In AMC, contrast *a ndo-m-gní* 'that which makes me' 1133, with a^N and independent construction versus *ina-m thoirched* 290 'that which might reach me', with dependent; cf. the others in the Glossary. B's reading *anroboi* in AMC 262 is treated as *an ro boi* in KM's edition, independent, cf. TTr.1 p. 187 l. 18 *an ro baí*; but *an roboi*, sp. for *an roba*, is of course also possible though perhaps less likely.

GLOSSARY

This is intended to be complete for all words. For very common words, or forms without noteworthy variation (most adverbs, non-conjugated simple prepositions, conjunctions, etc.), references are given to a few examples only. When a form in the text is an expanded contraction or an emendation, this is not normally mentioned here, and the actual manuscript form should be checked in the text and in the variants if there is doubt. References in roman figures preceded by '§' are to sections of the Appendix.

(1) *Terminology and arrangement*

The neuter gender is taken as obsolete except in a few stereotyped cases (§§ vii-viii), and nouns are given with their Middle Irish genders; when common gender, 'm./f.'; when the gender is unknown none is mentioned. When a preposition governed both acc. and dat. but the actual noun-case in an example is ambiguous, it is classed according to early Irish usage; so *isin tellach* 171 'acc.' but *hi tellach* 1156 'dat.' On the obsolescence of this distinction in Middle Irish see §§ xxiii-xxiv.

The term 'past indicative' distinguishes the form of the old perfect tense from that of the old preterite, the two having fallen together in Middle Irish in meaning but not in form. The old perfective subjunctive is called 'subjunct. w. *ro*' since this too is by now formal. The terms 'independent' and 'dependent' replace the conventional 'absolute/deuterotonic' and 'conjunct/prototonic' opposition (except where it is relevant to retain these terms), since these had already disappeared as living categories in most verbs; see §§ lxix-lxxiv. Where there is no evidence in the text of a deuterotonic form of an old compound to establish that such survived, the pres. ind. sg. 3 independent is used as head-word; so **frecraid** not *fris-gair*, but **do-meil** not *toimlid*. A hyphen before a verb-form indicates that it is dependent; so *ticc* 160 but *-ticc* 86.

Loose nominal compounds, i.e. nonce-creations or those where each element has its separate meaning, are printed hyphenated, and the two elements are treated separately in the Glossary, the number, case, and (with nouns and adjectives) gender being given under the second elements only. But close compounds, where the two combine to change the meaning, or those of prep. plus noun or adj., are treated as single words. Thus *fír-gruth* 'genuine curds' but *fíriasc* 'salmon', *fritháilem* 'attendance', *forórda* 'gilded'.

A superscript L, N, or H indicates that the word in question lenites, nasalises or prefixes h to a following word. Oblique forms are given only if they differ from the headword. Where number-references are followed by 'n.', this means that there is a comment on the word in question in the Notes.

(2) *Finding words in the Glossary*

Forms not lemmatised are cross-referenced except where they would occur within very few lines of the headword. Words in *hV-* (with the exception of **hirophin**) should be sought under the appropriate vowel.

Middle Irish spelling varies a good deal and certain features which affect the Glossary may be noted here.

(a) VOWELS. The use of *i* to indicate the glide before C^j is commonly ignored by B. Headwords with these omissions are ranked alphabetically as if the missing *i* were present; thus, e.g., **céle**, **celebrad** and **célide** follow **ced** and precede **céim**.

142 GLOSSARY

Before C^w, *ea* sometimes appears for the normal *e*. This is treated alphabetically as *e* not *ea*; thus, e.g., **seag** follows **séda**.

In absolute final position after -C^j, -*e* and -*i* are interchangeable, both denoting the same higher allophone of /ə/; e.g. *aislingi* for *aislinge*. Similarly after -C^w, -*a* and -*ai* denote the same lower allophone of /ə/; e.g. *cadlai* for *cadla*. In such cases the headwords are given in -*e* and -*a* respectively.

The original diphthong or diphthongs, now monophthongised, usually written in the text as *ae* and *aí*, may also be spelt *oe* and *oí* (the second in both cases spelt, rarely, *aeí* and *oeí* and very rarely *uí*); e.g. *baeth*, *baíth*, *boíth* and *gaeth*, *goeth*. When more than one of these spellings occurs for a given word, the headword appears alphabetically where **ae** or **aí** belong, but under *aeí*, *oe*, *oí*, *oeí* or *uí*, whichever is appropriate, when they are the only spellings of a word in the text; e.g. **goeí** after **gob**.

(b) CONSONANTS. The phonemes /p, t, k, b, d, g, f, s/ are most usually written single (initially always so) but may sometimes be doubled. These doublings are all ignored in the alphabetical order, e.g. **abb** comes between **a** and **aball**.

On the other hand *ll*, *nn*, and *rr* are phonemically distinct from *l*, *n*, and *r* and are therefore always alphabetically separate in the glossary. In AMC, *nn* is more often spelt *nd*, and hence it has been found convenient here to order words containing *nn*, irrespective of historicity, alphabetically under *nd*.

No alphabetical distinction is made between -*m*- and -*mm*- when representing /m/; thus, e.g., **imim** follows **immglan**.

1 **a**^{L} particle before vocs. 150, 220, 236, etc.

2 **a**^{H} particle before numerals in counting 1 to 10, see 1 **dó** and **trí**.

3 **a** possess. adj. Sg. 3 m. *a*^{L} 'his' 9, 14, 17, etc.; f. *a*^{H} 'her' 41, 628, 1066, etc.; pl. 3 m./f. *a*^{N} 'their' 48, 292, 1343 n., etc.

4 **a**^{N}, **an** demonstr. rel. antecedent 'those who, that/those which' 262, 366, 519, 523, 696, 747, 1133. See 1 **ina** and § cviii.

5 **a**^{N} prep. see **i, hi**.

6 **a**^{H} prep. w. dat. 'from, out of' (see § xl) 25, 285, 603, etc. *A llos* see **los**. W. def. art., sg. *as(s)in* 129, 171, 297, etc.; pl. *as na* 746. W. suffixed obj. prons., sg. 3 m. *ass* 632, 1104, 1342; f. *e(i)ssi* 138, 256, 707, etc., *esti* 1116. W. possess. sg. 1 *as mo* 1052; 3 m. *as a* 635, 1077.

-**a**^{N}, -**sa**^{N} rel. particle suffixed to preps. '(to) whom, (with) which' etc. (see individual preps.); e.g. *ima* 'about which' 188, *forsa* 'on which' 588, etc.; w. 2 **ro** (q.v.) *for ar* 293.

1 **abb** m. 'abbot'. Sg. nom. 149; gen. *abbad* 342; dat. *abbaid* 194.

2 **abb** interj. 'ho!' 1035 n.

aball f. 'apple-tree'. Pl. dat. *ablaib* 473.

abann f. 'river'. Pl. nom. *aibne* 462.

abland f. 'small loaf'. Sg. acc. *ablaind* 224.

acca, accum see **oc, ic**.

-**acca(i)** see **at-chí**.

acaillid 'addresses, speaks with'. Subjunct. w. 2 **ro**, pres. sg. 1 (w. infix) *ru-s acailler* 1253.

acallam f. (v.n. of **acaillid**) '(act of) addressing, speaking with'. Sg. nom. in comp. *mín-accallam* 'gentle conversation' 1175; gen. in adjectival comp. *so-acallma* 'affable' 1160.

acallmach adj. in comp. *so-acallmach* 'fair-spoken, affable; easily discussable'. Sg. acc. m. 1190.

acht conjunction (see § xliv) 'but' 132, 233, etc. *Acht co* 'provided that' 569, 901; negat. *acht ná* 200. *Acht mina* see **mina**. As prep. 'except', w. nom. or acc., 203, 209, 224, 307, 324, 331, 609.

accobar m. 'desire, wish; greed'. Sg. nom. 896; dat. 1010, 1130.

ac(c)obrach adj. 'desirous; avid, greedy'. Sg. nom. *is acobrach dam fritt* 'you have made me greedy' 892, in comp. *so-accobrach* (w. gen. of thing desired) 'very avid' 95.

accra f. (v.n. of **acraid**) '(act of) prosecuting'. Sg. dat. 1311.

acraid 'accuses; charges (someone) with (some offence)'. Fut. sg. 3 rel. *aicéras* 274.

adaig f. 'night; eve (of the following day)'; see RC XXV, 115 f. Sg. nom. 51, for acc. of time (§ xxi) 103, 685, 1290, for dat. (§ xxi) 291, in comp. *cét-adaig* 'first night' 1340; acc. (of time) *aidche* 97, 205, 720, *aidchi* 520, *oidche* 695; gen. *aidche*

127, 156 etc., *oidche* 347; dat. *aidche* 125, 298, 837, *oidche* 516. Pl. acc. (of time) *aidche* 1291; dat. *aidchib* 227.

adáither see **atáid**.

adarc f. meaning uncertain in compound comic name, sg. nom. *Ug-Adarc* 963 n.

adastar m. 'bridle'. Sg. nom. 957.

adbul adj. 'great, vast'. Pl. dat. m. *aidble* 997. In comp. see **mór**.

adbar m. 'material, substance; cause'. Sg. nom. 689; dat. 1259.

ad-chuirethar deponent 'restores, removes'. Pres. ind. sg. 3 (w. infix) *atom-chuirethar* 'I betook myself' (?) 1052 n.

admat m. 'invention, contrivance'. Pl. nom. *admait* 195 n.

ad-uaid see **ithid**.

aegaire m. 'shepherd'. Sg. gen. 1012.

aen, oen, oín, én cardinal numeral preceding and compounded w. the following noun 'one, a single, one and the same'; *aen* 218, 298, 516, etc.; in comps. see **aenfher, aentuma, galar**; *oen* 55, 291, 307, etc., following rather than preceding, *lá n-oen* 'one day' 647; *én* in comp. see **gel**. As noun 'one person/thing, some/any one/thing'; sg. nom. *aen* 83, 162, 164, 265; acc. 128, 152, 1139, *oen* 612, 613, 625, etc., *cach n-oen* 1300; dat. *cach aen* 1337 f., *oín* 610.

aenach m. 'assembly, congress'. Sg. gen. *aenaig* 1203.

aenar m. 'single person'. In appositional dat. w. possessive, sg. 2 *t' aenur* 'you alone' 722 f.; 3 *a aenar/-ur* 'he alone' 525, 557, 602.

aenfher m. 'one man, a single man'. Gen. *oenfhir* 804; dat. 165.

aenta m./f. 'oneness, unity, association'. Sg. dat. *aentaid* 516.

aentuma adj. 'unmarried'. Pl. gen. f. 1194.

aer, aír f. 'satire, (act of) satirising'. Sg. nom. *aír* 234; acc. *aer* 86, *aír* 1044; dat. *aír* 573.

aeraid 'satirises'. Imperf. sg. 3 *no aerad* 85.

aes m. (coll.) 'people'. Sg. nom. *aes ciúil* 7 *airfitig* 'musicians and minstrels' 1286 f.

ag m./f. (orig. neut. *s*-stem) 'ox, bullock'. Sg. nom. 14; acc. *ag n-allaid* 'deer' 1013 f. n.; gen. *oige* 1104.

agaid f. 'face'. Sg. nom. 1166; acc. 1294, 1296; dat. 1119; *i n-agaid* 'against' 24, 1273.

ahél (sp. for disyllabic *aél*) m. 'flesh-fork'. Sg. nom. 490 n.

aí, aeí pronominal, see **cechtar** and **dala**.

aíbell, oíbell f. 'spark, ember'. Sg. acc. *oíbill* 173 n. Dual nom. *oíbell* (sic) 159; acc. *oíbill* 170. Pl. nom. *aíble* 1164 n.

aíbind adj. 'pleasant'. Sg. nom. m. 496. Superl. *aíbne* 1289.

aibne see **abann**.

aicce see **oc**.

aicenta adj. 'natural'. Sg. nom. m. *demon aicenta* 'a demon by nature' 1259; sg. gen. m. of time *lathi aicenta* '24 hours' 1078.

aicéras see **acraid**.

accidit f. 'disease, attack of illness'. Sg. nom. 1145.

aicsed m. 'observer'. Sg. nom. 1176.

acsin f. (v.n. of **at-chí**) '(act of) seeing'. Sg. nom. 602.

aidble see **adbul**.

aidche, aidchib see **adaig**.

a(i)dmilled m. '(act of) destroying; blighting by magic'. Sg. dat. 46, 57, 718, 1261.

aíge, oíge m. 'a guest'. Sg. gen. in comp. *fiad fhír-oíged* 'respect due to a rightful guest' 268. Pl. nom. *aígid* 150, *oígid* 343; gen. *aíged* 116, 118, 122, 126, *oíged* 161, 202, 215, 219.

aigen m. 'cooking-pot'. Sg. gen. *aigin* 992.

1 **ail** f. 'disgrace, reproach, insult'. Sg. nom. 422.

2 **ail** f. 'rock'. Pl. acc. *ailechu* 28.

áil f. 'wish, request, boon'. Sg. nom. (in phrase *cid is áil di* 'what is wanted of?') 752. Pl. gen. 603.

aile, ele adj. 'other'; cf. **ala**. Sg. nom. m. *aile* 152, f. 209, 324; acc. m. 121, f. 632, 294; gen. f. *ele* 59; dat. f. *aile* 584, 767. Pl. acc. f. *ele* 1262.

aille f. 'hymn of praise'. Pl. dat. *aillib* 141.

áille see **álaind**.

a(i)mser f. 'time'. Sg. nom. 4, 323; gen. *amsire* 511; dat. *aimsir* 7.

áne f. 'splendour; sportiveness'. Sg. gen. 1164.

-aineba see **anaid**.

anechtair, in(d)echtair advb. 'from/on the outside'. *Anechtair* 1055, 1224; *in(d)echtair* 1098, 1248.

aness advb. 'from the south' 31.

anfhial adj. 'shameless'. Sg. nom. m. 1042.

aingel m. 'angel'. Sg. nom. 347, 349, 352, 428, 1335; gen. *aingil* 351.

1 **anim(m)** f. 'soul, life'. Sg. nom. 507; acc. 1277; gen. *anma* 512, 513, *anmma* 1267; dat. *anmain* 901. In comp. see **anmchara**.

2 **anim** f. 'blemish, defect'. Sg. nom. 1176.

ainm m. 'name'. Sg. nom. 69, 71, 282, 916, 921; dat. *anmam* 1118 n. Pl. nom. *anmanna* 911.

antem adj. meaning uncertain, probably something like 'bold'. Pl. gen. m. 1001.

aír see **aer, aír**.

airaigid see **air(a)igid**.

airc(h)etal, oirchetal m. '(act of) training, teaching (by learning traditional lore in verse); poetry'. Sg. gen. *aircetail* 242, *airchetail* 1269, *oirchetail* 1039; dat. *aircetal* 691.

airchindech m. 'chief, leader'. Sg. acc. 485.

airde f. 'sign'. Sg. nom. 1273.

aire see 4 **ar**.

airecc, orecc m. '(act of) inventing, creating, producing'. Sg. gen. *airicc* 5, 9, 20, *oricc* 56.

airech, oirech m. 'packhorse'. Sg. nom. *airech* 941, *oirech* 949.

aré(i)r see **araír**.

áirem f. '(act of) counting; number'. Sg. nom. 19, 623.

airerdacht f. 'pleasure, delight'. Sg. acc. 1220.

airfitech, oirfitech m. 'music, minstrelsy'. Sg. gen. *airfitig* 1287, *oirfitig* 1039.

airget see **argat**.

air(a)igid, airige f. 'choice portion of food, tit-bit'. In comps. (meanings uncertain), sg. nom. *prím-airaigid* 17 n., *frith-airige* 559; acc. *frith-airaigid* 17; dat. *prím-airigid* 558, *frith-airigid* 560.

airísel adj. 'very low'. Sg. dat. m. 1156.

airlímaid 'sharpens, polishes'. Fut. pass. sg. -*airlímfathar* 897.

airm(m) f. 'place'; *airm(m)* i/a '(the) place in which' 193, 534, 761, 896.

ármide verbal of necessity 'to be reckoned'. Sg. nom. m. 615.

airnaigthe, ernaigthe f. 'prayer'. Sg. nom. *airnaigthi* 711, *ernaigthi* 712.

áirnechán m. diminutive of *áirne* 'sloe'. Sg. nom., comic name 912.

airscél m. 'famous tale'. Pl. nom. *airscéla* 494.

airshliab f. 'foothill, highland'. Sg. gen. *airshlébi* 1155.

airtecul m. 'article, part, division'. Sg. nom. 615.

ais 'back' in prep. phrases; *dar a ais* 'behind his back, over his shoulder' 285; *(f)ri a ais* 'on/at his back' 322, 490, 589 f., 759.

aisc f. '(act of) seeking; request, boon'. Pl. gen. 603.

aiscid see **ascaid**.

aisec m. '(act of) restoring, giving back'. Sg. nom. 870; acc. 529.

aisil f. 'part, portion; joint'. Pl. nom. *aisle* 979.

ais(s)linge, aislingthe f. (m. in 502 and 1297) 'vision, dream'. Sg. nom. 425, 778, *aislingi* 430, 785, (for acc.) 1297, *aislingthe* 815, *aislingthi* 361, 423, 1219; acc. *aislinge* 366, *aislingi* 500, 504, 505, 783, *aislingthi* 348, 362, 426; gen. *aislinge* 502, *aislingthi* 355, 428; dat. *aislinge* 1, *aislingi* 780, 781.

aisnéidid 'tells'. Pres. ind. pass. sg. -*aisnéther* 1343. Impv. sg. 2 *aisnéid* 1131. Fut. sg. 1 *asnédfit* 1132.

ais(s)né(i)s(s), faissnéis f. (v.n. of **aisnéidid**) '(act of) telling, relating'. Sg. acc. *aisné(i)s* 354, 878, *faissnéis* 1348; gen. *aisnéssi* 1345; dat. *aissnéis* 1345.

ait adj. 'pleasant'; as noun in comp. *sain-ait* 'a special dainty' sg. dat. 899.

áit(t) f. 'place'; *áit(t)* i/a '(the) place in which' 304 f., 309, 590, 1117, 1296.

aite m. 'foster-father, tutor'. Sg. nom. 110.

áith adj. 'sharp, keen'. Sg. nom. m. 192.

athbendachaid 'blesses'. Pres. ind. sg. 3 -*athbendach* 1125.

aithe m./f. '(act of) requital, reparation; retaliation, vengeance'. Sg. acc. 564; gen. *aithi* 233.

aithech m. 'tenant farmer, peasant'. Sg. acc. 1012.

athgére f. 'keen appetite, great hunger'. Sg. nom. *athgéri* 986.

aithindlat m. 'washing-water already used'. Sg. dat. 129.

athis f. 'reviling, disgrace, defamation'. Sg. nom. 869.

aithle 'remainder; track'. Sg. dat. in prep. phrase (w. following gen.) *d' aithle* 'after' 714.

aithne f. (v.n. of **aithnid**) '(act of) commanding, enforcing'. Sg. dat. 571.

aithnid 'entrusts'. Past ind. pass. sg. *ro h-aithned* 530.

aithrige f. '(act of) doing penance'. Sg. dat. 294.

attreb f. (v.n. of **aittrebaid**) '(act of) occupying, inhabiting'. Sg. dat. *attreib* 57.

aittrebaid 'dwells, inhabits'. Past ind. sg. 3 *ro aittrebastar* 1222.

ala pronominal in phrase *ind ala X* '(the) one (of two) X' (by contrast with *in X aile* 'the other X'). Sg. nom. f. 631.

álaind adj. 'beautiful, lovely, handsome'. Sg. nom. m. 1173, in comp. *fír-álaind* 'very beautiful' 598; acc. 332; dat. f. in comp. *fír-álaind* 734. Pl. nom. f. *áille* 1172.

alam 'herd, flock'. Pl. nom. *alma* 1243.

all 'rein'. Pl. dat. *allaib* 951 n.

allaid adj. 'wild'. *ag allaid* see **ag**.

allsmand m. 'necklet'. Pl. nom. *allsmaind* 482.

alt m. 'joint'. Pl. dat. *altaib* 1122.

alta adj. 'jointed' (?). Pl. nom. m. in comp. *sith-alta* 'having long joints' 1172 n.

altrom m. '(act of) fostering'. Sg. gen. in *mac mí-altromma* 'a son of bad fosterage, a badly brought up boy' 1127 f.

am see 1 **is**.

ám emphasising particle 'indeed, truly' 264.

amach see **immach**.

amal prep. w. acc. 'like' 211, 442, 527, 1012. Conjunction w. indicative 'as', w. subjunct. 'as if', 25, 354, 713, 731, 998, 1112, 1169, 1322.

amlaid advb. 'thus, so'; *is amlaid* introducing statement is usually little more than a slight emphasiser; 12, 118, 783, 1224.

amra adj. 'wonderful, glorious' etc. Sg. nom. m. 826, 827, 1046, *amru* 84.

1 **amuig** advb. 'on the outside' 472.

2 **amuig** advb. 'from outside' 1092 n.

1 **an** see 1 **in**.

2 **an** see 4 **a**.

an- negative prefix in e.g. **anfhurbithe** q.v.

án adj. 'splendid, brilliant'. Sg. gen. m. *áin* 1039.

ana m. 'wealth, riches, abundance'. Sg. acc. 663.

anaid 'stays, remains'. Fut. sg. 3 *anfaid* 31, *-aineba* 30 n. Pret. pl. 3 *ansit* 703.

anair-thuaid see **tuaid**.

anál f. 'breath'. Sg. dat. *anáil* 286.

anall advb. 'from beyond, from/on the other side'; *fri/re* + obj. + *anall* 'beyond, on the other side of ' 445, 1230.

anamail adj. 'unequalled'. Pl. gen. m. 1001.

and, ann see **i**.

annál m. 'annal, record, commemoration'. Pl. dat. *annálaib* 141.

andland m. 'condiment, relish'. Sg. acc. 1186; dat. 178. Pl. nom. *andlaind* 1185.

annsa adj. 'difficult, troublesome'. Sg. acc. 1037. Compar. 528, 557. *Ní h-annsa* (always abbreviated) 'it is not difficult (to answer)' 534, 722, 876, etc.

anfaid see **anaid**.

anfhurbithe participial adj. 'incomplete' (see **forpthe**). Sg. nom. f. *anfhurbithi* 623.

an-í see **-í**.

anm(m)a, anmain see 1 **anim(m)**.

anmchara m. 'confessor'. Pl. gen. *anmcharut* 1265.

anmanna see **ainm**.

anmunna m. 'animal, beast'. Sg. nom. 1222; dat. 55.

anocht see **innocht**.

anocul m. '(act of) protecting, sparing; quarter'. Sg. gen. *anocuil* see **maithem**; dat. 247.

anóir f. 'honour, respect'. Sg. gen. 1289.

anórdha adj. 'honourable, dignified'. Superl. *anórdha* 1289.

anuas advb. 'down, downwards' 1213; 'down to this point' 1219; *for/ar X anuas* 'in addition to X' 1140, 1208.

anund advb. 'over yonder, thither' 275 (i.e. 'to Hell'), 704 (i.e. 'to the other side of the house'), 1093 (i.e. 'inside'), 1229.

apair, -aprai see **as-beir**.

1 **ar**^N possess. adj. 'our' 309, 365, 1214; in sense 'my' 260.

2 **ar**^L see **-a**.

3 **ar** see 1 **ol** and 2 **ol**.

4 **ar**^L prep. w. dat. 'in front of, before; for, because of, for the sake of, in place of, in exchange for' etc. 45, 51, 765 n., see also 1 **for**; with verbs of taking, carrying etc. 'from' 1107; in oaths and adjurations 'by' 666. *Ar umalóit* 'in obedience, obediently' 303. W. suffixed obj. pron. sg. 3 m./neut. *aire* 84, 87, 506, 644. By MI confusion, used with senses of 1 **for**, q.v., in which cases it may not lenite

accs. 66, 177, 178, 593, 951, 952, 1197.
5 ar^N see **iar.**
6 **ar** conjunction 'for, because' 40, 90, 124, etc.
ár m. 'slaughter, defeat'. Sg. gen. *áir* 79; dat. 76.
ára f. 'kidney'. Sg. gen., comic name *Árand* 386.
arada f. 'rein'. Pl. acc. (for dat., § xxiii) *aradnu* 959.
araile, arole pron. and adj. 'another, the other, a certain '. Pron., sg. acc. m. 591, *aroli* 611, f. *aroli* 647; *ón trath co 'raile* 1292 f. (see **tráth**); dat. f. 1333. Adj., sg. nom. m. 11; gen. *aroli* 648.
araír, aré(i)r advb. 'last night' 639, 675 etc., *aré(i)r* 221 n., 361 etc.
arán m. 'bread, loaf'. Sg. acc. 187; dat. 177. In comps., sg. nom. *tur-arán* 'dry bread' 1197; gen. *min-aráin* 'bread of fine ground flour' 561, 645, 663, *tur-aráin* 1096; dat. *garb-arán* 'coarse bread' 1074, *tur-arán* 453.
arbor m. 'grain, corn'. Sg. nom. 867.
ard adj. 'high, raised up; chief'. In comps. see **coire, cosnamaid, gabáil, gaiscedach, rí**; second element in close comps. see **comard** and **forard**. As noun m. 'a height'; sg. nom. in comp. *leth-ard* (lit. 'a half-height, inequality of height') 'unevenness, unfairness' 871.
argat, airget m. 'silver'. Sg. gen. *argait* 1244, in comp. *find-argait* 'white silver' 764, *find-airgit* 735.
aridise, doridise advb. 'again, back again' *aridisi* 155, 847, *doridise* 878, *doridisi* 559.
aroli see **araile.**
1 **as(s)** m. 'milk'. Sg. nom. 867; gen. in comic name *Loch (n)Ais(s)* see **loch;** dat. 403, 1208 f.
2 **ass** m. 'shoe'. Pl. acc. *assai* 834; dat. *assaib* 1065.
3 **as**^(L) see 1 **is.**
4 **as(s), as(s)in** see 6 **a.**
as-beir, at-beir 'says, declares'; w. *fri/re* 'names, calls'; w. obj. (or *do* plus obj. meaning 'word, oath') 'declares'. Pres. ind. sg. 1 *at-biur* 168, 363, 875, 1145, *as-berim* 998, *at-berim* 326; pl. 1 *at-beram* 365; 3 *at-berut* 428, 1290, *at-berat* 1292, *at-berait* 1245 (see § lxvi). Pass. sg. *as-berair* 1231 (see § lviii). Imperf. pass. sg. *at-bertha* 85, 87. Impv. sg. 2 *apair* 249, 252, *abair* 670, *-apair* 680. Pres. subjunct. sg. 3 *-aprai* 1211 n. Past subjunct. pass. sg.

it-berad 1323. Fut. sg. 1 *at-bér* 252, 730, *-epér* 249, 671. Pret. sg. 3 *as-bert* 149, 306, 552, *at-bert* 43, 163, 264, 426, 751, 1034, 1036, 1275, *-epert* 245, *-ebert* 846.
asae adj. 'easy'. Compar. *asu* 1241.
asblad meaning obscure 549 n.
asc(c)aid, aiscid f. 'request, favour, boon'. Sg. nom. 246, 311, 312, 324, 327; acc. 528, 667, *aiscid* 674; gen. *ascada* 669.
asna m. 'rib'. Pl. dat. *asnaib* 952.
aspal m. 'apostle'. Pl. acc. (for dat., § xxiii) *aspalu* 626; gen. *aspal* 623 n., 624.
astig see **istaig.**
at see 1 **is.**
att m. 'hat'. Sg. acc. 738.
atá substantive verb (see §§ xcvi-c) 'is; there is' etc.; for phrase *atá do X* see **di.** Pres. ind. Sg. 1 *-tó* 209, *-tú* 296; 3 *atá* 668, 731, 754, 1129, 1297; *má 'tá* 882; *ní-s tá* 328 n. Pl. 1 *atáum* 723, *atám* 1260 (see 1256 n.), *-támm* 511; 3 *atáut* 295, *atát* 511, 512, 1338; *-tát* 297, w. infixed pron. 1035 n. Impers. *atáthar* 715. W. 2 **ol**, sg. 1 *oldú* 'than I (am)' 265; 3 rel. *oldás* 'than (is)' 526, *oltás* 524, 685, 695, 1305, *inás* 630; non-rel. forms *oldá* 266, *oltá* 238, 1295. Rel.: sg. 3 *fil* 169, 196, 253, etc.; impers. *filter* 359. Dep.: on negatives, sg. 3 *ní fhil* 690, *nocon fhil* 182, *ná fil* 300, 891, pl. 3 *ní fhilet* 151; on interrogative, sg. 3 *in fil?* 164, 882, pl. 3 *in filet?* 150; on prep. *i* (plus rel. particle), sg. 3 *i fil* 179, 534, 687, 1296; responsive sg. 3 *fil* 164, 197, 882. Indep. introducing statement-clauses (other than responsive) 225, 258, 336, 559, 688, 1252, *fail* 1037, pl. 3 *fileat* 881. (See also **do-fil.**) Habitual pres. ind. Sg. 3 *-bí* 655; rel. *bís* 924. Imperf. Sg. 3 *no bíth* 144, *no bíd* 285, 286, 1085, *-bíd* 1088. Pres. subjunct. (see also fut.). Sg. 1 *beó* 572; 2 *bé* 682 n., 1299; rel. *bess* 508. Pl. 3 *-bet* 250, 603. W. 2 **ro**, sg. 3 *-raib* 207, *-rab* 730 n., *-roib* 1175; pl. 3 *-rabat* 569, 671. Past subjunct. Sg. 1 *-beind* 1262; 3 *no beth* 1318, *bed* 711, *-beth* 712, 1263, 1268. Pl. 3 *-betís* 363. Fut. (on confusion here w. subjunct. forms see § xcviii). Sg. 1 *biat* 299, *bet* 293, 294, 516 (see § xcviii); rel. *bess* 234. Pl. 3 *-bet* 1340. Impers. *-bether* 717. Pret. Sg. 1 *-bádus* 1046; 3 *boí* 9, 12, 13, etc., *buí* 587. Pl. 3 *bátar* 582, 812, etc., *-bátar* 218, 310,

704. Impers. *-bás* 716, *-bádus* 544.
PAST IND. Sg. 1 *ro bá* 289, *in tan ro mbá* 'when I was' 841 n. (§ cvii); 3 *ro boí* 262 n., 845, *-roba* 745, *-raba* 788, *rabi* 162.

atáid 'kindles'. Pres. ind. sg. 3, 739; pass. sg. *adáither* 1248.

at-aig see **atn-aig, at-aig**.

at-chí 'sees'. Pres. ind. sg. 1 *it-chiú* 1316. Past ind. sg. 1 *at-chonnarc* 485, 488, *it-chonnarc* 152, 785, *it-chondarc* 815; *-acca(i)* in *co n-acca(i)* 787, 789, 791, 819, 850, 1019, 1063, 1092, 1098 f., 1102, 1113.

at-chluin 'hears'. Past ind. sg. 1 *rochuala* 81, *at-chuala* 62, 82, *it-chuala* 779, *-cuala* 843; 3 *at-chuala* 37, 94, 1338, *-cuala* 594; pass. sg. *-closs* 139.

at-fét 'tells'. Pres. ind. pl. 3 *at-fiadat* 138, 592, 708, 1232 f. Past ind. pl. 1 *it-chótamar* 898; 3 *at-chódutar* 1333.

athair m. 'father'. Sg. nom. 77; gen. *athar* 33, 517.

athard(h)a 'paternal heritage; fatherland'. Sg. gen. 602, 1345.

athchuinchid f. '(act of) asking for, begging for'. Sg. dat. 610.

athlaech m. 'unqualified priest'. Sg. nom. 866.

athluime f. 'nimbleness, agility'. Sg. dat. 1017.

atlaigid (w. 1 **buide**) 'gives thanks'. Pret. sg. 3 *atlaigis* 278.

atlugud m. (v.n. of **atlaigid**) 'thanks'. Sg. acc. 1238.

atn-aig, at-aig (see 355 n.) 'puts, places, sets; brings; sets about, begins; proceeds, goes'. Pres. ind. sg. 1 *atn-aigim* 1102, *at-aigimm* 1112; 3 *atn-aig* 170, 240, 584, 584, 647, 1229, 1274, *at-aig* 355, 768, 771; pl. 3 *atn-agut* 193; pass. sg. *atn-agar/-ur* 110, 239, 240, 250, 1239, *at-agur* 754, 1331.

ató prep. 'from' 509 n.

atom- see **-dam-**.

at-raig 'rises; gets up and goes; swells up'. Pres. ind. sg. 1 (deponent) *atomregar* 1006 n.; 3 *at-raig* 309, 1294. Impv. sg. 2 *érig* 732, *eirc* 843 n. Fut. sg. 1 *-érus* 170. Pret. sg. 3 *at-racht* 104, 217, 705; pl. 3 *at-rachtatar* 262, 1122. Past ind. sg. 1 *atom-raracht* 848, 1010. As simple proto. (§§ lxix ff.), pres. ind. rel. *érgius* 699; s-pret. sg. 3 *érgis* 585, 698, 729.

atuaid advb. 'from the north' 27.

auroslaicid 'opens'. Pres. ind. impers. *auroslaicther* 219.

1 **ba, -ba** see 1 **is**.

2 **ba** see **fo** and 2 **im(m)**.

bá see 2 **im(m)**.

1 **-bá** see **atá**.

2 **-bá** see **báid**.

bac m. 'hook, clasp, staple'. Pl. nom. (for acc., § xx) *baic* 757.

bachall f. 'staff'. Sg. dat. *bachaill* 1087.

bádaid see **báidid**.

-bádus see **atá**.

baeth, baíth, boíth adj. 'silly, reckless; wanton, licentious'. Sg. acc. f. *baíth* 863; gen. *boíthe* 860. As noun 'fool, idiot', pl. dat. *baethaib* 864.

báid 'dies'. Pres. ind. sg. 3 *-bá* 80.

báidid, bádaid 'drowns, quenches'. Pres. subjunct. w. 2 **ro**, sg. 3 *ro báde* 848, 852; *ro báda* 848. Past. subjunct. sg. 3 *no báided* 747. Past indic. pass. sg. *ro báide(a)d* 1109, 1234.

ba(i)le m. 'place'; *ba(i)le a/i* 'the place in which'. Sg. nom. *bali* 1182; dat. 219, 297.

bánbiad m. (coll.) 'whitemeats' i.e. curds, cheese, and other milk products. Sg. gen. *bánbíd* 96 n., 1135.

bainde see **banna**.

banrígan f. 'queen'. Sg. gen. *banrígna* 1013, 1194.

ba(i)rgen f. 'bread, loaf, cake'. Sg. acc. in comp. *leth-bairgin* 'half-loaf' 1086; gen. *ba(i)rgine* 654, 1185. Dual acc. *bairgin* 256, 277; dat. 100. Pl. nom. *bairgena* 1184; gen. 15.

bairgenach adj. 'bready, loafish'. Sg. nom., comic name 913.

bathis m./f. 'baptism'. Sg. nom. 619.

báitsech f. 'rain, shower'. Pl. dat. (for acc., § xxiv) *báitsechaib* 1026 n.

balcc adj. 'strong, firm, vigorous'. Sg. nom. m. 817.

balla adj. meaning uncertain but probably for *ballda* 'spotted, mottled'. Sg. gen. f., as epithet in comic name, *ballai* 391.

bam see 1 **is**.

ban see **ben**.

bán adj. 'white, pale, fair, bright; white-haired'. Sg. nom. f. 72, in comp. *dond-bán* 'brownish-white' 807; gen. m. in comp. *brec-báin* 'bright-speckled' 375. As noun, acc. f. *báin* 1275 n. See **bánbiad, glan, méith**.

banamail adj. 'womanly'. Sg. nom. f. 1161.

band m. 'movement, effort, action, deed'. Sg. acc. (of respect) 927. Pl. gen. 64.

banna, bainde m. 'a drop (of liquid)'.
Sg. nom. 285, 1295; acc. 267; gen.
bainde 378, 1089; dat. *bainde* 1086.
barᴺ**, for**ᴺ possess. adj. pl. 2 'your' 328,
1037, 1253, *for* 288.
bár see 3 **im(m)**.
bárach 'morrow'. In phrases (1) *iar n-a
bárach* 'on the next day' 104, 217,
358, 705, 1294, *ar n-a bárach* 849, *ar
a bárach* 228, 563; (2) *i mbárach*
'tomorrow' 208, 209 f., 339, 702 f.
barr m. 'top, tip, surface, crest; sprout'.
Sg. acc. 930, 1114; gen., comic name
bairr 410; dat. 468. In comps. see
bind, corccra.
barrach adj. 'branchy'. Sg. acc. m. 819.
bás m. 'death'. Sg. gen. *báis* 334; dat.
298.
-bás see **atá**.
bat, batir see 1 **is**.
(-)bátar, bé see **atá**.
bec(c) adj. 'little'. Sg. nom. m. 227,
420, 519, 521, 1019, 1206; acc. 353,
(of time) 116, 153; acc. f. *bic(c)* 224,
667, 1275; dat. m. 1313. Pl. nom.
m. *beca* 195. As neut. noun (§ viii
(5)) 'small amount', sg. nom. 337,
340, 774; acc. 99. Compar. *luga*
1295.
-bed see **atá**.
bedg m. 'a start, leap'. Pl. acc. *bidgu*
899.
béccid 'roars, yells'. Pres. ind. sg. 3,
776.
bein f. (v.n. of **benaid**) with **di** '(act
of) taking off'. Sg. dat. 198, 581.
-ben see **atá**.
beirbthe past partcp. (cf. **berbad**)
'boiled'. Sg. dat. in comp. *lán-berbthi*
'fully boiled' 1284.
beirid 'bears, sustains; carries off'; *beirid
fri* 'applies to, presses against'. Pres.
ind., pl. 1 rel. *berma* 1237 n.; pass.
sg. indep. *berair* 244, 280, 1240, *berar*
157, rel. *berair* 319 (§ lviii). Imperf.
sg. 3 *no bered* 1106 f. Impv. pass. sg.
berar 237, *berair* 1242 n. Pres. subjunct. w. 2 **ro**, sg. 2 *-ruca* 782; 3
-ruca 30. Past subjunct., sg. 1 *-beraind*
780; 3 *no berad* 92, 1322. Fut. sg. 2
béra 1148; 3 *-béraba* 34 n.; pass. sg.
-bérthar 1341. Condit. sg. 1 *-béraind*
781; 3 *no bérad* 1271. Pret. sg. 3 *beris*
620, 1229, *bertais* 634 n., 707. Past
ind. sg. 3 *ruc* 368; pass. sg. *ruccad*
158.
be(i)th (v.n. of **atá** and 1 **is**) '(state of)
being, to be'. Sg. nom. 125, 685,
837, 883, w. possess. adjs. 222 f.,
718, w. copula *nír beith* 'it was not

a case of being' 223; dat. *do beith*
'being' 1232.
-bether see **atá**.
-betís see **atá** and 1 **is**.
bél m. 'mouth'; in pl. (of single person)
(1) 'lips', (2) 'face'. Sg. acc. 771, 784
(§ xxiii); gen. *beóil* 582; dat. *beól* 766,
768. Pl. nom. *beóil* 899, 1121, 1169;
acc. *beólu* 591, 607, 768, etc.; acc.
(for dat., § xxiii) 595, 775, in phrase
ar/for bélu 'in front of' 1030, 1234
(see 4 **ar** and 1 **for**); gen. 1224; dat.
ar a bélaib 649. In comps., *so-beóil*
'eloquent' 1161; see **corccra**.
bela see 1 **beóil**.
belach m. 'gap, defile'. Sg. gen. *belaig*
1031.
bélaide, béla(i)the adj. 'fatty, greasy,
juicy'. Sg. nom. f. 1049, 1199; gen.
m. 976, f. in personal name see
Index s.v. **Becnat**; dat. f. 467. Pl.
nom. f. 980; dat. 1026.
ben f. 'woman, wife'. Sg. nom. 903,
928, 1159; acc. *mnaí* 487, 863, 868;
gen. *mná* 860, 938; dat. in comp.
droch-mnaí 'bad woman' 871. Pl.
nom. *mná* 1123 n.; gen. *ban* 1194.
benaid 'strikes, cuts'; *benaid a* 'takes
out'; *benaid di* 'takes off/out'; *benaid
fri* 'touches'. Pres. ind. pass. sg.
bentair 340, 357. Imperf. pass. pl.
-bendais 1078. Pres. subjunct. w. 2
ro, sg. 3 *ro bena* 1157. Fut. sg. 3
-benfa 1176; pass. sg. *benfaider* 337.
Pret. sg. 3 *benais* 129, 137, 257, 321,
662, 763, 767, 770, *bendais* 763 n.,
-ben 256. Past ind. sg. 3 *ro ben* 282 n.;
pl. 1 *ro bensum* 313, *-r bensumm* 439;
pass. sg. *ro benad* 212, 270.
bend f. 'point, tip, peak, corner'. Sg.
nom. in comic name *Bend Grotha*
'Curd Peak' 1030 n.; dat. *beind* 109.
Dual nom. *beind* 760.
bendach, bennach adj. 'pointed,
peaked'. Sg. gen. m. *bennaig* 417;
dat. f. *bendaig* 830 (see 829 n.).
bendachaid w. direct obj. or 2 **do**
'blesses; says farewell'. Impv. sg. 2
bennach 370; 3 *bendachad* 831. Pret.
sg. 3 *bendachais* 110.
bendacht f. 'blessing'. Sg. nom. 303;
acc. *bennachtain* 38. Pl. acc. *bendachtu*
663, 1300.
bendais see **benaid**.
1 **beó** adj. 'alive'. Sg. nom. m. 659.
2 **beó** see **atá**.
beóchail 'gravy'. Sg. nom. 847, 853,
1002; gen. *beóchla* 1004.
beóchlaide adj. 'gravy-soaked'. Sg.
nom. m. 1020; gen. 1089; dat. 1086.

GLOSSARY 149

1 **beóil** 'fat, grease, meat-juice'. Sg.
nom. 848; gen., comic name *Bela*
373 n., in comp. *drúcht-bela* 'dew of
meat-juice' 1026.
2 **beó(i)l, beóla/-u** see **bél**.
beóir f. 'beer'. Sg. gen. *beóri* 462, comic
name 378.
beós advb. 'still, also; continually' 23,
567, 665.
bera(ib) see **bir**.
berbad '(act of) boiling, cooking'. Sg.
dat. in comp. *cét-berbad* 'recent
boiling' 795.
bertais see **beirid**.
bes(s) see **atá** and 1 **is**.
bés m. 'custom, practice'. Sg. nom. 642.
(-)bet, (no) beth see **atá**.
1 **betha** m. 'life'. Sg. nom. 90.
2 **betha** see **bith**.
b(h)us see 1 **is**.
-bí see **atá**.
biad m. 'food'. Sg. nom. 182, 775; acc.
147, 193, 223, 224, 685, 769; gen.
bíd 368, 421, 494, etc., in comic
name 910, 1002, 1003; dat. *biúd* 331,
788, 811, etc. Pl. nom. *biada* 736,
975, 1142; acc. (for dat., § xxiii)
biadu 897; gen. 838, 1221; dat. *biadaib*
997, 1208 (for acc., § xxiv) 973. In
comps., sg. gen. *deg-bíd* 'good food'
414, see **bánbiad**; pl. acc. *il-biadu*
'many foods' 1205.
biail m. 'axe'. Sg. nom. 320.
biait f. one of the Eight Beatitudes. Pl.
nom. *biati* 620 n.
biat see **atá**.
biathad m. '(act of) feeding; paying
food-rent'. Sg. dat. 1344.
bid, bidat see 1 **is**.
bíd see **biad**.
-bíd see **atá**.
bidgu see **bedg**.
bilech adj. 'tree-grown'. Sg. acc. m.
819.
bille 'seal' (on document). Pl. acc. (for
dat., § xxiii) 1071.
bind adj. 'melodious, sweet-sounding;
pleasing'. Sg. gen. f. *binde* 379. Pl.
acc. m. *binde* 179. In comps., sg.
nom. m. *tét-bind* 'sweet as harp-
strings' 1174; gen. f. *barr-binde*
'having a melodious surface' i.e.
'whose surface-ripples make music'
75.
bir m. 'spit, stake, spike'. Sg. acc. 741.
Pl. nom. *bera* 759; acc. *bera* 735, 761;
dat. (for acc., § xxiv) *beraib* 737, 744.
bís, (no) bíth see **atá**.
bith m. 'the world'. Sg. gen. *betha* 435,
621, 1143.

bíthe adj. 'smooth, tender'. Sg. gen. f.
410.
blad f. 'renown'. Sg. dat. 1316.
bladach adj. 'famous, splendid'. Sg. dat.
f. *bladaig* 799.
bladmar adj. 'famous, splendid'. Sg.
gen. m. *bladmair* 404.
bláith adj. 'smooth'. Sg. gen. m. 435,
f. *bláthi* 376; dat. f. 830. Pl. nom. f.
bláthi 980. In comps. see **gel**, 2 **lind**,
milis.
blass m. 'taste; a tasty bit, a dainty'. Pl.
acc. in comp. *il-blassa* 'many dainties'
35, 48; gen. *il-blass* 1135 n.; dat. (for
acc., § xxiv) *il-blassaib* 45, 47.
blassachtach f. '(act of) tasting (noisily),
smacking the lips'. Sg. dat. *blassachtaig* 584.
blasta adj. 'tasty'. Sg. nom. m. 463;
gen. 900.
bláth m. 'flower; bloom, blossom'. Sg.
dat. 474.
bláth- see **bláith**.
bláthach f. 'buttermilk'. Sg. gen.
bláithche 1025, comic name 377.
bliadain f. 'year'. Sg. gen. *bliadna* 1337,
in comp. *leth-bliadna* 'a half year' 59.
Pl. acc. (of time) *leth-bliadna* 1260,
1262; gen. *leth-bliadan* 58, 607, 719.
Blichtucán m. comic pet-name (affectionate diminutive of *blicht* 'milk')
'Little Milky'. Gen. 914.
blog f. 'piece, fragment, scrap (of food)'.
Pl. acc. *blogu* 649; gen. 647, 774;
dat. *blogaib* 291, 648.
blonac f. 'lard, suet'. Sg. nom. *blonoc*
1049, comic name *Blonag* 928; gen.
blonci 471, *blongi* 1021, 1079, 1103,
comic name 1065 (see also s.v. 2
mael); dat. *blonaig* 799, 1072. Pl.
nom. *blongi* 980; dat. (for acc.,
§ xxiv) in comic tribal name *Blongib*
982, 1005. In comp. see **tinbe**.
bó f. 'cow'. Sg. nom. 680, 1302, 1327,
1346; gen. 1085. Pl. acc. *bú* 30. In
comps. see **bósha(i)ll** and **ger**.
boc(c) adj. 'soft; easy'. Sg. nom. m. in
comp. *so-bocc* 'very easy' 1042, f. *boc*
942; acc. m. *buic* 404, 411, 900; dat.
f. *buic* 802, 1087. Pl. nom. f. *bocai*
797, *boca* 1170. In comp. see
brechtán.
bocht adj. 'poor'. Compar. *bochta* 260.
As m. noun in pl. 'the poor culdees',
nom. *boicht* 315, 343; gen. 229 n.;
dat. *bochtaib* 262.
bodar adj. 'deaf'. In comps. see **usce**
and **sáith**. As noun 'deaf person' sg.
acc. 855.
bodbda adj. 'warlike'. Sg. dat. m. 586.

(-)boí see **atá**.

bolcsén m. 'middle'. Sg. acc. 109.

boinne adj. meaning uncertain, perhaps 'smooth'. Sg. nom. m. *boinni* 645.

boíth see **baeth**.

bolg/-c m. 'bag, bubble, swelling' etc.; 'bellows' or 'quiver'. Sg. nom. 76 n. In comps. see **midbolc** and 1 **lind, onfad, sliss**.

bolgach/-c- adj. 'bubbly'. Sg. acc. f. *bolgaig* 1198; dat. m. *bolcach* 1209.

bolgán m. 'belly'. Sg. gen., comic name *Bolgáin* 411.

bolgum(m)/-c- m. 'mouthful, sip'. Sg. nom. *bolcum* 1212; acc. 1212; gen. *bolgaim* 1206. Pl. gen. in comp. *ferbolcumm* 'of man[-sized] sips' 1207.

bond m. 'sole of the foot; foot'. Sg. acc. 1177. Pl. acc. *bunnu* 1065.

borr adj. 'swollen, thick, fat'. In comps. see **croth, torad**.

boss f. 'palm of the hand'. Sg. nom. in comp *clé-boss* 'left palm' 1239; gen. *bossi* 1238.

bósha(i)ll f. 'corned beef' (comp. of **bó** and **sa(i)ll**) cf. Lucas, Gwerin III, ii, 10. Sg. nom., comic name 934; gen. *bóshaille* 486, 733, 979, etc.

both f. 'hut, monastic cell'. Sg. acc. *boith* 648; dat. *boith* 289, 647.

brá f. 'eyebrow'. Dual nom. 1167.

brafud m. 'moment'. Sg. acc. 1204 n.

brága f. 'neck, throat, gullet; breast'. Sg. acc. *brág(a)it* 760, 1211, 1233, 1270; dat. *brágait* 10, 14, 20, etc., short dat. (§ xvi) 1231.

bragitóracht f. 'farting; buffoonery'. Sg. nom. 548 f.

braichles f. 'wort, malt'. Sg. dat. *braichlis* 464.

braine m. 'prow'. Sg. dat. 1021.

brainech adj. 'foremost, outstanding'. Sg. nom. f. 942.

braisech f. 'kale, cabbage; cabbage soup, pottage'. Sg. nom. 807, 1199; gen. *braisce* 930, comic name 410; dat. *braisig* 467.

bran m. 'raven'. Pl. gen. 1318.

bras(s) adj. 'boastful; violent; huge' etc. Sg. nom. m. 965; gen. m. *braiss* 494. In comp. see Index of Names of Persons s.v. **Becnat**.

brat(t) m. 'cloak, mantle'. Sg. nom. 645, 935, 1165, etc.; acc. 681; gen. *bruit* 1163; dat. *brut(t)* 107, 1166. In comp. see **gel**.

bratach adj. 'wearing a cloak'. Sg. nom. f. 1162.

bráth m. 'Doomsday'. Sg. acc. in phrase *co bráth* 'till Doomsday, for ever'

hence, w. neg., 'never' 183, 717; gen. *brátha* see **bruinne**.

bráthair m. 'brother, kinsman'. Sg. nom. 43, *bráthair bunaid* 'kinsman by ancestry' 678; gen. *bráthar* 41.

brec(c) adj. 'spotted, speckled, many-coloured'. Sg. dat. f. *bricc* 830. Pl. nom. *brecca* 1120. In comps. see **bán** and **find**.

bréc f. 'falsehood, deceit'. Sg. nom. 288.

brechtán m. 'butter, custard' etc. Sg. nom. 1196, comic name 922; gen. *brechtáin* 797, 1073, 1097, comic name 377, in comps. *boc-brechtáin* 'of soft custard' 1095, *ro-brechtán* 'of great custard' 444.

breó f. 'flame, conflagration'. Sg. dat. *briaid* 1250.

breth f. (v.n. of **beirid**) '(act of) carrying, taking; passing judgement, interpreting'. Sg. nom. 237, 279; gen. *brethi* 239, 1043 (see **buide**); dat. *breith* 154, 239, 779.

brethach adj. 'giving judgement, judicial'. Voc. in comp. *ríg-brethaig* 'of royal judgements' 620.

Bretnach adj. 'British, Welsh'. Sg. nom. m. 1328; acc. m. 565.

bretnusach adj. 'wearing a brooch'. Sg. nom. f. 1162.

briaid see **breó**.

briathar f. 'word, declaration, pledge'. Sg. nom. 672; acc. *bréthir* 317, 326, 365, 523, 1145; gen. *bréthri* 1267; dat. *bréthir* 363, 673. Pl. gen. 360. In comp. see **senbriathar**.

bríg f. 'power, vigour; value, efficiency'. Sg. gen. *bríge* 817.

brisc adj. 'brittle, breakable'. Sg. dat. m. in comp. *nem-brisc* 'unbreakable' 1259.

briscén m. 'tansy'. Sg. acc. 1194 n.

brisid 'breaks'. Pres. subjunct. pass. w. 2 **ro**, *ro brister* 200. Past partcp. sg. nom. m. *briste* 'broken' 1196.

br(i)ugu m. '(rich) landowner'. Pl. nom. *brugaid* 569, *briugaid* 571.

brocóit f. 'bragget'. Sg. gen. *brocóti* 462, 1076, comic name 379.

brogaid 'increases, multiplies'. Pres. ind. sg. 3 rel. *brogas* 943.

broimnech f. '(act of) farting'. Sg. dat. *broimnig* 860.

bro(i)nd see 1 **brú**.

brón m. 'sorrow, grief'. Sg. nom. 1163.

bronnad '(act of) using up, consuming'. Sg. nom. *bronnud* 1135; dat. *brondad* 900.

brothar 'hair, fur'. In comps. see **ceirt** and **lum(m)an**.

brothchán m. 'pottage, gruel'. Sg. gen. *brothcháin* 1193, comic name 374.

1 **brothrach** f. 'blanket, garment' (of hairy cloth ? cf. **brothar**). Sg. dat. *brothraig* 486.

2 **brothrach** adj. meaning uncertain. Sg. nom. f. 1049 n.

brothrachán adj. meaning uncertain. Sg. gen. *brothracháin* 1095 n.

1 **brú** f. 'abdomen, belly'. Sg. acc. *broind* 55, 885, 891; gen., comic name *Brond* 391 (see 388 n.).

2 **brú** f. 'brink, border'. Sg. acc. 29; dat. 75, 465.

bruach m. (old neut.) 'edge, hem'. Sg. acc. 1162 (see § iv).

brúchtach f. 'a belch'. Sg. acc. *brúchtaig* 1198.

brugaid see **br(i)ugu**.

bruinne m. 'limit, brink'. Sg. acc. in phrase *co bruinne (m)brátha* 'till the brink of Doom' 422, 694 f., 731.

bru(i)t see **brat(t)**.

brúit f. 'brute'. Pl. voc. *brúti* 329.

bruithe past partcp. (cf. **berbad**) 'boiled, cooked'. Sg. nom. f. 807; dat. f. 1072 (see 1049 n.), 1088. Pl. nom. m. 1190.

brus 'refuse, leavings'. In comp. see **garbán**.

bu see 1 **is**.

bú see **bó**.

buadach adj. 'victorious, gifted; peerless'. Sg. gen. f. *buadaige* 1079.

buaid, buad f. (old neut.) 'victory; acme, perfection; talent'. Sg. nom. *buaid* 626, 1343, neut. in verse (see § viii) *buaid mbainde* 'perfection of drink' 378; acc. *buad* 79. Pl. acc. (for dat., § xxiii) *buadu* 626.

buaidrén meaning uncertain, 'stirabout'? Sg. gen., comic name 374.

buan adj. 'long-lasting; constant'. Pl. nom. f. *buana* 979; acc. 1026.

buanad '(act of) perpetuating'. See 1315 n.

buar m. 'diarrhoea, flux'. Sg. nom. 1218.

buarannach adj. 'suffering from diarrhoea, fluxy'. Sg. nom. m., comic name 879.

bud see 1 **is**.

budessin see **fén**.

budesta advb. (see **fecht**) 'now, henceforth' 836.

buí see **atá**.

1 **buide** f. 'thanks; a subject for satisfaction'. Sg. nom. in phrase *is*

buide la 'is happy' 32; acc. 278 (see **atlaigid**); gen. in phrase *fer brethi budi* 'one who expresses thanks' 1043.

2 **buide** adj. 'yellow'. Sg. gen. f. in comp. *cúl-budi* 'yellow-haired' 990 n.; dat. m. 1209. Pl. nom. f. 1120, in comp. *derg-buide* 'reddish-yellow' 977.

buidech adj. 'satisfied, contented, pleased'. Pl. nom. m. *budig* 899.

buiden f. 'host, company'. Pl. acc. *buidne* 79; dat. *buidnib* 64, 577.

bulbing m. 'loaf'. Sg. acc. 1054.

bulle f. 'blow'. Sg. acc. *bulli* 1056.

buinde m. 'torrent, gush'. Pl. dat. *buindib* 1076.

bunad m. 'stem, origin, basis; ancestry'. Sg. nom. 1315 n.; gen. as attributive adj. see **bráthair**. In comp. see **gende**.

bunat(t)a adj. 'fundamental, original'. Sg. nom. f. 145, 211.

bundraisse meaning uncertain. Sg. gen. 1088 n.

bupthaid adj. 'terrifying'. Sg. acc. m. 1025.

búraid 'bellows'. Pres. ind. sg. 3, 776.

c' see 1 **cia**.

'ca see **oc, ic**.

cab m. 'mouth'. Sg. gen., perhaps in comp. comic name *Elc-Caib* 879 n.

cacc m. 'excrement, dung'. Sg. gen. *cacca* 270, 329.

caccaid 'excretes'. Pres. ind. pl. 3 *-caccut* 1155.

cach, cech pronominal adj. (see § xxxix) 'each, every'. Sg. nom. m. *cach* 147, 240, *cech* 463; nom. f. *cach* 1186; nom. neut. *cach^N* 545 n., 546, 691; acc. m. *cach^N* 143, 953, 1186, 1217 n., 1300; gen. m. *cach^L* 680, 681, 1087, 1141 (2), 1258, 1303 (2), 1304, 1327 (2), 1328, *cech^L* 484, 804, *cacha^H* 95, 143, 567, 889 (2), 900, 1048, 1089; gen. f. *cach* 1327, 1332, *cacha^H* 567, 681, 741, 889 (c. h-ithe), 890, 1072, 1185, 1332; dat. m. *cach* 896, 1086, 1337; dat. f. 3, 1304. For *cacha díbside* see 888 n.

cách pron. 'everybody, each one'; sometimes 'everyone else'. Sg. nom. 525; acc. 85, 1197; gen. *cáich* 432; dat. *cách* 298, 515, 630, 658, 1141. In phrase *asu a chách* 'easier than

M

anything else' 1241 f. For *cacha díb-side* see 888 n.

cade interrog. pron. 'what (is) ?' 1150.

1 **cadla** m. (coll.) 'the small intestines'. Sg. nom. *cadlai* 823.

2 **cadla** adj. 'handsome, beautiful'. Sg. nom. m. 927. Pl. nom. m. *cadlai* 824.

caelán m. 'intestine, gut'; in pl. 'chitterlings'. Pl. acc. *caelánu* 1201, (for dat., § xxiii) 1071, 1101, 1105; gen. *coelán* 810; dat. *coelánaib* 483.

caemna f. 'provision of entertainment'. Sg. gen. 1133, in comp. *mí-chaemna* 'bad provender' 1134.

caer f. 'berry'. Pl. nom. *caera* 868; dat. *coeraib* 409.

caera f. 'sheep'. Sg. nom. 1304, *caeru* 1328; acc. 567; gen. *caerech* 925. Pl. gen. *coerach* 403, *caerech* 1202.

caill f. 'a wood'. Pl. acc. *caille* 1026.

caillech f. 'old woman, hag, witch'. Sg. nom. 31, 72, 865. Dual gen. 25.

caimme see **camm**.

caín adj. 'beautiful, fine, handsome'. Sg. nom. m. 816, 1167, f. 1063, 1166; acc. f. 739; gen. m. 407; dat. f. 841.

cainnend f. (coll.) 'leeks'. Sg. gen., comic name *Cainninde* 380; dat. *cainnind* 477, in comp. *fír-chainnind* 'fresh leeks' 1069 n.

cáinte m. 'satirist'. Pl. nom. 569, 574.

cáintecht f. '(act of) satirising'. Sg. nom. 548; gen. *cáintechta* 550.

caircib see **carraic**.

cairde m./f. 'delay, respite, truce'. Sg. nom. 316, 425.

cáise m. 'cheese'. Sg. gen. in comp. *sen-cháise* 'old cheese' 455; dat. in comp. *tirm-cháisi* 'dry cheese' 984 f. Pl. dat. *cáisib* 483.

caisel m. 'stone rampart'. Sg. nom. 447, 821.

cáith f. (coll.) 'chaff, husks'. Sg. gen. in comp. *síl-chátha* 'seed-husks' 159, 171.

caithem f. (v.n. of **caithid**) '(act of) consuming, eating; an expense'. Sg. dat. 253, 571.

caithid 'consumes, eats, uses up; passes (time)'. Pres. ind. pass. sg. w. 2 **ro**, *ro caiter* 'is needed; must be' 1039 n. Imperf. sg. 1 -*caithind* 291. Impv. pl.

1 -*caithium* 315. Pret. sg. 3 *caithis* 277. Past ind. sg. 1 *ro chaithes* 268, w. 4 **a** and 2 **ro**, *ar chaithius* 293.

calath m. 'landing-place'. Sg. acc. 1029.

1 **calma** f. 'courage, deeds of valour'. Sg. nom. 727.

2 **calma** adj. 'strong, bold'. Superl. 755, 1115.

camm adj. 'crooked, twisted'. Sg. gen. f. *caimme* 380.

cammrand m. 'quatrain sung extempore in alternating contention'. Dual acc. 26, 176.

can interrog. advb. 'whence ?' 877.

canaid w. 2 **do** 'sings about'. Past ind. pass. sg. *ro canad* 61 n.

cantaicc f. 'canticle'. Pl. dat. *cantaccib* 142.

cantain f. (v.n. of **canaid**) '(act of) singing, reciting'. Sg. acc. 138.

capall m. 'horse'. Sg. gen. *capaill* 13; dat. 1073.

cara m. 'friend'. Sg. nom. 1253; dat. *carait* 883.

carna f. 'flesh, meat'. Sg. acc. in comp. *lán-charna muii*. 'plentiful mutton' 733; gen., comic 1ame 399, in comp. comic epithet *Tirm-Charna* 'Dried Meat' 913; dat. in comps. *tirm-charnu* 452, *lón-charna* 'rump steak' 1100.

carr f. 'scab'. In comp. see **matrad**.

carrach adj. 'scabby, knobbly'. Sg. nom. m. 821.

carraic f. 'rock'. Pl. dat. (for acc., § xxiv) in comp. *cruad-chaircib* 'hard rocks' 1027.

cartaid 'sends'. Pres. ind. sg. 3, 48.

carthain '(act of) loving'. Sg. nom. 1133.

cas adj. 'curly, tangled, dense'. In comp. see **draigen**.

cath m. 'battle'. Sg. dat. 1343.

cátha see **cáith**.

cathair f. 'stone enclosure' (of fort, city, monastery, etc.). Sg. acc. *cathraig* 139, in comp. *prím-chathraig* 'chief enclosure' 1058.

cathaír f. 'chair, throne'. Sg. acc. (for dat., § xxiii) 866.

cáttu m. 'honour, esteem'. Sg. nom. 1289.

cé see 1 and 2 **cia**.

cech see **cach**.

cechtar pronominal, indecl., 'each (of two)'. Sg. gen. w. petrified nasalisation *cechtar n-aí* 'of/for each of the two of them' 257; dat. 582, 1076.

ced see 1 **cid**.

céle m. 'companion, mate'; in phrase *a chéle* 'the other, another'. Sg. acc. 109; dat. 260.

celebrad m. 'celebration' (of service, office, etc.). Sg. nom. 228; acc. 314.

célide m. 'a visit'. Sg. gen. *fir chélide* 'of a visitor' 1195.

céim m./f. (v.n. of **cingid**) 'step, stride, pace'. Sg. voc. *a chéim fhosad* 'oh you of the firm pace' 416; dat. 586. Pl. gen. *míle cémend* 'a thousand paces, a mile' 139.

céin see **cian**.

cenél m. '(noble) kindred, family group; kind, sort'. Sg. gen. *ceneóil* 656; dat. *ceneól* 575, 601. Pl. acc. *ceneóla* 713. In comp. see **socheneóil**.

ceirt f. 'rag'. Pl. dat. in comp. *brotharchertib* 'hairy rags' 1095.

cétemain see **cétamain**.

cethre numeral adj. m. (where m. for f. see § xxix) 'four'. Nom. *cethri* 759, 1207 (*cethair* 612 n.), for f. 1248; acc. *cethri* 735; dat. *cethri* 1074, for f. 1073, 1140, *cethra* 746 n. In comps., *cethar-*, see **dorsech, drumnech, lán, li(u)bar, ochair, scoltech**.

cel m. 'death'. Sg. acc. in phrase *dul for cel* 'to die' 253 f.

cell f. 'church, monastic settlement'. Sg. gen. *cille* 681, 1328; dat. *cill* 1304.

cémad see 1 **is**.

cen (usually *cen^L*) prep. with acc. 'without' 121, 147, 202, etc. As conjunction w. 3 **co**, *cen co^N* (*cein co^N* 224), as neg. of 2 **cia**, 'though not, if not, unless; that not' 296, 689, 782. W. pres. subjunct. of copula (see 1 **is**) *cen cop* 501; past subjunct. *cen co bad* 1315.

cena see **c(h)ena**.

cenbar meaning uncertain; KM 'a chafer'; DIL C 513.8 suggests = *crebar* 'gadfly' or 'screech owl'. Sg. gen. *cenbair* 1245.

cend m. 'head; end, beginning'. **(A)** Sg. nom. 865; acc. 58, 427, 590, etc.; gen. *cind* 1035, in comic name *Lethir-*

Chind 'Leather-Head' 915; dat. *cind* 118, 286, 633, etc. In comps. see **faelid, ísel, lethchend, mullach. (B)** Prepositional (w. dep. gen.) and adverbial phrases. (1) W. 2 **co**, *co cend* 'entirely, completely' 315; 'to the end of; throughout' 290, 292. (2) W. 1 **for**, *for cend* (acc.) 'to meet; towards' 155 (for 4 **ar**); *for cind* (dat.) 'before; awaiting' 118, 511, 1019. (3) W. i^N, *i cend* 'for the purpose of; towards' 112, 239, 840, 1141. (4) Dat. without prep., *cind* 'at the end of' 828 (see DIL C 122.3-8).

cennphort m. 'introduction, preface'. Sg. nom. 424; acc. 355, *cennphurt* 353 n.

cenglaid 'binds'. Pres. ind. sg. 3, 540. Fut. pass. sg. *-cengéltar* 337 n. Past ind. pass. sg. *ro cenglad* 340, 756. Past partcp. *cengalta* 539.

cenmothá prep. w. acc. 'except, besides' 17, 1216.

1 **ceó** 'mist'. Sg. acc. *ciaig* 741.

2 **ceó** 'milk'. Sg. dat. 808.

ceól m. 'music'. Sg. gen. *ciúil* 1287.

cérba see 2 **cia** and 1 **is**.

cerc f. 'hen'. Sg. gen. *circe* 1196. Pl. gen. *cercc* 1204. Cf. **rercherc**.

cerd f. 'skill, craft, art'. Pl. acc. (for dat., § xxiii) *cerdu* 550.

cernach adj. 'having corners'. Sg. acc. f. *cernaig* 886.

cerrbacán m. (coll., cf. DIL C 142.70) 'carrots'. Sg. nom. 1195; dat. 477.

césad m. 'suffering; the Passion'. Sg. acc. 309. In comp. see **crand**.

cét m. (cardinal) numeral 'a hundred'. Gen. *praind chét* 'a banquet for a hundred (people)' 889; *cori cét* 'a cauldron of a hundred (measures)' 1283; *secht fichit cét* 'fourteen thousand' 1046 f.

cét- (ordinal) numeral prefixed to noun 'first; fresh, new' 21, 92, 274, etc.

cétal m. '(act of) singing; song'. Sg. dat. in comp. *clas-chétul* 'choral song' 511.

cétamain, cétemain m. indecl. 'May-day, May'. Sg. gen. 134, 204.

cethar, cethra see **cethre**.

cetharda 'group of four; four things'. Sg. nom. *cethardai* 3.

cétna adj. (1) (ordinal) numeral preceding noun 'first' 615; (2) following noun 'same' 771; as pronominal sg. acc. m. 427.

chaidche advb. 'always; henceforth' 1149.

c(h)ena advb. 'moreover, indeed, then, so; in particular; besides' 208, 308, 773, *chenai* 853. W. preceding *ol* (*ar* 713, *acht* 132, 1015 n.) 'besides, as well' 346, 696, 1261 f., 1336 f., *chenai* 1330.

chuc(c)a, chucat, chuice see 2 **co.**

1 **cia, cé, c'** m. (f. early *cissí*, later *cia*); for neut. cf. 1 **cid.** Direct and indirect interrog. pron.; indef. pronominal and adj., 'who? what? which?; whoever, whatever'. *Cia do thoísechaib is gératu?* 'which of the chiefs is most valiant?' 1003; *cia thégi* 'to what (place) you are going' 877. With nouns (copula understood) *cia a n-anmanna?* 'what (are) their names?' 911; *cia h' ainm?* 'what (is) your name?' 916; *cissí ascaid?* 312; *cia lóg?* 505 f., 518, 562. *Cia fot?* (lit. 'what (is) the length?') 'how long?' 772; *cia h-airmm?* 'where?' 533 f.; *c' áit?* 1296. Indirect interrog. *ro scrútustar cia leth* 'he considered (in) what direction' 91; indef. *cia bali* '(in) whatever place' 1182. In advb. phrases 'however, whatever' etc.: *cé fota bé* 'however long you may be' 1298 f.; in phrase *cia* plus substantive vb. *di/do* (plus possessive) plus noun, e.g. *cia boí dia sheircc aicce* (lit. 'whatever she had of love for him') 'however much she loved him' 40 f.; *cia boí d' immbud ecnai leó* lit. 'whatever they had of abundance of learning' 241 f.; *cia boí dia slemnu* (lit. 'whatever there was of its smoothness') 'however smooth it was' 595; *cia roba do mét* 'however big it was' 745.

2 **cia^L, cé^L, gé^L** (see § xliv) w. indep. constr. (but see 513 n.) 'though'. When introduced by phrase meaning 'I should be pleased, I don't care, it's all one to me' it means rather 'if, whether, that'. See 248 (*cé*), 328,

508, 513, 625, 1213, 1318. W. copula see 1 **is.** Negative see s.v. **cen.**

ciaig see 1 **ceó.**

ciall f. 'mind, sense, wisdom, prudence'. Sg. nom. 863, 898; acc. (of respect) *céill* 1324, in comp. *glan-chéill* 'pure reason' 1323.

cian adj. 'long, lasting; far-distant'. Pl. dat. f. *ciana* 603. In comp. see *fota.* As noun f. 'length of time, period', sg. acc. as conjunction (*in*) *céin* 'as long as' 285, 349, 572, 659; pl. dat. as advb., *ó chianaib* 'recently, just now' 153, 293 f.

ciar adj. 'dark, black'. See Index of Names of Persons s.v. **Mael Chiar.**

cícaras m. 'greed'. Sg. gen. *cícarais* 1200 n.

1 **cid, ced** direct, indirect, and indef. interrog. pron. neut. (see 1 **cia**) 'what (is)?, what (is), whatever (is)'. Direct w. rel. clause, 196, 554, 596, 651, 670, 721, 752, 1241, 1280. As advb. w. *sin/ón* 'how/why is that?' 876, 884, 999, 1002; *cid ná dénum?* 'why don't we make?' 176. Indirect w. rel. clause, 169, 252. Indef. *cid ed* lit. 'whateve. it (be)' 308.

2 **cid** conjunctio (see 1 **is**) 'though (it be), that (it be)'; as advb. 'even'. W. adj. 227, 365, 552, 556, 557; *cid duitsiu* 'even by you' 677; *ní festa cid mó no ríssed aen uaib a less* 'it might not be discovered *that* it may be more (that) some one of you might need' 264 f.

cimas f. 'edge, border, limit'. Sg. dat. *cimais* 654.

cind see **cend.**

cindus (= *c' indus* 'what way?') interrog. advb. 'how?' 359, 715.

cingid 'steps, strides; goes'. Pret. sg. 3. *cingis* 540, 543.

cír f. 'crest, top'. Sg. dat. 471.

cirrad '(act of) mangling, cutting up'. Sg. nom. in comp. *min-chirrad* 'mincing fine' 1134 n.

cissí see 1 **cia.**

ciúil see **ceól.**

cland f. 'one's children, sons and daughters; kindred, descendants'. Sg. dat. *cloind* 575. Pl. acc. *clanna* 599; gen. *clann* 810.

clas f. 'assembly; choir'. In comp. see cétal.

clé adj. 'left'. Sg. dat. f. *clíi* (sp. for *clí*) 1094. In comps. see **boss** and **lám**.

clérech m. 'priest, member of the clergy'. Sg. nom. 660; voc. *clérig* 236, 370, 423. Pl. nom. *clérig* 520, 661; dat. *clérchib* 662.

cléthe f. 'top, crown (of the head)'. Sg. acc. *cléthi* 738; dat. *cléthi* 1048. Pl. dat. *cléthib* 1116.

cléthi see **cléthe** and **cliath**.

cleth f. 'house-post, pole'. Sg. acc. *cleith* 634.

clí f. 'pillar, support, prop'. Sg. voc. 371.

cliab m. 'basket; the (human) chest'. Sg. acc. 867. In comp. see **galar**.

cliath f. 'partition, panel; a hurdle; the rib-cage'. Sg. acc. *cléith* 856; gen., comic name *Cléthi* ('Ribs') 387. Pl. dat. *cliathaib* 122.

cliathán m. 'loin, flitch'. Pl. acc. *cliathánu* 1202.

clíi see **clé**.

clith 'covering, protection'. Sg. acc. 332 n.

clithmaire 'protection, shelter, comfort'. Sg. dat. *clithmaire* 845 (see s.v. **di**).

cloc m. 'bell'. Sg. nom. 228, 357; acc. *clog* 865. Pl. acc. *cluca* 179, *clucu* 313. Cf. **clucín**.

cloch f. 'stone, rock'. Sg. acc. *cloich* 592, 594; gen. *clochi* 855; dat. *cloich* 349. Pl. dat. *clochaib* 127 n. In comp. see **drochat**.

cloicend m. 'skull'. Sg. dat. 1181.

cloidem m. 'sword'. Sg. nom. 646.

cloind see **cland**.

closte verbal of necessity of *cloisid* 'hears'. *Ní closti* 'is not to be heard' 1337.

closs see **at-chluin**.

cloth adj. 'famous'. Sg. voc. f. 371.

clú m./f. 'fame'. Sg. nom. 1111.

cluas f. 'ear'. Sg. gen. *cluaisi* 1332. Dual gen. 1115. Pl. dat. *cluassaib* 1074.

clucín m. 'little bell'. Sg. dat. 1081, 1082.

clúm f. 'feathers, down'. In comp. see **déraigid**.

cnáim m. 'bone'. Pl. nom. *cnámu* 200; acc. (for dat., § xxiii) *cnámu* 200.

cnám m. '(act of) gnawing'. Sg. nom. 1135. In comp. see **fial**.

cnó f. 'nut'. In comp. see 1 **mess**.

1 co^N prep. w. dat. 'with' 12, 13, 84, etc.

2 co^H, cu^H prep. w. acc. (see § xl) 'to, as far as' 58, 93, 109, etc.; *cu* 1304. W. def. art. (see 1 **in**) sg. *cosin* 510, 1190, 1191, 1197, 1199, *cusin* 169, 358, 563, 774; pl. *cosna* 973, 1201, *cusna* 982 (2), 1005 (2). W. art. and -í, *cusint-í* 197. W. suffixed obj. prons., sg. 2 *chucat* 187; 3 m. *chuice* 43, *chuci* 348, *chuc(c)a* 48, 137, 172, 706. W. adj., to form advb., see e.g. **dedbirech, dian, díscir**, etc.

3 co^N conjunction 'with the result that; and; so that; until; that' (with dependent statement clause, see **cen**) 30, 55, 115, 120, 135, 178, etc. W. 2 **ro**, *co ro* (before *C*-) 199, 305, 342, (before *V*-) 199; *cor* (before *C*-) 439, 1228, (before *V*-) 146. W. copula see 1 **is**.

'co see **oc, ic**.

cobair f. 'help'. Sg. acc. 724.

cobraid 'helps'. Pres. subjunct. sg. 3 -*cobra* 529.

cocad m. 'war'. Sg. dat. 1051.

cochall, cocholl m. 'cowl, hood'. Sg. nom. 519, 521, 525, 527, 1306, 1316; acc. 525, in comp. *gerr-chochall* 'short cowl' 545; gen. *cochaill* 532; dat. 907 (see 906 f. n.), 1068. See **cochlín**.

cocnum m. '(act of) chewing'. Sg. acc. in comp. *slucud-chocnum* 'chewing and swallowing' 1210.

codlad, codulta see **cotlad**.

codut adj. 'harsh'. Sg. nom. m. 876.

coecat m. 'fifty; a set of fifty'. Sg. gen. *coecait* 143.

coelach m. 'roof-wattling' (under the thatch). Sg. nom. 810.

coelán see **caelán**.

coem adj. 'beautiful, lovely'. Sg. nom. m. 443.

-coem see **cumcaid**.

coer see **caer**.

coera see **caera**.

coic m. 'a cook'. Sg. gen. in comp. *dag-choca* 'of a good cook' 1126 f.

cóic numeral adj. 'five'. Sg. nom. 614; gen. 290. Cf. **cúiger**.

coíc- numeral prefix 'five-times, five-fold'. See **diabulta** and **dorn**.

cóiced m. 'a fifth part'; one of the traditional Fifths (provinces) of early Ireland; here, Munster. Sg. acc. 713; gen. *cóicid* 622.

cochlín m. 'a little cowl'. Sg. dat. 1313.

coiclid 'spares'. Fut. sg. 2 *-coicéla* 1182.

cocrích f. 'borderland'. Sg. dat. 536, 542.

coícthiges f. 'a fortnight'. Sg. gen. *coícthigis* 334.

coidlide adj. 'made of hide, leather'. Dual acc. m. 102.

coilech m. 'a cock'. Sg. nom. 1196 n.

co(i)llid 'destroys, violates'. Pres. ind. sg. 3 rel. *choilles* 167. Past ind. pass. pl. *ro collit* 166.

comberbad m. '(act of) boiling together (with something)'. Sg. dat. 1282.

Coimde m. 'the Lord' (God). Sg. dat. *Coimdid* 345.

coimdetta adj. 'pertaining to the Lord; the Lord's'. Sg. gen. f. 1273.

co(i)mét m. '(act of) keeping safe, guarding'. Sg. gen. in phrase *lucht coiméta* 'guardians, warders' 287, 320 f.; dat. *comét* 304.

cométach m. '(act of) guarding'. Sg. gen. *cométaig* 280 n. (see 2 **lín**).

coimge, comga f. 'protection, safeguard'. Sg. nom. 810, 1337.

comgne 'traditional learning'. Sg. dat. 371 n.

comlethan adj. 'very broad'. Sg. acc. f. *comlethain* 886.

comlis see **con-meil**.

compert f. 'procreation, conception'. Sg. nom. 619.

comriachtain f. '(act of) meeting, reaching equality with'. Sg. acc. 884.

comscísachtach f. '(act of) becoming wearied in company with'. Sg. dat. *comscísachtaig* 604.

coin see **cú**.

connel f. 'candle'. Sg. gen. *connli* 747.

cóir adj. 'straight, proper, just, seemly'. Sg. nom. m. in comp. *so-chóir* 'very suitable' 1165. Pl. nom. m. *córa* 1171; dat. f. *córaib* 906. Compar. *córu* 260.

As noun f. 'right, proper order; justice', sg. acc. 221; dat. 1153.

co(i)re m. 'cauldron, pot'. Sg. nom. 805, 1230, *cori* 1247, 1283 (see **cét**), in comp. *lón-choire* 'food cauldron' 1231 (see 1230 f. n.); acc. 1230, 1236; gen. *cori* 991, in comp. *ard-chori* 489.

corén m. 'little pot'. Sg. gen. in comp. comic name *Lón-Chorén* 'Little Food Pot' 907. Pl. dat. (for acc., § xxiv) *corénaib* 1188.

cóirgid 'arranges, sets right'. Pret. sg. 3 *cóirgis* 172.

corrmíl m. 'midge'. Sg. nom. 1016.

corthe m. 'pillar, standing stone'. Sg. nom. *corthi* 589; acc. 348, 358, 860; dat. 338, 341.

coiss(e) see **cos**.

coitchend adj. 'common, universal'. Sg. acc. m. 50 n. (The 'eight universal things' are natural phenomena common to the whole world.)

coland f. 'body'. Sg. nom. 865; acc. *colaind* 865.

colba m. 'bench, bed, bed-rail'. Sg. acc. 1159; dat. 590. Pl. nom. *colbai* 824; acc. *colbadu* 578; dat. *colbaib* 121, 842, *colbadaib* 220.

colc f. 'sword'. In comp. see **dírech**.

colcaid f. 'feather bed, mattress'. Sg. acc. 1113, *colcid* 1286.

1 **coll** m./f. '(act of) destroying, violating'. Sg. nom. 165, 167.

2 **coll** m. 'a hazel'. Sg. gen. in comp. *find-chuill* lit. 'white hazel' perhaps a special kind of hazel, 735.

colpa m. 'calf' (of the leg). Pl. nom. *colptha* 1171.

'com see **oc**.

coma f. 'gift, bribe, condition (of treaty etc.)'. Sg. acc. 689.

comad see 1 **is**.

comadas m. 'suitability, fittingness'. Sg. gen. (attributive) in *ainm comadais* 'suitable name' 69, and predicative in *nárba comadais* 'which was not fitting' 548.

comainm m. 'surname, by-name; name'. Sg. nom. 923, 926, 938, 1064. Pl. nom. *comanmand* 65.

comair in phrase *i comair* 'in front of, in the presence of' 1143.

comarce f. 'protection, defence, safeguard, surety'. Sg. acc. (of respect) *comarci* 1003; dat. *comarci* 1001.

coma(i)rle f. 'counsel, advice; decision, plan'. Sg. nom. 207, 209, 324; acc. 893, *comarli* 207, 892.

coma(i)thech m. 'fellow tenant, neighbour'. Sg. gen. (distributive) *coma(i)thig* 681, 1303, 1327.

comall m. 'fulfilment'. Sg. acc. 251, 671.

comallad m. '(act of) fulfilling'. Sg. dat. 570.

comarc 'agreement, plan' (?). Sg. acc. in comp. *luath-chomarc* 302 n.; dat. 302.

comard adj. 'equally high'. Pl. nom. m./f. *comarda* 1168.

comba see 1 **is**.

combruthe past partcp. of *con-berba* 'boils (together)'. Sg. nom. m. *combruthi* 1283. Cf. **comberbad**.

comga see **coimge**.

comla f. 'door'. Sg. nom. 452, 1051; acc. *comlaid* 1056, 1060. In comp. see **iarcomla**.

comlán adj. 'complete, perfect'. Sg. nom. m. 69.

comnart adj. 'very firm'. Sg. acc. m. 1029.

comorba m. 'heir'. Sg. acc. 1340.

comrac m. 'conflict'. Sg. dat. 1343.

comrád m. 'conversation, speech'. Sg. nom. in comp. *mín-chomrád* 'gentle speech' 1175.

comraircnech adj. 'blundering'. Sg. voc. f. 330.

comrarcu/-gu, comrorcu f. 'mistake, misunderstanding, guilt'. Sg. nom. *comrargu/-cu bunat(t)a* 'original sin' 145, 211, *comrorcu* 676 (for acc., § xx).

comthromm adj. 'of equal weight, well-balanced'. Sg. acc. m. 108.

comur m. 'meeting-place, meeting'. Sg. acc. 81.

con see **cú**.

co-na see **-da-**.

conáb, conadam see 1 **is**.

conar f. 'path'. Sg. gen. *conaire* 437.

cond(a)igid 'asks, enquires; asks for, begs, demands'. Pres. ind. sg. 1 *condaigim(m)* 247 f. n., 679, *connaig-*

imm 327, *condigim* 519; 2 *condigi* 518, 671, *condige* 252; pass. *condagur* 559. Pres. subjunct. sg. 1 *cuinger* 328 n. Verbal of necessity *cuintesta* 'should be enquired about' 3 n., 4.

congaib f. 'gathering, assemblage, muster'. Sg. nom. 437.

connice prep. w. acc. 'as far as' 537.

conid see 1 **is**.

con-luí 'goes, proceeds'. Pres. ind. sg. 1 *con-ludimm* 1062 n.

con-meil, comlid (deutero. and simple proto., see §§ lxix ff.) 'rubs'. Fut. sg. 2 *con-melfi* 1152. Pret. sg. 3 *comlis* 744.

conu see **cú**.

cop see 1 **is**.

1 **cor, cur** m. (v.n. of **cuirid**). (1) '(act of) putting, scattering, sowing'. (2) 'contract, bond, guarantee, pledge; guarantor'. (3) 'occasion'. (1) Sg. nom. *cor* 200, 201, 856, *cur* 870; dat. *cur* 45. (2) Pl. nom. *cuir* 250, 295; acc. *curu/-a* 252, 576, 671 (for nom., § xxii). (3) Sg. dat. *don chur-sa* 'on this occasion' 1147.

2 **cor** see 3 **co** and 2 **ro**.

corab see 1 **is**.

corand f. 'chaplet, circlet'. Sg. dat. *coraind* 1070; pl. dat. *cornib* 1068.

corc(c)a m. 'oats' (perhaps 'oatmeal porridge' at 158, 185 and 186). Sg. nom. 158 n., 1184; gen. 159, 171, 185, 186, 407, 1074.

corcair f. 'pink colour'. In comp. see **glan**.

corccra adj. 'purple, pink'. Sg. nom. m. 1165, in comp. *dond-chorccra* 'brownish pink' 1296, f. in comp. *bél-chorccra* 'red lipped' 1161; dat. in comp. *barr-chorccra* 'pink tipped' 474. Pl. nom. m./f. 1168; dat. f. 409.

corgas m. 'Lent'. Sg. gen. *corgais* 1196.

corma see **cuirm**.

cornib see **corand**.

corob see 1 **is**.

corp m. 'body'. Sg. nom. 507; acc. 1277; gen. *cuirp* 846; dat. 901.

1 **corr** adj. 'pointed'. Dual acc. m. *corra* 102. Pl. acc. f. 1060. As noun f. 'point, tip', sg. acc. *cuirr* 1089. In comp. see **corrmíl**.

2 **corr** f. 'heron'. Sg. gen. (attributive) *cuirre* 632, *curri* 1186.

3 **corr** f. 'pool, pond, puddle'. Sg. gen. *cuirre* 657.

corrach adj. 'unstable, shifty'. Sg. voc. f. 330.

corrán m. 'hook, staple'. Pl. acc. *corránu* 757.

córu see **cóir**.

corup see 1 **is**.

cos(s) f. 'foot, leg'. Sg. nom. 636; acc. *coiss* 1112; gen. *coisse* 163, *cossi* 1245. Dual nom. *coiss* 762. Pl. acc. *cossa* 132, 1073 (for dat., § xxiii); gen. 135. In comp. see **lúthmar**.

cosc m. '(act of) preventing'. Sg. nom. 860.

cosin, cosna see 2 **co**.

cosnaid 'contends; strives for'. Pres. ind. pl. 3 rel. *chosnait* 1191.

cosnamaid m. 'contender, defender'. Sg. nom. 23, in comp. *ard-chosnamaid* 'chief defender' 599; voc. 622.

'cot' see **oc**.

cota, cotib see **cuit**.

cotlad m. (v.n. of **cotlaid**) '(state of) sleeping; sleep'. Sg. nom. 729; gen. *cotultai* 846, *codulta* 1288; dat. *codlad* 1292.

cotlaid 'sleeps'. Fut. sg. 1 -*coitél* 731.

craebach adj. 'branching'; of liquids 'streaming in branches, forks'. Sg. gen. m. *craebaig* 408.

craes m. 'gullet; gluttony'. Sg. gen. *craes* 896, *craís* 1143, in phrase *lon c.* 'demon of gluttony' 13, 20, 56, *craeis* 9 n. In comp. see **lon**.

craíbechán m. 'porridge, gruel'. Sg. nom. 1201; gen. 968, comic name 408; dat. 991, 993.

craiccend m. 'skin, hide'. Sg. acc. 199.

crand m. 'tree'. Sg. acc. 323, 855, in comp. *césad-chrand* 'passion-tree' (the gallows on which MC was to be hanged) 321.

crebar m. 'gadfly'. Sg. nom. 1016.

credb 'shrinking, decaying, corroding, wearing away'. Sg. gen. *credba* 1132 n.

créduma m. 'bronze, brass'. Sg. gen. (attributive) 843.

crét interrog. advb. 'for what reason, why?' 699.

criathar m. 'sieve, (honey-)comb'. Sg. gen. *créthir* 861. Pl. dat. *criathraib* 734.

crích f. 'end, limit; land, district' (the pl. may have sg. sense). Sg. acc. 112, 300, 323, 692; gen. *críche* 1031. Pl. nom. *crícha* 310; acc. *crícha* 713; dat. *críchaib* 603.

cride m. 'heart'. Sg. gen. 896.

cris(s) m. 'belt'. Sg. dat. 763, 1067.

crithir f. 'spark'. Sg. acc. 741, 747.

crob f. 'hand, claw, paw'. Dual acc. 1228.

croch f. 'cross'. Sg. gen. *crochi* 1273.

crochad m. (v.n. of **crochaid**) '(act of) hanging'. Sg. nom. 209, 238, 324; acc. 313; dat. 304.

crochaid 'hangs' (trans.). Pres. subjunct. pass. sg. -*crochthar* 235 n., 237. Past subjunct. pass. sg. -*crochthá* 243, w. 2 **ro** *ro crochtha* 305 n.

cross f. 'a cross'. Sg. gen. *crossi* 1202.

croth f. 'cream, curds'. Sg. gen. *crothi* 989, in comps. *sen-chrothi* 'of sour cream' 458, 1076, comic name *Borr-Chrothi* 'of Thick Cream' 376.

1 **crú** m. 'gore' (see 961 f. n. and 970 f. n.). Sg. acc. 971; gen. 962.

2 **crú** m. 'hoof'. Pl. acc. (for dat., § xxiii) 1074.

cruaid adj. 'hard, tough'. Sg. nom. m. 646, 875; gen. f. *cruadi* 990. In comp. see **carraic**.

cruind adj. 'round, compact'. In comp. see **mag**.

cruit m. 'harper; harp'. In comp. see 2 **fiach**.

cruithnecht f. 'wheat'. Sg. nom. 1183, in comp. *gel-chruithnecht* 'white wheat' 447; gen. *cruithnechta* 256, 906, comic name 400; dat. in comp. *fír-chruithnecht* 'pure wheat' 15.

Cruithnechtán m. comic pet-name (diminutive of **cruithnecht**) 'Little Wheat'. Nom. 919.

cruth m. 'shape, shapeliness'. Sg. acc. 953.

cú m./f. 'hound'. Sg. acc. *coin* 861; gen. *con* 13, 858, 926. Pl. voc. *conu* 270, 329. In comp. see **téll**.

1 **cuachán** m. 'little bowl, cup'. Sg. nom. 158 n., 185, 186.

2 **cuachán** m. in *miach cuachán* sg. gen. 560, perhaps 'a bushel of oatmeal porridge' (see 158 n.).

cuairt m./f. 'circuit, visitation'. Sg. acc. in comp. *cét-chuairt* 92 n.; dat. 93 n.

-cuala see **at-chluin**.

cuarán m. 'sandal, shoe'. Dual acc. 102. Pl. acc. *cuaránu* 129, 130, 131.

cubaid adj. 'fitting, appropriate'. Sg. nom. m. 717; pl. nom. m. *cuibde* 65. In comp. *in-chubaid* 'inappropriate' 424 f. n.

cubus m. 'conscience'. Sg. acc. *cubais* 753 (see 752 f. n.), 754.

cuchtar f. 'kitchen'. Sg. acc. *cuchtair* 1102; dat. 1109.

cúiger m. 'five people; a legal family unit, family'. Sg. gen. *cúigir* 1200 n.

cuil f. 'fly, gnat; flea'. Sg. nom. 1016.

cúil f. 'corner, nook'. Sg. nom. 629.

cuill see 2 **coll**.

cuimgess see **cumcaid**.

cumne f. 'memory, remembrance'. Sg. dat. *cumni* 421.

cuimrech m. '(act of) binding, fettering'. Sg. gen. *cuimrig* 280, 287.

cuinchid (v.n. of **condaigid**) '(act of) asking, begging, seeking'. Sg. nom. 858; dat. 603, 669.

cunnid m. 'prop, one who sustains; a champion'. Sg. acc. 1195.

-cuinger, cuintesta see **cond(a)igid**.

cuir see 1 **cor**.

cu(i)rid 'puts, throws, sends' (see **fo-cheird** and **láid**) simple proto. replacing OI *ro-cuirethar*. Pres. ind. pass. sg. *-curther* 1117. Pret. sg. 3, *cuiris* 612, 614.

cuirm f. 'ale'. Sg. nom. 1195; gen., comic name *Corma* 399, in phrase *nua corm(m)a* (lit. 'the new of ale') 'new ale' 16, 226, 1198.

cuirp see **corp**.

cuirr see 1 **corr**.

cuirre see 2 and 3 **corr**.

cuit f. 'share, portion; rations, provision, food'. Sg. nom. 189, 226, 1136; acc. 14; gen. *cota* 155. Pl. dat. *cotib* 616.

cu(i)tig f. 'portion of food, rations, meal'. Sg. nom. 154, 157; dat. in comp. *prím-chutig* 558 (see 17 f. n.).

cúl m. 'the back part, rear; the back of the head, neck'. Sg. acc. 956; dat. in phrase *for cúl* (w. gen.) 'at the back of' 478. In comp. see 2 **buide**.

cumma in phrase *(is) cumma la X* 'it is of no importance to X, X does not care' 508, 513. As advb. in *cumma no bered tinne . . . 7 lón-longén* 'he was bringing out flitches . . . and sausages [?] alike' 1106 f.

cum(m)aid 'creates, forms, shapes, composes'. Pres. ind. sg. 3 *cumaid* 353. Pret. sg. 3 *cummais* 101.

cumair adj. 'short'. As noun 'a summary, an abstract' sg. nom. 360.

cumal f. unit of value (the worth of three milch cows). Pl. gen. 1317.

cummascaigid 'mixes'. Past partcp. *cummascaigthe* 1108.

cumcaid, cuimcid 'can, is able to'. Pres. ind. sg. rel. *chuimges* 1348 n. Pl. 1 *-cumgam* 1256 n. Past ind. sg. 3 *-coem* in *nír choem ní* 'could do nothing' 1251 (see DIL C 446.15).

cumdachta adj. 'well-made, decorated'. Sg. dat. f. 842.

cumra adj. 'sweet-smelling'. Sg. nom. m. in comp. *fír-chumra* 'very fragrant' 1295. Pl. nom. m. 1203; dat. f. in comp. *fír-chumra* 473.

cundrad m. 'trading; bargain, contract'. Sg. gen. *cundartha* 872.

1 **cur** 'warrior, hero'. Sg. gen. *curad* 589.

2 **cur, curu** see 1 **cor**.

curchán m. 'little boat, coracle'. Sg. nom. 433.

cusin, cusint-í, cusna see 2 **co**.

cutrum(m)a adj. 'of equal weight; symmetrical, well-proportioned'. Sg. acc. m. 108, 1029; dat. m. 985. Pl. nom. m. 1171.

d', da see **di** and 2 **do**.

-daN- infixed obj. pron. Class C sg. 3 m. 'him, it'. Two forms: (1) *n(d)a*, after 3 co^N, 135, 711 f. (indirect obj. 'so that he might have', 2 exx.); (2) *-t-*, after preverbs *do, ro,* and *no*, 108, 966, 1216, 1301. See § xxxvi.

1 **dá**L numeral adj. m. 'two', f. *dí*L (for MI confusion between the genders see § xxix). Nom. m. *dá* 159, 597, 906, 1329; f. *dí* 762, 797, 1170, *dá*

(for *dí*) 159, 760, 784 (see **mír**), 1167. Acc. m. *dá* 176, 1162, 1209, *dí* (for *dá*) 26, 101, 172, 837; f. *dí* 170, 256, 277, 1228. Gen. m. *dá* 809; f. *dá* ('correct') 25, 539, *dí* ('incorrect') 582, 1076, 1115. Dat. (OI *dib*) f. *dí* 1099, *dá* 100, 1075.

2 **dá** see 2 **do**.

3 **dá** see 4 **dia**ᴺ.

dabach f. 'vat'. Sg. nom. 16. Pl. gen. 1088.

dag-, deg- adj. prefix 'good'. See **biad, coíc, duine, fritháilem, mac(c), már**.

1 **dáig** prep. w. gen. 'as regards' 18. As conjunction (see § xliv) 'because' 21, 1039, 1044; (*ar*) *dáig co/ná* 'so that, so that not' 206, 995.

2 **dáig** see **dóig**.

dáil see 1 **dál**.

daíne see **duine**.

dair f. 'oak-tree'. Sg. gen. *darach* 857; dat. *daroich* 1154.

daire m. 'grove, thicket'. Sg. nom. 476.

1 **dál** f. 'meeting'. Sg. nom. 1140 n.; dat. (for acc., § xxiv) in phrase *i ndáil* 'to meet' 334, 965.

2 **dál** f. 'delay, respite'. Sg. nom. 312, 317, 362, 366, 425, for acc. (§ xx) 364, 427; gen. *dála* 337.

dala pronominal 'one (of two)' in phrase *in dala n-aeí* 'one of (the two of) them', nom. 163.

dam see 2 **do**.

-damᴸ**-, -dom**ᴸ**-** infixed obj. pron. Classes B and C sg. 1 'me'. Class B in *atom-* (= *ad-dom-*) 848, 1006, 1052; see **at-raig** and **ad-chuirethar**. Class C w. 3 **co**ᴺ and 4 **dia**ᴺ (*-nam, -nom*) 570, 627, 1114. See §§ xxxv and xxxvi.

dám f. 'company, party'. Sg. nom. 223; acc. *dáim* 1037.

dámad see 1 **is**.

damaid 'allows; grants'; *damaid fri* 'endures, tolerates'. Pret. sg. 3 *-dam* 580; pass. sg. *-damad* 346. Past ind. pass. sg. *ro damad* 273.

dán m. In phrase *a ndán* 'foretold, fated' 167.

da-ní see **do-gní**.

1 **dar** 'seems, seemed' with **la**. *Dar lium(m)* 'I thought' 806, 812.

2 **dar** (occasionally **dar**ᴸ), **tar** (see § xl) prep. w. acc. 'across, over, past, about'; in asseverations 'by'; *tidecht taris* 'to transgress it'. *Dar* 28, 29, 33, etc. *Tar* 756, 768, 872, etc. W. def. art. sg. *darsin* 1007, 1113, 1211, *dar in* 121, 163. W. suffixed obj. prons., sg. 1 *torum* 333; 3 m. *taris* 340, 687, 1067. W. possess. sg. 1 *daro m'* 'by my' 716 n. In phrase *dar fíarlaít/fíarut* 'across' 152, 540, 587. *Dar ná dlegar oirbire* 'about which one ought not to grumble' 225.

darach, daroich see **dair**.

dath m. 'colour'. Pl. dat. *dathaib* 1318.

de see **di, de**.

1 **dé** f. 'smoke'. Sg. nom. 1157; acc. *diaid* 740.

2 **Dé** see 1 **Dia**.

dead f. (orig. neut.) 'end'. Sg. dat. (for acc., § xxiv) in *co deód n-aidche* 'till the end of the night' 728, (*i n*)*deód* (*n-*)*aidche* 'at the end of the night' 353 (see § xvi), 698. See 2 **diaid**.

debroth oath or asseveration 'God's doom'. On the form and the meaning see 168 n. In phrases *at-biur mo debroth* 168, 875; *do m' debroth* 565 f., 683, 780, 1276; *dar mo debroth* 993 f.; *daro m' debroth* 716 n.; *ba m' debroth* 685 (see **fo**).

decáid 'a decade, set of ten psalms'. Pl. dat. *decáidib* 142.

-dechad, -dechaid, -dechumar see **téit**.

dechmad ordinal numeral adj. 'tenth'. Sg. nom. m. 622. As noun f. 'tenth part; a tithe', sg. nom. 265 n., 275, 276; acc. *dechmaid* 257, 258, 261; gen. *dechmaide* 263.

déda 'two things, a couple'. Sg. nom. 610.

deg- see **dag-**.

deichᴺ numeral adj. 'ten' 614, 1060, 1084, 1338.

décsin f. '(act of) looking'. Sg. dat. 263.

dedbirech adj. 'hasty'. As advb. w. 2 **co** 'hastily' 538 n.

dédenach, dédinach adj. 'last, latest'. Sg. nom. m. 726, f. 1285, neut. 691 (see 545 f. n.); acc. m. 1212.

déne f. 'swiftness, speed'. Sg. dat. *déni* 1017.

dé(i)nmnetach adj. 'impatient, hasty' 1041. As advb. w. 2 **co** 'impatiently' 152, 538, 586, 1011.

derbshiúr f. 'sister'. Sg. nom. 22.

deriud m. 'end'. Sg. nom. 336, 502; acc. 501.

dermitnech adj. 'disreputable, infamous'. Sg. acc. m. 1254.

descert m. 'the southern part, the south'. Sg. dat. 684. In comp. see 1 **leth**.

descertach adj. 'southern'. In comp., sg. dat. f. *iarthar-descertaig* 'south western' 664.

desel m. 'clockwise direction, right-hand course'. Sg. dat. as prep. (w. gen.) *desel relci* 'clockwise round the graveyard' 110.

-dessid, -dessitar see **saidid**.

desmberecht m. 'example, specimen'. Sg. dat. 1339.

de(i)t(t) see 2 **do**.

de(i)thbir adj. 'fitting, proper, reasonable, natural'. Sg. nom. 85, 124, 845, 1009, 1043. In comp. *so-dethbir* 'very natural' 638, 1125, 1128. As noun 'reason, cause', sg. nom. 652.

delb f. 'form, appearance'. Sg. nom. 1063.

delc/-g m. 'pin, brooch'. Sg. nom. 286; gen. *delci* 284, *delgai* 285, *delca* 286; dat. 1347.

demun m. 'devil, the Devil'. Sg. nom. 274, 608, 718, 1250, 1275, *demon* 1259.

-dén, -déna, -dénann, -dénum see **do-gní**.

dénam m. (v.n. of **do-gní**) '(act of) doing, making'. Sg. acc. 1256; gen. *dénma* 9; dat. 700, 727, 1143, 1302.

dénmus m. 'making, forming'. Sg. dat. 99.

deód see **dead**.

deog, deoch f. 'drink'. Sg. nom. 656; acc. *dig* 147, 224, 656, *deog* 1206; dat. in comp. *do nua-dig* 'as a fresh drink' 1282.

deóin f. 'will, consent'. Sg. dat. in *dia bar ndeóin* 'by your free will, willingly' 328.

deól m. '(act of) sucking'. Sg. nom. 857.

deórad m. 'stranger, wanderer, pilgrim'. Pl. acc. *deóradu* 663.

dér m. 'tear'. Pl. gen. 709.

déraigid 'spreads; makes a bed'. Pres. ind. pass. sg. *déraigther* 1286. Past partcp. in comp. *clúm-déraigthi* 'feather-spread' 1286.

derc/-g adj. 'red, ruddy; red-haired'. Sg. nom. m. in comp. *ór-derg* 'golden-red' 1166, f. *hó-derg* 'red-eared' 1346; dat. f. *deirg* 1154. Pl. nom. m. *deirg* 1169; dat. *dercaib* 480.

dergnat f. 'flea'. Pl. nom. *dergnatta* 135, *dergnuta* 204.

dergnatach adj. 'full of fleas'. Sg. nom. m. 124.

dermáir adj. 'huge'. Sg. nom. 587; pl. nom. f. *dermára* 1248.

-derna, -dernad, -dernais, -dernsamm, -dernsat see **do-gní**.

deróil adj. 'insignificant, mean, humble'. Sg. acc. f. 720.

dess adj. 'right, right-hand'. Sg. gen. f. *dessi* 1238; dat. *deiss* 1055, 1099. In comp. see **lám**.

dét m. 'tooth'. Pl. nom. *déta* 897, 1169; acc. *détu* 1152; gen. 592, 594.

dethach f. 'smoke, vapour'. Sg. dat. *dethaig* 655.

di¹, de^L (do^L, da^L) prep. w. dat., 'from, of' etc. Almost all forms except the prep. prons. have fallen together w. 2 **do** (q.v.) which may cause ambiguity. The 3rd pers. prep. prons. often suffix anaphoric **-side** q.v. For phrase *atá do* (plus possessive) plus abstract noun cf., e.g., *ro boí do chlithmaire mo lepthai* 'so comfortable was my bed' 845; *mina beth dia n-uaisle* 'if it were not for their nobility' 1263; see also s.v. 1 **cia**. The original forms of the simple prep. *di/de* survive in 6, 740, 1068; otherwise *do* 15, 16, 75, etc. Before *cach/cech* it becomes *da* 3, 811, 1199. The *-V* may be elided before *V-* or *fhV-* 156, 201, 203, etc. W. def. art. sg. *don* 83, 344, 584, etc.; pl. *do na* 582, 1225. W. suffixed obj. prons., sg. 1 *dimm* 271; 2 *dít(t)* 337, 563; 3 m. *de* 56, 129, 196, etc.; 3 f. *di* 553, 591; pl. 3 *díb* 54, 704, 741, etc. W. possessives, sg. 3 m. *dia^L* 40, 86, 154;

162 GLOSSARY

pl. 2 *dia bar* 328; 3 *dia*^N 1263-4. **W.**
-a^N (rel. particle), *dia*^N 'from whom/
which' 1077.

1 **dí** see 1 **dá.**

2 **dí** see 2 **do.**

di- negative and privative prefix 'in-,
un-'. See **díchonnercle, díchumci,
dífhreccra.**

1 **Dia** m. 'God'. Nom. 831; voc. *Dé*
312; acc. 295, 677, 1237; gen. *Dé*
348, 523, 1256, 1335; dat. 264, 600,
618, 724, 1276.

2 **dia** m. 'day'. Sg. gen. (of time) 117,
230.

3 **dia, dia**^N see **di** and 2 **do.**

4 **dia**^N, **dá**^N conjunction 'if, when' 25,
32 n., 34, etc. The later form *dá*^N
730. See also s.v. 1 **is.**

diabul m. 'devil, demon'. Sg. nom.
1255.

diabulda adj. 'devilish, diabolical'. **W.**
2 **co** 'like a devil' 586.

diabulta adj. (past partcp. of *diablaid*
'doubles') 'doubled, folded'. In
comps., sg. nom./acc. f. *coíc-diabulta*
'five-fold' 539, 1166; pl. acc. m. *lúb-
diabulta* lit. 'loop-doubled' 1201.

1 **diaid** see 1 **dé.**

2 **diaid** late form of sg. dat. of **dead**
(q.v.), in comp. prep. (w. gen.) *i
ndiaid* 'after, behind' 67; *i n-a diaid*
'behind him' 760, 948 n.; *i n-a ndiaid*
'after them' 292. As advb. *i n-a diaid*
'afterwards' 694.

diamad see 1 **is.**

dian adj. 'swift, brisk, vehement'. Sg.
nom. m. 1040, f. 1160. **W.** 2 **co**
'swiftly' 543, 1011.

dianad see 1 **is.**

dianechtair advb. 'from/on the outside'
206, 594, 1054.

diapsalma 'diapsalm', a musical pause
in singing the psalms. Pl. dat.
diapsalmaib 141.

dias f. personal numeral 'pair, couple,
two people'. Sg. dat. (of accompaniment) *dís* '(there being) two (of us)'
786; w. 1 **ar**, *ar ndís* 'the two of us'
1214.

díb see **di.**

díbad m. 'inheritance, legacy'. Sg. nom.
856.

díbe f. 'hunger and thirst'. Sg. nom.
1140.

dícend see **glám.**

díchonnercle f. 'unkindness'. Sg. nom.
1138.

díchor m. '(act of) banishing, expelling'.
Sg. dat. 9.

-dichsed see **téit.**

díchumce f. 'powerlessness, inability'.
Sg. dat. *díchumci* 883.

didiu transitional advb. 'moreover,
however, then, well now' etc.; 8,
536, 665, etc.

dífhreccra adj. 'incomparable; im-
mense'. Pl. acc. f. 737.

dig see **deog.**

-dig, -diged, -digset see **téit.**

dígbaid 'takes away, deprives, dimin-
ishes'. Past ind. sg. 3 (w. infix) *ra-m
dígaib* 657.

díglaid 'avenges, punishes'. Pres. subjunct. pass. sg. *-dígailter* 196.

-dignesta, -dignestar see **do-gní.**

dímór adj. 'great, huge'. Sg. gen. m.
dímóir 1059.

dín m. 'protection, defence'. Sg. nom.
944.

dingbaid 'keeps away' (trans.). Past
subjunct. sg. 1 *-dingbaind* 563.

-dingen see **do-gní.**

dírech adj. 'straight'. Sg. nom. m. in
comp. *coílc-dírech* 'straight-bladed'
646; dat. f. *dírig* 1055, 1154. Pl. acc.
m. in comp. *fír-dírge* 'very straight'
735.

dís see **dias.**

díscir adj. 'bold, wild, shameless'. Sg. nom.
m. 1040; acc. f. 720. **W.** 2 **co**
'boldly' 152, 538, 585, 1010 f.

dísert, dísiurt m. 'a retreat in the wilds,
hermitage'. Sg. nom. 894 n., 1046,
1091; gen. *díserta* 894, 1031; dat.
dísiurt 1147.

díthat f. 'meal, snack'. Sg. gen. *díthata*
890. Pl. nom. *díthata* 889.

diúltad m. '(act of) rejecting; refusing
to admit'. Sg. nom. 1137.

dixit (Latin) 'said' 174, 429, 988.

dlaí f. 'tuft, bundle, wisp' (of thatch).
Sg. acc. 635.

dliged m. 'law, justice; legal argument
in justification'. Sg. acc. 244; gen.
dligid 273, 347; dat. *dligud* 243.

dligid 'has a right/claim to, deserves; ought to'. Pres. ind. sg. 3 -dlig 686; pl. 2 -dligthi 276; pass./impers. sg. -dlegar 'is proper' 225, 254.

1 **do**^{L}, **da**^{L}, **t'**^{L}, **th'**^{L}, **h'**^{L} possessive sg. 2 'thy'. Do 168, 337, 507, etc.; da 564. Elided forms before V-, fhV-: t' 188, 247, 507, etc. (note t' sh- 1122; i t' C- 1180 f.), th' 666, 781, 1121, h' 234, 916, 1119.

2 **do**^{L}, **da**^{L} (see **di** for their coalescence). Prep. w. dat. 'to, for, against' etc.; can express the agent 'by'; governing v.ns., making quasi-infinitives. Before cach, cech, it becomes da 1337. Do 9, 23, 36, etc.; w. elision before V- 39, 650. W. def. art. sg. don 4, 5, 45, etc.; pl. do na 580 (2), 700, 996, 997. W. art. and -í, dont-í 1348. W. suffixed obj. prons., sg. 1 dam 246, 250, 255, etc.; 2 duit 234, 337, 361, etc.; de(i)t(t) 224, 877, 1207, 1260; 3 m. dó 18, 22, 39, etc.; 3 f. dí 6, 38; pl. 1 dún 311, 316, 370, etc.; 2 dúib 275; 3 dóib 60. W. possessives, sg. 1 do m' 364, 571, 683; 2 do t' 574 f. (2), 1268; 3 m. dia^L 92, 110, 136, etc., f. dia$^{(H)}$ 41; pl. 3 dia^N 48, 342, 573 f. (2), 574, 682, dá^N 570. W. -a^N (rel. particle) dia^N 'to whom/which' 1146, 1267; see also s.v. 1 **is**.

1 **dó** cardinal numeral, w. 2 **a** in counting, a dó 'two' 607, 616.

2 **dó** see 2 **do**.

do-adbat 'shows' (trans.), 'appears' (intrans.). Past ind. sg. 3 (w. infixed pron. sg. 1) do-m-árfaid 'appeared to me' 361 n.; pass. sg. do-m-árfas 424, 430, 779, do-árfas 827, -tárfas 817.

do-airis 'stands, stops; consists'. Pres. ind. sg. 3, 615. Past ind. sg. 1 -tarrusar 1114.

do-airngir 'prophesies; promises'. Past ind. pass. sg. do-rarngired 618.

do-ánaic see **ticc**.

do-beir 'gives, puts, brings'; do-beir for 'confers on'. Pres. ind. sg. 1 do-biur 522 f.; 3 do-beir 79; pass. sg. do-berar 255, do-berair 320 (see § lviii). Imperf. pl. 1 do-bermis 1032; 3 do-bertis 1226; pass. sg. do-berthí 1225, pl. do-bertis 35. Impv. sg. 2 tabair 362, 617, 666,

983; 3 tabrad 1178; impv. (from stem tuc(c)-) sg. 2 -tuc 637; pass. sg. tuc(c)thar 235 n., 254. Pres. subjunct. (from stem tuc(c)-) pass. sg. -tucthar 425. Past subjunct. (from stem do-rat-) sg. 2 -tarta 687. Fut. sg. 1 do-bér 527, 528, 567, 893, -tibar 528 n., -tibér 365; 3 -tibre 525; pass. sg. do-bérthar 670, 672, 693, 984, 1305. Condit. sg. 1 do-béraind 564, 1277; 2 do-bértha 562; 3 do-bérad 506, -tibred 427, 632; pl. 1 do-bérmais 260; 3 -tibratis 364. Pret. sg. 3 do-bert 38. Past ind. (a) (from stem tuc(c)-) sg. 1 tucus 1112; 3 tuc(c) 92, 137, 706; pass. sg. tuc(c)ad 52, 302, 307, 694, 1227, 1236, 1283; (b) (from stem do-rat-) sg. 1 -tardus 527; 3 do-rat 101, 282; pl. 3 -tardsat 640, 675; pass. sg. do-ratad 272, -tartad 214.

doccair adj. 'troublesome, difficult; full of hardship'. Superl. doccra 205.

do-chóid see **téit**.

dochta f. 'niggardliness'. Sg. nom. 1137.

do-chuir, tochraid 'puts, sends; throws; happens (to be); meets; invites, summons'. Do-chuir do X 'meets X'; do-chuir do X fri Y 'X has a (hostile) encounter with Y'. Pres. ind. sg. 3 do-t-cuir 'which summons him' 966; pl. 3 -dochrat in a dochrat duit 'in which they meet you, where you find them' 1183 n. Pret. pass. sg. -tochrad 441, 1033. Past ind. sg. 3 do-rala 118, 639, 675, -tarla 1146.

dochum(m)^N prep. w. following gen. 'to, towards' 299, 510. W. possessive a dochumm 'to him' 38. W. pleonastic possessive and following gen. 281, 543, 902, 995. As comp. prep. i ndochumm: (a) w. gen. 279; (b) w. possessive, e.g. i n-a dochumm 'to him' 44, 136, a m' dochumm 850.

do-chummlai 'sets off'. Pres. ind. sg. 3, 112.

doennacht f. 'humanity, kindness; act of kindness'. Sg. acc. 609.

do-fil 'is at hand, approaches'. Pres. ind. sg. 3 w. infixed obj. pron. (=logical subj.) do-s-fil 'he approaches' 27 (see § xxxiii).

do-foichell 'promises'. Past. ind. sg. 3 do-ruachell 44 n.

dogaillsi f. 'grief, dejection'. Sg. nom. 1140.

do-gair 'summons'. Pres. ind. pass. sg. *do-garar* 668. Pret. pass. sg. *do-garad* 38.

do-géba see **fo-geib**.

do-gní 'does, makes, causes' (trans.), 'acts' (intrans.). *Do-gní X Y ar Z* 'X does Y as Z asks/orders'; impers. w. acc. obj. plus *di* 'becomes'. Pres. ind. sg. 3 *do-gní* 554, 596, 1133, 1309, *daní* 1210, *-dénann* 553; pl. 1 *-dénum* 176; pass. sg. *do-gníther* 710, 712. Imperf. sg. 1 *do-gnínd* 290. Impv. sg. 2 *déna* 177, 1255. Pres. subjunct. sg. 1 *-dén* 178; pass. sg. *do-gnether* 508. Past subjunct sg. 3 *do-gneth* 128. Fut. sg. 1 *do-gén* 769, 1255, *-dingen* 731 (see § lxxxvii (2), sg. 3); pl. 3 *do-génut* 604; pass. sg. *do-géntar* 1280, 1298, 1302, *-dignestar* 422 n. Condit. pass. sg. *-dignesta* 564 (see 422 n.). Past ind. sg. 2 *do-rindis* 231, *-dernais* 188, 221, 421; 3 *do-rigne* 53, 196, 197, *cid do-t-rigne?* 'what has made you [behave so]?' 637 f., 651, *-derna* 609, *co nderna lon craís de* 'so that it became a demon of gluttony' 55 f.; pl. 1 *-dernsamm* 232, 314; 3 *do-rigset* 302, 625, *-dernsat* 26; pass. sg. *do-rónad* 8, 339, *do-rigned* 211, 1283, *-dernad* 421, 777, 1110, pl. *do-rónta* 823.

dogra f. 'sorrow'. Sg. nom. 1337.

dóib see 2 **do**.

do-icc see **ticc**.

doichell f. 'grudging, inhospitality, sullenness'. Sg. nom. 1137; gen. *doichle* 1165.

dóig adj. 'likely'. Sg. nom. w. copula 58, 143; gen. m. (qualifying noun) *dáig* 'certain' 965 (see 964 ff. n.).

doíl f. 'beetle'. Sg. gen. (qualifying) *doíle* '[as] of a beetle, as [black as] a beetle' 1167.

doilig adj. 'difficult, troublesome, vexatious'. Sg. nom. m. 556, 557. Compar. *duilge* 86, *doilge* 558; compar. in *-de*, *doilgide* 559.

doíne see **duine**.

doinmech adj. 'wretched'. Sg. nom. m. 90.

doirrseóir m. 'doorkeeper, porter'. Sg. nom. m. 1092; acc. 1063.

dorsech 'having doors/openings'. Sg. acc. f. in comp. *cethar-dorsig* 'having four openings, gaps' 740.

dóit f. 'upper arm; hand'. In comp. see **gel**.

dóitech adj. Sg. nom. m. in comp. comic name *Lám-Dóitech*, meaning unclear but perh. used in sense 'right-handed' 914 f. n.

dol, dul, dula m. (v.n. of **téit**) '(act of) going'. Sg. nom. *dol* 89, *dul* 197, 786, *dula* 93; acc. *dol* 254; dat. *dul* 149, 253, 275, 303, 334, 965, 1093, 1211.

do-lína 'fills, gluts'. Imperf. pass. sg. *do-línta* 665.

do-lluid see **do-thét**.

do m' see 2 **do, da**.

do-meil 'consumes, eats'. Pres. ind. sg. 1 *-tomlim* 1137. Impv. sg. 2 *tomil* 168. Past subjunct. w. (infixed) 2 **ro**, sg. 1 *-tormolaind* 996. Fut. sg. 1 *-toimél* 731; 3 *do-méla* 189, 775. Past ind. sg. 1 *nír thoimless* 267; 2 *ro thomlis* 773; 3 *do-romel* 53, *do thomail* 1285 (see § l); pl. 3 *ro thomailset* 343.

Domnach m. 'Sunday'. Sg. nom. 336; acc. 315; gen. in *adaig Domnaig* 'Saturday night' 226 f., 227, 229 f.

do-muin 'supposes'. Pres. ind. sg. 1 *do-munim* 880.

don see **di** and 2 **do**.

dond adj. 'light brown, dun; dusky'. Pl. nom. f. *donna* 977. In comps. see **bán, corccra**, 2 **fiach** and **lethar**.

do-rala see **do-chuir**.

do-rat(ad) see **do-beir**.

dorcha adj. 'dark, gloomy'. Superl. 205.

doridise see **aridise**.

do-rigne, do-rigned, do-rigset, do-rindis see **do-gní**.

dorn m. 'fist'; a measure of 4 to 6 inches, a 'hand'. Sg. gen. in comp. *coíc-duirn* 'of five hands' 108, 885. Pl. acc. *dorni* 1152; dat. *dornaib* 857.

do-roich 'comes to, reaches, arrives; happens'. Pres. ind. sg. 3, 466 n. Imperf. sg. 3 *-toirched* 290 n. Pres. subjunct. pl. 3 *-torsit* 570 (see § lxvi).

do-romel see **do-meil**.

do-rónad, do-rónta see **do-gní**.

do-ruachell see **do-foichell**.

dorus m. 'doorway, gateway'. Sg. nom. (for acc., § xxi) 121; acc. 160, 1053; dat. 120, 1031.

-dos- infixed obj. pron. Class C. Sg. 3 f. *-nos-* 1146. Pl. 3, 1144, 1180, 1182. See § xxxvi.

do t' see 2 **do, da**.

do-thét 'comes'; sometimes 'goes'. Pres. ind. sg. 3 *-taet* 327. Pret. sg. 3 *dolluid* 109, 352, 510, 1310, 1325. Past ind. sg. 1 *-tudchad* 894; 2 *-tudchad* 1266.

draigen m. 'blackthorn bush'. Sg. nom. in comp. *cas-draigen* 'dense blackthorn bush' 1047.

drechongdás meaning uncertain, prob. '(brow-)band' (of horse). Sg. dat. 1079 n.

dremun adj. 'furious, frantic'. Sg. nom. m. 1040.

dressán m. 'spleen'. Sg. dat. 1080.

drithle f. 'spark'. Pl. acc. *drithlenna* 133 n.

droch- adj. prefix 'bad'. See **ben, flaith, ithir**.

drochat m. 'causeway, bridge'. Sg. dat. in comp. *cloch-drochat* 'stone causeway' 1097 n.

drol m. 'ring, loop'. Sg. acc. 284.

drúcht m. 'dew'. Sg. nom. 50; acc. 134, 204, 352; gen. *drúchta* 1295. In comp. see 1 **beóil**.

druimm m. 'back, ridge'. Sg. acc. 634; gen. *drom(m)a(i)* 107, 283, comic name 393.

drumnech adj. 'having ridges'. Sg. acc. f. in comp. *cethar-drumnig* 'made of four ridges' 739.

drús f. 'lust'. Sg. dat. *drúis* 861.

drúth m. '(professional) jester'. Sg. gen. *drúith* (applied to a low-grade poet) 1314.

dú f. 'place'. Sg. dat. 960, 969; *dú a* 'the place in which' 1155.

duan f. 'song, poem'. Pl. nom. *duana* 549.

dub adj. 'black'. Sg. acc. m. 1162 n. In comp. see **gorm**.

dubach adj. 'gloomy, melancholy'. As noun 'a melancholic' sg. dat. 856.

dubán m. '(fish-)hook'. Sg. dat. 1103.

dubánacht f. '(act of) angling'. Sg. dat. 1106.

dublathe adj. 'melancholy'. Sg. nom. m. *dublathi* 1040.

dúib see 2 **do**.

Dúilem m. 'the Creator'. Gen. *Dúilemun/-an* 208, 273, 994, 1213; dat. *Dúilemain* 234, 278, *Dúilem* 600.

dulesc m. 'dulse, edible seaweed'. Sg. gen. *dulisc* 1077.

duilge see **doilig**.

duille f. 'leaf (of a book)'. Sg. gen. 651.

duillech adj. 'leafy'. Sg. nom. f. 807.

duine m. 'person, man'; indef. sense 'anybody'. Sg. nom. 147; acc. 811; dat. 421. Pl. nom. *doíne* 603; gen. in comp. *dag-daíne* 'gentlefolk' 1217.

duirn see **dorn**.

duit see 2 **do**.

dul, dula see **dol**.

dulas m. meaning uncertain, perh. 'depression' or 'hunger'. Sg. nom. 898 n.

1 **dún** m. 'fort, fortress'. Sg. acc. 1244; gen. *dúine* 910, 1098, 1234.

2 **dún** see 2 **do**.

dúnad m. 'encampment, fort'. Sg. nom. 443; gen. *dúnaid* 543, 593, 904, etc.; dat. 1147.

dúthchus m. 'hereditary right'. Sg. nom. 414.

dúthracair 'wishes, desires'. Pres. ind. sg. 1 *dúthracur* 1008 (see § lvi).

é, hé personal pron. sg. 3 m. 'he, him, it'. See §§ xxx-xxxii and xxxviii. Following 2 **is** see § xxx. As subj. of pass. verb 214, 280, 549, 665, 756, 1240; obj. of trans. verb 528, 563. W. copula: (1) as subject: 742, 744; w. anaphoric demonstr. *e-s(s)ide* 24, 124, copula understood 12, 84; w. 'emphasising' suffix *e-ssium* 558; (2) as predicate: 8, 20, 71, 274, 276, 318, 904, 1047, 1064, 1271, 1312, 1345; *e-ssium* 661; w. demonstr. *(h)é so/sin* 56, 501, 909.

éc(c) m. 'death'; *téit (i n-)éc(c)* 'dies'. Sg. acc. 297, 304, 515. Pl. (see DIL E 9.15) nom. *éca* 1123.

ech m. 'horse'. Sg. nom. 565 (see § xvi), 1328.

echlasc f. 'horsewhip'. Pl. nom. *echlasca* 198, 213, 271; acc. 1271.

ecla f. 'fear'. Sg. nom. 161.

eclais f. 'church'. Sg. nom. 221; gen. *eclaisi* 210, 222, 236, *eclasa* 158; dat. 225, 226, 420.

écmais f. 'absence'. Sg. gen. 21 n.

ecna f. 'learning'. Sg. gen. *ecnai* 242, 1257; dat. 611, 690.

écnach m. '(act of) slandering, reproaching; complaining, scoffing'. Sg. acc. 604; dat. 221.

ecnaid m. 'scholar, sage'. Sg. gen. *ecnadu* 344.

ecnaide 'wisdom'. Sg. dat. 1269.

ecnaidecht f. 'wisdom, knowledge, learning'. Sg. dat. 1263.

ecor m. 'array, rank'. Sg. nom. 473.

écosc m. 'appearance, aspect' (dress, ornaments etc.). Sg. nom. 1165.

écsamail adj. 'various; unusual, outstanding, incomparable'. Pl. gen. m. 839, 1221, f. 774.

1 e(a)d m. 'space' (of time). Sg. dat. (of extent) 758 (cf. 116 n.).

2 e(a)d personal pron. sg. 3 neut. 'it' (see §§ x and xxxi f.). Used in AMC as predicate of copula only; 4, 138, 144, 227, 247, 289, 302, 308, 424, 592, 640, 674, 676, 679, 708, 1142, 1232, 1236.

écin adj. 'some, any'. Sg. acc. f. 724.

ele see aile.

eill m. 'opportunity of harming, taking advantage of'. Sg. acc. 1195.

éill see iall.

eimeltius m. 'weariness, disgust'. Sg. nom. 135.

enech m. 'face; honour, generosity; mercy, protection'. Sg. gen. *enig* 1267, *muinnter enig* 'a generous company' 479; dat. *i n-enech* 'in [compensenation for an insult to] the honour of' 210 (2), 235, 236. Pl. dat. (sg. sense) *inchaib* 1164; *ba h-athis i n-inchuib* 'it would be defamation as compensation for an insult' 869.

-eper, -epert see as-beir.

epistil f. 'epistle; written charm as amulet' (see 482 n.). Sg. gen. *episle* 1072. Pl. nom. *episle* 482; dat. *epislib* 1070.

erbe f. 'hedge, fence, paling'. Sg. nom. 470.

eirg see téit.

éirge f. (v.n. of at-raig) '(act of) getting up, rising'. Sg. gen. *érgi* 704.

érgius, érgis see at-raig.

erriud m. 'apparel, garment'. Sg. nom. 1325.

éis, éisse f. 'track'. Sg. dat. in phrase *dia éssi* 'after him, after his time' 86.

éisc see iasc.

e(i)ssi, esti see 6 a.

e-ssium see é.

éstecht f. '(act of) listening'. Sg. dat. 709.

éit f. 'herd of cattle'. Pl. nom. *éte* 1243.

eter prep. w. acc. 'between' 524, 1030, 1162, 1209. W. suffixed obj. pron. pl. 3 *etarru/-a* 469, 475.

ethiar m. 'ether, upper air'. Sg. acc. 1278.

ethre m. 'end, tail'. Sg. acc. *ethri* 936.

etir (*eter* + pron. sg. 3 neut.) advb. 'at all' 422.

et(t)ne m. 'kernel'. Pl. nom. *ettne* 35, *etneda* 1204 (see § xiii).

elada, elatha f. 'literary composition'. Sg. dat. *eladain* 4, 5; *elathain* 3.

éláid 'escapes'. Past subjunct. sg. 3 w. 2 ro, *ro élád* 206 f.

elc adj. 'mischievous, bad'. In comp., perhaps, see cab.

ellach m. 'harness'. Sg. nom. 957.

ém transitional emphasising advb. 'indeed' 519, 717, 851, etc.

emnach adj. 'twinned, double'. As noun, pl. dat. (for acc., § xxiv) *emnaigib* 'twins' 1201.

én m. 'bird'. Sg. acc. 1202.

én- see aen and gel.

eó m. 'brooch'. Sg. nom. 1166.

eólach m. 'a learned man'. Pl. nom. *eólaig* 138, 592, 1245, 1290.

eólas m. 'knowledge, experience, learning'. Sg. gen. *eólais* 84, 242.

eórna f. 'barley'. Sg. nom. 1184.

epaid f. 'spell, charm'. Sg. gen. *eptha* (i.e. 'magic') 54, 856.

éra f. (v.n. of éraid) 'refusal'. Sg. nom. 87.

éraid 'refuses'. Past ind. pass. pl. *ima ro éraid clérig* 'about which the clergy were refused' 520 n.

erard see **irard**.

erb f. 'doe, roe'. Sg. acc. *eirb* 742.

erchra f. '(act of) perishing; decay'. Sg. acc. 300.

erdam m. 'porch, barbican'. Sg. gen. *erdaim* 1053 n.

erdraic(c) adj. 'well-known, famous'. Sg. nom. m. 67, f. 1110. Compar. *errdarcu* 550.

erdrochat m. 'causeway, steps, front-path'. Sg. nom. 446.

erfhuirgid 'holds back, restrains, keeps'. Past ind. pass. sg. *-r erfhuirged* 146.

erlam adj. 'ready'. Sg. nom. m. 18, *erlum* 701.

erlám f. 'custody, possession'. Sg. dat. *erláim* 528, 530.

érnaid 'escapes'. Fut. sg. 3 *-érnaba* 32 n.

ernaigthi see **airnaigthe**.

ernail f. 'section, category'. Pl. dat. *ernalib* 141.

eros m./f. 'poop, stern'. Sg. dat. *erus* 1021.

errandus m. 'part, portion, share'. Sg. nom. 653.

errchaide adj. 'vernal, of spring'. Sg. acc. f. 743.

errdarcu see **erdraic(c)**.

ersaind see **ursa(n)**.

-érus see **at-raig**.

esairgid 'strikes, shoves'. Past ind. sg. 3 *ro esairg* 606 f.

essamain adj. 'fearless'. Sg. gen. m. in comic name 879.

essamna f. 'confidence, boldness'. Sg. acc. 1141 (see 1140 n.).

esbuid f. 'deficiency'. Sg. nom. 229.

ésca m. 'the moon'. Sg. nom. 50.

escomlád m. '(act of) departing'. Sg. nom. 254.

esorcu f. (v.n. of **esairgid**) '(act of) striking, beating'. Sg. nom. 857 n.

esparta f. 'vespers'. Sg. gen. *espartan* 310, 323; dat. *espartain* 116, 153.

espoc m. 'bishop'. Sg. gen. *espuic* 529, 530, 532, 866. Pl. gen. 1264.

étach m. 'clothing, cloth'. Sg. acc. in comp. *gerr-étach* 'short garment' 545; gen. *étaig* 198, 202, 213, etc.; dat. 203, 332.

étan m. 'brow'. Sg. nom. (for acc., § xxi) 1196; dat. 1165.

etaraissnéis f. 'a digression'. Sg. nom. 665.

etarra, etarru see **eter**.

etarscaraid 'separates, parts'. Pres. subjunct. sg. 3 w. 2 **ro**, *ro etarscara* 199.

etarthráth m. 'midday'. Sg. dat. 1287.

ethar m. 'boat'. Sg. nom. 1019; dat. 1053.

et reliqua (Latin) 'et cetera' 619, 1111.

étrom adj. 'light'. Sg. acc. 332.

etrud m. 'milking-time, evening'. Sg. acc. 1287.

fábull m./f. 'romance, narration'. Sg. gen. *fáible* 840; dat. 836.

fácbaid 'leaves'. Pres. ind. sg. 3, 662. Pret. sg. 3 *fácbais* 1300. Past ind. sg. 3 *-fárcaib* 120, 634; pass. sg. *ro fácbad* 532, *-fárcbad* 1245.

fácbáil f. (v.n. of **fácbaid**) '(act of) leaving'. Sg. dat. 90.

faebar m. 'edge' (of sword etc.) Pl. nom. *faebra* 589.

faelid adj. 'glad, exultant'. As advb. in comp. *co cend-fhaelid* 1007 n.

faen adj. 'prostrate, supine'. Sg. acc. m. 283.

faesam, foesam m. 'protection'. Sg. dat. 988, 989, 991, 992, *faesum* 1001.

-fagba, -fagtha, -fagbad see **fo-gaib**.

fagbáil f. (v.n. of **fo-gaib**) '(act of) getting'. Sg. dat. 95.

faide see **fota**.

fadessin see **fén**.

1 **fail** f. 'arm-ring'. Sg. nom. 1328; acc. *falaig* 565.

2 **fail** in phrase *i fail* (w. possess. or gen.) 'beside, in the company of' 682, 1155.

3 **fail** see **atá**.

fa(i)llsigid see **follsigid**.

fairre see **farr**.

faissnéis see **ais(s)né(i)s(s)**.

faitches m. 'caution, heed'. Sg. nom. 848.

faithche, faithge f. 'lawn, green, cleared space outside fort or monastery'. Sg. nom. *faithchi* 245; acc. *faithchi* 322; gen. *faithgi* 153, *faithchi* 541; dat. 236, *faithchi* 351.

fáthliaig m. (comp. of *fáith* 'prophet' and *liaig* 'physician') in personal name *in Fáthliaig* 'the Prognostic Physician'. Nom. 1036, 1038, 1117, 1120, 1131, 1145; acc. 1051, 1099; gen. *Fáthlega(i)* 895, 902, 903, 1032, 1094, 1103, 1110.

falaig see 1 **fail**.

fán m. 'slope'. Sg. acc. 539.

fannaigid 'grows weak'. Past ind. pl. 3 *ro fhannaigsetar* 1121.

fannall f. 'a swallow'. Sg. acc. *fannaill* 743.

-fárcaib, -fárcbad see **fácbaid**.

farr f. 'post, prop'. Pl. nom. *fairre* 459.

farrad in phrase *i n-a fharrad* 'beside/ near him' 1108.

fás adj. 'empty'. In comp. see **taeb**.

fásach m. 'wilderness, waste'. Pl. acc. *fásaige* 1018.

fásaid 'grows'. Pres. ind. sg. 3 rel. *fhásus* 1155. Past ind. pl. 3 *-r fhásatar* 55.

fáth m. 'cause, reason, motive'. Sg. nom. 5, 9, 20, 56.

fecht m. 'journey; time, occasion'. Sg. acc. 786; dat. *i fecht-sa* 'on this occasion, now' 1298, whence **budesta, festa, fodecht-sa**.

fégad '(act of) looking at, scanning, observing'. Sg. dat. 794.

feib conjunction 'as, how, as if; when' (see § xliv) 205, 308, 543, 650, 758, 1205, 1288, 1331, 1333, 1334, 1335.

féic f. 'ridge-pole, roof-tree; roof'. Sg. acc. 1250.

féich see 1 **fiach**.

féig adj. 'keen-sighted'. Sg. nom. m. 1176.

fén indecl. pronominal (see § xxxix) 'self, himself' etc.; 'his own' etc., referring to a possessive. *Fén* 129, 212, 303, etc.; *fodé(i)n* 146, 312, 354, etc.; *fadén* 616; *fessin* 265, 316, 516, 705, 724; *fadessin* 137; *fodessin* 1118, 1218; *budessin* 246.

fénnid m. 'champion'. Sg. voc. in comp. *ríg-fhénnid* 'royal champion' 689.

feiss (see 18 n.) 'evening meal, supper; feast'. Sg. nom. in comps. *lón-fheiss* 'a feast of food' 334, *mór-fheiss* 'dinner' 18; gen. *mór-fheiss* 18.

-fesser see **ro-fitir**.

fes(s)id 'spends the night; stays, rests'. Pres. ind. sg. 3, 204, 215, 347; pl. 3

fessait 219. Pret. sg. 3 *fesiss* 1287; pl. 3 *fessaiter* 1288.

fessin see **fén**.

féith f. 'sinew'. Pl. nom. *féthi* 1121.

fellaid w. 1 **for** 'cheats in respect of'. Pres. subjunct. pass. sg. *-felltar* 573.

fendóc f. 'scald-crow'. Sg. nom. (for acc., § xx) 1013.

feóil f. 'flesh'. Sg. nom. 199; gen. *feóla* 656; dat. 1122.

fer m. 'man'. Sg. nom. 240, 493, 600, 1043 (see 1 **buide**), 1256; acc. 143; gen. *fir* 484, 923, 1195 (see **céilide**). Pl. nom. *fir* 514, 801, 803; voc. *firu* 1252; gen. 58, 345, 578, 781; dat. *feraib* 1330, 1336. In comps. see **bolgum, ferglacc, lám**.

feraid 'grants, supplies'; 'affects, afflicts' [?; see 1163 n.]. Pres. subjunct. sg. 3 w. 2 **ro**, *ro fhera* 1163. Pret. sg. 3 *ferais* 625.

ferg f. 'anger'. Sg. acc. *feirg* 631.

ferglacc f. 'a man's hand' (a measure of height). Pl. gen. 15 (see 14 f. n.).

fern f. 'alder-wood'. Sg. gen. *ferna* 1159.

ferr see **maith**.

fessait, fessaiter see **fes(s)id**.

-fesmais, -festa, -f sur see **ro-fitir**.

festa advb. (see **fecht**) 'now' 279, 973, 982, 1188, (h)i festa 1241, 1280.

fét(t)a adj. 'smooth, highly-polished, handsome, goodly'. Sg. nom. m. 1295; dat. f. 734.

fétaid 'gets'. Pres. ind. sg. 3 *ro-fhétand* 1044 n. Imperf. pass. sg. *-fétta* 87.

-fetar, -fetara see **ro-fitir**.

1 **féth** m. 'condition, appearance'. Sg. nom. 1120, 1126, 1127.

2 **féth** 'art, skill'. In comp. see **snas**.

féthán m. (diminutive of 1 **féth**) 'poor condition'. Sg. nom. 1119.

fia see 3 **fiad**.

1 **fiach** m. 'payment due; a rightful (legal) due'. Pl. nom. *féich* 575; acc. *fiachu* 1202; gen. 570, 571, 573, 683; dat. *fiachaib* 573.

2 **fiach** m. 'raven'. In comp. names *Donn-Fhiach* and *Cruit-Fhiach*: see Index of Names of Persons.

1 **fiad** m. 'honour, respect'. Sg. acc. 268 see **aíge**.

2 **fiad** adj. 'wild'. In comp. see **uball**.

3 **fiad**^{L,N} (written *fia* before *d*-) prep. w. dat. (see § xl). In oaths 'before' 234, 264, 1276. W. suffixed obj. pron. 'in the presence of, in the eyes of' sg. 1 *fiadum* 522; 2 *fiadut* 521 n.

fiadain adj. 'wild, uncultivated'. Sg. nom. m. *uball fiadain* 'crab-apple' 609.

fiadnaise f. in phrase *(h)i f(h)iadnaise* (w. possess. or gen.) 'in the presence of'; 'before' in oaths; 208, 273, 432, 500, 523, 762, 783, 839, 994, 1213, 1221.

fial adj. 'generous, noble'. Sg. gen. m. in comp. *cnáim-fhéil* 'generous with food' (lit. 'generous in [supplying] gnawing') 412.

fiar adj. 'bent; curling, wavy'. Sg. acc. m. 1153.

fiarfaige see **iarfaige**.

fiarlaít see 2 **dar**.

fiarut see 2 **dar**.

fiche m. numeral 'twenty, a score'. Dual gen. *dá fhichet* 'forty' 809. Pl. nom. *cethri fichit* 'fourscore' 1207, *secht fichit cét* 'fourteen thousand' 1046 f.; acc. *trí fichte* 'three score' 15; gen. *deich . . . fichet* 'thirty' 1084, 1338, *ceithri . . . fichet* 'twenty-four' 1140.

fid m. 'wood'. Sg. nom. 474. Pl. acc. *feda* 1017.

fidbach some kind of corn. Sg. nom. 1184.

fidchell f. 'a gaming board'. Sg. nom. 829 n.

figled m. (v.n. of **figlid**) '(act of) scrutinising'. Sg. dat. 650.

figlid 'watches; scrutinises'. Pret. sg. 2 *figlis* 648, 649.

fil, file(a)t see **atá**.

file m. 'poet' (professional poet-sage). Pl. nom. *filid* 569, 573.

filidecht f. 'poetry; the profession of *file*'. Sg. acc. 90, 549; gen. *filidechta* 92.

fillte past partcp. 'folded'. Sg. dat. m] in comp. *secht-fhillte* 'folded seven times' 102.

filter see **atá**.

fín m. 'wine'. Sg. gen., comic name *Fína* 398; dat. 461.

find adj. 'white, bright; true'. Sg. nom. f. 760, 1328; acc. m. 787, f. 105, 282, 567; gen. m. 790. Pl. nom. *finda* m. 1084, f. 459. In comps.: sg. nom. m. *sám-fhind* 'gentle and true' 1042, f. *brecc-fhind* 'white-spotted' 1346; see also **argat**, 2 **coll, gel, litte**.

finda m. 'a hair'. Sg. acc. 1153.

findach adj. 'hairy, shaggy'. Sg. nom. m. 1158.

1 **fír** m. (neut. in 272 and 346; see § viii) 'truth, justice; right; attestation, proof, evidence'. Sg. nom. *fír (n)dligid* 'rightful justice' 273, 346 f., *fír n-indligid* 272, *fír flatha* 'the honour of a prince' 686; acc. 730, *fír doichle* 'evidence of sullenness' 1164 f.; gen. *scél fíre* 'a true story' 42; dat. 39.

2 **fír** adj. 'true, real; rightful; pure'. Sg. nom. m. 606. As first element of comps. ('true, real, truly') it may have no more than an intensive or vaguely commendatory force; see **aíge, álaind, cainnend, cruithnecht, cumra, dírech, fíriasc, fírluss, gamain, gruth, iarthar, scaílte**.

firend adj. 'male'. Sg. dat. m. 765.

firián, fíreón adj. 'just, righteous'. Sg. nom. f. 238. As noun m. 'righteous person, one of the elect', sg. nom. 509; acc. 510.

fíriasc m. 'salmon'. Sg. gen. *fírésc* 1067.

fírluss (coll.) meaning uncertain. Gen. *fírlossa* 476 n.

fiss m. '(act of) finding out; knowledge'. Sg. nom. 154, *fiss scél* 'information' 881; gen. *fessa* 1269; dat. *dia fhiss* 'to enquire about him' 136.

fís f. 'a vision'. Sg. nom. 827.

fithir m. 'teacher'. Sg. dat. 110.

fiú adj. 'worthy, fitting'. In phrase *is fiú* (w. acc.) 'is worth, equivalent to' 1218, 1317.

flaith f. (1) 'lordship'. (2) 'lord, prince'. (1) Sg. dat. 666. (2) Sg. gen. *flatha* 672, 686, 1344; dat. in comp. *droch-fhlaith* 871. Pl. dat. *flathib* 1348.

fleochad m. 'rain'. Sg. nom. 119.

fo^{L} prep. w. acc. and dat. (see § xl) 'under, towards; according to, as regards' (w. some contamination by senses of 2 **im(m)**) 121, 122, 282,

283, 319, etc.; *co ra-m dígaib fo m'*
nert 'so that it has deprived me of
my strength' 657. W. def. art. sg.
fon 339, 541, 543, etc., *fonn* 770. W.
suffixed obj. pron., sg. 2 *fót* 636,
1158; 3 m. *foe* 1073, 1237, *foí* 1232;
pl. 3 *fou* 1074, *fóthib* 736. W.
possessives, sg. 1 *fo m'* 657, *ba m'*
685; 3 m. *fo a* 282, 1071.

1 **fó** adj. 'good'. In phrases *fó liumm* 'I
am satisfied' 248, *fó fer* 'happy is the
man (who)' 493 n.

2 **fó** conjunction 'or' 162.

fóbair 'begins, sets about' (see 138 n.).
Pret. sg. 3 *fóbrais* 783. Past ind. sg.
3 *fo-róbairt* 138, 591, *fo-rórbart* 707,
fo-rórbairt 348, 546.

foccal m. 'word'. Pl. nom. in comp.
mí-fhoccuil 'bad words, abuse' 195 n.

fochartad m. '(act of) clearing away'.
Sg. dat. 1096.

fo-cheird 'puts, throws' (see **cuirid** and
láid). Pres. ind. sg. 1 *fo-s-cerdimm*
1057, 1061; 2 *fo-s-cerdi* 1187. Impv.
sg. 2 *fo-t-cherd* 1000, *fo-dos-ceirdi* 1180.

fócraid 'orders'. Pret. sg. 3 *fócrais* 777.

foccus 'proximity'. In phrase *i fhoccus*
(w. gen.) 'close to, near' 593.

fodail f. 'division, part'. Pl. dat. *fodlaib*
1140.

fodecht-sa advb. (see **fecht**) 'on this
occasion, now' 533.

fo-d-era see **fo-fera**.

fodé(i)n see **fén**.

foe, foí see **fo, ba**.

foelustar see **fo-loing**.

fo-fera (w. petrified infix) 'causes'. Pres.
ind. sg. 3 *fo-d-era* 676. Past ind. sg.
3 *Iss ed fo-t-ruair dam an-í-sin frit-siu*
'It is that which caused me [to do]
that to you' 640 f.

fo-gaib, fo-geib 'gets, finds'. Pres. ind.
sg. 3 *-fagaib* 1144; pass. sg. *fo-gabar/
-ur* 230, 338, 736. Imperf. sg. 3 *fo-
gebed* 645, *-fagbad* 124. Pres. subjunct.
sg. 2 *-fagba* 724. Past subjunct. sg. 2
-fagtha 224. Fut. sg. 2 *fo-géba* 895,
998, *do-géba* 673 (see § l), *-fuigbe* 335,
(see § lxxvii *fo-gaib*). Pret sg. 1 *fuarus*
269, *-fuarus* 268; 3 *-fuair* 128; pass.
sg. *-fríth* 242.

fogluim f. '(act of) learning, studying'.
Sg. gen. *fogluma* 91.

fognam m. '(act of) rendering service'.
Sg. nom. 871.

fogur m. 'sound, noise'. Sg. gen. *foguir*
144.

fochéim m./f. 'gait, step'. Sg. nom.
1173.

foíded m. '(act of) sending'. Sg. dat.
344.

foigdech m. 'beggar'. Sg. acc. 855.

follsigid, fa(i)llsigid 'shows, manifests'.
Pret. sg. 3 *follsigis* 173. Past ind. sg.
3 *ro fhaillsig* 428; pass. sg. *ro fa(i)llsiged*
502, 504, 749, 753, *ro fhaillsiged*
354 n.

foillsiugud (v.n. of **follsigid**) '(act of)
showing, revealing'. Sg. dat. 349.

foímmthecht f. 'gait'. Sg. nom. 1174.

foimtin f. '(act of) guarding against,
taking precautions'. Sg. acc. 1050.

forcend m. 'end'. Sg. acc. 692.

forcetal m. '(act of) teaching, advising'.
Sg. nom. 873.

forcipol m. in advb. phrase *i forcipul*
'folded, pleated' 106.

foirend f. 'set of pieces in board-game'.
Sg. dat. *foirind* 829.

foriadaid 'shuts'. Impv. pass. sg. *foriatar*
206.

forlethan adj. 'very broad'. Sg. nom.
f. 1167.

forpthe participial adj. 'perfect, complete' (cf. **anfhurbithe**). Sg. nom. f.
forpthi 624, 626.

forrgid 'overpowers'. Pres. subjunct.
sg. 3 w. 2 **ro**, *ro-m fhorrgi* 333.

fola see **fuil**.

folam adj. 'empty, unoccupied'. Sg.
nom. m. 125.

follus adj. 'evident, manifest'. Sg. nom.
m. 25. In comp. see **gnéthech**.

folmnach adj. 'tied, fastened up'. Sg.
acc. f. *folmnig* 862.

fo-loing 'supports, endures'. Pres. ind.
sg. 3, 1210. Imperf. pl. 3 *fo-loingtis*
460. Fut. pass. sg. rel. *foelustar* 1146.

folt m. (coll.) 'the hair of the head'.
Sg. dat. *fult* 1153.

foltnide adj. 'hairy'. Sg. acc. m. 1153.

foluamnigid 'flies'. Pret. sg. 3 *foluamnigis* 1278.

fomnaid 'takes care, heeds, bewares'.
Impv. sg. 3 *fomna* 847.

1 **for** prep. (non-mutating) w. acc. and dat. (see § xl) 'on, on to; in addition to, along with; at, by' 79, 89, 93, 109, etc. W. verbs of asking, requesting 'from' 328, 669. W. personal names 'was called' 68, 73, 74. By confusion w. 4 **ar** (q.v.), w. or without lenition, 36, 39, 49, 91, etc. W. def. art. sg. *forsin* (before *V-*, *forsind* 420) 236, 349, 764, 1251, 1338, *for in* 348, 590; pl. *forsna* 583, 737, 758, *for na* 551, 1207. W. def. art. and -*í* (q.v.) *forsint-í* 196. W. suffixed obj. prons., sg. 1 *form* 238, 272, 274, etc.; 2 *fort* 564; 3 m. *fair* 39, 88, 206, etc., *air* 1140; 3 f. *furri* 19, 1052, 1057, 1061 1114, 1163; pl. 2 *foraib* 328; 3 *forru* 264. W. possessives, sg. 1 *for m'* 573, 1016; 2 *for h'* 1119; 3 m. *for a déni* 'for all its swiftness' 1017. W. rel. particle -**a**, *forsa* 588; negative *forsná* 300. In adj. comps. see **forard, forlethan, forlán, forórda**.

2 **for** see 1 **ol**.

3 **for** see **bar**.

forard adj. 'very tall'. Sg. nom. m. 476.

forba m. 'completion, culmination'. Sg. dat. 143.

forbaílid adj. 'joyful, cheerful'. Sg. nom. f. 1160.

forcutbide m. 'a jester' (?). Sg. nom. in comp. *so-fhorcutbide* 'a good jester' (?) 1043 n.

forlán adj. 'very full'. Sg. acc. m. 787.

form see 1 **for**.

fo-ró(r)ba(i)rt see **fóbair**.

forórda adj. 'gilded over'. Pl. dat. m. 842.

forsin(d), forsint-í, forsna see 1 **for**.

for-t-gella (w. petrified infix) 'affirms, calls to witness, invokes'. Pres. ind. sg. 1 *for-t-gillim* 64, 335, 781 f., 1212, *for-t-gellaimm* 295.

fortócbálta participial adj. 'raised, tucked up'. Sg. acc. f. 106.

fosad adj. 'firm, steady'. Sg. voc. f. 416.

fosaic f. 'the washing of the feet'. Sg. acc. 128, 579.

fostán adj. 'steady, firm'. Sg. voc. f. 416.

fot m. 'length'. Sg. nom. 711; acc. 722; dat. *fut* 1057.

1 **fót** m. 'sod'. Dual nom. 160; acc. 172.

2 **fót** see **fo**.

fota adj. 'long, far'. Sg. nom. m. 1146, 1298, 1299; acc. f. in comp. *cian-fhota* 'long and lengthy' 886; gen. m. in comp. *sír-fhota* 1048. Compar. *faide* 630.

fo-t-ruair see **fo-fera**.

fou see **fo**.

fraig f. 'wall'. Sg. nom. 454; dat. *fraigid* 131. Pl. (or sg.) gen. *fraiged* 1202.

frass f. 'a shower'. Pl. acc. *frassa* 709.

frecnairc adj. 'present'. Sg. acc. m. 510.

frecnarcus m. 'presence'. Sg. dat. 299.

frecraid 'answers'. Past ind. sg. 1 *ro fhrecrus* 844.

frestul m. 'receiving, meeting, welcoming'. Sg. dat. 513.

fri^H, **fria**^{H} prep. w. acc. (see § xl) 'towards, to, against; for; on behalf of, on the part of; in accordance w.; occupied in'. W. equative adj. 'as' e.g. *liridir fri* 'as many as' 133. W. possess. and v.n. 'to' e.g. *ri a indisi* 'to tell it' 496. *Fri* 126, 133, 134, etc., *fria* 22, 581, 599, etc. (confusion w. **la** 143, 1085), *re* 415, *ra* 89, *fris* (form preceding pronominal *nach*) 1139. W. def. art. sg. *fris(s)in* 161, 592, 594, etc.; *resin* 445; pl. *frisna* 713. W. suffixed obj. prons., sg. 1 *frim* 509, 653, 670, etc.; 2 *frit(t)* 641, 677, 892, 998; 3 m. *fris(s)* 85, 87, 212, etc., *riss* 806; 3 f. *fria* 43, 250. W. possessives, sg. 1 *fri m'* 295; 2 *fri(a) t'* 604, 878; 3 m. *fri a* 309, 322, 529, etc., *ri a* 490, 496, *ré* 354; pl. 3 *fri a* 251. W. rel. particle -**a**, *frisi* 115, *risi* 1176, *fria* 588. (*Fri a* is monosyllabic, as is *fria*, but the distinction is made here for the sake of clarity.)

frith- (composition-form of **fri**) 'additional, extra', see **air(a)igid** and **frithpian**.

fríth see **fo-gaib**.

fritháilem f. '(act of) waiting on, serving, attending to'. Sg. nom. in comp. *deg-fhritháilem* 'good attendance' 1040; acc. 579.

frithbac m. 'recess'. Sg. nom. 629 n.

frithing in advb. phrase *'n-a fhrithing* 'on his way back' 155.

frithpian f. 'extra punishment'. Sg. nom. 338.

fuacht m./f. 'coldness'. Sg. nom. 333.

fuaim m. 'sound, noise'. Sg. acc. 594.

fuair, fuarus see **fo-gaib**.

fuathrócc f. 'apron'. Sg. acc. in comp. *lín-fhuathróicc* 'linen apron' 738.

fuigell m. 'judicial sentence, judgement'. Sg. acc. 872.

fuil f. 'blood'. Sg. gen. *fola* 1127.

fuilled m. 'addition, increase'. Sg. acc. 233.

fullid 'adds to, increases'. Fut. sg. 2 *fullfi* 566.

fuirgid 'delays, keeps waiting'. Past ind. pass. sg. (w. infix) *ra-m fhuirged* 169.

fu(i)rmid 'puts, sets'. Pres. ind. pl. 3 *furmit* 755. Imperf. sg. 3 (w. infix) *no-s fuirmed* 1089 f. Past ind. pass sg. *ro fuirmed* 213 f.

fuirseóracht f. 'buffoonery, clowning'. Sg. acc. 547.

fuísidid 'confesses'. Pres. ind. sg. 1 *fuísidim* 232.

fulang m. '(act of) enduring, supporting, tolerating'. In comp. adj. *so-fhulaing* 'easily borne, tolerable' 350 n.

furachair adj. 'wary, alert'. Sg. nom. m. 1176.

'ga see **oc, ic**.

gabaid, gaibid, geibid 'takes, seizes, takes possession of, accepts; goes; sings'; *gabaid im* 'puts on' (dress etc.); *gabaid feirg X* 'X is enraged'; *gabaid immach* 'extrudes'. Pres. ind. sg. 1 *gebim* 1054; 3 *gabaid* 104, 105, 257, 263, 545, 631, 632, 737, *-gaib* 1136; pass. sg. *-gabar* 987. Impv. sg. 2 *geb* 187. Pres. subjunct. sg. 1 *-gabar* 689. Past subjunct. sg. 1 *-gabind* 1036 (see 1035 n.); pass. pl. *-gabdaís* 1270. Fut. sg. 1 *gébut* 568; pl. 3 *gébdait* 195 n.; pass. sg. *gébthair* 985, rel. *gébthar* 566, *-gébthar* 688. Condit. sg. 3 *no gébad* 1215. Pret. sg. 3 *-gaib* 135; pl. 3 *gabsat* 579 (see § lxvii). Past ind. sg. 3 *ro gab* 11, 108, 161; pl. 1 *ro gaibsium* 1029; pass. sg. *ro gabad* 213, 271.

gabáil f. (v.n. of **gabaid**) '(act of) taking hold; a hold; (act of) singing'; *gabáil X do Y* 'to ply X on Y; to sing X against Y'. Sg. acc. 1137; dat. 198, 228, 549, 574, in phrase *i n-ard-gabáil* 'in a raised, fixed position' 104 f., 759.

gabul m./f. 'branch of a stream'. Pl. dat. *gablaib* 405.

gabur m. 'goat'. Sg. dat. 859.

gaeth, goeth f. 'wind'. Sg. nom. 119, 120, 1007; acc. *gaíth* 743; dat. *gaíth* 655.

gáidetar see **guidid**.

galbech adj. 'fierce, violent'. Sg. gen. f. *gaibigi* 1124.

gaimen m. 'skin, hide' (cf. **gemen**). Sg. dat. 868.

gainem m. 'sand'. Sg. nom. 180, 181; acc. 133, 856.

gaire f. 'proximity'. Sg. gen. 81 n.

gáire m. 'laughter, a laugh'. Sg. acc. 732.

gairid 'calls, summons'. Fut. pass. sg. rel. *gairfither* 910.

gairmid 'calls, summons'. Past ind. pass. sg. *ro gairmed* 44.

gaiscedach m. 'warrior, hero'. Sg. voc. in comp. *ard-gaiscedaig* 'chief hero' 688.

gal f. 'steam'. Sg. gen. *gaile* 405.

galar m. 'disease, sickness'. Sg. nom. 1215, 1216, 1217, 1271; acc. 1131, 1217, in comp. *aen-ghalar* 1216; gen. *galair* 1009, 1120, 1129, 1148, in comps. *trom-galair* 'serious illness' 1125, *cliab-galair* 'disease of the chest' 1192.

gamain m. 'a yearling calf'. Sg. gen. in comp. *fír-gamna* 'a genuine yearling calf' 1158.

gar m. 'a while'. Sg. dat. (of time) 153 (see 116 n.).

garb adj. 'rough, coarse'. In comp. see **arán**.

garbán m. 'coarse meal, bran'. Sg. gen., comic name *Garbáin* 407, in comp. *brus-garbán* 'refuse of coarse meal' 1054.

garg adj. 'rough; flocculent'. Sg. gen. f. *gairge* 406.

garr m. 'ordure, offal'. Sg. gen. *gairr* 1013.

gasta adj. 'sprightly, alert'. Sg. nom. m. 1173.

gat m. 'withy, osier'. Sg. nom. 856.

gataid 'steals, takes away, deprives'. Impv. sg. 2 -*gat* 637.

-gébad, gébdait, ge(i)b etc., see **gabaid**.

gebbad '(act of) cropping'. Sg. dat. 1014.

gemen m. 'skin, hide' (cf. **gaimen**). Sg. nom. 1158.

gein f. 'birth'. Sg. nom. 619.

gende past partcp. 'begotten, born'. Sg. nom. m. in *peccad bunad-gendi* 'original sin' 145 f.

genelach m. 'pedigree'. Sg. acc. 421; dat. 368.

gentlecht f. (coll.) 'heathen spells'. Sg. acc. 47.

ger f. 'lard, suet, tallow'. Sg. nom. in comp. comic name *Bó-Ger* 'Beef-Suet' 941; gen. *gered* 433, 1020, 1028, 1051, *geriud* 1056.

gére f. 'sharpness; hunger, greed'. Sg. nom. *géri* 1135; dat. *géri* 12, 1257.

gerrcend m. 'bolt, bar'. Sg. nom. 1052.

gerthide adj. 'fatty, greasy, suety'. Sg. gen. f. 433, 1028.

geiss f. 'a taboo, supernatural prohibition'. Sg. gen. *gessi* 165. Pl. nom. *gessi* 166.

gel adj. 'bright, white, fair'. Sg. gen. f. *gile* 402; pl. nom. m. *gela* 1169. In comps. sg. nom. f. *dóit-gel* 'white armed' 1160; acc. m. *find-gel* 'bright white' 1159, f. *én-gil* 'all-white, pure white' 1113; gen. f. *brat-gile* 'white-mantled' 471; pl. nom. f. *bláth-gela* 'smooth and white' 1170, *tonn-gela* 'white-skinned' 1172; see **cruithnecht**.

gelbond m. 'sparrow'. Pl. nom. in comp. *min-gelbuind* 'little sparrows' 1156.

gem m. 'winter'. In comp. see **secul**.

gémad see 1 **is**.

gen f. 'a smile'. Sg. acc. 732, 929.

gérata adj. 'heroic, valiant'. Superl. *gératu* 1003.

gerr adj. 'short'. Compar. *girru* 545. In comps. see **cochall** and **étach**.

1 **gile** f. 'brightness, brilliance'. Sg. nom. 933 (see 932 f. n.).

2 **gile** see **gel**.

gilla, gille m. 'lad, servant'. Sg. nom. 170, 197, 963, in comp. *gláim-gilla* 'a satirist lad' 1039; gen. 1233. Pl. nom. *gille* 834.

gillid 'vows, pledges, promises'. Pres. ind. sg. 1 *gillim* 233.

gin m. 'mouth'. Sg. acc. 1238, 1239; dat. 1260.

glacc f. 'the partly open hand; a grasp, handful'. Pl. nom. *glacca* 1078. In comp. see **ferglacc**.

glaine f. 'cleanness, purity'. Sg. dat. 403.

glanide adj. 'clean, bright'. Pl. nom. m. 1169.

glám f. 'satire'. Sg. dat. in phrase *gláim dícind* 'extempore satire' 574 (see 573 f. n.). In comp. see **gilla**.

glan adj. 'clean, pure, bright'. Sg. dat. m. 1314. In comps., sg. acc. f. *mór-glain* 'big and bright' 1059; gen. m. *bán-ghlain* 'bright white' 411, *trebar-gloin* 'substantial and clean' 1044; pl. acc. f. *corcar-glana* 'bright pink' 1060; see **ciall** and **immglan**.

1 **glass** m. 'lock, bolt'. Sg. dat. 1056, 1061.

2 **glass** adj. 'blue, blue-grey'. Sg. nom. m. 1167.

glé adj. 'clear, pure, bright'. Sg. nom. neut. 70 n., 1310.

gleó m. 'combat'. Sg. acc. 806.

glomar m. 'bridle bit'. Sg. gen. *gilla glomair* 'bridle boy' i.e. 'horse-boy' 963.

glond m./f. 'deed, exploit'. Pl. gen. 933 (see 932 f. n.).

glún m. 'knee'. Sg. acc. 591.

gnáth adj. 'usual, customary'. Sg. nom. m. 125, 714.

gnéthech adj. 'active'. Sg. nom. m. in comp. *follus-gnéthech* 'manifestly working' 146, 212.

gníid 'makes, produces'. Pret. sg. 3 *gnídis* 624 n.

gním m. (v.n. of **gníid**) 'action, activity, work'. Sg. gen. in comp. *lér-gníma* 'diligent activity' 791; dat. in comp. *lér-gním* 'busy work' 1100.

gnímach adj. 'active'. Sg. acc. m. in comp. *mí-gnímach* 'inactive, sluggish, listless' 1133.

gob m. 'beak'. Pl. dat. *gobaib* 1124.

goeí m. 'spear'. Sg. nom. 804.

goeth see **gaeth**.

gorid 'warms'. Impv. sg. 2 *-gor* 1153. Pres. subjunct. sg. 3 w. 2 **ro**, *ra gori* 1156.

goirt adj. 'hungry, starved; bitter, sour'. Sg. nom. m. 180.

gona see **guin**.

gorm adj. 'dark blue'. Pl. nom. f. in comp. *dub-gorma* 'blue-black' 1168.

gort m. 'field, field of grain'. Sg. gen. *guirt* 1014.

gorta f. 'hunger, starvation, famine'. Sg. nom. 184, 1124, 1139, 1272, *gorti* 1135; gen. 1124.

gotha see **guth**.

1 **grád** m. 'love'. Sg. dat. 40, 51.

2 **grád** m. 'grade, rank, order'. Sg. nom. 622; pl. nom. *gráid* 512, 621.

gráin f. 'horror, loathing'. Sg. nom. 161.

greim m. 'a grip'. Sg. acc. 1137.

grés in advb. phrase *do grés* 'always' 1330.

1 **grian** f. 'the sun'. Sg. nom. 50.

2 **grian** m. 'gravel, sand; earth, ground'. Sg. nom. 181, in comp. *mur-grian* 'sea sand' 442, 1033.

grianad m. '(act of) sunning'. Sg. acc. 124.

gríbda adj. 'fierce'. Sg. dat. 601.

gríss f. 'heat; hot ashes'. Sg. nom. 1157.

gruad m./f. 'cheek'. Sg. nom. 636. Pl. nom. *gruade* 1168.

gruiten f. 'salt butter, small curds'. Sg. gen. *gruitne* 804.

gruth m. 'curds'. Sg. nom. in comp. *sen-gruth* 'old curds, sour curds' 1193; gen. *grotha* 1021, 1075, 1108, in comic name *Bend Grotha* 1030, *sen-grothai* 1028, *fír-grotha* 'real curds' 459; dat. 798.

gruthrach f. 'curds, flummery'. Sg. gen., comic name *Gruthraige* 406.

gual m. 'charcoal'. Sg. acc. 857.

guala f. 'shoulder'. Sg. gen., comic name *Gualand* 387; dual gen. *gualand* 539.

guidid 'prays, begs'; *guidid for X im Y* 'prays in the name of X for Y to be granted'. Past ind. pl. 3 *ro gáidetar* 49 (see 50 f. n.).

guilbniugud '(act of) biting, nibbling'. Sg. dat. 135.

guin f. '(act of) wounding, killing'. Sg. gen. *gona* 803.

guth m. 'voice, word'. Sg. nom. 843; acc. 1034; gen. *gotha* 140, 1266.

h' see 1 **do**.

hirophin m. (coll.) 'cherubim'. Acc. 512.

i[N], **hi**[N], **a**[N] prep. w. acc. and dat. (see § xl) 'into, in'. Nasalisation of *V*- occasionally spelt *nd*- 226, 515, 516, 611. *i* 7, 9, 24, 26, etc.; *hi* 119, 127, 142, 239, etc.; *a* 167, 170, 516, 532, etc. W. def. art., sg. *isin* 55, 131, 132, etc., *isind* 225; pl. *isna* 45, 47, 227, etc. W. suffixed obj. prons., sg. 3 m., 'in(to) him, it; there, as far as that; then', *ann*, *and* 97, 98, 130, etc., *ind* 127, 204, 276, etc.; 3 f. *innte* 644, 655, 1114, *inde/-i* 182, 1084; pl. 3 *intib* 747. W. possessives, sg. 1 *i mm'* 210, *a m'* 253, 850, 1009; 3 (i) *n-a* 13, 44, 155, etc.; pl. 2 *in bar* 1037; 3 *i n-a* 292. In rel. construction (see GOI p. 312) *i* 179, 297, 451, etc., *a* 193, 305, 703, 1117, 1182. W. 4 **a**, *i n-a* 'in that which' 1137. W. **cach**, *in cach* 745, 960, 969, 1086.

.i. abbreviation for *edón* 'namely, that is to say, i.e.' 4, 9, 50, etc.

í, **hí** personal pron. sg. 3 f. 'she, her, it'. See §§ xxx-xxxii and xxxviii. As subj. of pass. verb *indisfither hí* 782, *ima ngabar hí* 987. Obj. of trans. verb *oslaicis hí* 255. W. copula *is í* 157, *conid hí* 1284, *ba h-í* 16, 625, *comba . . . hí* 633. W. 2 **is**, *'s í* 'and she' 1160-62.

-í indecl. demonstrative, combined w. article as relative antecedent *int-í* 'the one (who)'. Sg. nom. 307; acc. 260, 987; reduced form *tí* sg. nom. 966. W. preceding preps. see 2 **co**, 2 **do**, 1 **for**. In non-relative construction *an-í-sin* 640.

iadaid 'shuts, fastens'. Pres. ind. pass. sg. *iatar* 1247. Impv. pl. 2 *iadaid* 1253. Pret. sg. 3 *iadais* 697.

iarshliss m. 'flank, hindquarter'. Sg. nom., comic name *Hiarshliss* 925.

GLOSSARY 175

iarsinní conjunction 'because' 87.

iall f. 'lace, thong'. Sg. acc. in comp. *leth-éill* 'one of two shoe-laces' 581. Pl. nom. *ialla* 1084.

iar^N, ar^N prep. w. dat. (see § xl) 'after; according to; because of' 63, 241, 244, etc. W. demonstr. *iar sin* 'after that, thereupon' 42, 99, 215, etc., *ar sin* 596. W. def. art. sg. *iarsan* 1285. W. possessive sg. 3 m. *iar n-a* 344, 610. In phrase (*i*)*ar n-a bárach* see **bárach**.

iarcomla f. 'back-door'. Sg. acc. 1017; dat. *iarcomlaid* 1077.

iarfaige f. '(act of) enquiring; question'. Sg. nom. 752, *fiarfaige* 754; acc. 916.

iarnaide adj. 'made of iron'. Sg. nom. m. 106.

1 iarraid 'asks for, demands'. Pret. sg. 3 *iarrais* 732.

2 iarraid f. '(act of) seeking'. Sg. nom. 859.

iarthar m. 'back part, western part'. Sg. dat. 684, in comp. '*n-a fhír-iarthar* 'just behind it' 461. See **descertach**.

iarum advb. 'thereupon, thereafter, then, afterwards; moreover' 35, 53, 129, etc.

iasc m. 'fish'. Sg. gen., comic name *Éisc* 396. In comp. see **fíriasc**.

iat personal pron. pl. 3 'they' (w. copula only) 190, 631, w. demonst. 796.

iatar see **iadaid**.

ibar m. 'yew-tree'. Sg. gen. *ibair* 858.

ic see **oc**.

íc(c), híc(c) f. (v.n. of **ícaid**) '(act of) curing; remedy'. Sg. acc. *hícc* 895; gen. *ícce* 1130; dat. *do híc* 505, *d' ícc* 1148.

ícaid 'cures'. Fut. sg. 3 -*ícfa* 1216.

ícide m. 'a healer'. Pl. gen. *ícidi* 1010.

íchtarach adj. 'lower'. Sg. acc. m. 546.

icon see **oc**.

idnocul m. '(act of) escorting, conveying, delivering'. Sg. dat. 531.

iffern(n) m. 'hell'. Sg. acc. 516, 692, 1277; gen. *iffirn(n)* 299, 1279.

il adj. 'many'. Pl. nom. m. *ile* 975. Adj. prefix in pl. noun comps. see **biad** and **blass**.

ilarda, ilerda adj. 'abundant, numerous, varied'. Pl. nom. m. 1142; dat. 897.

ille advb. 'to the present' 776; *ó shin ille* 'from then till now' 766.

1 im(m) m. 'butter'. Sg. nom. 446, 1281; gen. *im(m)e* 470, 656, 829, 858, 1021, 1067, 1114, in comic names 381, and see s.v. 2 **mael** and **sliab**; dat. *imim* 958, *imm* 792, 798.

2 im(m)^L, ba^L (cf. **fo**), ma^L, um^L prep. w. acc. (see § xl) 'round, about, as regards, for, beside, with, in the company of'; of putting on clothes, 'on'. *im* 51, 172, 481, etc., *imm* 1247; *ba* 738; *um* 1288. W. def. art. sg. *im(m)on* 472, 1138; pl. *im na* 172, *ma na* 744 (2). W. suffixed obj. prons., sg. 1 *im(m)um* 968, 984; 2 *imut* 986; 3 m. *imme* 106, 111, 545, etc., *ime* 738, *imbe* 1101 n.; 3 f. *impe* 1166; pl. 3 *immpu* 905. W. possessives, sg. 3 *im(m)a* 132, 1065, 1066; *imo* 760; *má* 487, 1111; *bá* 742, 1081, 1100, 1240. W. rel. particle -*a*, *ima* 188, 519, 987, (w. 2 **ro**) *bár* 520. As intensifying prefix w. adjj. see **imchialla, imchian, imdorcha, immglan, imlán, imlom**.

immach advb. 'outwards' 140, 633, etc., *amach* 157, 704.

im(m)ad m. 'large amount, abundance'. Sg. acc. 94, 773; dat. 84, 1264, *immbud* 242, 1269.

immaille advb., in phrase *immaille fri* 'along with' 321.

imarcide (-g-), imorcide adj. 'due, proper, appropriate'. Pl. gen. m. 839, f. 774. W. 2 **co** 'duly' 258.

im(m)aire m. 'ridge (of ground), dyke; row of vegetables on a ridge'. Sg. nom. 351; acc. 350; dat. *oc imaire* 'constituting a dyke' 470. Pl. nom 1069.

imman m. 'hymn'. Pl. dat. *immnaib* 142.

imarbág f. 'strife, contest'. Sg. dat. *imarbáig* 25.

imarchraid 'carries'. Pret. sg. 3 -*imarchair* 322.

imarcraid f. 'excess, superfluity'. As adj. *ro-imarcraid* 'very excessive' 233.

ima-sech advb. 'each by each, across each other' 457, 763.

imbe see 2 **im(m)**.

imbualad m. 'a fight'. Sg. gen. *imbualta* 1050.

immbud see **im(m)ad**.

immchassal m. 'coating, varnish'. Sg. dat. 1020.

imchialla adj. 'very sensible, intelligent'. Sg. nom. f. 1160.

imchian adj. 'very long'. Sg. acc. m. 758.

imchomarc m. '(act of) questioning, interrogating'. Sg. acc. 878.

imchubaid adj. 'suitable, fitting'. Sg. nom. m. 354.

1 **im(m)da** f. 'bed, couch'. Sg. acc. *immdaid* 148. Pl. nom. *imdadai* 799; acc. *im(m)dadu* 579, (for dat. § xxiii) 220; dat. *immdadaib* 122.

2 **im(m)da, iumda** adj. 'many, abundant'. Pl. nom. m. 1142, *iumdai* 800; gen. m. 838, 1221; dat. m. 897.

imdecht f. (v.n. of **imthét/imthigid**) '(act of) travelling'. Sg. gen. *imdechta* 112.

imdorcha adj. 'very dark'. Sg. acc. m. 162.

im(m)dorus m. 'porch, outer gateway, guard-chamber at outer entrance to fort' (see 1053 n.). Sg. acc. 1055, 1097, 1098, 1203; gen. *imdorais* 1053, 1057.

im(m)e see 1 and 2 **im(m)**.

imechtrach adj. 'outer'. Sg. gen. m. *imechtraig* 1058.

immel m. 'edge, rim, border'. Pl. gen. 652.

immerta past partcp. of **imrid**. Sg. gen. m. in comp. *lán-immerta* 'fully covered' 1101 n.

imfhuilngid 'causes'. Past ind. sg. 3 *ro imfhulaing* 144 f.

imfhulang m. (v.n. of **imfhuilngid**) '(act of) supporting; maintenance'. Sg. dat. 571 n.

immglan adj. 'very pure'. Sg. gen. m. *immglain* 383.

imim see 1 **im(m)**.

immlán adj. 'very full, whole, complete'. Sg. acc. m. 570.

immlige f. '(act of) licking round'. Sg. dat. 1223.

imlom adj. 'very bare, bleak'. Sg. acc. f. *imluim* 743.

immnaib see **imman**.

imnaiscid 'binds round, wraps round'. Pret. sg. 3 *imnaiscis* 132.

imo, immon see 2 **im(m)**.

imorcide see **imarcide**.

imorbus m. 'transgression, sin, offence'. Sg. gen. *imorbois* 318; dat. 623, 625.

imorro transitional advb. 'however, moreover' 143.

impe see 2 **im(m)**.

immpide f. 'intercession, the right to intercede'. Pl. gen. 1329 n.

impód m. (v.n. of **impóid**) '(act of) turning'. Sg. dat. 651.

impóid, impáid 'turns round, revolves' trans. and intrans. Pres. ind. pass. sg. *impáither* 1230. Pres. subjunct. pl. 3 w. 2 **ro**, *ru-s impóat* 1181.

im(m)pu see 2 **im(m)**.

imráid 'rows, navigates'. Pret. pl. 1 *imrásium* 1023

im(m)ram m. (v.n. of **imráid**) '(act of) rowing; voyage'. Sg. nom. 497, 867.

imrid 'applies, inflicts, employs, practises'. Past ind. pass. sg. *ro h-imred* 272.

imscing f. 'enclosure, apartment; bed, couch'. Sg. dat. in comp. *ríg-imscing* 'royal apartment' 1246. Pl. acc. *imscinge* 578.

imthét 'goes round'. Pres. ind. sg. 3, 932 n.

imthigid 'sets off, departs; dies'. Impv. sg. 2 *imthig* 533. Pres. subjunct. sg. 1 *imthiger* 667 n.

immthús m. 'guidance'. Sg. nom. 864.

im(m)um, imut see 2 **im(m)**.

1 **in, an** definite article (see § vi). On forms of sg./pl. acc./dat. when suffixed to prepositions see s.v. 6 **a**, 2 **co**, 2 **dar, di**, 2 **do, fo, for, fri, i, iar**, 2 **im(m)**, 2 **ó, oc, ós, tria**. SINGULAR Nom. m. *in* 12, 43, 46, etc.; *in t-* before *V-* 349, 505, 609, etc., for acc. 1297 n. Nom. f. *in*ᴸ 31, 120, 189, etc., occasionally *ind* before *V-* 323, 631, 1145, 1219. Acc. m. *in*⁽ᴺ⁾ 42, 121, etc., *ind* 485, *an-i-sin* 640 (see § vi); visibly nasalising *V-* 187, *C-* 99, 193, 769, etc. Acc. f. *in*⁽ᴺ⁾ 205, 348, 426, etc.; visibly nasalising *V-* 172 (where *ind=in n-*). Gen. m. *in*ᴸ 9, 97, 122, etc.; occasionally *ind*ᴸ before *(fh)V-* 233,

894, 902, 903, 1031, 1102; *in ts(h)*
170 f., 613, 620, 653, 1233, 1285.
Gen. f. *na*[H] 127, 153, 156, etc.; *ina*[H]
210. Dat. m. (before *s*- 547, 1274)
see preps. Dat. f. (prepositionless, of
time) *an* 24, 60, 699; see also preps.
DUAL m./f. Nom. *in* 906. Acc. *in*
26, 172. Gen. *in* 25. PLURAL m./f.
Nom. *na*[H] 43 etc.; *ina* 48. Acc. *na*[H]
53, 195 etc.; see also preps. Gen. *na*[N]
51, 571 (*na fh*-), 1001, 1198. Dat. see
preps.
2 **in** see **i.**
3 **in** see **sin** and **so.**
4 **in** interrogative particle (direct and
indirect) 150, 162, 164, 882. As
copula form see s.v. 1 **is.**
in- negative prefix, see **cubaid.**
1 **ina**[N] later form of 4 **a** (q.v.), 290 n.,
684, 687, 1137.
2 **ina** see 1 **in.**
inad m. 'place'. Sg. dat 635.
inailt f. 'maidservant'. Sg. gen. *inalta*
938.
inand adj. 'same', *ní h-inand 7 indé* 'it
is not the same as yesterday' 1299 f.
inar m. 'tunic'. Sg. nom. 968; dat. *hinar*
1066.
inás see s.v. **atá.**
inbe f. 'entrails, tripe'. Sg. gen. 961,
1105, comic name 401, *inbi* 1071 n.
1 **inber** m. 'a cooking spit; a bar for
carrying a cauldron'. Sg. acc. 932;
dat. *inbiur* 489.
2 **inber** m. 'river-mouth, estuary'. Pl.
dat. (for acc., § xxiv) *inberaib* 1025.
See Index of Names of Places and
Peoples.
inbert 'load, bundle, package; horse-
pack, saddle-bag' (meaning not certain). Sg. nom. 961.
inbuid f. 'time, occasion'. Sg. dat. (of
time) *an inbuid-se/-sin* 'at this/that
time' 24, 60, 699; *inbuid ro bá* 'while
I was' 289.
inchinn f. 'brains, intelligence'. Sg. gen.
(attributive) *inchinni* 479 n.
inchuib see **enech.**
incipit (Latin, lit. 'begins') 'the beginning' 1,836.
1 **ind** m. 'end, tip; top of the head'. Sg.
acc. 1176.
2 **ind** see 1 **in.**
3 **ind** see **sin.**
4 **ind** see **i.**
1 **inde** f. 'inner part, bowels'. Pl. dat.
indib 1222.
2 **inde/-i** see **i.**
indé advb. 'yesterday' 266, 1300; *ó 'né*
'since yesterday' 701.

in(d)echtair see **anechtair.**
indeó interjection 'alas' 627, 658.
indile f. 'cattle, herd of cattle'. Pl. nom.
1243.
indis(s)e f. (v.n. of **indis(s)id**) '(act of)
telling'. Sg. acc. 496, 1349; gen.
indisen 1220; dat. *indissi* 39, 1299.
indis(s)id 'tells'. Pres. ind. sg. 1 *indisimm*
431. Impv. sg. 2 *indis* 504, 1297.
Pres. subjunct. sg. 3 (w. 2 **ro**) *ro*
indise 366. Fut. sg. 1 *indisfet* 362,
1259, *innisfet* 426; pass. sg. *indisfither*
782, -*indisfither* 1340. Past ind. *ro*
indis 39, 42, 500, 783 f.; pass. sg. *ro*
h-indissed 301.
indiú advb. 'to-day' 115, 359, 716,
1299.
indlaid 'washes hands and/or feet'. Pret.
sg. 3 *indlais* 129. Past ind. *ro indail*
706.
indlat see **indmad.**
indlid 'prepares, arranges, adjusts'. Pret.
sg. 3 *indlis* 757.
indliged m. 'illegality, injustice'. Sg.
gen. (attributive) *fír n-indligid* 272
(see § viii).
indligtech adj. 'law-breaking, lawless'.
Sg. nom. m. 1222.
indmad, indlat m. (v.n. of **indlaid**)
'(act of) washing hands and/or feet;
water for this purpose'. Sg. acc.
indlat 147; dat. *indmad* 849, *innmad*
1152, in comp. see **aithindlat.**
indmas(s) m. 'wealth, treasure, goods'.
Sg. dat. *innmas* 1246. Pl. nom.
indmassa 1244.
innocht, anocht advb. 'tonight' 151,
167, 537, etc.; *anocht* 62, 1037, 1278.
indorsa advb. 'at this time, now' 719.
indracus m. 'worthiness, integrity,
innocence'. Sg. dat. 1264, 1266, 1268.
indraicc adj. 'fitting; meeting legal
requirements; fair'. Sg. nom. f. 238.
As advb. w. 2 **co**, *co h-indraicc*
'lawfully, fairly' 258.
indraithid 'devastates, destroys'. Fut.
pass. sg. -*indraithfither* 898.
innram m. 'service'. Sg. dat. *ar th'*
innram 'in the name of the service
due to you' 666.
indrechtán m. 'sausage'. Sg. gen.
indrechtáin 1087, comic name 382.
Pl. acc. (for nom., § xxii) *indrechtána*
1084, (for dat.) *indrechtánu* 1085.
in(d)r(i)ud m. (v.n. of **indraithid**) '(act
of) invading, devastating; harm,
injury'. Sg. nom. 1141; acc. 1132;
dat. 719.
indsib see **inis.**

indsma (v.n. of **indsmaid**) '(act of) penetration; consummation'. Sg. dat. 862.

indsmaid 'thrusts in, drives in'. Pres. ind. 1 *indsmaimm* 1059. Imperf. pass. pl. *-indsmatís* 588. Pret. sg. 3 *indsmais* 590.

inntlecht m. 'mind, understanding'. Sg. nom. 192; gen. *inntlechta* 1257.

1 **ingen** f. 'daughter, girl'. Sg. nom. 902, 931, 1178, 1308; acc. *ingin* 22; gen. *inghene* 1174; dat. *ingin* 35, 52. Pl. nom. *ingenai* 579.

2 **ingen** f. 'finger-nail'. Pl. nom. *ingne* 1172; acc. *ingne* 1060; dat. *ingnib* 1123.

ingerta adj. 'suitable for manure'. Sg. gen. m. 1097 n.

ingnad adj. 'unheard-of, marvellous, wonderful'. Sg. nom. f. 431. Pl. nom. m. *inganta* 975, 1142; dat. *inganta* 897, 997, *ingantaib* (for acc., § xxvi) 973.

ingor 'anchor'. Sg. acc. *ingur* 1200.

inis f. 'island'. Pl. dat. (for acc., § xxiv) *indsib* 1027

inmain adj. 'dear, lovable'. Sg. nom. m. 1139.

inmaine f. 'affection'. Sg. dat. 37, 51.

inmar m. 'fat, juice, rich gravy'. Sg. gen., comic name *Inmair* 385; dat. 747.

inmarda adj. 'rich, juicy, fatty'. Sg. dat. m. *inmardai* 331.

inmedónach adj. 'internal, midmost'. Pl. dat. f. *inmedónachaib* 1222 f.

int-í see **-í**.

inund advb. 'over there' 203.

irard, erard adj. 'very high'. Sg. dat. m. 1156. As advb. w. 2 **co**, *co h-erard* 'very loftily' 1006 f.

irchuitbed '(act of) excusing; making excuses'. Sg. nom. 854 n.

irguide f. '(act of) begging'. Sg. dat. 336.

1 **is** the copula (see §§ ci–cv) 'is'. PRES. IND. Sg. 1 **am** 299, 1259; w. 3 dependent neg. *nacham* 1139; w. 3 **co**, *conadam* 'so that I am' 1138. 2 *at* 1256, *it* 779, *isat* 678. 3 *is* 8, 20, 51, etc. (occasionally *iss* before personal pronouns sg. 3, § xxxii); rel. *is^L* 25, 227, 238, etc., *as^L* 3, 4, 205 (2), 628, 695, *us^L* (a contraction) 366; negat. *ní^H* 247, 327, 422, etc., *nocon* 419, 1232, negat. rel. *nát* 1206, 1208; interrog. *in* 'is it?' 729, negat. *nach* 506; w. 3 **co**, *conid* 56, 87, 552 (see 551 f. n.), etc.; w. 3 **dia** (2 **do** + -a^N) *dianad* 281, 493; w. **má** 'if' *mása*

881. Pl. 3 *at* 896 (rel.), 1120 (2), 1121; negat. *nidat* 65. IMPV. Sg. 3 *bat* 1337. PRES. SUBJUNCT. Sg. 1 *bam* 659. 3 rel. *bhus* 900, *bes* 1337; rel. negat. *nába* 901; w. 3 **co** (negat.) *conáb* 1008, (plus 2 **ro**) *corob* 338, *corab* 1173 (2), 1174, 1179, *corup* 334; w. 2 **cia** see s.v. **cid** and (negat.) **cen**; w. **má**, *mad* 997. PAST SUBJUNCT. Sg. 3 rel. *bud^L* 260, *bid* 354 n.; w. 2 **cia** (for neg. see s.v. **cen**) *cémad* 1317, *gémad* 1321; w. 3 **co**, *comad* 701, 1008, 1271; w. 4 **dia**^N, *diamad* 642, *dámad* 523; w. **mina**, (treated as prep. w. acc.) *minbad in mbáin mbic* 'but for the little fair woman' 1275. Pl. 3 *betís* 1170. FUT. Sg. 2 *bidat* 1148 n. 3 *bid* 32, 318, 775, 908; rel. *bus* 702; negat. *níba* 209, 234, 274, 1146, 1342. Pl. 3 w. **i**, *i mbat* 899. CONDIT. Sg. 3 *bid* 856; rel. *bud* 811; w. 2 **ro**, *robad* 524. PRET. Sg. 3 ('was', and modally 'would be') *ba* (before *C-*) 23, 70, 90, etc., *ba^H* (before *V-*) 16, 67, 69, 71, 83, 192, 625, 796, 1046, 1142; rel. *ba* 755, 770, 1251, *bu* 86; neg. *níba* 125, 265, 1295; w. 3 **co**, *comba* 17, 633. Pl. 3 *batir* 1083. PAST IND. Sg. 3 (before *V-*) *rop* 41, 752, *rob* 223; negat. *nírbo* (before *fhV-*) 221, *nírb* (before *V-* and *shV-*) 883, 1314, 1320, *nír* (before *C-*) 223; dependent negat. (before *C-*) *nárba* 548, *co nár* 629 f.; w. 2 **cia**, *cérba* (before *C-*) 725, 837.

2 **is** conjunction 'and' 422, 462, 798, 1323; *'s* 490, 1160–61.

ísa see **ithid**.

ísel adj. 'low; plebeian'. Sg. voc. in comp. *cend-ísel* (lit. 'low-headed') 'hangdog' 330. As noun m., sg. nom. 296; dat. 709.

isin, isna see **i**.

istad m. 'treasury'. In comp. see **loc(c)**.

istaig, astig advb. 'inside' 481, 603, 1225.

istech advb. 'inwards' 759, 1113.

it see 1 **is**.

it-berad, it-chonnarc, it-chótamar, it-chuala see **as-beir, at-chí, at-fét** and **at-chluin** respectively.

íth f. 'fat, lard, grease'. Sg. nom. *híth* 951; gen. *hítha* 905, 959, 1189, comic name 386.

ithamail adj. 'greedy'. Sg. nom. m. 1042.

íthascach f. 'suet' (?). Sg. dat. *íthascaig* 907 n.

ithe f. (v.n. of **ithid**) '(act of) eating'. Sg. acc. 51; gen. 889; dat. 1181. Pl. nom. 887.

ithemraige f. 'voracity'. Sg. nom. 1136.

ithid 'eats'. Fut. sg. 2 *-ísa* 627. Condit. sg. 1 *-ísaind* 183. Past ind. sg. 3 *ad-uaid* 276 (see § lxxvi).

ithir f. 'corn-land, tilth'. Sg. acc. in comp. *droch-ithir* 'bad tilth' 870.

ítmaire f. 'thirst'. Sg. nom. 1136.

iuchanta adj. 'pink'. Pl. nom. f. 1173.

iumdai see 2 **im(m)da**.

la[H] prep. w. acc. (see § xl) 'with, along with; in the opinion of, on the part of '; introducing the agent 'by'. *la* 15, 229, 256, 681, 735. W. suffixed obj. prons., sg. 1 *lium(m)* 197, 248, 723, 806, 812, 995, 1139, *lem(m)* 508, 523, 528, etc., *leam(m)* 513, 1138; 2 *lat(t)* 196, 366, 420, etc.; 3 m. *lais(s)* 14, 32, 132, 356, 546, *le(i)s(s)* 155, 202, 531, 696, 838, 1229, f. *lee* 41, 121, 1165, *lé* 1167, 1168; pl. 1 *lind* 315, 695, 702, 1242; 2 *lib* 235; 3 *leó* 193, 242, 324, etc.

lá(a) m. 'day'. Sg. nom. 50, 119, 318, 904, 908, 909; acc. 647 (acc. of time, § xvi), 719, 837; gen. *laí* 336 (of time), 364; dat. *ló* 125. Pl. acc. *láa* 1291 (of time).

labra f. 'speech, words'. Sg. acc. 831.

labrad m. 'speech'. Sg. gen. *laburthae* 243.

lacha see **loch**.

lachtmar adj. 'milky; milk-fed'. Sg. gen. m. *lachtmair* 1126.

Lachtmarán m. comic pet-name (affectionate diminutive of **lachtmar**) 'Little Milky'. Nom. 914.

laech, loech m. 'warrior'. Sg. nom. 12, 600; voc. *laích* 1131. In comps. see **lestar, mál** and **athlaech**.

laechda adj. 'warrior-like, heroic'. Sg. nom. f. 437.

laechrad f. (coll.) '(group of) warriors'. Sg. dat. *laechraid* 755.

laeg m. 'calf, fawn'. Sg. acc. in comp. *cét-laeg* 'first fawn' 742; gen. *laíg* 1126.

1 **laí** f. 'rudder'. Sg. acc. 867.

2 **laí** see **lá(a)**.

láid 'puts, places; throws' (cf. **cuirid** and **fo-cheird**); *láid bidgu* 'throws fits'; *láid for* 'afflicts, vexes'. Imperf. sg. 3 *-láud* 293. Fut. sg. 3 *-láife* 898. Past. ind. sg. 3 *ro lá* 46, *ro-s lá* 'she went' 940; pass. pl. *ro láithea* 834 n.

laíd f. 'poem, lay'. Sg. nom. 61.

láir f. 'mare'. Sg. gen. *lára* 860.

lais(s) see **la**.

lathe m. 'day'. Sg. nom. *lathi* 317; gen. *lathi* (see **aicenta**) 1078; dat. *lathi* 119.

lám f. 'hand, arm'; *dol do láim* 'going to communion'; *fri láma X* 'on behalf of X'; *lám-ar-cách* '(that which) persuades everyone'; *dar láim X* (asseveration) 'by the hand of X'. Sg. nom. (for acc., § xxi) 1197; acc. *láim* 33, 320, 1294; dat. *láim* 254, 532, 1055, 1083, 1088, 1093, 1099, 1103, 1228. Dual gen. *lám* 582. Pl. nom. *láma* 1120; acc. *láma/-u* 131, 263, 278, 706, 756, (for dat., § xxiii) 1096, 1126; gen. 849, 1152; dat. *lámaib* 1100, (for acc., § xxiv) 295. In comps., sg. nom. *leth-lám* (lit. 'half-hand' i.e. one hand) 'a seat at the side of' 1330; acc. *des-láim* 'right hand' 109; dat. *clé-láim* 'left hand' 646; pl. gen. *fer-lám* 'a man's hand' (a measure of height) 1105; see also **dóitech**.

lamaid 'dares'. Past ind. sg. 1 *ro lámus* 806.

lámand f. 'gauntlet, glove'. Dual dat. *lámaind* 1099.

lán adj. 'full, ample, plentiful'. Sg. nom. m. 463, 805, 808; acc. f. in comp. *cethar-láin* 'four times filled' 886; gen. m. *láin* 991, 992. As noun m. 'the fill of; a full amount', sg. nom. 648, 1088. In comps. see **berbthe, carna, forlán, immerta, immlán, méith, te**.

lánomain f. 'married couple'. Sg. nom. 1339. Pl. dat. *lánamnaib* 1347.

lár m. 'surface, floor, ground; middle (of a space)'. Sg. nom. 629; acc. 101, 466, 746, 1087, 1090; dat. 547, 790.

lárac f. 'thigh, haunch'. Sg. gen., comic name *Láirce* 389. Pl. gen. 105, 540, 1015.

lassaid 'lights, sets fire to'. Pret. sg. 3 *lassais* 173.

lassar f. 'flame, blaze'. Sg. nom. 1157.

latrand, latrann m. 'robber'. Pl. voc. *latrannu/-nda* 269, 288, 329.

lat(t) see **la**.

lé, lee see **la**.

leba, lebaid see **lepaid**.

lebar adj. 'long, flowing'. Compar. *libru* 546. In comp. see **técht**.

leba(i)r, lebruib see **li(u)bar**.

lecc f. 'stone slab'. Sg. nom. 589.

lécar see **lécid**.

leccda adj. 'flat, like a slab'. Sg. acc. m. 738.

lécud m. (v.n. of **lécid**) '(act of) allowing'. Sg. dat. 202, 507.

légaid 'reads'. Pres. ind. pass. sg. *légaither* 1334. Condit. sg. 3 *no légfad* 1301.

léibend m. 'platform, dais'. Sg. nom. 798.

lécid, lécaid 'leaves, allows, lets go'. Pres. ind. pass. sg. *lécar* 947 n. Pres. subjunct. pass. sg. -*lécther* 360, 362. Fut. pass. sg. *lécfithir* 366. Past ind. sg. 3 *ro léic* 283; pl. 3 *ro lécsit* 343.

légend m. (v.n. of **légaid**) '(act of) reading, studying; studies'. Sg. nom. 90; gen. *légind* 99, in phrase *mac légind* 'student' 553, 597, 638, etc.

leiges m. 'cure, remedy, healing medicine'. Sg. acc. 1192; gen. *legis* 1010, 1130.

léne f. 'shirt'. Sg. nom. 1346; acc. *lénid* 104, 540, 1015.

léir adj. 'diligent'. In comp. see **gním**.

lére f. 'assiduity'. Sg. dat. *léri* 1257, in phrase *do léri* 'entire(ly)' 355 n.

le(i)s(s) see **la**.

lethchend m. 'cheek'. Sg. gen., comic name *Lethchind* 390.

lethenach m. 'page'. Sg. acc. 649, 650.

le(a)m(m) see **la**.

lemnacht m. 'new/fresh milk'. Sg. nom. 1194, 1281; gen. *lemnachta(i)* 789, comic personal name 383, and in comic place-name see **loch**.

Lemnachtán m. comic pet-name (affectionate diminutive of **lemnacht**) 'Little Fresh Milk'. Gen. 919.

lenaid w. direct obj. or w. obj. governed by **di**, 'follows, importunes, persists'. Pres. ind. pass. sg. *lentar* 766. Pres. subjunct. sg. 2 -*lena* 627. Fut. sg. 1 -*lenab* 773; 2 *lenfa desin* 'you will persist in that' 772.

lenda, lenna see 2 **lind**.

leó see **la**.

lepaid f. 'bed'. Sg. nom. 629; acc. 150, *leba* 761; gen. *lepthai* 845; dat. *lebaid* 123, *lepaid* 841, *lepa* 171.

le(a)r m. 'sea, ocean'. Sg. nom. 464; acc. 498; gen. *lir* 438.

lerg f. 'slope'. Sg. acc. *leirg* 283, in comp. *stuag-leirg* 'curving slope' 107.

1 **less** m. 'benefit, profit'; *ric a less* (lit. 'attains its profit') 'needs' (see **ric**). Sg. acc. 265.

2 **less** f. 'buttock'. Sg. gen., comic name *Lessi* 390.

lessaigid 'cares for, maintains, preserves'. Condit. sg. 3 *no lessaigfed* 1301.

1 **lessaigthe** past partcp. (of **lessaigid**) 'well cared for'. Sg. gen. *lessaigthi* m. 1126, f. 1127.

2 **lessaigthe** see **lessugud**.

lesc adj. 'repugnant, unwelcome'. Compar. *lesciu* 695.

lesca f. 'sloth, reluctance'. Sg. dat. 154.

lestar m. 'vessel'. Sg. nom. 808, 1023; acc. in comp. *loech-lestar* 'warship' 436; gen. *laech-lestair* 497.

lessugud m. (v.n. of **lessaigid**) '(act of) caring for; maintenance, (foster-)care'. Sg. gen. *lessaigthi* 572, in comp. *mí-lessaigthi* 'bad foster-care' 1128.

1 **leth** 'side, direction' etc. Sg. nom. 91; dat. 584, 664, in comp. *i ndescert-leth* 'on the south side' 245, in prep. phrases *do leith* (w. gen.) (lit. 'from the side of') 'in avoidance of' 1012 n., *i lleith fri* 'with respect to' 653, 677, adverbially *fo le(i)th* 'separately, individually' 890, 1070.

2 **leth** 'half'. Sg. nom. 616. Prefixed in comps., 'half, one of a pair; un-', see 1 **ard, bairgen, bliadain, iall, lám, lethchend**. In Index of Names of Places and Peoples, see **Leth Moga**.

lethan adj. 'broad'. In comps. see **forlethan** and **mag**.

lethar m. 'leather, hide'. Sg. dat. 1067, in comp. *dond-lethar* 'brown leather' 102. In comic name see **cend**.

lettromm adj. 'lop-sided, unequal'. Sg. nom. m. 872.

lia m. 'a stone'. Sg. nom. in comp. *nertlia* (lit. 'strength-stone') 'a stone needing great strength to lift it' (used as a test of strength?) 587.

liath m. 'grey'. Pl. nom. f. *liatha* 1121.

lib see **la**.

libair see **li(u)bar**.

lige m. 'bed, lair'. Sg. dat. 858.

lilicca sg. gen. f. 'of a milch cow' 1126; for OI and MI nom. forms see DIL L 244.70 ff.

lilithir see **liridir**.

1 **lín** m. 'linen'. Sg. dat. in comp. *nua-lín* 'new linen' 1346. See **fuathróc** and **scóit**.

2 **lín** m. 'full number'. Sg. nom. of associative apposition *lín a chuimrig 7 a chométaig* 'with enough (men) to bind him and secure him' 280; *lín atáum* 'being all we are, as many as there are of us' 723.

línad m. '(act of) filling, sating'. Sg. dat. 1143.

línaide adj. 'made of linen'. Sg. acc. m. 738.

1 **lind** f. 'pool, lake, sea'. Sg. dat. 435, 1234. Pl. acc. in comp. *bolc-lenna* 'seething pools' 438.

2 **lind** m. '(alcoholic) drink, liquor, ale'. Sg. nom. 463, 864; gen. *lenda* 572, 1344, in comp. *bláith-lendai* 'of smooth ale' 464; dat. 331. Pl. dat. *lendaib* 996.

3 **lind** see **la**.

lingid 'leaps'; *lingid dar* 'outruns'. Pres. ind. sg. 3, 631. Pret. sg. 3 *lingis* 323, 1227, 1250.

lir see **ler**.

liridir equative adj. 'as many'; 'as many *as*' expressed w. *fri* 133 or w. acc. of the compared noun 204 (the latter w. by-form *lilithir*, see § xxviii).

liss m. 'courtyard'. Sg. acc. 819; gen. (distributive) 680, 1303, 1327.

lista adj. 'wearisome'. Sg. nom. m. 1138.

litte f. 'porridge, gruel'. Sg. nom. in comp. *find-litte* 'white porridge' 1200; gen. in comic name *Find-Litten* 402.

literdha adj. 'literate'. Pl. voc. f. in comp. *nem-literdhai* 'illiterate' 329.

líth m. 'festivity'. Sg. nom. 832.

li(u)bar, lebar m. 'book'. Sg. gen. *libair* 101 n., 107, 130, 137, 253, 255, 283, 706; dat. *liubar* 1334. Pl. nom. *libair* 139, 708, 1292, *libuir* 593, *lebair* 613, 614; dat. *lebruib* 1236.

lium(m) see **la**.

ló see **lá(a)**.

loan see 1 **lón**.

loc(c) m. 'place; passage or authority in a text'. Sg. nom. 4, 5, 242; dat. in comp. *istad-luc* lit. 'treasury-place' 1215.

loch m. (old neut., see § viii) 'lake, firth; pool'. Sg. nom. 467; acc. 445, 789; gen. *lacha* 1018, 1019; dat. 1106 n., 1107, 1109. In comic names: sg. nom./acc. *Loch nAiss* 'Milk Lake' 1030 n.; acc. *Loch Lemnachta* 'Fresh Milk Lake' 940, 1032; gen. *Locha L.* 434, *Locha A.* 498, *Lacha L.* 1024; dat. *Loch L.* 1051.

locht m. 'fault, blemish'. Sg. nom. 1175; acc. 978.

lodmar see **téit**.

loech see **laech**.

lóg, luag m. 'price; reward'. Sg. nom. 506, 507, 518, 562, 1345, *luag* 1245. Pl. acc. *lógu* 44.

loimm f. 'sup, drop; milk'. Sg. gen., comic name *Lommai* 392; dat. *lomum* 1210 n. (see § xvi), *loimm* 1284.

lo(i)ngén/-ín m. occurring only in comp. *lón-l.*, meaning obscure (see 388 n.). Sg. nom., comic name 906; acc. 1107, 1191; gen. in comic names 388, 914.

lo(i)ngthech adj. 'greedy'. Sg. nom. m. in comp. *moch-loingthech* 'greedy early' (i.e. greedy for breakfast) 1041; gen. in personal name *Brass-Longthig* 'Hugely-Gluttonous' see Index of Names of Persons s.v. **Becnat**. For *Moch-Longthi* see **longad**.

lo(i)scid 'burns'. Pres. ind. sg. 3 *-loisc* 1342. Pres. subjunct. w. 2 **ro**, sg. 3 *ro losci* 1157. Past ind. pass. sg. *ro losced* 1237.

lommai, lomum see **loimm**.

lómar adj. 'fleecy'. Sg. gen. m. *lómair* 1347.

lom(m)nán m. 'abundance'. Sg. nom. 788. As adj. 'full to overflowing', sg. nom. m. 808; pl. nom. f. *lomnána* 978.

lon m. 'demon'. Sg. gen. *luin* 1247; dat. *lun* 1285, in comp. *craes-lon* 'gluttony-demon' 1231. In phrase *lon craís* see **craes**.

1 **lón, loan** m. 'fat; food, feast'. Pl. acc. *lúnu/-a* 1189 n. Dual nom. in comic name *in dá Loan* 'the two Fatties' 906. In comps. see **co(i)re, corén, feiss**.

2 **lón** m. 'haunch, rump'. In comps. see **carna** and **lo(i)ngén**.

lonn adj. 'fierce, angry' etc. As noun, sg. nom. *cid lonn lat-su* 'though it be a cause of anger to you' 365 f.

1 **long** f. 'ship'. Sg. gen. *luinge* 867.

2 **long** f. meaning obscure, see 388 n. Sg. gen. in comic name *Loinge Brond* 391.

longad m. '(act of) eating, consuming; diet'. Sg. nom. 858; acc. 874; gen. *longthe/-i* 883, 890, in comp. *moch-longthi* 'early eating' 1134, in comic name *crích hUa Moch-Longthi* 'land of the Descendants of Early Eating' 1031, *Síth Longthe* 'Fairy Mound of Eating' 880; dat. 13, 882, 900.

longan noun, meaning unknown but apparently some textile material (wool?) used for cloaks. Sg. gen. *longain* 1347.

lór m. 'fill, satiety'. Sg. acc. 996. Adj. 'enough' sg. nom. m. 1339.

lorg f. 'club, staff'; here apparently 'peg'. Sg. acc. *luirg* 131 (see 130 f. n.).

los in phrase *a llos* 'by means of' 417.

lossa see **lus**.

182 GLOSSARY

lothomur m. 'bath-tub'. Sg. nom. 126.

luaba meaning uncertain, perhaps 'porridge'. Sg. gen., comic name *Luabann* 389; dat. *luabin* 805.

luachair f. (coll.) 'rushes'. Sg. acc. 862.

luag see **lóg**.

luaith f. (coll.) 'ashes'. Sg. acc. 654; gen. *luatha* 121.

luamnach adj. 'flying, active'. Sg. dat. f. *luamnig* 1180.

Luan m. 'Monday'. Sg. gen. *Luain* 230.

luasc f. 'swinging/jerking motion'. Sg. dat. *luaisc* 1180.

luath adj. 'swift, brisk'. Sg. nom. m. 950. Equative *luathithir fria* 'as swift as' 742. In comp. see **comarc**.

lúb, lúp f. 'loop, circle, a winding'. Sg. gen. (qualifying) *immram lúipe* 'circuitous voyage' 497. In comp. see **diabulta**.

lucht m. 'people'; w. defining gen. of v.n. X 'those who do X, people to do X'. Sg. nom. 287, 320 ('guards'); dat. 222.

luchtaire m. 'head-waiter' (?). Sg. acc. 488 n.

luga see **bec(c)**.

luidid 'goes' (see 1062 n.). Impv. sg. 3 *luid* 641.

luige m. '(act of) swearing; oath'. Sg. nom. *ba luige dó-sam* 'he used to swear by' 644.

luin, lun see **lon**.

lum(m)an f. 'cloak'. Sg. nom. 759; acc. *lum(m)ain* 105, 282, 539. Pl. dat. in comp. *brothar-lumnib* 'hairy cloaks' 1094.

lúna/-u see 1 **lón**.

lúp see **lúb**.

lurc m. 'young pig' (?). Sg. gen. *luirc* 1127 n.

lurga f. 'shin, shank'. Pl. gen. *lurgan* 1104; dat. (for acc., § xxiv) *lurgnib* 1066.

luss m. (sg. and coll.) 'herb(s)'. In comp. see **fírluss**.

lúthmar adj. 'vigorous, agile'. As advb. (w. 2 **co**) in comp. *co cos-lúthmar* 'with nimble feet' 1006 f.

1 **-m-ᴸ** infixed obj. pron. sg. 1, Class A, 'me'; see § xxxiv. 169, 272, 290, 292, 333, 361, 424, 430, 553, 575, 627, 657, 692, 779, 880, 1035, 1117, 1133.

2 **-m-** nasalisation of *b-* caused by (elided) proleptic infixed obj. pron. sg. 3 *(a)*ᴺ (see § xxxiv); 38, 282.

m(m)' see **mo**.

ma, má see 2 **im(m)**.

máᴸ conjunction 'if' 166, 882; see also s.v. 1 **is**; for neg. see **mina**.

mac(c) m. 'son, boy'; *mac(c) légind* 'student' (see **légend**). Sg. nom. 11, 28, 37, etc., in comp. *dag-mac* 'good son' 906 f.; voc. *me(i)c* 553, 621, 638, etc.; gen. *me(i)c* 7 n., 21, 24, etc.; dat. 23, 36. Pl. nom. *me(i)c(c)* 195, 642. See also Index of Names of Persons.

macdacht adj. 'adolescent, marriageable'. Pl. nom. f. *macdachta* 579.

mad see 1 **is**.

1 **mael** f. 'head of close-cropped hair'. See Index of Names of Persons s.v. **Mael Chiar**.

2 **mael, moíl** m. in personal names followed by gen. 'Devotee, Disciple, or Servant of X'. See Index of Names of Persons. In comic names, sg. nom. *Óc-Mael Blongi* 'Young Devotee of Lard' 915, *Mael Saille* 'Devotee of Bacon' 1064; gen. *Maíl Imme* 'Devotee of Butter' 1064.

maelán m. some kind of corn; 'bere' (?). Sg. nom. 1183.

maer m. 'official, steward, collector of dues'. Sg. nom. 681. Pl. dat. *maeraib* 1348.

maeth adj. 'soft, tender'. As noun, sg. acc. *maeth bóshaille* 'the tender part of corned beef' 733.

maethal, moethal f. 'lump of soft cheese' (see Lucas, Gwerin III, ii, 18 f.). Sg. gen. *maethla* 945, 949, 1061, 1118; dat. *maethail* 1081, *moethail* 802. Pl. gen. *moethal* 1027, in comic names 397, *Maethal* 1050; dat. *maethluib* 454, in comic names (for acc., § xxiv) *Maethlaib* 982, 1005.

mag m./f. 'plain, field'. Sg. acc. in comp. *lethan-mhag* 'wide plain' 1024; gen. *muige* 790. Pl. acc. *maige* 1017; dat. in comp. *crund-muigib* 'compact fields' 905.

maidid 'breaks, bursts' (intrans.). Pres. subjunct. sg. 3 *-muide* 199.

magister m. 'master'. Sg. nom. 309.

maín f. 'wealth, treasure'. Sg. nom. 690; acc. 1199.

mairg 'woe, sorrow'. As interjection, w. acc. and rel. clause, 'alas for him (who), woe to him (who)' 189, 525.

maisech adj. 'fine, handsome'. Sg. gen. m. *maisig* 1045.

maith adj. 'good'. Sg. nom. 11, 359, 414, etc.; in phrase of type *is maith lium* 'I like' 995, 997. As interjection introducing speech, 'well now' etc., 194, 220, 358, etc. As noun (1) 'reward' (lit. 'something good'), sg. nom. 1301; (2) 'nobleman', pl. dat. *maithib* 556. Compar. and superl. *ferr* 153, 222, 238, 526, 610, 683, 701, 1305; *is fherr cach ngalar* 'which is better than any disease' 1217 n.

maithem f. 'forgiveness'. Sg. nom. *maithem n-anocuil* 'granting of mercy, quarter' 327 (on the nasalisation see § viii).

maithius m. 'goodness' etc.; 'prosperity'. Sg. nom. 712; gen. *maithiusa* 1258.

mál m. 'prince'. Sg. nom. in comp. *laech-mál* 'warrior prince' 12.

mallacht f. 'curse'. Sg. nom. 41; acc. *mallachtain* 637, *mallacht* 39, 676; gen. in *in mac mallachtan* 'the accursed one' 1227 f.; dat. *mallachtain* 678, 693.

manach m. 'monk'. Sg. acc. 1254 (here ironical).

mang f. 'doe, hind'. Sg. acc. *maing* 742.

már see **mór**.

mara see **muir**.

marb adj. 'dead'. As noun 'dead person, corpse', sg. nom. 1342.

marbad m. '(act of) killing'. Sg. acc. 652, 777; dat. 642.

marbnaid f. 'elegy'. Sg. nom. 1100.

marc m. 'horse'. In comp. see **slóg**.

marcach m. 'horseman'. Sg. gen. *marcaig* 1083.

margócán diminutive of **mairg**. As interjection 1146 n.

maróc f. 'sausage'. Sg. gen. *maró(i)ce/-i* 1052, 1057. Pl. nom. *maróca* 795.

mart m. 'ox, cow' (specially the carcass). Sg. nom. 14.

Márta m. 'March'. Sg. gen. 744.

mass adj. 'fine, handsome'. Sg. acc. f. *maiss* 487.

mása see 1 **is**.

matad m. 'cur, tyke' (cf. **matrad**). Sg. nom. 307; gen. *mataid* 307. Pl. voc. *matadu/-uda* 269, 288, 328.

mataidecht f. 'doggishness, currishness'. Sg. nom. 1214.

matan m./f. 'morning'. Sg. acc. f. *mata(i)n* 206, 216, 217 n., 313, 316, 352 (of time), 355, 703, 849; acc. m. *matan* 357 (of time), 939; dat. f. *matain* 134.

máthair f. 'mother'. Case uncertain 77 (see § xliii, *sceó*).

matrad m. 'cur, tyke' (cf. **matad**). Sg. voc. in comp. *carr-matraid* 'scabby tyke' 1213.

matroga meaning uncertain, perhaps 'a currish decision' 306 n.

mé personal pron. sg. 1, 'I, me'. *Mé fén* 364. As subject of copula (expressed or understood) 167; w. 1 **-sa**, *messi* 852, *mis(s)e* 775, 1216. *Ol mé* 'said I' 1118, *ol smé* 851 n.

mebraigid 'commits to memory'. Pret. sg. 3 *mebraigis* 192.

mecan m. 'root'. Pl. dat. *mecnaib* 858.

medg m. 'whey'. In comp. see **usce**.

medón m. 'middle'. Sg. acc. 347, 748; dat. 54, 159, 170, *ar medón* 'in the middle' 593.

medónach adj. 'central, midmost'. Sg. acc. f. *medhónaig* 1059; dat. f. *medónaig* 1246.

medrach adj. 'merry, high-spirited'. Sg. gen. m. *medraig* 1045.

médithir see **métithir**.

megel f. 'bleating'. Sg. acc. in comp. *slaim-megil* 'clotted/gurgling bleating' 1210 f.

melid (1) 'grinds, sharpens'. Imperf. pass. pl. *-meltís* 588. (2) 'consumes'. Imperf. sg. 3 *no meled* 14.

messe 'ram' (?). Pl. gen. *messi* 1190 n.

messi see **mé**.

méith adj. 'fat'. In comps., sg. gen. m. *lán-méith* 'full and fat; very fat' 382; dat. m. *lán-méith* 1100; gen. f. *bán-méthi* 'white and fat' 1085.

mether m. 'outer garment, covering'. Sg. acc. 202.

métithir/-d- equative adj. 'as big'; 'as big *as*' expressed w. *ocus* or *fri* (§ xxviii) 633, 1179, 1186. For the sense in 1016 see Note.

metríne m. 'small wooden vessel, small measure'. Sg. nom. 1206.

mela see **mil**.

mell m. 'round mass, bulge'. Pl. dat. *mellaib* 105, 540, 1015.

mellach adj. 'delicious'. Sg. dat. m. 955, f. *mellaig* 802.

mellaid 'flatters, dupes'. Imperf. pl. 3 *melltais* 1312.

menma m. 'mind'. Sg. acc. *menmain* 89, 97; dat. *menmain* 91.

mer adj. 'mad, wild'. Sg. acc. m. 596.

mér m. 'finger'. Sg. acc. 284. Pl. nom. *méra* 1172.

merachad m. '(act of) going astray'. Sg. acc. 999.

1 **mess** m. (coll.) 'nuts, fruit'. Sg. gen. in comic names *Messai* 384, comp. *Cnó-Messa* 'of Nut-Fruit' 412.

2 **mess** m. 'judgement, the Last Judgement'. Sg. gen. *messa* 869.

mesc adj. 'intoxicating'. Sg. dat. m. in comp. *so-mesc* 'good and intoxicating, very intoxicating' 332.

mescaid 'mixes, dips'. Pret. sg. 3 *mescais* 130.

mescán m. 'lump of butter'. Pl. gen. in comic name *fri Tuathaib Mescán* 'against the Tribes of Butter-Lumps' 1050.

messu see **olc(c)**.

mét f. 'greatness, size'. Sg. dat. 745.

métal f. 'paunch'. Sg. dat. *métail* 1082.

mí m. 'month'. Sg. dat. *mís* 1014.

mí- pejorative prefix 'bad, ill-, un-'. See **altrom, caemna, foccal, gnímach, lessugud, rath**.

miach f. 'bushel'. Sg. nom. 560, 561.

miadach adj. 'noble, dignified'. Sg. acc. f. *miadaig* 487.

mian m. (orig. neut., see § x) 'desire, eagerness, appetite'. Sg. nom. 1134, 1142; acc. 1194 (see §§ iii and xxi), 1198; dat. 1258. Pl. gen. 895.

mianach adj. 'eager, avid'. Sg. nom. m. 1041. Advb. w. 2 **co**, *co mianach* 'eagerly' 1011.

miass f. 'dish'. Pl. nom. *miassa* 977.

míchuirdech adj., meaning uncertain, possibly 'like a freak, a monstrosity'. Advb. w. 2 **co**, *co míchuirdech* 1011.

mid m. 'mead'. Sg. acc. 1192; gen. *meda* 1025, comic name 398.

midbolc f. (comp. of *mid-* 'middle' and **bolg**) 'belly'. Sg. gen. comic name *Midbuilce* 372 n.

midchuairt f. 'central hall, banqueting hall'. Sg. gen. in *taige midchuartai* 'of a house with a banqueting hall' 1044 f.

midchuine f. 'medicine'. Sg. acc. 1148.

midnocht 'midnight'. Sg. dat. 63.

mif(f)rech adj. 'melancholy, despondent'. Sg. acc. m. 554, 1133.

mil f. 'honey'. Sg. acc. 442, 733, 744, 764, 768; gen. *mela* 857, 1075, 1108, in comic name 372 n.; dat. in comic name 922.

míl m. 'beast, creature; louse'. Sg. gen. 55; dat. 765 n. Pl. nom. *míla* 54, 134, 204; acc. *míla* 53.

mílach adj. 'full of lice'. Sg. nom. 123.

míle f. 'a thousand'. Sg. acc. 139 (see **céim**).

mílech m. 'brooch'. Sg. nom. 106.

mílid m. 'soldier, warrior'. Pl. gen. *míled* 588.

milis adj. 'sweet'. Sg. nom. 415. Superl. *millse* 1199. In comps., sg. nom. m. *téth-milis* 'warm and sweet' 1174; gen. m. *bláth-milis* 'smooth and sweet' 900; dat. m. *so-milis* 'very sweet' 332; pl. dat. m. *so-millsi* 996.

millid 'destroys'. Past subjunct. sg. 3 *no milled* 58 f. Condit. sg. 1 *no millfind* 1262.

millsén m. 'curds' perhaps sweetened (cf. Lucas, Gwerin III, ii, 19 f.). Sg. nom., comic name 931; gen. 1033, 1188, comic name 397.

min adj. '(ground or broken) fine, small'. In comps. see **arán, cirrad, gelbonn, scellec, scomartach**.

mín adj. 'smooth, calm; gentle, courteous'. Sg. gen. m. 1045; dat. f. 802. Pl. nom. f. *míne* 579; acc. m. *míne* 1188. Superl. *míne* 1199. In comps. see **acallam** and **comrád**.

mina conjunction (neg. of **má**) 'if not, unless' 196, 575; *acht minu-s tecma gorta* 'unless famine befalls it' 184;

mina-m shaera 'unless it frees me' 692. *Mina beth do* 'if it were not for' 1263, 1268. W. copula see 1 **is**.

minde 'speck'. Sg. acc. 120.

mír m./f. 'morsel, mouthful, portion'. Sg. nom. 1179, 1186, in comp. *cétmír* 276; acc. 267, 656, 763, 767, 770; gen. *míre* 766, comic name 392. Dual nom. 784. Pl. acc. *mírenda* 1180; gen. *mírend* 1178.

mís see **mí**.

miscais f. 'hatred'. Sg. nom. 1134.

mis(s)e see **mé**.

Mithem m. 'midsummer, June'. Sg. gen. *Mitheman* 1014 n.

mná, mnaí see **ben**.

moᴸ, **m(m)**ʼᴸ (elision before *V-, fhV-, shV-* and before *C-* after some preps.) possessive sg. 1 'my'. *Mo* 78, 168, 190, etc.; *m' V-* 33, 266. For elision following preps. see 2 **dar**, 2 **do**, **fo, for, fri, i, oc**.

mó, móu see **mór**.

moch adj. 'early'. As advb. sg. dat. 104, 231. In phrase *mata(i)n moch* 'early in the morning' 217 n., 358, 849, 939. In comps. see **loingthech** and **longad**.

mod m. 'way, manner'. Sg. dat. (adverbial) plus rel. clause, '(in the) way (that)' 80 n.

moethal see **maethal**.

mog m. 'slave'. Pl. nom. *mogaid* 1094; gen. *mogad* 864.

móin f. 'peat'. Sg. gen. in comp. *úr-mónad* 'raw peat' 172; dat. *úr-mónaid* 160.

mórthimchell m. lit. 'great circuit'. Sg. dat. in phrase *i mórthimchell* 'right round' 793.

móit f. 'desire'. Sg. nom. 89.

molad m. (v.n. of **molaid**) 'eulogy, panegyric'. Sg. acc. 1044, (of respect) 87.

molaid 'praises'. Imperf. sg. 3 *no molad* 85.

molt m. 'wether'. Sg. gen. *muilt* 733, in comp. *sen-muilt* 'old wether' 1081. Pl. nom. 1190.

monar m. (old neut., see § viii) 'work, task'. Sg. nom. m. 495; neut. 1310.

monuar interjection 'alas' 319.

mór, már adj. 'big, great'. Sg. nom. m. 12, 506, 518, etc., in comp. *ramór* 'very big' 805, *ro-mór* 'too big' 1206, f. 5, 89, 552, etc.; acc. m. 850, 1112; gen. m. *móir* 1098, f. *móire* 1265; dat. f. *móir* 1225, 1246, in comp. *adbul-móir* 'vastly great' 1250. Pl. acc. m. *móra* 45, 881, in comp. *deg-máru* 'good and big' 737. Compar. *mó* 264, 266, 628, *móu* 664; *ro-mó* 'much more' 838. As first element in comps. see **feiss, glan, mu(i)nce, pian, slóg** and, in Index of Names of Places and Peoples, **Leth Moga**.

mórad m. '(act of) magnifying, exalting'. Sg. nom. 863.

muad adj. vague term of praise 'noble, honourable' etc. Sg. nom. m. 80.

mucc f. 'pig'. Sg. nom. 14. Pl. acc. *mucca* 1189; gen. 823.

muich (see DIL M 183.83 ff.) f. 'gloom, dejection'. Sg. dat. 1128.

-muide see **maidid**.

muige, muigib see **mag**.

mulend m. '(water-)mill'. Sg. gen. *mulind* 1234.

muime f. 'fostermother, nurse'. Pl. nom. 1163.

muin f. 'the back'. Sg. dat. 946.

mu(i)nce f. 'collar'. Sg. nom. in comp. *mór-mhuince* 955; dat. *munci* 1080, 1081.

muincech adj. 'wearing a necklace'. Sg. nom. f. 1162.

muncend f. 'expanse'. Sg. acc. *muncind* 440.

mu(i)n(n)ter f. '(monastic) community'. Sg. nom. 218, 310, 311, etc.; voc. 246, 259, 270, etc.; acc. *mu(i)n(n)tir* 251, 639, 675, 1036, 1279; gen. *mu(i)n(n)tire/-i* 207, 501, 679, 693, 1265; dat. *mu(i)n(n)tir* 241, 297, 301, etc. Pl. nom. *muintera* 1243.

muir m./f. 'sea'. Sg. nom. 50, 469; gen. *mara* 133. In comps. see 2 **grian, torad, trácht**.

muirn f. 'mirth, jollity'. Sg. nom. 553.

mulchán m. 'hard cheese' (cf. Lucas, Gwerin III, ii, 20 f.). Sg. dat. 955.

mullach m. 'top'. Sg. dat. 1101; gen. in comp. *cend-mullaig* 'the top of the head' 739, 1048, 1116.

mur- see **muir**.

múr m. 'wall'. Sg. acc. 472. Pl. nom. *múir* 1035.

na see 1 **in**.

-na see **-da-**.

'n-a see **i**.

1 **ná, nád/nát, nach, ná ro, nár** negative particle, introducing dependent and certain main clauses; 'that not, who(m) not, which not'. See §§ li–liii. **(A)** In logically main clauses. **(a)** responsive *nád* 772. **(b)** interrogative *ná* 554, w. copula pres. ind. *nach* 506. **(c)** imperative *ná*^H 315, 637, 680, 724, 726. **(d)** jussive subjunct. (w. 2 **ro**) *ná ro* 200, w. infixed pron. sg. 2 *ná ro-t* 848, 852, *ná ra-t* 1002. **(B)** In dependent clauses. **(a)** interrogative past ind. *in rabi fó ná rabi* 162. **(b)** relative clauses: (i) direct rel. *nád* 1035, *ná* 421, 422, 629, 635, 971; w. infixed prons. *ná-t* 1124, *ná-dos* 1144, perhaps *nach* 525 (see § liii (i)), in past ind. *ná ro-s* 709; w. copula, pres. ind. *nát* 1206, 1208, pres. subjunct. *nába* 901, past ind. *nárba* 548; (ii) w. prepositional rel. clause *dar ná* 225; (iii) w. conjunctions taking rel. in MI, *ó ro-siacht* 7 *ná dlig* 686, *ór ná fil* 891; (iv) w. dependent clauses introduced by verbs of saying, thinking, wishing, etc., *ná* 317, 427, 550, 1016, 1292; *nát* 593, 708; *co ná* 326, 364, and w. copula pres. subj. *conáb* 1008. **(c)** in consecutive clauses, *co ná* 120, 628, 632, 634, 655, 1136, w. copula, pres. ind. *conadam* 7 *nacham* 1139, past ind. *co nár* 629 f. **(d)** in final clauses (w. subjunct. plus 2 **ro**) *dáig ná ro élád* 206 f., *co ná roib* 1175, w. infixed prons. *ná ro-m* 333, *co ra-t* . . . *ná ro-t* . . . *ná ro-t* 1156 f.

2 **ná** conjunction 'nor' 564, 694.

nába see 1 **is** and 1 **ná**.

1 **nach** indef. pronominal adj. 'any, whatever, some, a certain' (cf. **nech**). Sg. nom. m. 1176; acc. 49, 1139; gen. 656; dat. 1246.

2 **nach, nacham, nád** see 1 **is** and 1 **ná**.

naeb adj. 'holy, blessed'. See s.v. **spirut**.

naidm f. 'surety; bond, pledge'. Pl. nom. *nadmand* 250.

na(i)dmid (w. 1 **for**) 'binds; lays as a legal obligation (on someone)'. Pret. sg. 3 *na(i)dmis* 251, 576.

-nam see **-dam-**.

nam(m)á advb. 'only' 200, 691, 998.

1 **nár** adj. 'glorious'. Sg. gen. m. *náir* 78.

2 **nár, nárba** see 1 **is** and 1 **ná**.

nát see 1 **is** and 1 **ná**.

'né see **indé**.

nech indef. pronominal 'anyone, anything, someone, something' (cf. 1 **nach** and 1 **ní**). Sg. nom. 136, 164, 704; gen. *neich* 266; dat. *neoch* 654 n., 755, 1144.

nem m./f. 'heaven'. Sg. nom. 50; acc. 512, 637; gen. *nime* 78, 134, 508, 512, 621; dat. *nim* 299, 690.

nem- negative prefix w. nouns and adjs., see **brisc** and **literdha**.

némand m. 'pearl'. Pl. nom. *némaind* 1170; acc. *némannu* 1203.

nert m. 'strength'. Sg. dat. 657. In comp. see **lia**.

nessa compar. and superl. adj. 'nearer; nearest, next' 144, 630, 764, 770, 1251. Old superl. *nes(s)am* 228, 1241.

-ni see 1 **-sa**.

1 **ní** m. (old neut.) indef. pronominal 'a thing, something, anything'. Sg. nom. 214, 965 (see 964 ff. n.); acc. as obj. of verb 343, 485, 843, 1019, as obj. of prep. 292, 839; gen. *neich* 602. Dual nom. 597. *In ní-sin* 'that thing' sg. nom. 306, 508; acc. 37, 335, 844. *Aen ní (chena)* 'one thing (however)' 308, 522, 773, 853. W. rel. clause 274, 548, 746. W. rel. copula plus compar. adj. *ní as mó* 'any more' 628, *ní as lesciu* 'more repugnant' 695, *ní is messu* 'any worse' 716 f.; but *ní bes dogra* 1337 is literal, 'anything which may be (a cause of) sorrow'.

2 **ní**^L negative introducing main clauses 'not' 18, 30, 34, etc. W. 2 **ro**, before C-, *ní ro* 268, 273, 313, *nír* 267, 1251.

3 **ní, níba, nidat** see 1 **is**.

nia m. 'warrior, champion'. Sg. voc. in comp. *ríg-nia* 'royal champion' 621.

nícon[L] negative introducing main clauses (see also **noc(h)o(n)**) 128, 162, 365, 580, 585, 659, 671, 688, 746.

nim, nime see **nem.**

nír see 1 **is** and 2 **ní.**

nírb(o) see 1 **is.**

níth m. 'fight, conflict'. Sg. gen. *nítha* 964 n.

nithó negative advb. 'not so, no' 701.

no preverbal particle (see § xlv). (a) Prefixed to secondary tenses 14, 85, 747, 1086, 1215, 1271; omitted: 350, 457, 660, 1312. (b) With other tenses, to infix pronouns 321, 337, 627, 1007, 1117, 1153, 1205, 1216.

nó co-ordinating conjunction 'or' 8, 19, 120, etc.

nochta f. 'nakedness'. Sg. gen. 1204 n.

1 **noc(h)o(n)**[L] negative w. main clauses (later form of **nícon**) 'not' 170, 182, 183, 346.

2 **nocon** see 1 **is.**

nó co[N] conjunction 'until' 169.

noí numeral adj. 'nine' 512, 621, 887, 888, 1178.

-nom see **-dam-.**

nómaide f. 'period of four and a half days [or more loosely three]; several days'. Sg. gen. 292; dat. *ré nómaide anocht* (lit. '(already) before some days tonight') 'some days before tonight' 1277 f., of time (see § xvi and 116 n.) 293, 294.

nónbur m. personal numeral 'nine people'. Sg. nom. 304; gen. in *ól nónbuir* 'enough drink for nine men' 887 f.

nua adj. 'new, fresh'. In comps. see **deog, 1 lín, torad.** As noun see s.v. **cuirm.**

numir f. 'number' (cf. **umir**). Sg. nom. 624.

1 **ó** m./f. 'ear; corner'. Dual acc. 1163 n. In comp. see **derc.**

2 **ó**[L] prep. w. dat. (see § xl) 'from, of, by; w. respect to, concerning, about' 35, 52, 116, etc. *Ferr déda hó oín* 'two things are better than one' 610; *ó shin, ó shund* see **sin** and **sund.** W. def. art. sg. *ón* 109, 563, etc. W. suffixed obj. prons., sg. 1 *uam* 1273,

uaimm fodén 'on my own part' 1320; 2 *uait* 689; 3 m. *uad* 342, 350, 352, *uad fodén* 'about himself' 354; pl. 1 *uaind* 327, *uann* 1315; 2 *uaib* 265, 266; 3 *uadib* 263. W. possess. sg. 3 m. *ó a* 615. W. rel. particle *-a*, *(h)ó*[N] 'from whom/which' 307, 894, 1265.

3 **ó** conjunction 'since, because' 169, 686, 722.

oc, ic prep. w. dat. (see § xl) 'at, with, by'. In phrase of type *atá Y oc X* (1) 'X is in possession of Y'; (2) X = v.n. 'Y is doing (act of) X'. *oc* 98, 140, 163, etc.; *ic* 98, 135, 262, etc. W. def. art. sg. *icon* 560. W. suffixed obj. prons., sg. 1 *occum* 360, *accum* 652, 689; 3 m. *occa* 1225, *acca* 99, 887, f. *aicce* 41; pl. 1 *occaind* 150; 3 *occu* 223. W. possess. adj., sg. 1 *'com'* 289, 1116; 2 *'cot'* 718, 1146; 3 f. *'ca*[H] 1299; pl. 3 *oca*[N] 1181. W. rel. particle *-a*, *'ca* 296, *'ga* 209.

óc adj. 'young'. As noun 'young man, warrior'. Pl. gen. 1001; dat. *ócaib* 480. In compound comic name *Óc-Mael Blongi* 'young M. B.' 915.

occurach adj. 'hungry, ravenous'. Sg. nom. m. 1042.

occuras m. 'hunger, craving'. Sg. nom. 986.

ochair f. 'side'. In comp. adj. *cethar-ochair* 'four-sided, square'. Sg. acc. 886; dat. 985.

ochra f. 'leggings'. Pl. dat. *ochraib* 1066.

ocht[N] numeral adj. 'eight' 619, 1154, 1181, 1184, 1185.

ochta m. 'group of eight things, an octad'. Sg. acc. 49.

ochtar m. personal numeral 'eight people'. Sg. nom. 60, 1115; acc. 62, 82; dat. 83.

óclach m. 'young man, warrior; servant'. Sg. gen. *óclaig* 1063.

ocus co-ordinating conjunction 'and'. Contracted as 7 passim; occasionally *ocus* 46, 902, or *et* (v.l.) 916 .

odarda adj. 'dun, brownish'. Sg. nom. m. 645.

oen see **aen.**

og m./f. 'egg'. Sg. nom. 633; acc. 1179, 1186. Pl. nom. *uga* 1204; gen. 16. In comp. see **adarc.**

188 GLOSSARY

oibéil adj. 'meddlesome' (?). Sg. acc.
m. 1254 n.

óbéla adj. 'wide open'. Sg. acc. m. 161.

oíbell see aíbell.

oidche see adaig.

oiffrend m. 'Mass'. Sg. acc. 229, 314.

oige see ag.

óge f. 'chastity; perfection'. Sg. dat. ógi
1264, 1269.

oíge, oíged see aíge.

óil see 1 ól.

óinmit f. 'fool'. Sg. dat. 863.

óir see 1 ór.

oirbire f. 'reproach'. Sg. nom. 225; acc.
231; gen. oirbiri 1043.

oirchetal see aircetal.

oirdnid 'ordains'. Past ind. pass. sg. ro
h-oirdned 600.

oirecc see airecc.

oirech see airech.

oirer m. 'pleasure, satisfaction'. Sg. acc.
94.

oirerda adj. 'pleasant, delightful'. Pl.
gen. m. 1221; dat. m. (see § xxvi)
973.

oiret f. 'length'. As conjunction (w. rel.
clause) 'as long as' 682.

oirfitech see airfitech.

oirfited m. 'entertainment, delight'. Sg.
nom. 493.

oirmitnech adj. 'honoured, revered'.
Sg. gen. m. oirmitnig 1267.

oirther m. 'eastern part'. Sg. acc. 684.

1 ol 'says, said'; later forms ar, for, or.
W. pron. subject see mé and 2 sé.
W. noun subject: ol 151, 154, 167,
etc. (approx. 80 exx.); ar 31, 164,
166, etc. (approx. 37 exx.).; for 606;
or 197, 554, 597, etc. (approx. 35
exx.).

2 ol^{L/N} prep. (originally probably 'beyond'). Leniting in ol chena, see
c(h)ena. Nasalising in oldá (etc.), see
atá.

3 ol conjunction 'because' 525.

1 ól m. '(act of) drinking'. Sg. nom.
1282; acc. 887; gen. óla 889; dat.
294, in comp. sain-ól 'choice drink'
899, 1284. Pl. nom. óla 887.
Adjectival comp. so-óil 'good to
drink' 331 (cf. 350 n.).

2 ól (orig. neut.) 'vat' or other large
liquid measure. Sg. nom. in comic

name Ól nOlar 'Vat of Creams'
937 n.

olann f. 'wool'. Sg. gen. olla 859.

olar m. 'fat, grease, cream'. Sg. acc.
732; gen., comic name Holair 385.
Pl. gen. in comic name see 2 ól.

olarda adj. 'greasy, fatty'. Sg. gen. m.
olorda(i) 468, 1027; dat. m. 331.

olc(c) adj. 'bad, evil'. Sg. nom. 419,
1119, 1145. Compar. messu 717. As
noun m., sg. nom. 505; dat. 156. As
advb. w. 2 co, cu h-olc 'in a bad
way' 718.

oldá, oldás, oldú, oltá, oltás see atá.

oll adj. 'great, ample'. Sg. acc. m. 936.

olla see olann.

omun m. 'fear'. Sg. nom. 41.

on m. 'blemish, disfigurement'. Sg.
nom. 1175.

1 ón demonstr. pron. 'that, the aforesaid'
86, 124, 419, 884, 1002, 1009, 1044,
1255. W. demonstr. force weakened
to an anticipatory particle, do-bér-sa
ón comairle duit 'I will give you
(that), advice' 893.

2 ón see 2 ó.

onba some kind of food, unidentified.
Sg. nom. 826 n.; gen., comic name
401.

onfad 'storm, turbulence, furious
waves'. Sg. acc. in comp. bolg-onfad
'swelling storm-waves' 1025.

opar f. '(hard) work'. Sg. nom. w.
copula understood a n-opar (lit. '(it
was) their hard work') 'their work
(was) cut out for them' 1115.

or see 1 ol.

1 ór m. 'gold'. Sg. nom. 1321; gen. óir
565, 1244, 1328. In comp. see derc.

2 ór conjunction 'because, for' 98, 154,
295, 299, 328, 891, 1040, 1256.

oráit, oróit f. 'prayer'. Sg. nom. 1118;
acc. 188.

orba m. 'inherited land, patrimony'.
Sg. gen. orbai 1344.

orbaind apparently for arbainn, MI
form from arbar 'corn' (see DIL A
378. 37 ff. and O 153. 17 ff.). Sg.
gen. 1184. Pl. nom. 1182.

ord m. 'order, sequence, rank; ordi-
nance; ceremony, customary observ-
ance'. Sg. gen. uird 794; dat. urd 241,
745, 1225, 1226.

órda adj. 'gilded' see **forórda**.

ordaigid 'orders, ordains, appoints'. Pret. sg. 3 *ordaigis* 1205. Past ind. sg. 3 *ro ordaig* 1334.

ordan m. 'dignity, honour'. Pl. gen. 1163 n.

ordu f. 'piece, portion'. Sg. gen. *ordan* 741.

oróil, uróil f. 'abundance, excess' (see DIL F 353. 56 ff., esp. 62-3). Sg.nom. in phrase *nírb oróil* 'it would not have been excessive' 1314, 1320.

oróit see **oráit**.

ósᴸ, **uas**ᴸ prep. w. dat. 'above, over'. *ós* 105, 435, 465, etc.; *uas* 286, 1048. W. def. art. pl. *ós na* 1168. W. suffixed obj. pron. sg. 3 m. *uasu* 106 n.

os(s)la(i)cid 'opens'. Impv. pass. sg. *osslaicther* 1091. Pret. sg. 3 *oslaicis* 255. Past ind. sg. 3 *ro oslaic* 706. Past partcp. *osla(i)cthe* sg. nom. m. 118; acc. 161.

osnad f. 'complaint'. Sg. acc. *osnaid* 640.

óthá prep. w. acc. and dat. 'from' 428, 1097, 1176. See **ató**.

ottrach m. 'dung, sewage'. Sg. gen. *ottraig* 1096.

pars m. 'a piece of the Host'. Sg. nom. 253.

pater f. 'the Paternoster; a written copy of it'. Sg. nom. 986. Pl. dat. *paitrib* 142.

peccad m. 'sin'. Sg. nom. 145, 212.

pecdach m. 'sinner'. Pl. acc. (for dat., § xxiii) *pecdachu* 869.

pennait f. 'penance, expiation'. Sg. gen. *pennati* 318.

persu f. 'person'. Sg. nom. ('author') 4, 6; acc. *persaind* 720; dat. *persaind* 548.

petta m. 'pet'. Sg. nom. *petta cuirre* 'pet heron' 632.

pian f. 'punishment'. Sg. nom. 837; dat. *péin* 838, in comp. *mór-phéin* 'main punishment' 339. Cf. **frithpian**.

ponc m. 'point, moment'. Sg. dat. *punc* 511.

popul m. 'people; community (of a monastery)'. Sg. nom. 336, 365.

port m. 'port; place, abode; fort'. Sg. gen. *puirt* 1235; dat. *purt* 434, 1019.

praind, proind f. 'meal, dinner'. Sg. nom. 157, 889 (see **cét**); acc. 168, 173, 277.

praindiud '(act of) dining, feasting'. Sg. dat. 682.

precept f. '(act of) preaching; sermon'. Sg. nom. 702, 710; acc. 229 n., 314, 707, 710; gen. *preceptai* 714.

prím- adj. prefix 'first, chief' see **air(a)igid, cathair, cu(i)tig, rath**.

psalm see **salm**.

punc see **ponc**.

puirt, purt see **port**.

pupall f. 'tent'. Sg. nom. 905.

-r see 2 **ro**.

1 **ra** see **fri**.

2 **ra** see 1 and 2 **ro**.

-rab, -raba, -rabat, -rabi, -raib see **atá**.

ráidid 'says'. Pres. ind. pass. sg. *-ráiter* in *frisi ráiter* 'which is called' 115. Impv. sg. 2 *-ráid* 724, 726. Past ind. pl. 1 *ro ráidsium* 1331; pass. sg. *ro ráided* 305.

'raile see **araile**.

ráma m./f. 'oar'. Sg. nom. 1032. Pl. dat. *rámaib* 1022.

rán adj. 'noble, glorious'. Sg. dat. m. 68.

ráncamar, ránuc see **ric**.

rand m. 'stanza, quatrain'. Sg. acc. 177, 178. Pl. acc. *runda* 192, 195, *runna* 194, *rundu* 1309. In comp. see **cammrand**.

rann, rainn m./f. 'part, division; portion (of meat), share; fate'. Sg. acc. *raind* 1111 n. Pl. acc. (for dat., § xxiii) *rainde* 615 (see 614 n.). In comp. see **tarthrann**.

rath m. '(divine) grace, favour; good fortune, prosperity; value, benefit'. Sg. nom. 502, in comp. *mí-rath* 'ill luck' 146; acc. 662, 1300; dat. 1256, 1258. Pl. nom. in comp. *prím-ratha* 'chief benefits' 1338.

1 **ráth** m./f. 'surety, guarantor; guarantee, pledge'. Pl. nom. *rátha* 250.

2 **ráth** m./f. 'rampart'. Pl. dat. *ráthaib* 444.

ráthaigid 'notices, observes'. Pret. sg. 3 *-ráthaig* 585.

re see **fri**.

1 **ré** f. 'period of time'. Sg. acc. 607, 719.

2 **ré**ᴺ, **ria**ᴺ prep. w. dat. (see § xl) 'before'. *ré* 253, 658, 965, 1141, 1277, 1343; *ria* 116, 153, 298, 334, 515. W. def. art. sg. *résin* 339. W. suffixed obj. prons., sg. 1 *romum* 422; 3 m. *remi* 'before his time' 86 (and as advb. see **remi**); pl. 1 *remaind* (lit. 'before us') 'what I have written thus far, the aforegoing' 665; 3 *rempu* 219.

3 **ré** see **fri**.

recaid 'sells'. Pres. ind. sg. 3, 99.

Recht m. 'law; the Old Testament'. Sg. gen. **Rechta** 614.

-rega, regmait, regut see **téit**.

refed m. 'rope'. Pl. nom. *refeda* 340, 751, 755.

relic f. 'graveyard'. Sg. gen. *relci* 110.

remes m. 'period; (length of) reign'. Sg. acc. 712.

remi advb. (see 2 **ré**) 'before, previously' 127, 205, 590, 694 n., 716, 753, 1289.

réir see **riar**.

rercherc f. 'full-grown hen' (cf. **cerc**). Sg. gen. *rerchirce/-i* 16, 633, 1179.

résin see 2 **ré**.

résiú conjunction 'before' 667.

rethe 'a ram'. Sg. gen. *rethi* 1211.

rélad m. '(act of) revealing, declaring'. Sg. dat. 360.

rell 'a block' (?). Sg. nom. 587 n.

remaind, rempu see 2 **ré**.

renda see **rind**

renna see **rinn**.

ressamnach adj., personal epithet, sg. nom. m. 1307 n.

ri see **fri**.

rí m. 'king' (sg. nom. written *rig/ríg* (see v.ll.) 78, 1287, 1294, 1342; cf. MID p. 232). Sg. nom. 11, 23, 78, etc., in comp. *ard-rí* 'high king' 598; voc. 636; acc. *ríg* 661, 711, 864, 866; gen. *ríg* 22, 93, 535, 1221, 1226, 1227, 1267; dat. *ríg* 1282, 1284, 1286, 1319, 1347. Pl. nom. *ríg* 569, 570, 1243. In comps. see **brethach, fénnid, imscing, nia, rígthech**.

ria see **fri** and 2 **ré**.

riam advb. (see § xl (v)) 'ever, never; before' 166, 550, 662; *riam remi /*

remi riam 'ever before' 205, 716, 1289.

riar f. 'will, wish'. Sg. acc. in phrase *fri a réir* 'under his authority' 1322; dat. in phrase *do m' réir* 'obedient to me' 364.

ric 'arrives at, reaches'. Pres. subjunct. sg. 2 *-rís* 901. Past subjunct. sg. 1 *-rísaind* 995; 2 *-rísta* 643; 3 *no ríssed* (see 1 **less**) 265; pl. 3 *-rístís* 629. Fut. sg. 2 *ricfa* 904, 908. Past ind. sg. 1 *-ránuc* 1017; pl. 1 *ráncumar* 443.

ríched m. 'heaven'. Sg. gen. *ríchid* 510.

rig f. 'forearm'. Pl. nom. *rigthi* 1170.

ríg see **rí**.

rígan f. 'queen'. Sg. dat. *rígain* 1347. Pl. nom. *rígna* 1243. In comp. see **banrígan**.

ríge f. (old neut., see § viii) 'rule, kingship, sovereignty'. Sg. nom. 818; dat. 666.

rigin adj. 'hard, tough'. Sg. gen. f. *rigne* 400.

rígrad f. (coll.) '(group of) kings'. Sg. nom. 1288, 1301.

rígthech m. (comp. of **rí** and **tech**) 'royal house, kingly house, palace'. Sg. gen. *rígthige* 122 n., 547, 587, 634, 757, 1250; dat. *rígthig* 1115.

rigthi see **rig**.

rím '(act of) counting'. Sg. nom. 18.

rind m. 'point, spearhead'. Sg. acc. 284. Pl. nom. *renda* 589.

rinn m. 'star'. Pl. acc. *renna* 134.

1 **ro**ᴸ, **ra**ᴸ adj. prefix 'very, great, excessive, excessively' etc. See **brechtán, imarcraid, mór, te, técht**.

2 **ro**ᴸ, **ra**ᴸ rarely **ru**ᴸ (**ro**ᴴ before passives in *V*-). See §§ xlvi-l. Preverbal particle w. perfective subjuncts. and past inds. (original perfects); enclitic on negat. particles, some conjunctions, and preps. plus 4 **a** and **-a**, in all of which cases the *-V* may be apocopated, leaving *-r*. The form *ra-* seems particularly common before infixed pronouns. The late substitution of *do* for *ro* occurs once. W. perfective subjunct., *ná ro* 200, 333, 847 f., 848, 1157, 1163; *co ro* 199, 305, 342, 366; *ná ra* 1002; *co ra* 1156, *co ru* 1180 f., 1253. Past ind. *ro* 39, 44, 49, etc.; *ro*ᴴ w. passives 272, 301,

530, 600, *ní ro* 268, 273, 313, etc.; *co ra* 657; *ó ra* 169, 722; *nír* 267, 1251; *cor* 146, 439, 1228; *co nár* 1245. W. prep. plus **-a**, *bár throiscset* 'about which they fasted' 520; plus 4 **a**, *for ar chathius* 'on that which I ate' 293. W. *do* for *ro*, *do thomail* 1285 n. See also 1 **is**.

rob, robad see 1 **is**.

roba see **atá**.

robud, robad m. 'warning'. Sg. nom. 854; acc. 852.

ro-chóid see **téit**.

rochtain f. '(act of) reaching'. Sg. dat. 42.

ro-chuala see **at-chluin**.

rodbaid 'destroys'. Pres. subjunct. w. 2 **ro**, sg. 3 *ra-t rodba* 1002 n.

ro-fhétand see **fétaid**.

ro-fitir (old preterito-pres.) 'knows'. Pres. ind. sg. 1 *-fetar* 877; 2 *-fetara* 555. Pres. subjunct. sg. 1 *-fessur* 169 n. Past subjunct. pl. 1 *-fesmais* 259. Condit. pass. sg. *-festa* 264. Pret.(-pres.) pl. 3 *-fetar* 162 n.

roga m. 'choice; decision, conclusion'. Sg. nom. 307. See **matroga**.

roib see **atá**.

ro lá see **láid**.

romum see 2 **ré**.

rop see 1 **is**.

ro-saig 'reaches, arrives at; finishes'. Past ind. sg. 1 *-ruachtus* 1058; 3 *ro-siacht* 281, 544, 650, *ro-siacht do fhír flatha* (lit. 'your honour of a prince has come to pass') 'your princely word has been passed' 686, *-roacht* 501.

rosc m. 'eye'. Sg. nom. 1167. Pl. acc. (for dat., § xxiii) *rosca* 1168.

ruadán m. 'buckwheat'. Sg. nom. 1183.

ruaimnech f. 'fishing-line'. Sg. dat. *ruaimnig* 1103, 1106.

ruathar m. 'rush, onset'. Sg. dat. 586.

ruc, ruca, ruccad see **beirid**.

rún f. 'secret, mystery'. Sg. nom. 863. Pl. dat. (for acc., § xxiv) *rúnib* 140.

runda, runna see **rand**.

ruri m. 'great king, over-king'. Sg. voc. 620.

ruth m. '(act of) running; a course'. Sg. nom. 950.

-s- infixed obj. pron. 3rd persons, sg. and pl., Class A, 'him, her, (it), them' see § xxxiv. Sg. 3 m./neut.: 27, 124, 136, 161, 283, 286, 321, 328, 775, 986, 999, 1007, 1253, 1277. Sg. 3 f. (for (*a*)^N see 2 **-m-**): 184, 189, 275, 282, 564, 747, 940, 1057, 1061, 1089, 1187. Pl. 3: 34, 101, 313, 709, 1181, 1205, 1226, 1309.

's see 2 **is**.

1 **-sa** etc., enclitic pron. attached to indep. subj. prons.; to groups of preverb plus infixed obj. pron. plus verb; to verbs, referring to their subj.; to groups of possess. adj. plus noun; and to prep. pron. comps.; all to draw attention to the person and number of the main pron., expressed or (w. verbs by themselves) understood. Sg. 1 *-sa* 152, 178, 209, etc.; *-su* 721; *-se*/*-si* 78, 207, 232, 604, 998; *-sea* 183, 266, 682, 880, 1266. Sg. 2 *-sa* 997, *-su* 177, 196, 366, 420, 555, 782; *-siu* 188, 361, 574, etc.; *-se*/*-si* 187, 537, 553, 781; *-sea* 605. Sg. 3 m. *-som* 368 etc.; *-sum* 753; *-sam* 644; *-sium* 157, 212, 352, 353, 427, (*e-ssium*, see **é**). Pl. 1 *-ni* 723. Pl. 2 *-si* 275.

2 **-sa** see **so**.

3 **-sa** see **-a**.

sacart m. 'priest'. Sg. gen. *sacairt* 1233. Pl. gen. 1198.

sádaile f. 'ease, comfort'. Sg. dat. 846.

sadall m. 'saddle'. Sg. nom. 945; dat. 1078.

sádchib see **sáithech**.

saegal m. 'life; the world'. Sg. gen. *saegail* 653, 711.

saer adj. 'noble'. Sg. nom. m. 600.

saerad m. (v.n. of **saeraid**) '(act of) delivering, rescuing'. Sg. dat. 678.

saeraid 'delivers, rescues'. Pres. subjunct. sg. 2 *-saera* 692.

saeth m. 'distress, grief'. Sg. nom. 602, 1144.

saethar m. 'toil, toilsomeness'. Sg. gen. *saethra* 944 n.

sáidech see **sáithech**.

saidid, suidid 'sits, settles down, halts, rests'. Pret. sg. 1 (deponent, § lvi) *-sessar* 1114; 3 (active) *saidis* 635, 762,

1251. Past ind. (old perfect) sg. 3 -dessid 115; pl. 3 -dessitar 578.

sáidid 'sets, fixes, implants'. Pret. sg. 3 sáidis 322, 741, 761. Past ind. sg. 3 -r sháid 1228.

saiget f. 'arrow'. Sg. nom. 859.

saigid f. '(act of) seeking'. Sg. dat. in phrase do shaigid 'to seek' 503, 533, 1266.

sail f. 'joist, beam'. Pl. nom. sailghe 456.

sa(i)ll f. 'bacon'. Sg. nom. sall 942, saill 820; gen. sa(i)lle 456, 656, 809, 988, 1073; gen. in comic names (see also 2 **mael**) 381, 912, 920; gen. in comp. sen-shaille 'matured bacon' 100, 256, 278, 733, 1047, 1061, 1065, 1107, 1193, comic name 916. See also **bósha(i)ll**.

sain- adj. prefix 'special, choice', see **ait** and 1 **ól**.

sain-chan advb. 'here and there' 1248.

saindrud advb. 'exactly; to be precise, in particular' 26, 98, 117, 544, 1159.

sáith f. 'sufficiency, fill; full meal'. Sg. nom. 291, 1085, 1284, 1285, in comp. bodar-sháith 201 n.; acc. 331, 645.

sáthech, sádech adj. 'satisfied, flourishing'. Pl. dat. m. in comp. tenn-shádchib 'vigorous and flourishing' 480.

saland, salann, salond m. 'salt'. Sg. nom. 862, 1203; acc. 734, 745.

sall see **saill**.

salm m. 'psalm'. Pl. nom. sailm 228; gen. 138, 140.

saltair f. 'psalter'. Sg. acc. 137, 707.

-sam see 1 **-sa**.

sám adj. 'gentle, pleasant'. In comp. see **find**.

samaigid 'sets up, establishes, arranges; settles down'. Pret. sg. 3 samaigis 696, 736.

samail f. 'likeness, similarity'. Sg. gen. (descriptive) mo shamla (lit. 'of my likeness') 'like me' 720 f. In advb. phrases, sg. acc. fon samail-sin 'in that guise, thus, so' 339, 541, 547, 756; fonn samail cétna 'in the same way' 770.

samaisc f. 'heifer'. Sg. gen. samaisce 1080.

samlaid advb. 'thus, so' 1283.

sanais f. 'a whisper'. Sg. nom. 855.

sanntach adj. 'greedy'. Sg. nom. m. 95.

sant f. 'strong desire, greed'. Sg. gen. santi 1144.

sarophin m. (coll.) 'seraphim'. Acc. 513.

sárugud m. '(act of) violating, flouting, disobeying'. Sg. nom. 873.

sás(s)ad m. (v.n. of **sásaid**) '(act of) feeding'. Sg. acc. 229, 316.

sásaid 'satisfies, feeds'. Past subjunct. w. 2 **ro**, pass. pl. ro sásta 342 f. Past ind. pass. pl. ro sásta 314 f. (see §§ lx, lxxxi, xcv).

Satharn m. 'Saturday'. Sg. gen. aidche Sathairn 97 f. n.; dia Sathairn 117.

Saxanach adj. 'English'. Sg. acc. m. 734.

scaiblín(e) m. 'pottage, pot-meat'. Sg. gen. scaiblíne 1066, comic name Scaiblín 404.

scaílte participial adj. 'scattered, loosened'. Sg. nom. f. in comp., fír-scaílti 'very loose' 760.

scál m. 'spectre, apparition'. Sg. nom. (as proper name) 852, 876, 879, etc.; acc. 850.

scaraid 'spreads out, separates'. Impv. pass. sg. scarthar 1157. Fut. pl. 3 -scérat 1340.

scáth m. 'shade, shelter'. Sg. dat. in phrase for scáth (= ar scáth) 'near, beside; engaged in' 91.

sceïd 'vomits, gushes'. Imperf. sg. 3 no sceed 1089.

scellec m. 'piece of rock'. Pl. dat. in comp. min-scellcib 'small chunks of rock' 821.

scéith see **sciath**.

scél m. 'story'. Sg. nom. 301, 1345; acc. 42; gen. sceóil 1346; dat. sceól 1338, in comp. cét-sceól 'first tale' 1341. Pl. nom. scéla 190, 881; gen. 881.

scélaige m. '(professional) tale-teller'. Pl. nom. 1233, 1290.

scell 'a grain'. Pl. dat. scellaib 859.

sceó conjunction 'and' 77 n.

-scérat see **scaraid**.

scian f. 'knife'. Sg. acc. scín 763.

sciath m. 'shield'. Pl. nom. scéith 800; gen. 801.

sciathrach f. 'shield-strap'. Pl. dat. sciathraigib 801.

scibar m. 'pepper'. Sg. gen. *scibair* 859.

scób f. 'broom, bundle'. Sg. dat. *scóib* 1077.

scoltech adj. 'having cleavages, divisions'. Sg. acc. f. in comp. *cetharscoltig* 'divided in four' 740.

scóit m. 'sheet, cloth'. Pl. nom. in comp. *lín-scóti* 'linen cloths' 1240.

scolaige m. 'scholar, student, pupil'. Sg. nom. 44, 94, 96, 128, 750, *scolaigi* 47, 84, 192; voc. 555; gen. 97, 140, 710, 777; dat. 89, 529, 1290, *scolaigi* 45.

scolb m. 'wattling; thatch-rod'. Sg. acc. 635. Pl. nom. *scuilb* 796.

scolóc(c) f. 'monastic servant, lay-brother'. Sg. voc. 150, 175, 191, *scolóic* 190 n.

scomartach (coll.) 'fragments'. Sg. dat. in comp. *min-scomartaig* 'small fragments' 1104 n.

scor m. 'stud, herd of horses'. Pl. nom. (for acc., § xx) *scuir* 943.

scríbaid 'writes'. Pres. ind. pass. sg. *scríbthar* 1334.

scrútaid 'investigates, considers'. Past ind. sg. 3 *ro scrútustar* 91.

scrútain m. (v.n. of **scrútaid**) '(act of) investigating, considering'. Sg. dat. 93.

scuabad m. '(act of) sweeping'. Sg. acc. 121.

sculmare m. 'scull, oar'. Pl. dat. *sculmaraib* 1022.

1 **-se, -sea** see 1 **-sa**.

2 **-se, -sea** see **so**.

1 **sé** numeral adj. 'six'. Gen. 290.

2 **sé** personal pron. sg. 3 m. 'he'. Only in *ol sé* 150, 164, 169, 264, 673, 893, 909, 1297, *or sé* 359 f., 652, 1119, and *ar sé* 151, see 1 **ol**. For 7 *sé* see § xxx.

sebcaide adj. 'hawk-like'. Pl. nom. f. 1171.

1 **sech** prep. w. acc. (see § xl) 'past, beyond' 771, 784, 953, 1026. W. suffixed obj. prons., sg. 1 *seocham* 1008, *sechum(m)* 1057, 1062; sg. 3 m. *secha*, as advb. 'past, by' 552, 1062, has little or no force (cf. DIL S 123. 47-67), though KM's 'said aside' in 552 is perhaps acceptable. See **imasech**.

2 **sech** conjunction, introducing negat. main clause co-ordinate w. another, *sech ní . . . ní* 'neither . . . nor' 643.

sechna f. '(act of) avoiding, doing without'. Sg. nom. 524.

sechnón prep. w. gen. 'throughout' 1271. As advb., 'all around' 583.

secht^N numeral adj. 'seven' 482, 887, 888, 1068, 1069, 1070, 1071, 1078, 1088; *trí secht* 'twenty-one' 1317; *secht fichit cét* 'fourteen thousand' 1046 f. As noun, *in secht* 'the [group of] seven [things]' 618. In comps. see **fillte** and **trom(m)**.

sechtach adj. 'sevenfold'. Sg. gen. m. *sechtaig* 1258.

sechtair^L prep. w. acc. 'out of, outside' 139. As advb. 'out, outwards' 1077.

secul m. 'rye'. Sg. nom. 1183; gen. in comp. *gem-shecoil* 'winter rye' 1014.

séda adj. 'sixfold'. Sg. nom. f. *in umir shéda* 'the sixfold number' (i.e. 'six') 616.

seag m. 'strength, vigour'. Sg. nom. 655.

ségda(e) adj. 'fortunate; pleasant'. Sg. nom. m. 449. Pl. nom. f. 1171.

seche f. 'hide' (used as tablecloth). Sg. acc. *sechid* 628, 868. Pl. dat. *sechedaib* 583.

seim m. 'rivet'. Pl. nom. *semmunna* 588.

senbriathar m. 'saying, proverb'. Sg. nom. 754, 767, 776.

-sene indecl. anaphoric demonstrat. sg. 3 and pl. 3, enclitic on noun or pron., 'that, those, the aforementioned'. Sg. dat. f. *furri-sene* 19.

senistir f. 'window'. Pl. nom. *senistre* 508.

sesbéim m. 'oar-stroke'. Pl. acc. *sesbémend* 439.

sessed numeral adj. 'sixth'. As noun, *in sessed* 'the sixth one', sg. acc. 617.

sétid 'blows'. Pret. sg. 3 *sétis* 172.

sétige m. 'blanket' (?). Sg. nom. 122 n.; acc. 132, 203.

sel m. 'a while, a spell'. Sg. dat. (of time) 116 n.

selg f. '(act of) hunting, a hunt, hunting-party; quarry'. Sg. gen. *selga* 67.

se(a)n adj. 'old'. Pl. nom. m. *sena* 458; dat. *senaib* 996. As noun, sg. nom. 1192. Otherwise only as prefix: in comps. see **cáise, croth, gruth, molt, sa(i)ll, senbriathar, torcc.**

sénad '(act of) denying, witholding (the truth)'. Sg. dat. 39.

senchaide m. 'historian, teller of (antiquarian) tales'. Pl. nom. 708, 1333.

senóir m. 'old/venerable man; ancestor'. Pl. nom. *senó(i)re/-i* 592, 708, 1333.

seo see **so.**

seocham see I **sech.**

seruán (sp. for *serbán*) m. 'wild oats'. Sg. nom. 1183.

serc(c) f. 'love'. Sg. gen. *sercci* 1164; dat. *seirc(c)* 36, 40.

sercoll m. 'titbit, delicacy'. Sg. acc. 1192.

sercus m. 'love'. Sg. nom. in comp. *cét-shercus* 21 n.

serndaid 'arrays oneself' (reflexive). Imperf. pl. 3 *serndais* 457.

sess m. 'thwart, bench of boat; beam'. Pl. nom. *sessa* 458; dat. *sessaib* 1021.

-sessar see **saidid.**

1 **sét** m. 'path, way; journey'. Sg. gen. *sétta* 112; dat. 268.

2 **sét** m. 'precious thing, treasure'. Sg. nom. 1305.

seta adj. 'long, slender, graceful'. Pl. nom. m. 1172.

1 **-si** see I **-sa.**

2 **-si** see **so.**

siar advb. 'back, backwards' 1077.

-side indecl. anaphoric demonstrative 'that, those, the aforementioned', enclitic on: (a) copula, or possess., plus noun; (b) indep. pron; (c) prep. pron. (a) *derbshiúr-side* (copula understood) 'that one (was) a sister' 22; *a míla-side* 204. (b) *e-s(s)ide* 12, 24, 84, 124; *cade-side?* 'what (is) that?' 1150. (c) *de-sside* 'from that' 721; *díb-side* 'of those' 752, 1070, 1087, etc.; *dóib-side* 'about those' 60 etc.; *ann-side* 'there, then' 705 etc.; *les-side* 'in the opinion of that one' 155.

sifind f. 'rush, reed'. Sg. acc. 120.

síl m. (old neut. in *síl nÁdaim*, see § viii) 'seed, grain; progeny'. Sg. nom. 363. Pl. gen. 870. In comp. see **cáith.**

sílad m. '(act of) scattering, disseminating; publicising'. Sg. dat. 574.

silled m. '(act of) looking'. Sg. acc. 263.

sin, in sin 'that (one), those (ones)'. **(A)** Demonstr. pron. (stressed), sg. and pl.; cf. **so.** (a) subject: of active verb *feib tairnic sin* 'when that had come to pass' 758; of pass. verb *at-agur dó sin uli* 'all that was brought him' 1331; of substantive verb *oltás sin uile* 'than all that (is)' 1305; of copula *ba h-í in sin* 'that was' 16, *conid hé sin* 56, 909, *ní h-áil etir sin* 422, *nocon ed sin* 1235 f., *rop iarfaige sin* 752 f.; w. copula understood *ó t' anocul sin?* '(is) that a question of sparing you?' 247, *maith in sin* 'that (is) good' 850. (b) object of verb: *do-s-rat sin* 'he put those' (proleptic *-s-*, § xxxiv, pl. 3) 101; *gébut-sa sin* 568; *nícon ráthaig sin* 585; *ná ráid ind sin* 724 f.; *ná ráid-siu ind sin* 726. (c) object of simple prep.: *amal sin* 211; *ar sin* 'at that' 596; *co sin* 'till that' 661; *iar sin* 42, 99, 215, 228, 347, 426, 427, 1153; *ó shin* 728, 766; *óthá sin* 428; exceptionally, with prep. pron., *ind sin* 276, 368, 537, 1219, *ann sin* 211, 239, 310 f., 1327. **(B)** Demonstr. adj. (enclitic), sg. and pl., **-sin.** (a) def. art. plus noun plus *-sin: in laech-sin* 12; *an inbuid-sin* 24, 60; *in ní-sin* 37, 97, 306, etc.; *isna h-il-blassaib-sin* 47; *isin anmunna-sin* 55; *don ochtar-sin* 83; *in tan-sin* 324; *fon tochim-sin* 543 (see also s.v. **samail**); *in aidche-sin* 728; *asin ruaimnig-sin* 1105 f.; *in ingen-sin* 1178. (b) def. art. plus demonstrative *-í* plus *-sin: an-í-sin* 640. (c) qualifying prep. prons.: *air-sin* 'on that' 1140; *de-sin* 'about that, from that' 196, 351, 754, 772, 1215.

sinchán m. diminutive of *sinnach* 'fox'. Sg. acc. 1012.

sínid 'stretches out'. Pres. ind. pl. 3 *sínid* 263. Pret. sg. 3 *sínis* 650.

sinsalma 'synpsalm' (choral psalm-singing). Pl. dat. *sinsalmaib* 142.

sír adj. 'long'. In comp. see **fota.**

sís advb. 'downwards, below (in text)' 286, 428, 746, 1083, 1106, 1211.

sísana advb. (expanded form of **sís**) 836.

sith- adj. prefix 'long'. See **alta.**

síth m./f. 'fairy mound'. Sg. dat. in comic place-name *Síth Longthe* 880.

síthalta participial adj. 'filtered, clarified'. Pl. dat. m. *síthaltai* 996.

síthfe m. 'a ridge'. Sg. dat. *síthfi* 101.

-siu, -sium see 1 **-sa**.

siúr f. 'sister'. Sg. nom. 38, 40.

siút demonstr. pron., indecl., 'that, yon, that one' (person or thing) 235, 424.

sláinte f. 'health'. Sg. acc. 1218.

slam 'snowflake; clot'. In comp. see **megel**.

slán adj. 'well, healthy'. Sg. nom. m. 1148, 1324.

slat f. 'lath, (fishing-)rod'. Sg. acc. *slait* 635; dat. *slait* 1105.

sleg f. 'spear, javelin'. Pl. nom. *slega* 588.

sleith f. legal term '(act of) surprising a sleeping woman for the purpose of intercourse'. Sg. dat. 1013.

slema(i)n adj. 'smooth, polished, slippery'. Sg. acc. f. 1060; gen. f. *slemni* 988, comic name 912. Pl. nom. m. *slemnai* 455, f. *slemna* 1170; gen. m. *sleman* 1047; dat. m. *slemna* 1065.

slemda adj. 'smooth, slippery'. As advb. w. 2 **co** 1012.

slemna f. 'smoothness'. Sg. dat. *slemnu* 595.

sliab m. 'mountain'. Sg. nom. 475; acc. in comic name *Sliab nImme* 'Mountain of Butter' 883, 1030 (see § xxi).

sliasait f. 'thigh'. Pl. nom. *sliasta* 1171.

slipre 'rod'. Pl. nom. 198, 213, 271, 1270.

sliss m. 'side, wall, plank; side (of bacon)'. Sg. nom. 1159; acc. 634; gen., comic name *Slessa* 915; dat. 756, in comp. *bolg-shliss* 'bulging side' (probably = 'middle' here) 743. Pl. gen. *slessai* 1022.

slisne m. 'chip, chunk (of wood)'. Pl. dat. *slisnib* 1155 (see 1154 f. n.).

slithemda adj., meaning uncertain, possibly 'gliding' (see DIL S 278. 6). As advb. w. 2 **co** 1012.

slóg, sluag m. 'host, army; company'. Sg. nom. in comp. *mór-shluag* 557; dat. 547, 728, in comp. *marc-shlóg* 'cavalry' 577 f. Pl. nom. *slóig* 1191, 1242; acc. (for dat., § xxiii) *slógu*

707; gen. 545; dat. *slógaib* 580, 700. First element in comp. see **tech**.

slógad, sluaiged m. 'military service, military expedition'. Sg. nom. 658, *sluaiged* 652; acc. 661, 662.

sluasat f. 'shovel'. Pl. dat. *sluastib* 1096.

slucud m. '(act of) swallowing'. In comp. see **cocnum**.

sluindid 'names, tells, describes'. Impv. sg. 2 *sluind* 673. Past ind. *ro shluind* 1335.

smé see **mé**.

smir m. 'marrow'. Sg. nom. 1104; gen. *smera* 1022.

snas m. 'chipping, carving; finish; appearance'. Sg. gen. in comp. *féth-shnais* 'artistic-carving' 1119.

snechta m. 'snow'. Sg. nom. 119.

snechtaide adj. 'snowy'. Pl. nom. f. 1171.

snedid, snidid 'throws'. Pret. sg. 3 *snedis* 611, 628; *snidis* 617.

snige f. '(act of) dripping'. Sg. dat. 285.

so, in so, seo 'this (one), that (one), those'. **(A)** Demonstr. pron. (stressed). (a) subj. of copula, *is ed in so* 'it is this' 674; *cen cop é so a deriud* 501 f.; *bid biad duit-siu seo* 775; with copula understood, *a thosach so* 'this is its beginning' 765. (b) obj. of simple prep., *amal seo* 527. **(B)** demonstr. adj. (enclitic and reduced), sg. and pl., **-sa, -se/-si, -sea**. Def. art. plus noun plus *-sa* (etc.): *don chur-sa* 'on this occasion' 1147; *in dechmad-sa* 275; *isin istad-luc-sa* 1214 f.; *in t-olc-sa* 505; *cusin trát(h)-sa* 169, 774; *ón tráth-sa* 563; *in chuit-si* 189; *in dechmad-si* 265; *don eladain-se* 4, 5; *an inbuid-se* 699; *in laíd-se* 61; *in sceóil-sea* 1345 f.; *don tig-sea* 165.

so- adj. prefix 'good; fit, proper; easy; very' see **acallam, acallmach, accobrach, bél, boc(c), cóir, deithbir, forcutbide, fulang, mesc, milis,** 1 **ól, socheneóil.**

soccair adj. 'steady'. Sg. nom. m. 1023.

sochaide f. 'crowd, host'. Sg. gen. 703. Pl. nom. 1243; dat. *sochaidib* 580.

socheneóil adj. 'of good family, honourable kindred'. Sg. nom. m. 601, f. 1161. As noun m., sg. gen. 1192.

sochla adj. 'of good reputation'. Sg. nom. f. 1160.

soichid 'approaches, seeks'. Impv. sg. 2 *soich* 537.

soscéla m. 'the Gospels; a copy of the Gospels'. Sg. nom. 111 (see 110 f. n.), 984; acc. 983; gen. 613, 620; dat. 1274. Pl. gen. 873.

-som see 1 **-sa**.

son m. 'sound'. Sg. nom. 140, 144.

sonba m. 'beam' (?). Sg. nom. 825.

sond, sonn m. 'stake, post'. Sg. gen. *suind* 1048. Pl. gen. *sonn* 1047.

sondach m. 'palisade'. Sg. nom. 448, 820.

sop(p) m. 'wisp, bundle'. Sg. acc. 171, 173; gen. *suip(p)* 159, 171. Pl. acc. *suppu* 172.

spirtálta adj. 'spiritual'. Pl. dat. f. 141.

spirut m. 'spirit'; *in Spirut (Naeb)* 'the Holy Spirit'. Gen. *in Spiruta (Naíb)* 517, 1258.

spled 'sport, play, feats'. Pl. dat. *spledaib* 551.

spréde f. 'wealth, property'. Sg. gen. *sprédi* 99.

srian f. 'bridle'. Sg. nom. 959.

srogell 'whip'. Dat. sg. *srogill* 1083.

srón f. 'nose, nostril; headland'. Dual gen. 1076. Pl. dat. (for acc., § xxiv) *srónaib* 1028.

sruith m. 'reverend person, sage'. Pl. nom. *sruthi* 1333; gen. *sruthi* 1217.

sruth m. 'stream'. Pl. dat. *srothaib* 1075.

staic(c) f. 'steak, chop'. Sg. nom. 1225, 1227; acc. 745, 1228; gen. *staci* 745; dat. 763, 767, 770. Pl. nom. *staci* 751, 976; acc. *stacci* 736; dat. *stacib* 746, 1226.

stuag f. 'arch, bow, loop'. In comp. see **lerg**.

-su see 1 **-sa**.

suairc adj. 'pleasant'. Sg. nom. m. 449, 825, 1165.

suan m. 'sleep'. In comp. see **torthim**.

suas advb. 'upwards, up' 262, 698, 1052, 1214, 1250.

subach adj. 'happy, cheerful'. Sg. acc. m. 553.

súg m. 'juice; vigour, energy'. Sg. nom. 655.

súgud m. '(act of) sucking, absorbing'. Sg. dat. 655.

súgmar adj. 'juicy'. Sg. gen. f. *súgmaire* 456, 912, 920, 988.

suide f. (v.n. of **saidid**) '(act or state of) sitting'. In phrase *i n-a shuide* (lit. 'in his sitting') 'seated' 636, 762.

suidid see **saidid**.

suidiugud m. 'position, situation'. Sg. nom. 449.

súil f. 'eye'. Sg. nom. 631, 1124; acc. 632. Dual dat. 1075. Pl. nom. *súile* 1121, 1181; acc. (for dat., § xxiii) *súli* 1122.

suind see **sond**.

suipp, suppu see **sop(p)**.

-sum see 1 **-sa**.

sund, sunn demonstr. advb. 'here, now' 164, 258, 775, 1253, 1297; *ó shund (immach)* 'from now on' 660, 773.

sursan adj. 'fortunate, lucky'. Sg. nom. m. 883.

suthain adj. 'everlasting, perpetual'. Sg. acc. f. 1218.

t' see 1 **do**.

1 **-t-**[L] infixed obj. pron. sg. 2, Class A, 'thee'; see § xxxiv. 337, 596, 638, 848 (2), 852, 1000, 1002, 1123, 1124 (2), 1125, 1153, 1156, 1157 (2), 1215, 1216, 1271.

2 **-t-** see **-da-**.

-tá see **atá**.

tabach see **tobach**.

tabair, tabrad see **do-beir**.

tabairt (v.n. of **do-beir**) '(act of) giving, putting'. Sg. nom. 669; dat. 163, 275, 606, 766, 1238.

tacar m. '(act of) collecting, mustering; provisioning'. Sg. nom. 165 n.

tachor, tochar m. '(act of) putting, sending; opposing, fighting; a quarrel'. Sg. nom. *tochar* 674; dat. *tachor* 43, *tachur* 653.

taccra f. '(act of) arguing, disputing; prosecuting'. Sg. dat. 240.

taeb, toeb m./f. 'side, body'; *taeb fri X* 'trusting X'; *fri taeb X* 'as well as X'. Sg. nom. *taeb* 861; acc. 697 (see § ii), 1305, *toeb* 283; gen. *toíb* 1080; dat. *taíb* 127. Dual nom. *taeb* 1170. Pl. nom. in comic name *Fás-Taíb* 'Empty-Sides' 913.

-taet see **do-thét**.

taidbse f. '(act of) showing; appearance, vision, fantasy'. Sg. nom. *taidbsi* 431, 869.

taidlid 'visits, touches; harms'. Pret. sg. 3 -*tadaill* 986. Past ind. sg. 3 (w. infix) *ro-t táraill* 1124, 1125.

taig, taige see **tech**.

tain see **tan**.

tainghe see **tanach**.

-táir see **tárraid**.

tairbirid, toirbirid 'subdues; serves'. Impv. sg. 3 *toirbired* 1159. Past ind. pl. 3 (w. infix) *ro-t tairbirsetar* 1123.

tairicid 'comes, comes to an end, is finished'. Past ind. sg. 3 *tarnic* 710, 758; pl. 3 *tarnactar* 750 n.

tairissid 'stays, stops'. Past subjunct. sg. 3 -*tairissed* 1016.

tairmchell 'circuit; border'. Sg. dat. *tairmchéill* 1321 n.

tairmthecht f. 'transgression'. Sg. acc. 625.

tair(r)sech m./f. 'threshold'. Sg. nom. 453; acc. 164, 1113.

taiscelta participial adj. 'inspected, examined; choice'. Sg. gen. m. 1049.

taiscid f. '(act of) keeping, storing, hoarding'. Sg. nom. 291.

taisec m. '(act of) restoring, delivering'. Sg. acc. 570, 870.

taisselbad m. (v.n. of **taisselbaid**) '(act of) setting out, laying out'. Sg. dat. 1344.

taisselbaid 'shows, sets out, expounds'. Pres. ind. pl. 3 *taisselbait* 194.

taitnid 'shines, appears; is pleasing'. Pres. ind. sg. 3, 935.

talam m./f. 'earth; ground'. Sg. nom. 50; acc. *talmain* 1101, 1277; gen. *talman* 622, 781; dat. *talmain* 618, 690.

tallaid 'finds room'; *ní thalla X for/ar Y* 'Y does not admit of X'. Pres. ind. sg. 3 -*talla* 18, 1214. Condit. pl. 3 -*tallfatís* 887.

tám 'plague, disease'. Sg. nom. 1125.

-támm see **atá**.

tan f. '(point of) time'; as (temporal) conjunction 'when; before'. *In tan* 'when' 281, 350, 551, etc., *tan* 793; 'before' 581. *In tan-sin* 'then' 324. *Tan ann* 'on one occasion' 1227. *Iar tain* 'afterwards' 305, 451.

tana adj. 'thin'. Sg. gen. m. *tanai* 394; dat. m. 333. Pl. nom. f. 1172.

tanach f. 'pressed cheese' (cf. Lucas, Gwerin III, ii, 17 f.). Sg. nom. 1197; gen., comic name *Tainghe* 395; dat. *tanaig* 800. Pl. gen. 822, 1029.

tanaide adj. 'thin'. Pl. nom. m. 1169.

tar, taris see 2 **dar**.

-táraill see **taidlid**.

tárcud m. '(act of) providing; provision'. Sg. nom. 870.

-tardus, -tardsat, -tartad, etc., see **dobeir**.

-tárfas see **do-adbat**.

-tarla see **do-chuir**.

tarnic, tarnactar see **tairicid**.

tarr m. 'belly'. Sg. gen., comic name *Tarrai* 393.

tárraid 'overtakes, catches'; intrans. 'comes up, arrives'. Pres. subjunct. sg. 3 -*táir* 34 n. (see DF III, 326 f., DIL D 193. 17 ff. and 195. 16 ff.).

tarraing f. '(act of) pulling, dragging'. Sg. dat. 1116.

-tarrusar see **do-airis**.

tarthrann meaning uncertain. Pl. nom. *tarthrainn* 981 n.

tassa f. 'weakness'. Sg. acc. 832.

tascaid meaning uncertain. Sg. dat. 1068 n.

-tát see **atá**.

te, té, téith adj. 'hot, warm'. Sg. nom. m. in comp. *ro-the/(?)-thé* 'too hot' 350 n.; gen. m. in comp. *láin-te* 'very hot' or 'stuffed and hot' 388. First element in comp., see **milis**.

tecbaid 'raises'. Pres. ind. sg. 3, 131.

tech m. (old neut., see § viii (6)) 'house'; *tech aíged* 'guest-house'; *sluag-thech* 'assembly hall'; cf. **rígthech**. Sg. nom. 118, 206, 809, 1247, 1249, 1341; acc. 161, 202, 219 n., etc., 1249 (for dat., § xxiii); gen. *taige* 126, 160, 1044, 1100, *tige* 122, 220, 450, etc.; dat. *taig* 116, 535, 1251 (for acc.; see 219 n.), *tig* 144, 165, 215, etc.

techt f. (v.n. of **téit**) '(act of) going'. Sg. dat. 833.

técht adj. 'thick, viscous' (of liquids). In comps., sg. dat. m. *lebar-thécht* 'flowing and thick' 1209; *ro-thécht* 'very thick' 1208. As noun, *eter dá* *thécht* (lit. 'between two thicknesses') 'of medium thickness' 1209.

techtaid 'possesses'. Pres. ind. rel. *thechtas* 654.

teclumaid 'gathers'. Pres. ind. sg. 3, 131.

tecmaid impers. verb 'happens, happens to'. Pres. subjunct. sg. 3 *minu-s tecma gorta* 'unless famine befall it [i.e. Cork]' 184.

teglach m. 'household, family'. Sg. gen. *teglaig* 1204.

téig see **tiag**.

teilgid 'lets go, lets loose; sheds'. Past ind. sg. 3 *ro-s teilg* 709.

tene f. 'fire'. Sg. nom. 654 (see § xvi), 1251, 1342; acc. *tenid* 481, 739, 746, 1154, 1158, 1226, 1230; gen. *tened* 133, 159; dat. *tenid* 1225. Pl. nom. *tendti* 1248; dat. *tenntib* 744.

téit (see also **luidid**) 'goes, goes to'; in absolute context 'comes about'; w. **éc(c)** as obj. 'dies'. Pres. ind. sg. 2 *tégi* 877; 3 *téit* 427, *-téit* 971; pl. 3 *tiagat* 342 n. Imperf. sg. 3 *téged* 350 n.; pl. 3 *tégdis* 660 (see § xlv). Impv. sg. 2 *eirg* 503, 893, 998, 1151. Pres. subjunct. sg. 1 *-tias* 512; 2 *-téis* 999, 1151, *-téig* 999 n.; 3 (originally perfective) *-dig* 513; pl. 3 *-digset* 297. Past subjunct. sg. 3 *no téissed* 1008, *-dichsed* 635, *-diged* 304 n. Fut. sg. 1 *regut* 692, 983, 1214; 3 *-rega* 317, *-regu* 660; pl. 1 *regmait* 308. Condit. sg. 1 *no ragaind* 1270. Pret. sg. 3 *luid* 342, 537; pl. 1 *lodmar* 436. Past ind. sg. 1 *-dechad* 451; 3 *do-chóid* 748, 1233, *ro-chóid* 308 n., *-dechaid* 147, 704; pl. 1 *-dechumar* 1023.

terci see **terca**.

téith see **te**.

téll meaning uncertain, probably 'thong, leash'. Pl. nom. in comp. *coin-téill* 'dog-leashes' (or 'dog-whips'?) 1270.

tellach m. 'hearth'. Sg. acc. 171, 1229; gen. *tellaig* 828, 1197; dat. 1044, 1156.

tenn adj. 'strong, firm, vigorous'. Pl. nom. f. *tenna* 250. In comp. see **sáithech**.

tenga f. 'tongue; bell-clapper'. Sg. acc. *tengaid* 415, 650; gen. *tengad* 1332; dat. *tengaid* 1082.

teóra see **trí**.

terc adj. 'scanty, meagre; destitute'. Sg. nom. 1342 n.

terca, terce f. 'scarcity, rarity; want'. Sg. dat. *terci* 1010, 1129, *terca* 1341.

termund '(boundary of) monastery land, sanctuary'. Sg. nom. 524.

tess m. 'heat'. Sg. nom. 333.

tesarcain f. '(act of) delivering, rescuing, protecting'. Sg. acc. 1268; dat. 345, 526, 750.

tesc f. 'dish'. Sg. dat. *teisc* 734, 764.

tét f. 'cord, string; harpstring'. Pl. nom. *téta* 340, 751; dat. *tétaib* 758. In comp. see **bind**.

th' see 1 **do**.

thall advb. 'over there' 203.

thiar advb. 'in the west; at the back' 478.

thís advb. 'below' 738.

tí see **-í**.

1 **tiag** f. 'satchel'. Sg. nom. 255; acc. *téig* 101, 107, 130, 137, 255 n., 283, 706; dat. 253, 924.

2 **tiag-, tias-** see **téit**.

-tibar, -tibér-, -tibr- see **do-beir**.

tibid in phrase *tibid gen* 'smiles, laughs'. Pres. ind. sg. 3, 929.

tibrecht f. 'outburst, gushing out, overspill'. Sg. dat. 961.

tibrén m. 'little spring'. Sg. acc. 1027.

tic(c), tig (one ex. of deutero. form: see 880 n. and 1007 n.). (1) 'comes'; *tic(c) fri* 'harms'. Pres. ind. sg. 2 *tice* 877; 3 *tic(c)* 160, 347, 757, 758, *-tic(c)* 86, 1007; pl. 3 *tecat* 358. Pres. subjunct. sg. 2 *tís* 1213; pl. 3 *-tísat* 575. Past subjunct. sg. 2 *-tísta* 643; 3 *no thísad* 248. Past ind. sg. 1 *tánuc* 793; 2 *-tánac* 1267; 3 (w. infixed pron.) *do-m-ánaic* 880 n., *tánic* 89, 97, 211, etc., *-tánic* 86, 136, 550, 746; pl. 3 *táncatar* 310. (2) 'brings; gives' (pres. indic. only) see DIL D 303. 29-40 and IGT iii § 14. Pres. ind. sg. 1 *ticimm* 1056; 3 *tic(c)* 171, 619, 622, 648, *tig* 1294; pass. sg. *tecar* 1327.

tidecht f. (v.n. of **do-thét**) '(act of) coming'; *tidecht tar* 'to go against; to transgress'. Sg. nom. 155, 872; acc. 687; dat. 268, 269, 556.

tidnacid, 'tidnaisid (see 613 n.) 'grants, bestows, delivers'. Impv. sg. 2 *tidnais*

892. Pret. sg. 3 *tidnacis* 621, *tidnais* 613, 852. Past ind. pass. pl. *ro tidnacit* ⁻47 f.

tidnocul m. (v.n. of **tidnacid**) '(act of) bestowing, lavishing, delivering'. Sg. nom. 1332; dat. 49, 582.

1 **tig, tige** see **tech**.

2 **tig** see **tiug**.

3 **tig** see **tic(c)**.

tigadus m. 'housekeeping'. Sg. nom. 868.

timm adj. 'feeble, pliant'. Sg. dat. f. 800.

timmaircthe past partcp. 'bundled up'. Sg. nom. m. *timmaircthi* 123.

timchell m. '(act of) going round; a circuit'. Sg. acc. in *tánic for timchell* (lit. 'has attained your circuit') 'has circumvented you' 288.

timchillid 'one who surrounds; a guard'. Pl. gen. 304 n.

timna m. 'teaching, commandment; testament'. Sg. dat. 613. Pl. acc. (for dat., §.xxiii) *timnai* 614.

timoircid 'gathers, assembles'. Pret. pl. 3 *timoircsit* 54.

timmthasta past partcp. 'compressed, compacted'. Sg. nom. m. 123; dat. f. 1082.

timthirid m. 'servant'. Sg. nom. 151, 160, 168; acc. 48.

tinbe (v.n. of **tinmid**) '(act of) cutting, carving; a slice'. Sg. nom. in comp. *blonacc-thinbe* 'a slice of suet' 970.

tinne m. 'flitch (of bacon)'. Sg. acc. 1107.

tindram f. 'performance; story, history'. Sg. acc. 1260.

tinnsccra m. 'price paid a woman for cohabitation'. Sg. nom. 862.

tinmid 'cuts, carves'. Impv. sg. 2 *tinme* 768 n.

tinólid 'collects'. Past ind. pass. pl. *ro tinólit* 217 f.

tinól m. (v.n. of **tinólid**) '(act of) assembling; assembly'. Sg. gen. in *cloc tinóil* 'assembly-bell' 357; dat. 544.

tipra f. 'spring, well'. Sg. nom. 461; acc. *tiprait* 281, 285; dat. *tiprait* 849, 1151.

tír f. 'land, region'. Sg. acc. 114, 1008, 1108; dat. in comp. *Mumain-tír* 'the land of Munster' 1303.

tirm adj. 'dry'. In comps. see **cáise** and **carna**.

tirmaide adj. 'dry'. Sg. dat. m. 333, 1156. Pl. gen. f. 1029.

tís, -tísad, -tísat, -tísta see **tic(c)**.

tiug adj. 'thick, solid'. Sg. dat. f. *tig* 1082.

-tó see **atá**.

tobach, tabach '(act of) levying; enforcing (contracts etc.)'. Sg. dat. 572, 682, *tabach* 683.

tócbaid 'lifts up'. Pres. ind. sg. 1 *tócbaim* 1015; 3 *tócbaid* 278. Fut. pass. sg. rel. *tóicébthar* 905. Pret. sg. 3 *tócbais* 130, 539, 589, 596. Past ind. sg. 3 *tuarcaib* 107.

tócbáil f. (v.n. of **tócbaid**) '(act of) raising, lifting'. Sg. acc. 125, 126.

tochar see **tachor**.

tochosaig meaning uncertain; perhaps impv. sg. 2 of *tochsaigid* 'scrapes' 1152 n.

-tochrad see **do-chuir**.

tócht m. 'piece'. Sg. acc. 256; gen. *tóchta* 257; dat. 100, 277.

tocrád m. '(act of) vexing; a vexation'. Sg. nom. 901.

toeb, toíb see **taeb**.

toebán m. 'rafter'. Pl. gen. 809.

togairm (old neut., see § viii (4)) 'appellation'. Sg. nom. 70.

tóicébthar see **tócbaid**.

tochim '(act of) advancing; gait; appearance, manner'. Sg. dat. 543.

tomil, -toimél, -toimless etc. see **do-meil**.

toirbired see **tairbirid**.

-toirched see **do-roich**.

torsigid 'wearies'; w. reflexive infixed obj. pron. 'grows tired'. Past ind. sg. 3 *ro-s torsig* 286.

-torsit see **do-roich**.

torthim m./f. 'fit of sleep, torpor'. Sg. dat. in comp. *suan-torthim* 'sleepy torpor' 1288.

toísech adj. 'first'. Sg. nom. m. 1212. As noun m. (1) 'first-mentioned'. Sg. nom. 725. (2) 'a chief'. Pl. nom. *toísig* 910, 1001; dat. *toísechaib* 1003.

tol f. 'desire'; *is tol do X* 'is pleasing to X'; *is tol la X* 'X likes, wants'. Sg. nom. 366, 901; gen. *toli* 1143.

tolg m. 'sleeping-cubicle, box-bed'. Sg. dat. *tulg* 697.

toll adj. 'having holes'. Sg. acc. m. 867.

-tom-^L see **-dam-**.

tomad '(act of) aiming at, striking at'. Pl. nom. (for acc., § xx) *tomaid* 1274 n.

-tomail, -tomailset see **do-meil**.

tomailt, tomeilt f. (v.n. of **do-meil**) '(act of) grinding; consuming, eating'. Sg. dat. 592, 602, 647.

tomaltus m. 'meal'. Pl. nom. *tomaltais* 888.

tomus m. '(act of) weighing, measuring; measure, amount'. Sg. nom. 872.

tón f. 'bottom'. Sg. acc. *tóin* 861.

tond f. 'wave'. Pl. dat. in comp., *tromthondaib* 'mighty waves' 1004.

tonn f. 'skin'. In comp. see **gel**.

topar m. 'well, spring'. Sg. gen. *topair* 465.

torad m. 'fruit, produce'. Sg. gen., comic name *Toraid* 384, 913. In comps. sg. nom. *nua-thorud* 'fresh fruit' 226; acc. *mur-thorud* 'sea-produce' (here 'seaweed'?) 441; gen. in comic name *Borr-Thoraid* 'swollen fruit' 375.

torc(c) m. 'boar; boar-meat'. Sg. gen. *tuirc* 1049, in comp. *sen-tuirc* 'of old boar-meat' 1022. Pl. gen. 981.

-tormolaind see **do-meil**.

torrach adj. 'pregnant; swollen, lumpy'. Pl. gen. f. 822. As noun f. 'the lumpy one', sg. nom. (for acc., see § xxi) 1197.

torsann m. 'condiment, relish'. Pl. acc. (for nom., see § xxii) *torsnu* 1185.

torum see **dar**.

tós m. 'front, beginning'. Sg. dat. in phrase *i tós* 'at first' 662.

tos(s)ach m. 'beginning'. Sg. nom. 765; dat. in phrase *i tossaig* 'at first' 703.

tothlugud m. 'appetite'. Sg. acc. 1193.

trá transitional advb. 'well, then, moreover' etc. 20, 83, 92, etc.

tracht 'strength, vigour'. Sg. dat. 658.

trácht m. 'strand, shore'. Sg. gen. in comp. *mur-thráchta* 'sea strand' 440. Pl. acc. *tráchta* 1028.

traethad m. '(act of) abating, shrinking' etc. Sg. acc. 395.

traig f. 'foot'. Pl. nom. *traigthe* 1172.

tráth m. 'time, point of time, a whole day'; *ón tráth co 'raile* 'for 24 hours'; *ón tráth-sa cusin tráth ar a bárach* 'from this time to the same time tomorrow'; *cusin trát(h)-sa* 'till now'; *co cend cóic tráth* 'throughout five days'. Sg. acc. *tráth* 169, 563, 704, 774 (with delenition); dat. 563, 1293. Pl. gen. 290.

trebaire f. 'security, guarantee, bond'. Pl. nom. 251.

trebar adj. 'strong, substantial'. Sg. gen. m. *trebair* 1049. In comp. see **glan**.

trebarda adj. 'strong, firm, substantial'. Sg. gen. m. 450.

tréda m. 'a group of three things'. Sg. nom./acc. 225, *trédi* 559.

tresse f. 'strength, power'. Sg. dat. *tressi* 846.

tremanta a variety of whey. Sg. gen. *tremanta(i)* 465, 1024, comic name 394 n.

trén adj. 'strong'. Sg. gen. m. *treóin* 450. As advb. w. 2 **co**, *co trén* 'vehemently' 610.

trethan m. 'sea, stormy sea'. Pl. acc. *trethna* 1024.

trí m., **teóra** f. numeral adj. 'three'; in counting, w. 2 **a**, *a trí* 607, 616, 784. Nom. m. *trí* 887; f. *teóra* 1163, 1164, *trí* (MS *iii*, m. for f., see § xxix) 1123. Acc. m. *trí* 15, 1178, 1274, 1317; f. *teóra* 1260, 1262, 1291, *trí* (m. for f.) 709. Gen. f. *teóra* 14, 58, *trí* (m. for f.) 607, 719; by analogous confusion, *teóra* (f. for m.) 1291. As noun 'three things' gen. *teórai* 119.

tria^L prep. w. acc. 'through' 140, 284, 1282, 1323. W. def. art. sg. *triasin* 505. W. possess. sg. 3 m. *tria n-a* 1296. W. rel. particle **-a**, *triasa* 243.

trian m. 'a third'. Sg. nom. 617, 1329. Dual nom. 1329.

triar m. personal numeral 'three people'. Sg. dat. (of accompaniment) *triúr* '(there being) three (of us)' 786.

trícha m. numeral noun 'thirty'. Sg. nom. 16; dat. *tríchait* 1105.

trichemruad adj. 'blazing'. Sg. acc. f. *trichemruaid* 1154; dat. f. *trichemruaid* 1249.

trilis f. 'sheep-fold'. Sg. gen. *trillsi* 568.

Trínóit f. 'the Trinity'. Sg. gen. *Trínóti* 612.

triúr see **triar**.

tróg, truag adj. 'wretched, miserable'. Sg. acc. f. *tróig* 720. As noun 'wretch, poor creature', sg. voc. *tróig* 220, 359, 503, 851, 1092, 1254, *truaig* 843; dat. *tróg* 313.

troich see **trú**.

tro(i)scid 'fasts'; *troiscid la X fri Y im/ ba Z* 'fasts together with/on behalf of X against Y to obtain Z'. Pres. ind. pl. 3 *troscit* 696. Impv. sg. 2 *troisc* 724; pl. 1 *troiscem* 723. Pret. sg. 2 *troscis* 720; 3 *troscis* 695, 727. Past ind. sg. 2 *ro throscis* 719, *ra throscis* 722; pl. 1 *ro throscsium* 702; 3 *-r throiscset* 520 n.

trom(m) adj. 'heavy; grievous; vast, mighty'. Sg. nom. m. 725, f. 837; pl. nom. m. *troma* 981. Compar. and superl. sg. nom. m. *trumma* 691, in comp. *secht-truma* 'seven times more difficult' 726. See **galar** and **tond**.

troscud m. (v.n. of **tro(i)scid**) '(act of) fasting'; *troscud do X* 'fasting by X'. Sg. nom. 677; acc. 344.

trostán m. 'a staff'. Sg. acc. 108; gen. 417.

trú m./f. 'one fated to die'. Sg. dat. *troich* 854.

truag see **tróg**.

1 **trumma, truime** f. 'heaviness, severity, grievousness'. Sg. dat. 1009, 1129.

2 **trumma** see **trom(m)**.

tú indep. personal pron. sg. 2 'thou'. Absolute 682; predicate of copula 881.

tuaid in *anair-thuaid* 'on the north-east' 1158.

tuaiscert m. 'the north'. Sg. acc. 684.

tuathe f. 'sorcery'. Sg. acc. *tuathi* 47; dat. *tuathi* 45.

tuarcaib see **tócbaid**.

tuath f. '(petty) kingdom; tribe'. Sg. nom. 866; acc. *tuaith* 564. In comic names, sg. gen. *Tuathi in Bíd* 'of the Tribe of Food' 910; pl. gen. *Tuath*

Bíd 1002; pl. dat. (for acc., § xxiv) *fri Tuathaib Mescán* 'against the Tribes of Butter-Lumps' 1050.

tuc(c), tuc(c)ad, tucthar, tucus see **do-beir**.

-tudchad see **do-thét**.

tuga f. '(act of) thatching; thatch, thatched roof'. Sg. gen. 120; dat. *tugaid* 792.

tuicse f. '(act of) understanding'. Sg. acc. 803.

1 **tuicsenach** adj. 'choice' (cf. DIL T 354. 58, 355. 47-8). As noun, 'choice thing', sg. acc. 1190.

2 **tuicsenach** adj. 'understanding, intelligent'. Sg. gen. f. *tuicsinche* 1332.

tuir f. 'pillar, house-post'; metaphorically 'supporter; column (of fire)'. Sg. nom. 964; dat. 1249.

tuirem f. (v.n. of **turmid**) '(act of) enumerating, recounting'. Sg. nom. 838; acc. 1220.

turmid 'enumerates, mentions'. Pret. sg. 3 *-turim* (§ xci) 1205. Past ind. sg. 3 *ro thurim* 736.

tusliud m. '(act of) falling'. Sg. nom. 855.

tuitid 'falls'. Imperf. sg. 3 *no thuited* 1086.

tulg see **tolg**.

tum(m)aid 'dips'. Pret. sg. 3 *tum(m)ais* 284, 764, 767, 770.

tur adj. 'dry'. In comp. see **arán**.

ua m. 'grandson'; in tribal and family names 'descendant'. See **longad** and Index of Names of Places and Peoples s.v. **Uí Echach (Muman)**.

uachtar m. 'upper part; surface'. Sg. acc. 1033; dat. 1035.

uachtarach adj. 'higher, upper'. Sg. acc. m. 546, 591.

uad, uadaib, uaib, ua(i)m(m), ua(i)nd, uait see 2 **ó**.

1 **uair** f. 'time, occasion; an hour'. Sg. gen. in comp. *oen-uaire* 495; dat. 319.

2 **uair** conjunction 'because, for' 51, 86, 95, 504, 516, 753, 1256.

uaisle f. 'nobility, noble nature'. Sg. dat. 1263, 1268.

ua(i)tne m. 'prop, post, pillar'. Sg. acc.
uatni 635. Pl. nom. 455, 825; dat.
uatnib 842.

uas, uasu see **ós**.

uasal adj. 'high, noble'. Sg. nom. m.
1039; gen. *uasail* 1267. As noun m.
'a nobleman', sg. nom. 296; dat.
709.

uatha 'scarcity'. Sg. nom. 1123.

uathad m. 'small number, a few'. Sg.
nom. 223, 1339; dat. (of accompaniment) 703.

uball m. 'apple'. Sg. nom. 609, 1295;
acc. 623; gen. *ubaill* 606; dat. 617.
Pl. nom. *ubla(i)* 35, 629, 1203; acc.
ubla 43, 53; gen. 51, in comp. *fiad-
uball* 'of crab-apples' 560 f.; dat.
ublaib 582, 628.

uch interjection 'alas' 1144.

uchán interjection of grief 'alas' 1120.

ug, uga see **adarc** and **og**.

uí, uíb see **ua**.

uide m./f. 'journey'. Sg. nom. *uide/-i*
266.

uidecht f. 'journey'. Sg. dat. 1147.

u(i)le pron. and adj. 'all, every'. (a)
pronoun, subject of verb 812, *uli*
297, 358, 511, 676, 696, 723. (b)
adjective. Sg. nom. qualifying preceding def. subj. noun, *uli* 524; sg.
nom. qualifying preceding demonstr.
pron. 1305, *uli* 1331; def. sg. nom.
qualifying following subj. noun 509,
uli 1243; sg. acc. qualifying preceding
def. obj. noun *uli* 500, 1263; pl. acc.
qualifying preceding pl. infixed obj.
pron. *uli* 1145.

ulideta m. 'the entirety'. Sg. acc.
ulidetaid 198, (for nom., § xxii) 213,
271.

umir f. 'number' (cf. **numir**). Sg. nom.
611, 616, 626.

uindius f. 'ash-tree, ash-wood'. Sg. gen.
uindsend 1155; dat. *uindsinn* 740.

uinge f. 'ounce (of silver)'. Sg. nom.
681, 1303, 1327.

usce m. 'water'. Sg. nom. 861; gen.
295; dat. 126, 201, 292, in comps.
bodur-usce 'muddy water' 215, 657,
medg-usce 'whey water' 158, 225.

ulcha f. 'beard'. Sg. acc. *ulchain* 604,
605.

um see 2 **im(m)**.

umalóit f. 'humility, obedience, submission; serving'. Sg. acc. 308 (where
fri = la), 1255; gen. *umalóti* 1257;
dat. *umalóit* 136, 233, 303 (see 4 **ar**).

úr adj. 'fresh, new'. Sg. nom. m. 446,
1282; dat. 958. Pl. acc. f. *úra* 'newly
killed' 1189. In comp. see **móin**.

urchur m. 'a cast, shot'. Sg. acc. 617.

urd see **ord**.

uróil see **oróil**.

ursa(n), ersa 'door-post, jamb'. Sg.
gen. *ursand* 127, *ursainde* 697. Dual
nom. *ersaind* 797.

urslacthe past partcp. 'opened'. Pl.
nom. f. *urslacthi* 509.

us see 1 **is**.

usa compar. adj. 'easier, more tolerable'
524.

úsca 'lard, grease'. Sg. gen. *úsca(i)* 468,
1027, 1106, 1107.

út demonstr. advb. and adj. 'yonder;
that, those, yon' 45, 51, 129, etc.

INDEXES

Comic names which are simply common-nouns personified or localised — foods
etc. — are given in the Glossary.

NAMES OF PERSONS

Ádam Acc. 369, 509 ; gen. *Ádaim* 363, 413.

Ábél Acc. 509; gen. *Ábéil* 413.

Ancríst Antichrist. Gen. 873.

Anér, Aniér, Anéra name of Mac Con Glinne, 6 n., 74, 83, 85, 87, 253, 1038.

Barre, Barra patron saint of Cork. Acc. 296, 627, 659; gen. 209, 210, 235, *Barri* 523; dat. *Barri* 234.

Becán 76 (§ 8 n.).

Becnait 76 (§ 8 n.).

Becnat Bélathi ingen meic Baetáin Brass-Longthig the *Fáthliaig's* wife, 902 f.

Brigit saint. Nom. (for acc., § xxi) 1237; cf. 1275 n.

Caillech Bérre 72 (§ 8 n.).

Cathal mac Finguine king of Munster AD 721-742. Nom. 11, 34, 53, etc.; voc. *Cathail* 1276; acc. 93, 529; gen. *Cathail* 7 n., 10, 21, etc.; dat. 36, 49, 505, 631.

Comgán by-name of **Mac Dá Cherda**. Nom. 66 (§ 8 n.); dat. 1314.

Conn Cét-Chathach 'Conn of the Hundred Battles', legendary king of Tara. Gen. *clanna Cuinn Chét-Chathaig* (the noble families of Connaught descended from Conn) 599 f.

Críst Nom. *Íhsu Críst* 309; gen. *Críst* 613, 626.

Crítán by-name of **Mac Rustaing**. Nom. 68 (§ 8 n.).

Cruit-Fhiach 'Harp-Raven' son of **Roennu Ressamnach**, 1308.

Cú cen Gairm Gen. *Con cen Gairm* 7 n.

Cú cen Máthair Gen. *Con cen Máthair* 8 (see 7 n.).

Donn-Fhiach 'Dusky Raven'. Nom. 72 (§ 8 n.).

Dub Dá Thuath Nom. 70 (§ 8 n.).

Eógan evidently the *Fáthliaig's* real name. Gen. *Eógain* 1111.

Fergal mac Moíle Dúin King of Ailech (see 7 n.). Nom. 37; dat. 23.

Garb Daire by-name of **Mac Samán**. Nom. 73 (§ 8 n.).

Íhsu see **Críst**.

Lígach ingen Moíle Dúin Acc. *Lígaig* 22; dat. *Lígaig* 35, 52.

Mac Con Glinne/-nd- 'Son of the Hound of the Glen' see **Anér**. Nom. 6, 83 f., 164 f., etc.; voc. *Meic Con Glinne* 419, 993, 1280; acc. 239 f., 305 f.; dat. 74, 609 f., 630, etc.

Mac Dá Cherda Dat. 66 (§ 8 n.).

Mac Rustaing Dat. 68 (§ 8 n.).

Mac Samán Dat. 73 (§ 8 n.).

Mael Chiar 'Black Crop-Head' daughter of **Roennu Ressamnach**, 1308.

Ma(i)nchín (indecl. but the by-forms (acc.) *Manchéin* 1325 and (gen.) *Manchíne* 1306 both occur, the former in rhyme) 'Little Monk', Abbot of Cork, 149, 193, 194, etc.

Maire the Virgin Mary. Gen. 80 n.

Marbán Gen. 77 (§ 8 n.).

Mog Nuadat legendary ancestor of the Eóganacht. See **Leth Moga (Nuadat)** in Index of Names of Places.

Moýse Moses. Gen. *Moýsi* 614.

Pichán mac Moíle Finde king of the Uí Echach. Nom. 552, 555, 565, etc.; acc. 1288; gen. *Pichá(i)n* 535, 541, 551, 1235; dat. 729, 749.

Roennu Ressamnach poet. Nom. 1307 n.

Sáttan Satan. Nom. 13.

Stéléne Gen. 71 (§ 8 n.).

NAMES OF PLACES AND PEOPLES

ABBREVIATIONS

Bibliographical abbreviations coinciding with those of the *Dictionary of the Irish language* (DIL) are not included here.

ACL   *Archiv für celtische Lexikographie* (Halle 1900–1907)

AMC   Aislinge Meic Con Glinne (cf. KM)

AS   W. Stokes, *Acallamh na Senórach* (Irische Texte IV/1, Leipzig 1900)

AT 2   A. Aarne and S. Thompson, *The types of the folktale: a classification and bibliography* (2nd rev., FF Communications No. 184, Helsinki 1961)

B   Scribe of the Leabhar Breac and his copy of AMC

BBCS   *Bulletin of the Board of Celtic Studies* (London and Cardiff 1923—)

BDD   Togail Bruidne Da Derga

BDD U   Version of BDD in LU lines 6723–8037

BÓC   Brian Ó Cuív

BST   L. McKenna, *Bardic syntactical tracts* (Dublin 1944)

c.   *circa* 'about'

C   any consanant

C'   any palatalised consonant

C''   any non-palatalised consonant

CEMod.I   Classical Early Modern Irish

CGH   M. A. O'Brien, *Corpus genealogiarum Hiberniae* I (Dublin 1962)

Clare   E. Knott, 'An Irish seventeenth-century translation of the Rule of St. Clare', *Ériu* XV (1948, 1950)

CML 2   K. Jackson, *Cath Maighe Léna* (Med. Mod. Ir. Ser. IX, Dublin 1938)

CMT 1   W. Stokes, 'The second battle of Moytura' in RC XII (1891) 52–130, 306–8

CMT 2   B. Ó Cuív, *Cath Muighe Tuireadh: the second battle of Magh Tuireadh* (Dublin 1945)

COR   Cecile O'Rahilly

Corp. Gen.   See CGH

CR   W. M. Hennessy, *Chronicum Scotorum. A chronicle of Irish affairs, from the earliest times to A.D. 1135* (London 1866)

CRR   E. Hogan, *Cath Ruis na Ríg for Bóinn* (Todd Lect. Ser. IV, Dublin 1892) 2–59

Dánta G.   T. F. O'Rahilly, *Dánta grádha: an anthology of Irish love poetry (A.D. 1350–1750)* I (2nd edn, Cork 1926)

DF   E. MacNeill and G. Murphy, *Duanaire Finn: the Book of the Lays of Fionn* (Irish Texts Soc. VII, XXVIII, XLIII, Dublin and London 1908, 1933, 1958)

DIL   C. Marstrander et. al. (edd.), *(Contributions to a) Dictionary of the Irish language* (Dublin 1913–76)

DTL   K. H. Jackson, 'The date of The Tripartite Life of St. Patrick' in ZCP XLI (1986) 5–45

ECNP   K. Jackson, *Studies in early Celtic nature poetry* (Cambridge 1935)

EGQ   E. Gordon Quin

EIHM   T. F. O'Rahilly, *Early Irish history and mythology* (Dublin 1946)

EIL   G. Murphy, *Early Irish lyrics: eighth to twelfth century* (Oxford 1956)

EIM	G. Murphy, *Early Irish metrics* (Dublin 1961)
EMI	Early Middle Irish (see Introd. pp. xxii–xxiii)
EMod.I	Early Modern Irish
EU	C. O'Rahilly, *Eachtra Uilliam: an Irish version of William of Palerne* (Dublin 1949)
Fél.1	W. Stokes, *On the calendar of Oengus* (Trans. RIA, Ir. Manuscript Ser. I, Dublin 1880)
Fél.2	W. Stokes, *Félire Óengusso Céli Dé: The martyrology of Oengus the Culdee* (Henry Bradshaw Soc. XXIX, London 1905)
FEMN	E. Ua Riain (ed.), *Féil-sgríbhinn Eoin Mhic Néill* (Dublin 1940)
GOI	R. Thurneysen, *A grammar of Old Irish* (trans. D. A. Binchy and O. Bergin, Dublin 1946)
Gwerin	*Gwerin, a journal of folklife* (Oxford 1956–62)
H	(1) see LU H
	(2) scribe of TCD MS H.3.18 and his copy of AMC
Hull	V. Hull, 'The verbal system of *Aislinge Meic Conglinne*' in ZCP XXIX (1962–4) 325–78
IC	H. Pilch and J. Thurow (edd.), *Indo-Celtica: Gedächtnisschrift für Alf Sommerfelt* (Commentationes Societatis Linguisticae Europaeae II, München 1972)
IDPP	T. F. O'Rahilly, *Irish dialects past and present with chapters on Scottish and Manx* (2nd edn, Dublin 1972)
IE and IE	G. Cardona et al. (edd.) *Indo-European and Indo-Europeans: papers presented at the Third Indo-European Conference at the University of Pennsylvannia* (Philadelphia 1970)
IMI	Intermediate Middle Irish (see Introd. pp. xxii–xxiii)
IMN	*Irisleabhar Muighe Nuadhad* (Maynooth and Dublin 1906—)
ISP	E. Knott, *An introduction to Irish syllabic poetry of the period 1200–1600* (2nd edn, Dublin 1957)
JCS	*Journal of Celtic studies* (Baltimore Md. 1949–58, Santa Barbara 1981–)
JS	John Strachan
KM	(1) Kuno Meyer
	(2) idem, *Aislinge Meic Conglinne: The vision of MacConglinne a Middle–Irish wonder tale* (London 1892)
LAU	T. Ó Máille, *The language of the Annals of Ulster* (Univ. of Manchester Publications No. LIII, Celtic Ser. No. II, Manchester 1910)
LBr.	(1) Leabhar Breac (RIA MS 23 P 16)
	(2) *Leabhar Breac: the Speckled Book otherwise styled Leabhar Mór Dúna Doighre* (Manuscript facsimile, Dublin 1876)
LEIA	J. Vendryes et al. (edd.), *Lexique étymologique d'irlandais ancien* (Dublin and Paris 1959—)
LMI	Late Middle Irish (see Introd. pp. xxii–xxiii)
LMU	V. Hull, *Longes Mac n-Uislenn: the Exile of the Sons of Uisliu* (MLA Monograph Ser. XVI, New York and London 1949)
LU A	Scribe A of LU and his text in printed edition
LU H	Scribe H of LU and his text in printed edition
LU M	Scribe M of LU and his text in printed edition
M	see LU M
MC	Mac Con Glinne
McE	Gearóid Mac Eoin
MD	E. Gwynn, *The metrical dindshenchas* (Todd Lect. Ser. VII–XII, Dublin 1903–35)

MDúin	Immram Curaig Maíle Dúin in LU lines 1642–1937
MI	Middle Irish
MID	J. Strachan, 'Contributions to the history of Middle Irish declension' in *Trans. Phil. Soc.* (1905) 202–46
MIEIL	T. P. Cross, *Motif-index of early Irish literature* (Indiana Univ. Publications Folklore Ser. No. 7, Bloomington Ind. 1952)
MIM	G. Dottin, *Manuel d'irlandais moyen* (2 vols, Paris 1913)
MU 2	J. C. Watson, *Mesca Uladh* (Med. Mod. Ir. Ser. XIII, Dublin 1941)
MU LL	Version of MU in LL lines 34590–35211
MU U	Version of MU in LU lines 1430–1552
OI	Old Irish
PBA	*Proceedings of the British Academy* (London 1903—)
PIM	K. Meyer, *A primer of Irish metrics* (Dublin 1909)
Pr.I	Primitive Irish
PSIC	G. Mac Eoin et al. (edd.), *Proceedings of the sixth international congress of Celtic studies held in University College, Galway, 6–13 July 1979* (Dublin 1983)
SCC	(1) Version of 'Serglige Con Culainn' in LU lines 3220–4039 (2) M. Dillion, *Serglige Con Culainn* (Med. Mod. Ir. Ser. XIV, Dublin 1953)
Sc.G.	Scottish Gaelic
sed pr.	*sed prave* 'but wrongly'
sp.	spelling
SR 2	D. Greene and F. Kelly, *The Irish Adam and Eve story from Saltair na Rann* I (Dublin 1976)
ST	S. Thompson, *Motif-index of folk-literature* (6 vols, Copenhagen and Bloomington Ind. 1955–8)
TBC	Táin Bó Cúailnge
TBC I	First recension of TBC
TBC I R	C. O'Rahilly, *Táin Bó Cúailnge Recension I* (Dublin 1976)
TBC I U	Version of TBC I in LU lines 4479–6722
TBC I Y	Version of TBC I in YBL and variant readings in TBC I R
TBC II	Second recension of TBC
TBC II L	Version of TBC II in LL lines 7551–12421
TBC II R	C. O'Rahilly, *Táin Bó Cúalnge from the Book of Leinster* (Dublin 1967)
TBC St.	C. O'Rahilly, *The Stowe version of Táin Bó Cuailnge* (Dublin 1961)
TGSI	*Transactions of the Gaelic Society of Inverness* (Inverness 1872—)
TTr.1	(1) G. S. MacEoin, 'Das Verbalsystem von Togail Troí (H.2.17)' in ZCP XXVIII (1960–61) 73–223 (2) W. Stokes, *Togail Troi: The Destruction of Troy* (Calcutta 1881)
V(v).	verse(s)
V	any vowel
V^i	any front vowel
V^u	any back vowel
VGK	H. Penderson, *Vergleichende Grammatik der keltischen Sprachen* (2 vols, Göttingen 1909, 1913)
VSR	J. Strachan, 'The verbal system of the Saltair na Rann' in *Trans. Phil. Soc.* (1895) 1–76
VST	M. O Daly, 'The verbal system of the LL Táin' in *Ériu* XIV (1943–6) 31–139
VT 2 ⟍	K. Mulchrone, *Bethu Phátraic: the tripartite life of Patrick* I (Dublin and London 1939)
w.	with